10/22

LITHUANIA
700 YEARS

LITHUANIA
700 Years

Edited by DR. ALBERTAS GERUTIS

Translated by ALGIRDAS BUDRECKIS

Introduction by RAPHAEL SEALEY

H. Lang.

MANYLAND BOOKS
New York

LITHUANIA
700 YEARS

Library of Congress Catalog Card No. 75-80057

SBN: 87141

Published by MANYLAND BOOKS, INC.
84-39 90th Street
Woodhaven, N. Y. 11421

MANUFACTURED IN THE UNITED STATES OF AMERICA

Contents

Editor's Foreword

It is the intention of this volume to trace the development of the Lithuanian people and nation from the earliest known period to the present day, with special emphasis being placed on the formation and characteristics of the twentieth-century Independent Lithuanian State; the subsequent loss of Lithuanian independence; and the continuing efforts of Lithuanians throughout the world to re-establish that independence and free their homeland from Russian rule. Needless to say, a project of this size and scope cannot, to do the subject justice, be undertaken by one man. Therefore, when I began the task of compilation, I requested experts in specific areas of Lithuanian history to contribute detailed studies of their respective fields. Each contributor was free to develop his text as he wished, according to the materials and sources available to him.

Professor Jonas Puzinas (Philadelphia, Pa.) prepared the section dealing with Lithuania's pre-history and Professor Juozas Jakštas (Cleveland, Ohio) examined the evolution of the Lithuanian nation from the establishment of the Lithuanian Grand Duchy during the 12th - 13th centuries, through to World War I. I took it upon myself to describe the period of 1917-1940, in which Lithuania regained its independence and then lost it as a result of the Russian invasion and occupation of its territory. A detailed discussion of various movements designed to resist the Russian occupation by groups and individuals, both within Lithuania and among Lithuanian refugee colonies in the Free World, was submitted by Dr. Algirdas Budreckis (New York, N. Y.). Finally, the prospects of Lithuania's being able to regain independence in the future have been examined and evaluated by

Stasys Lozoraitis, Chief of the Lithuanian Diplomatic Service (Rome).

* * *

Situated along the southern shores of the Baltic Sea, Lithuania first emerged as a nation during the twelfth and thirteenth centuries. Known as the Grand Duchy of Lithuania, it played a dominant role in Eastern European affairs for several hundred years. Unfortunately, in the early part of the 19th century, the Grand Duchy fell under Russian domination—a domination which was to last over a hundred years, until World War I.

The close of the nineteenth century witnessed the revival of strong nationalist feeling in Lithuania; so much so, that by the beginning of the 20th century, Lithuanians were actively demanding political autonomy and national independence. It became evident that the spiritual and material interests of the people could best be served if the nation were allowed to take its destiny into its own hands. World War I provided a favorable opportunity for self-determination, and Lithuania formally declared its independence by the Act of February 16th, 1918.

This period of Lithuanian national independence, though it lasted only a little more than twenty years, nevertheless distinguished itself by unprecedented advances in all aspects of national life. Having freed itself from the progress-restraining bonds with Russia, the newly-created Lithuanian nation strengthened its ties to Western European culture and began to move towards material and spiritual well-being.

The independent status of Lithuania was terminated in 1939, because Communist Russia and Nazi Germany divided Eastern Europe between them. In the summer of 1940, Lithuania was overrun by Red Army troops and was subsequently absorbed into the Soviet Union. Except for a brief three-year period of German occupation, Lithuania has remained under Soviet control to this day, even though the majority of Western Democracies does not recognize the Russian occupation. Neither do the Lithuanian people. Diligently and uninterruptedly, efforts to attain the ultimate goal—independence—continue within and without the Lithuanian nation. The Declaration of February 16th, though issued fifty years ago, is still regarded as a permanent manifesto of the Lithuanian people's quest for self-determination, as well as a reminder that the realization of the quest must, sooner or later, be achieved.

* * *

This volume is directed to all readers who are interested in the history of Eastern Europe in general, and the history of Lith-uania in particular. It is also more specifically directed to those Lithuanians residing in the United States, especially to the younger generation, many of whom may find English a more palatable language than Lithuanian, but who are nevertheless interested in learning more about the land of their fore-fathers. Lithuania's national anthem urges her sons to draw strength from the past. Lithuania was under the rule of Czarist Russia when the words of the anthem were composed. Today it is once more in Russian hands, and its sons must still derive strength from the past glory of their nation—not only from the Grand Duchy, but also from the 1918 Republic, the achievements of which remain as a living and demanding inspiration to those who labor to re-establish Lithuanian independence. I sincerely hope that this volume will add, in some small way, to the success of those labors.

On behalf of myself and on behalf of my colleagues, I would like to thank the members of the Lithuanian Independence Fund, its chairman, Mrs. Emilija Čekas, and the Lithuanian-American community for making the publication of this volume possible.

ALBERTAS GERUTIS

Introduction

In August, 1941, the United States and Great Britain issued the Atlantic Charter and pledged themselves to uphold self-determination for all nations. But for most of the nations of East-Central Europe the outcome of the war brought a new foreign domination, with mass deportations, thought-control, secret police and all the other apparatus of modern totalitarianism. The sufferings of the three Baltic States, Lithuania, Estonia, and Latvia, have been especially severe.

Yet postwar indifference is more remarkable than wartime blunders. Both in governmental circles and in important sections of the press there has been a conspiracy of silence about the Baltic States for more than twenty years. It has been broken only when diplomats could use the misfortunes of the three nations to score a debating point, for example, during the Arab-Israeli War of June 1967. For the most part, wishful thinking has tried to pretend that Soviet imperialism does not hurt.

Those who prefer to face reality will be grateful to Dr. Albertas Gerutis for getting together a team of experts to prepare this book. The history of Lithuania has alarming significance for the present day. Lithuania was the last nation in Europe to accept Christianity; indeed, in the thirteenth and fourteenth centuries the early Lithuanian state was poised between the two cultures of the Roman Catholic West and the Orthodox East. In 1387, by accepting Christianity in its Roman Catholic form, Lithuania chose the West, and this choice was decisive for the further development of the nation. Thereafter the long centuries of ever closer association with Poland served to imbue the people with a profoundly Catholic and Western outlook.

xi

The link with Poland diminished drastically the national awareness of the Lithuanians but did not wholly destroy it. Some sense of separateness survived into the nineteenth century and provided a base for the national revival. Repressive measures taken by the later czars failed to check this revival; on the contrary, they seem to have stimulated it. Accordingly, Independent Lithuania, as it emerged from World War I, was a nation state of modern and progressive type.

The period of independence, marked by steady economic and cultural advances, was brought to an end by the Soviet and Nazi invasions of World War II. This does not mean that national consciousness has been destroyed. Under foreign rule at earlier times the Lithuanian nation showed itself remarkably resilient and capable of preserving its Western cultural inheritance. But Soviet domination, equipped with twentieth-century technology, is far more thorough than its predecessors. Whether a national culture of Western type can survive in the face of this threat is the question that now confronts the Lithuanians. It confronts the whole Western world.

RAPHAEL SEALEY
Department of History
University of California
Berkeley, California, 94720

The Origins of the Lithuanian Nation

by JONAS PUZINAS

I. EARLY THEORIES OF LITHUANIAN ORIGINS

One of the most interesting problems encountered in the study of the pre-history of Lithuania—and one to which a solution is not readily available—concerns the cultural origin and ancestral home of the Lithuanian people. Scholars and antiquarians have been fascinated by this question for centuries, as evidenced by the great number of ethnogenetic theories that have evolved. Lithuanians have been linked to various ancient peoples, among them the Romans, the Greeks, the Alans, the Herulli, the Thracians, the Phrygians, and the Slavs. Some of the older theories were based on nothing more than superficial comparisons of languages and religious customs, while others reflected a patriotic desire to gain national prestige by linking Lithuania with the renowned civilizations of the past. Not only Lithuanian scholars, but those of many other nations as well, were eager to claim descent from the great ancient powers for their native lands.

THE ROMAN THEORY OF LITHUANIAN ORIGIN

The Roman-origins theory is believed to have been postulated early in the fifteenth century, probably by Lithuanian scholars who were familiar with Roman history and who had discovered certain similarities of language, mores and religious ceremonies in the Lithuanian and Latin cultures. The Polish chronicler Jan Dlugosz (1415-80) was the first to bring this theory to public attention. His *Historia Polonica* maintains that the Lithuanians are descendants of Romans who fled from Rome either during the civil wars of Gaius Marius (156-86 B.C.) and Lucius Cornelius Sulla (138-78 B.C.), or later, during the civil wars between Gaius Julius Caesar (100-44 B.C.) and Gnaeus Pompeius Magnus (106-48 B.C.). Since Dlugosz was not an admirer of the Lithuanian people, there is reason to believe that the theory did not originate with him, but that it was simply recorded by him as a viewpoint popular at the time.

The Roman theory of Lithuanian origins received currency in the sixteenth century when the Lithuanians reacted against the boasts of the Polish *pans* about their origins. The interests and honor of Lithuania was defended by the Lithuanian magnates, who were descendants of the supporters of Vytautas the Great. This struggle is recorded in the *Chronicles of the Grand Duchy of Lithuania and Samogitia*, which contains an account of the Roman origins of the Lithuanians. The chronicle describes the Roman duke Palemonas (or Pilemonas) who with his family and 500 lords fled from Nero in the first century A.D. and sailed up the Nemunas, reaching the Dubysa, where they settled. It was this Palemonas who started the dynasty of Lithuania's dukes.

This theory of Roman origins strengthened the Lithuanian boyars in their quarrels with the Poles by raising their national ambitions. Therefore it is not surprising that in other writings of the period, the theory was repeated and even elaborated upon. One of the staunchest supporters of the Roman theory was Michalo Lituanus (probably in reality Mykolas Tiškevičius, the Lithuanian emissary to the Crimea). This writer, hiding under a pseudonym, and wishing to strengthen the statehood of the Lithuanians, wrote a memorandum to the King of Poland and Grand Duke of Lithuania Sigismund August wherein were offered suggestions for improving the order and customs of Lithuania. Fragments of this memorandum were printed in 1615 in Basel under the title "Michalonis Lituani De Moribus Tartarorum, Lituanorum et Moschorum." This piece also contained the account about the Roman origins. Michalo Lituanus was displeased with the Russian writings in the Lithuanian Chancellories (actually the documents were in Old Church Slavonic), for "the Russian language is foreign to us Lithuanians, i.e., to Italians, springing from Italian blood." He went on to argue "that this is so apparent from our semi-Latin language and from the old Roman customs, which had only recently ceased to exist, to wit: the cremation of the dead, augury, aveomancy and other superstitions, which until now have survived in some places, especially the veneration of Aesculapius in the same serpentine form as he was when he came to Rome from Epidaurus. Holy domestic gods, the dead souls, the guardians of cities, roads and homes, good domestic spirits, hills, caves, lakes and glens are worshipped. Recently Holy Water was used to quench the sacred and eternal fire which in the manner of the Romans and Hebrews was used for holocausts." Michalo Lituanus went on to give seventy-two words which in Lithuanian mean the same as in Latin. A few of them were Latin *ignis* (Lith. ugnis), *aer* (oras), *sol* (saulė), *mensis* (mėnesis), *noctis* (naktis), *ros* (rasa), *deus* (dievas), *vir* (vyras), *nasus* (nosis), *dentes* (dantis), *gentes* (gentrys), *semen* (sėmenys), *linum* (linai), *jugum* (jungas), and so forth.

Michalo Lituanus drew the story that the Romans came to Lithuania during the time of Caius Julius Caesar. At first they settled in Samogitia, later they went farther, conquering the Yatvingian nations, later the Ruthenians, etc. The Italian fore-fathers of the Lithuanians, called Litali, gave the name to the country.

The Polish historian M. Stryjkowski, in his Lithuanian history *Kronika Polska, Litewska, Żmodzka y wszystkiej Rusi. W Kro-lewcu 1582*, also makes the Lithuanians descendants of the Ro-mans. He even gives the genealogy of the Lithuanian dukes, starting with the Roman Palemonas. It was his opinion that the boyars of Lithuania and Samogitia came from Italian and Gothic stock, while the masses came from the Gepidae, Sudovians, Lita-lans or Alans. Stryjkowski brings Palemonas' trip to Lithuania up to the tenth century. Later historiographers of Lithuania be-lieved the Roman theory and repeated the story in their writings, thinking up one or two new versions.

At the beginning of the nineteenth century, Lithuania was touched by a new movement, romanticism. This was the period of the Lithuanian national renaissance. During this period an extraordinary interest was taken in Lithuania's past, the Lithua-nian language, customs and other national characteristics. This interest, to a large extent, was motivated by patriotic feelings: the desire to thwart the influence of the Poles in Lithuania. Polish influence was spreading throughout the country via the cities, rectories and estates. It met resistance in the villages. The Samogitians were especially nationalistic; even their boyars maintained their Lithuanian identity. A reaction set in against the alien Polish influence and spirit; everything that was Lithuanian was accentuated: the language was rehabilitated, the past was idealized, the beauty of the folk songs was praised, and so forth. Vilnius University also exerted an influence, as Lithuanian literature began to develop rapidly. Even non-Lithuanian writers began to use material taken from Lithuanian history. This national movement had great significance for the Lithuanian national renaissance, which manifested itself in force at the end of the nineteenth century. The newspaper *Aušra* spread ideas of the romantic school with great enthusiasm. Unfortunately, neither the romantic period, nor the end of the nineteenth century, witnessed any thorough historical or linguistic research. The trodden paths of the humanists were still being followed. It is no wonder that at the time, the old theories of Roman ethnogenesis cropped up with new variations. The Lithuanian historian Teodoras Narbutas (1784-1864), having written a nine-volume history of Lithuania in Polish, still believed in the Roman theory. In all of his works, he tried to show the past in the most honorable manner, created his own mythology, and even forged ancient Lithuanian documents, based on Runic, etc. Narbutas would have welcomed an independent Lithuania, not tied to Poland, as was characterized by his words at the end of the ninth volume: ''I wrote a history up to the time when the Lithuanian nation weakened. The later period belongs to Polish historians. The last free monarch of the Jogaila dynasty, Sigismund, died . . . and I break my pen over his grave.''

The last echoes of the Roman theories were still heard from the writers of the national renaissance at the end of the nineteenth century.

THE LITHUANIANS AND PRUSSIANS AS DESCENDANTS OF GREEKS

A very long time ago, the Prussians and Lithuanians were considered to be descendants of the Greeks. In the thirteenth century, Albertus Stadensis wrote that after the death of Alexander of Macedonia (323 B.C.) some of his army commanders wandered to Prussia and settled there. In the fifteenth century the Polish historian Jan Długosz wrote: "'Though the Prussian language and customs are related to those of the Lithuanians they are descended from the King of Bithynia Prusias [second century B.C.]."' That is, Prusias, after unsuccessful struggles in his own country, went north and settled in Prussia, which was named for him. According to Długosz, the Prussian language is similar to the Greek language, which was used by the Bithynians. Even now, he wrote, traces of the Bithynian nation can be found; the Prussians preserved their original words and can understand the Eolians, Dorians, Athenians and Ionians. For example, Jodochus Willichius of Reszlius-Reszel, Prussia, affirmed in the middle of the sixteenth century that the Prussian language is a corrupted Greek language and that he could converse with the Prussians in Greek. Johannes Behm (1578-1648), professor at Koenigsberg University, in the 1625 introduction to J. Bretkūnas' and J. Rėza's *Psalteras Dowido Wohischkai bei Lietuwischkai*, wrote that the Lithuanian language was a mixture of Greek and Latin. In order to demonstrate this, he used the Lithuanian proverb: "'Dewas dawe dantes, Dewas dos ir dones" (God gave teeth, God will give bread). This proverb was later to be used by all who pointed to similarities between the Greek and Lithuanian languages. The comparison of Lithuanian to Greek continued until the beginning of the nineteenth century.

During the romantic era, the Lithuanians were held to be related to the Greeks. But in the course of the period, the romantics themselves were not consistent regarding this theory. Teodoras Narbutas, who was a passionate follower of the Roman theory in his first volume of history, analyzes Lithuanian mythology, comparing it with that of the Greeks. In Lithuanian mythology, he found many more prominents than in the mythology of the other Northern European nations. Therefore, he reasoned that Lithuanian mythology had to be formed by people who had a high degree of civilization. From similarities between Lithuanian and Greek mythology, he concluded that the Greek and Roman gods driven from the south were brought to Lithuania, where they mingled with the local gods. Narbutas drew the conclusion that the religion of the Lithuanians was drawn from the same stock as that of the Greeks. However, in actuality the Lithuanian Olympus of gods was the creation of Narbutas' fantasy.

THE LITHUANIANS AS RELATED TO THE SLAVS

The Lithuanians were held to be related to the Slavs. In the fifteenth century, Enea Silvio de Piccolomini (1405-64), after 1458 Pope Pius II, in his work *De Europa* wrote in the twenty-sixth chapter that the Lithuanian language is Slavic. In the eighteenth century the Lithuanian pastor Mattheus Praetorius (1635-1707) of East Prussia held the Lithuanians to be related to the Germanic Ostrogoths, but he held the Prussian language, part of the same Baltic branch, to be Sarmatian, whose dialects were Polish, Russian, Czech and the other Slavic languages.

During the romantic period, we see antiquarians who confuse the Lithuanians with the Slavs. Even Lithuanian authors made up theories. Teodoras Narbutas did not doubt that a settlement of the Lithuanian nation had existed between the Oder and Elbe rivers; for earlier, Jan Potocki had found the names for gods there which were the same as those found and venerated along the Nemunas. Narbutas was convinced that the Lutichians and other Slavic clans were really Lithuanians. Narbutas thought that they could have moved along the Baltic Sea and eventually could have reached the Nemunas and Dauguva. The Slavs who came to Pomerania during the time of Charlemagne divided this Lithuanian nation into two parts: one part remained along the Nemunas, the other in its old settlements. The warlike Normans and Danes did not permit these two nations to maintain contacts, and for that reason, this nation with the same language and religion was cleaved in two.

The so-called traces of Lithuanians in western Slavic lands attracted the interest of correspondents of *Aušra* at the end of the nineteenth century. J. Šliupas, Mikalojus Akelaitis, Andrius Vištelis and others repeated Narbutas' line. This was especially done by Andrius Vištelis, who fled to Poznan after the 1863 Revolt. He found Lithuanian place-names throughout the province of

Poznan, and maintained that a thousand years ago the Lithuanians lived in this area.

THE RELATIONSHIP OF THE LITHUANIANS WITH THE HERULLI

The Lithuanians were held to be related to the Germanic tribes, especially the Eastern Germans, the Herulli. This rela-tionship was based on the so-called Herullian "Our Father," printed by V. Lazius in the sixteenth century with his comment that the language was still spoken in Mecklenberg. In reality it was a Latvian text of "Our Father," taken from the *Cosmographia Universalis* (1544) of the renowned Sebastian Münster. The Lithuanians were also held to stem from another Germanic tribe, the Viti.

At the beginning of the nineteenth century the Herullian theory found many supporters among Lithuanians and foreigners. The Lithuanians accepted the theory on purely patriotic grounds: they were impressed by Odoacer, who conquered Rome. The ro-mantics maintained that his name was Herullian and therefore Lithuanian. The most important advocate of this view was Rev-erend Ksaveras Bagužis (Bogusz in Polish) who wrote an impor-tant booklet about the origins of the Lithuanian nation and lan-guage, *O początkach narodu i języka Litewskiego* (Warsaw, 1808). In his preface, Bagužis bemoaned the fact that the Lithu-anian language—which once was spoken by Odoacer, Mindaugas, Kęstutis, Vytautas and other Lithuanian dukes—was being de-graded, that the intellectuals spoke Polish. He demanded that Vilnius University form a society to study the Lithuanian lan-guage, folklore and past. In his booklet, he analyzed historical sources from Herodotus to Wulfstan, covering the Lithuanian tribes. He related the Prussians, Curonians and the Iranian tribe of Alans, the Germanic Herullians and others to the Lithuanians. Bagužis was convinced that they all spoke Lithuanian and to-gether with the Lithuanians formed one nation. He held that the Herullians were Lithuanians.

Even the serious professor Joachim Lelewel of Vilnius Uni-versity was at first skeptical about the Herullian theory but later changed his mind and held that the Herullians, without doubt,

7

could be considered Lithuanians, and that the Lithuanian language had many Latin phrases which create the impression that the Lithuanians had once sojourned on Roman territory.

The view that the Lithuanians spring from the brave Herullians who conquered Rome in the fifth century had a special appeal to the Lithuanian romantic patriots. Silvestras Valiūnas (1789-1831), in one of his poems dedicated to Dionizas Poška, one of the participants in the patriotic movement, reminisced about the times when "a Samogitian ruled in Rome." Poška, in his poems dedicated to Kseveras Bagužis and Joachim Lelewel, speaks also about mighty Lithuania "when she defeated the Romans, Scythians, Slavs, Teutonic Knights, pagan Tartars . . ." Poška maintained that Palemonas was a Herullian who after the death of Odoacer returned to his fatherland. The Herullian theory was adhered to until the middle of the nineteenth century.

THE THEORY OF THRACIAN AND PHRYGIAN ORIGINS

One of the major advocates of the Thracian and Phrygian theory was the veteran of the Lithuanian National Renaissance, Dr. Jonas Basanavičius (1851-1927). This theory arose during his long sojourn in Bulgaria, where he began to search for Lithuanian origins among the relics of the Thracians and Phrygians: their language, place-names, customs, etc. Dr. Basanavičius devoted several decades in his attempt to prove the Thraco-Phrygian theory. He collected data in the museums and libraries of Sofia, Belgrade, Zagreb, Vienna, Prague, Berlin, and others. He announced his findings in the great study *Apie trakų-prygų tautystę ir jų atsikėlimą Lietuvon* (Vilnius, 1921), basing the relationship upon the similarity of Thracian words and place-names to the Lithuanian language. Of the 856 Thraco-Phrygian words which he compared to the Lithuanian, Prussian and Latvian languages, 600 were purported to be common in phonetics and semantics. Dr. Basanavičius concluded that all of Media in the East, i.e., all of southern Europe up to the Atlantic, was inhabited by the Thracians who were closely related to the Lithuanians, who had come to their habitat from Asia Minor, and that the epics that Homer sang about were the deeds of the ancestors of the Lithuanians.

8

The linguist Kazimieras Būga (1879-1924) criticized Basana-vičius' theories by pointing out that there are not enough similari-ties to warrant a close kinship. The Thracians and Phrygians belong to the satem group of eastern Indo-European languages. Since the Lithuanian language belongs to the satem group, there are of course some similarities in place-names and vocabularies.

OTHER THEORIES OF LITHUANIAN ORIGINS

There were other less widely circulated theories about the origins of the Lithuanians. For example, at the end of the eight-eenth century, Paul Ruhig, professor at Koenigsberg, sought sim-ilarities between the Lithuanian and Semitic languages. The nu-mismatist Dr. Aleksandras Račkus (1893-1966) in his book *Guthones (Goths) Kinsmen of the Lithuanian People* (Chicago, 1929), by using folk etymology, tried to trace the relationship of the Lithuanians to the Germanic Goths. He carried Lithuanian history back to Roman times. By his theory, all Gothic kings who ruled Rome became Lithuanians. Juozas Gabrys-Paršaitis (1880-1951) in his *La parenté des langues hettite et lithuanienne et la préhistoire* (Geneva, 1944) tried to prove that the Lithuanian language was related to the Hittite. He pointed out similarities of declensions and conjugation, as well as similar suffixes in the participles of both languages. It was his view that with the help of Lithuanian and Hittite, the meaning of many Indoeuropean place-names and personal names could be ascertained.

THE FALLACY OF THE EARLY AND LATER THEORIES OF
LITHUANIAN ORIGINS

By viewing all of the theories of Lithuanian origins from the period of humanism to our own day, we see that they were not based on scientific fact. There was no genuine scholarly research; all theories were based on the work of amateurs. The Roman theory could be understood as the product of humanism; that is, origins were sought in classical antiquity. The Lithuanian case had another motive. In 1413 at Horodlo, Poland, when the Lith-uanians and Poles signed acts bringing them together, forty-seven noble families of Lithuania received Polish coats of arms. Later, when Polish-Lithuanian relations were strained, the Polish nobles chided the Lithuanian magnates that they did not have coats of arms of their own but had received them from Poland. This of course teased the Lithuanian nobility; some of them returned the Polish devices and claimed to have descended from the Romans. According to the Bychowiec Chronicle, in the times of Vytautas the Great some of the Lithuanian nobles rejected the Polish offers, saying that the Poles were no nobles, that they had received their coats of arms from the Czechs while the Lithuanians were Roman nobles, and that they had coats of arms of their ancestors and therefore needed no foreign devices.

In later times, the origins of the Lithuanians were traced by means of false etymological analogies based on similar sounding names of nations and places which were to be found in old sources. The superficiality of this method could be seen from the fact that until the seventeenth century the Bible was used as a source to determine the origin of nations. For example, the Prussian historian Christoph Hartknoch said to chroniclers who sought to trace the Goths to Sweden: "There can be no doubt that nations divided at the Tower of Babel, that they came to our land from the east and not from the opposite direction." C. Hartknoch argued that the Tower of Babel stood in the east and not in Sweden.

At the beginning of the nineteenth century the romantics observed the paths taken by the earlier writers. By false etymologies, they sought to trace kinship to other nations and tribes by studying habitats and migrations. The main objective always was to elevate the past of the ancestors. Following this objective, some —like Narbutas—did not stoop to falsifying facts or forging ancient writings or images of ancient gods, and so on. During the romantic period, there were similar cases of falsifications among other nations. Let us remember the famed falsification of the Czech Vaclav Hanka, the Prague librarian who purportedly found (1817) in a church tower twelve parchment documents describing the campaigns of Czech heroes. The entire country was aroused by this find; the Czechs were jubilant in having discovered ancient documents about their glorious past. The documents were printed in Czech and later translated into German. For a

long time, no one doubted their authenticity. It was later discovered that the so-called *Kralovodvorski rukopis* (Manuscripts
of the Regal Court) were Hanka's forgeries.

At the start of the nineteenth century the science of comparative linguistics was born; its founder was the linguist Franz Bopp
(1791-1867). In 1816 his *Ueber das Conjugationssystem des
Sanskrit in Vergleichung mit jenem der griechischen, lateinischen,
persischen und germanischen (insbesondere gotischen) Sprache,*
Bopp compared Sanskrit, Greek, Latin, Persian and German con-
jugational systems, and determined that from Ireland to India
all of the languages have much in common and are of common
origin. In his later works, he compared the Lithuanian language
to other languages. Unfortunately, neither the Lithuanian romantics nor the later antiquarians devoted enough attention to this
scientific method, but chose to use folk etymologies and analogies.
Only at the beginning of the twentieth century did serious Lithuanian scholars appear who tore off the veil of emotions and did
pure scientific research. The question of Lithuanian origins took
on a new light.

II. The Origins of the Lithuanians in the Light of Linguistics

Language—the natural vehicle for human spiritual, community and cultural intercourse—is the first source for tracing the
history and relations of ethnic groups to their roots. The importance of linguistic data is paramount when there are not sufficient
historical sources. But this is not enough. In many cases, linguistics helps supplement and make precise the fragments of historical
evidence. Linguistics is the first auxiliary tool of archaeology, for
language reflects national origins and unveils spiritual and material culture. Language and words are a mirror of the material
and spiritual culture of a people, not only of their past but also
of their present. Native words bear witness to the creative
strength of a nation.

In addition to indigenous words, "loan words" are significant
to the history of a culture. Loan words show us the cultural influence of other ethnic groups, of neighbors and distant peoples.

11

They point to the source of cultural values; loan words bear witness to the relations with other nations in the course of history. A loan word is a phenomenon of linguistic culture. No nation lives an isolated existence; all have some rapport with neighboring and even distant nations; even people living in enclaves are not isolated. Relations with neighbors can be twofold: peaceful and warlike. Therefore, the interrelationships of loan words are varying. Peaceful rapport is related to the exchange of ideas, commerce and industry. The results of this intellectual and material exchange are reflected in the language. These peaceful relations flourish along old trade routes, along which go not only goods but also values and names for these goods. Warlike relations, especially during a long period of foreign occupation, also create conditions for the introduction of foreign words. The upper classes especially borrow form their conquerors terms which later filter down to the lower classes.

Finally, the names of places, especially names of rivers and lakes, are significant to studies. Place-names remain long after a nation has disappeared from the area. When no historical or other sources remain, place-names attest to the character of the autochtons and their relations with neighbors. Comparative potamology helps determine the oldest living species of ethnic groups. The merits of linguistics are very significant in solving problems of the past. Comparative linguistics, supported by grammar and vocabulary comparisons, is a reconstructive method for arriving at the nature of protolanguages and their relations with other languages, as well as for seeking solutions to questions dealing with the ancestral homeland of nations.

Therefore, let us acquaint ourselves with the information provided by the research of linguists before proceeding to utilize the data of archaeology which will help us solve the question of the ancestral homeland of the Balts and their descendants, the Lithuanians.

THE FIRST LINGUISTIC ATTEMPTS TO LOCALIZE THE LITHUANIAN ANCESTRAL HOMELAND

One of the first linguists to study the question of the ancestral homeland of the Lithuanians was the German linguist and archaeologist Adalbert Bezzenberger (1851-1922), who pointed out that the present-day Lithuanians and Latvians have resided in their present settlements since the Neolithic period. In his confirmations, he has used the Indoeuropean word *marios*, which was used in the place-name Kuršių Marios. According to Bezzenberger the name *jūra* (sea) appeared much later.

In studying the prehistory of the Lithuanians, place-names were analyzed. In 1897 the Russian slavist Aleksandr A. Kochubinskii (1845-1907), using river and lake names, drew the conclusion that Byelorussia was originally inhabited by the Lithuanians, that the Lithuanians had once inhabited the marshes of Pripet and the headwaters of the Dnieper, near the Berezina conflux.

Among the other Russian researchers who studied Baltic place-names in Byelorussia and Russia, one must count Aleksandr L. Pogodin (b. 1872); Aleksei I. Sobolevskii (1856-1929), who searched for the ancestral lands of the Lithuanians in the areas of Smolensk and Vitebsk, to the north of the Daugava and east of the headwaters of the Volga, and in the east near the influences of the Protva, lived the Galindians (called *Goliad'* in the Russian chronicles) A. I. Sobolevskii related the Protva Galindians of the eleventh to twelfth centuries (near Gzhatsk and Mozhaisk) with the Lithuanians. He drew the boundary between the Balts and the Finno-Ugrians through the former Tver, Smolensk and Moscow areas.

The Russian linguist Aleksei A. Shakhmatov (1864-1920) did not deviate much from this view. Shakhmatov sought the ancestral homeland in the headwaters of the Nemunas and in the northern sources of the Dnieper, the Slavs in the western Daugava and lower Nemunas basin, and the western Finns on both sides of the Pripet, while he located the Mordvinians in the headwaters of the Dnieper and along the Desna.

K. BUGA'S VIEWS REGARDING THE QUESTIONS OF THE LITHUANIAN ANCESTRAL HOMELAND, THE MIGRATION OF THE BALTS AND THEIR LIVING SPACE

Kazimieras Būga was one of the seminal Baltic linguistics specialists. By using linguistic data based on studies of place-names and loan words, he tried to trace the sources of the Baltic proto-nation, the Baltic living space, and relations with neighbors and Baltic chronology. Būga contributed the most to the study of the Lithuanian ancestral homeland. He based his findings on the study of place-names. He found many Baltic river names in the areas of Minsk and Smolensk, and to some extent in the regions of Vitebsk and Mogilev. Basing his conclusions on these Baltic place-names, he demonstrated that the ancestral homelands of the Lith-uanians and Latvians are to be found north of the Pripet (along the Berezina and Dnieper headwaters up to the Sozh' River) and near the headwaters of the Sozh' (in the Smolensk region). The ancestors of the Lithuanians and Latvians, therefore, lived near the ancestors of the Mordvinians. He based his findings on the number of Baltic words in the Mordvinian language. The Mord-vinians, for example, borrowed such words as *pantis, peilis, per-kūnas, sora, šikšna, tūkstantis*. The Balts contacted the Livonians, Estonians and Finns in the headwaters of the Daugava and Dnieper. In the southeast, they lived in near the Slavs. For some time, the Germanic tribes were the neighbors of the Slavs and Balts near the Pripet.

According to Būga, the Balts did not always live in their old settlements. The first to move were the Prussians, who left their home in the headwaters of the Nemunas and Neris and moved to the mouth of the Vistula before the Christian Era. They are mentioned by the Roman historian Cornelius Tacitus (55-120 A.D.) in his work *Germania* under the name Aistians (*Aestiorum gentes*). In the second century A.D., the Greek geographer Claud-ius Ptolemy mentions two clans, the Galindians and Sudovians (Galindai kai Soudinoi). The Prussians of the lower Vistula contacted the Germanic Goths.

Būga goes on to state that another Baltic group lived in the present lands of the Lithuanians and Latvians. For example, prior to the arrival of the Lithuanians and Latvians from the east, the Selians, Semigallians, Curonians, Yatvingians and Skalvians lived there. According to Būga, the Lithuanians and Latvians lived in present-day Byelorussia-Minsk, Mogilev and Smolensk until the sixth century A.D. The cause of this migration was the expansion of the Slavs which began in the sixth century, when they began

14

to move from beyond the Pripet into Lithuanian territory. The Lithuanians in the sixth and seventh centuries were forced to move from the headwaters of the Dnieper and the Sozh'-Berezina. The Latvians were being forced from between Vitebsk and Polotsk to cross the Daugava into the lands of the Livonians and Estonians.

After the Latvians came the Lithuanians, who took over the Selian lands in the environs of Zarasai, Dusetos, Obeliai and Rokiškis, and assimilated the Selians. Also, part of Latgala was taken over by the Lithuanians. The Lithuanian place-names with the suffix -iškiai or -iškēs attest to this. The Lithuanians reached the Daugava and crossed into present-day Kraslava, Daugavpils and Nicgale; some of them even crossed the Daugava to the right bank, for there are still many place-names with the suffix -iškiai, especially in the counties of Daugavpils, Drisa, Rēzekne and Ludza. The Lithuanian name Užvalda (Latvian Uzvalda) attests to this. Moving toward the sea, the Lithuanians met other Baltic nations: the Semigallians, Curonians, Skalvians and Yatvingians. The Lithuanians took over a large part of Semigallia, not only in Linkuva and Joniškis counties but in present-day Latvia as well. There are still many Lithuanian names in the counties of Bauska, Dobele and Tukums. Part of the Semigallians were assimilated by the Lithuanians, when they also assimilated part of the Curonians (near Klaipēda and in Samogitia), the Skalvians (in Tilsit and Ragnit) and the Yatvingians or Sudovians in Suvalkai.

As we can see, K. Būga touched on a whole complex of questions dealing with the ancient Balts and Lithuanians. The extent that Būga's views coincide with archaeology will be seen in the third part of this study.

RESULTS OF THE INQUIRIES OF OTHER LINGUISTS

Following Būga, the most serious tracer of place-names was the Berlin slavist Max Vasmer (1886-1962), who thoroughly delved into the problems of eastern Baltic boundaries. According to Vasmer, the Baltic tribes lived in the Smolensk and Kaluga regions, in the western part of the Moscow area, and in southwestern Tver and Pskov. These Baltic tribes were gradually pushed out by the Russians, although Russification did not advance at an even pace, and not everywhere. To the east of the Balts lived the Finno-Ugric tribes; in the south the Balts did not contact the Iranians, because the Slavs intervened.

Among other linguists who studied the problem were the slavist Nikolai S. Trubetskoi (1890-1938), the Finnish linguist Valentin Kiparsky (b. 1904), and Alfred Senn, professor at the University of Pennsylvania (b. 1899). After the Second World War, Soviet linguists became interested in Baltic linguistics, the relations between Baltic and Slavic, the questions of Baltic and Slavic ethnogenesis, and historical linguistic problems dealing with the Balts. One of the most exhaustive studies was published in 1962 by V. N. Toporov and O. N. Trubachev: *Linguistic Analysis of the Hydronymes of the Upper Dnieper*. Both authors divide the hydronymes of the headwaters of the Dnieper into three ethnic groups: Slavs, Finno-Ugrics, and Balts. The Slavic place-names are found east of the Dnieper. Both authors consider the Slavs to be newcomers who invaded the living space of the autochtonous Balts. The eastern Slavs pushed to the north and northeast along the rivers of the Dnieper Basin, as well as along the Sozh' and Desna. In the regions to the north of the Pripet and Nemunas headwaters, the eastern Slavs crept from the east, from the left banks of the Dnieper, and reached the edge of the Dnieper in historic times, driving out or assimilating the ancestors of the Lithuanians and Latvians. In the upper Dnieper, they met the Finno-Ugrics. There we find two types of hydronymes: Volga Finnish and Western Finnish. Most of the Finnish names of the Volga are concentrated in the eastern headwaters of the Dnieper (to the east of the headwaters of the Desna) and below the Don Basin. In the northern reaches of the upper Dnieper are traces of Finns; in this region, the Finns had contacts with the Balts. The Iranian element of the upper Dnieper localized itself from the mouth of the Pripet to the northeast.

The basic ethnic element of the upper Dnieper was formed by the Balts. Both authors investigated about 700-800 Baltic hydronymes in the territory from the headwaters of the Nemunas, Neris and Pripet to the west and northwest; from the Bobr to the Viazma River; from the headwaters of the Oka to Tuskor' Rat'; and eastward to Turiia in the Sluch headwaters, as well as

16

to the confluence of the Dnieper and Desna and to the Seym River in the south. V. N. Toporov and O. N. Trubachev thoroughly analyzed the Baltic remains, classifying the Baltic hydronymes by form and suffix, in addition to analyzing their etymology according to root, giving equivalents in Lithuanian, Latvian and Prussian. They gave due notice to materials of Lithuanian toponymics and hydronymics, for Lithuania is geographically connected with the upper Dnieper. Finally, they gave close attention to old Baltic loan words in the Byelorussian language and in the dialects of the southern Great Russians, especially in the Smolensk region. These loan words are connected with farm buildings, household items, vessels, food, nature, and so forth. Here are a few of the Baltic loan words in the eastern Slavic dialects: *arud* (Lithuanian *aruodas,* "granary"), *balanda* (Lith. *balanda* "orach"), *degot'* (Lith. *degutas* "tar"), *doilid* (Lith. *dailidē* "carpenter"), *dirvan* (Lith. *dirvonas* "fallow land"), *diaklo* (Lith. *duoklē* "tribute"), *jantar'* (Lith. *gintaras* "amber"), *kovsh* (Lith. *kaušas* "ladle," "scoop"), *kul'sha* (Lith. *kulšis* "haunch"), *kurpy* (Lith. *kurpēs* "shoes"), *lauma* (Lith. *laumē* "fairy"), *parsuk* (Lith. *paršiukas* "suckling pig"), *peled* (Lith. *pelēda* "owl"), *putra* (Lith. *putra* "soup"), *sviren* (Lith. *svirnas* "granary"), *vitina* (Lith. *vytinē* "barge"), and so on.

Toporov and Trubachev, summarizing their findings and those of the other linguists, try to establish the bounds of the Baltic lands in the east, southeast, south and north. The Balts in the east lived in the Oka basin, the upper Volga, and even near the Don. In the southeast, the Balts were touching the banks of the River Seym. Farther on, the Baltic boundary runs along the Seym to the confluence of the Seym and Desna. Up until now, it was believed that the Pripet formed the southern boundary of the Balts, but both authors found over fifty Baltic hydronymes to the south of the Pripet. The territory from the left bank of the Pripet to the Nemunas, Neris and western Daugava is full of Baltic hydronymes, for the Balts remained there the longest in historic times. The hydronymes of these regions have much in common with those of Lithuania and Latvia. For example, of the 300 hydronymes connected with the basin of the Berezina, about eighty are Baltic. To the north are many Baltic hydronymes

17

in the basin of the Sozh'; to the east of the Sozh', the Baltic hydronymes are less frequent.

As it has already been noted, Būga held that the Balts, being forced by the Slavs, retreated from their habitats to the north and the west. Toporov and Trubachev, completing their analysis of the hydronymes of the upper Dnieper, raised a new hypothesis, namely, that the mass of Balts in the upper Dnieper did not move to the northwest during the Slavic influx, but were gradually assimilated. Even after the Slavs had pushed farther to the north, there were many Baltic enclaves in the Dnieper region. These Balts remained intact for a long time, until the twentieth century. Toporov and Trubachev support this hypothesis with the fact that the Baltic names for even small riverlets remained intact for a long time and were only recently Slavonized phonetically.

Other Soviet linguists conclude that the process of Slavonization of the Balts was a long one. For example, M. J. Grinblat, using archaeological data and place names, maintains that the Lithuanians form the oldest elements of people in Byelorussia. In northwest Byelorussia, there are many Lithuanian names for lakes, rivers, villages and towns. Some locales (Rodunē, Varanavas, Astravas) as late as 1954 had Lithuanian-speaking inhabitants with Lithuanian surnames. There are many Lithuanian words in the Byelorussian language. Studying all of these facts, M. J. Grinblat concluded: "In the northwest territory of present-day Byelorussia, where there are many Lithuanian toponymes, two waves of colonization took place—from the northeast (by the Slavic Polochanians) and from the south and southeast by the Dregovichi and Volhynians. These two waves Slavonized the autochtons, the Highland Lithuanians, and part of the Yatvingians. The Slavonization of Lithuanians was a long process; it began between the sixth and nineth centuries and ended in the northwestern part of Byelorussia at the beginning of the twentieth century. The Slavic colonization of the Lithuanian territory took place under peaceful conditions and was not connected to the forcible expulsion of the natives."

CONCLUSIONS OF THE LINGUISTIC STUDIES

Condensing the findings of the linguists, we must acknowledge that they performed a great service by bringing light to the historic problem. The linguists determined that a great number of Asiatic and European languages are related and stem from a common source. In prehistoric times, there was one nation, which spoke one language; the name of this nation has not survived in historical records, therefore the proto-nation has been given a synthetic name: the Indoeuropeans or Indogermans (the latter form is preferred by German scholars). The primary nucleus of the Indoeuropeans is called the Indoeuropean Proto-Nation and its speech, the Indoeuropean Proto-Language. It is believed that around 3000 B.c. this Indoeuropean Proto-Language split into two dialects. Taking the word "hundred" as a criterion, the eastern dialectic group of Indoeuropean language was called the Satem Group (from the Iranian word *satem,* meaning "hundred"). The western group is called the Centum Group (from the Latin word *centum,* "hundred"). The Satem Group was composed of the Aryans, Slavs, Balts, Thracians, Phrygians, Albanians, etc., while the Centum Group consisted of the Greeks, Italics, Celts, Germans, etc. When the Indoeuropean Proto-Language split into dialects, separate Indoeuropean nations appeared: the Germans, Italics, Balts, Slavs, Iranians, etc. They in turn split into related nations with related languages.

Linguistics has determined that the Lithuanian, Latvian, Old Prussian (extinct since 1700), Curonian, Semigallian, and Selian languages were related and at one time formed a single language. Since the name of this nation has not survived in history, the Lithuanian linguists Kazimieras Jaunius and Kazimieras Būga suggested the name Aistians, for the proto-nation (based on the name given by Tacitus, *Aestiorum gentes*). German linguist Georg Heinrich Nesselmann in 1845 began using the collective term Balts, based on Pliny the Elder's term Balcia or Baltia. The latter term has been accepted in scientific literature. The linguists demonstrate that the Baltic languages stem from one basic root, that the Balts in ancient times spoke one language, called the Baltic Proto-Language, and that they formed a unitary nation, the Baltic Proto-Nation. Most linguists reject the hypothesis that in ancient times the Balts and Slavs formed a linguistic unity. Similarities between the Baltic and Slavic languages rise from the fact that they are both Satem groups and that they have been neighbors for very long. The linguists also maintain that around 1000 B.C. the Baltic Proto-Language split into two groups: the western and eastern Balts. The western Balts consisted of the Prussians with a number of clans (the Sudovians, Sambians, Skalvians, Nadrovians, and others); the eastern Balts—Lithuanians, Latvians, Semigallians, Curonians, Selians and the Galindians living west of Moscow—formed the second group. Loan words help determine the relations with the Finno-Ugrics, Iranians, Slavs and Germans. Hydronymes help determine the boundaries of the Baltic living space. According to linguistic data, the northern Baltic boundary went along the modern Latvian-Estonian border to the east, up to the upper Volga, and past Tver to Uglich. In the east, the boundary ran west from Moscow to Tula. In the southeast, the Balts lived as far as the right bank of the Seym River, up to the Desna River. In the south, the Balts spread south of the Pripet, from which they later spread to the mouth of the Vistula. In the west, they settled along the Baltic Sea coast from Pomerania to the mouth of the Daugava. In the sixth century, the Slavs pushed them west, but the majority remained in their original lands and were Russified.

III.   THE PREHISTORY OF THE LITHUANIANS

By summarizing the work of the linguists, we see that they helped lay a firm foundation for further inquiries into the origins of the Lithuanians, their living space, and their cultural history. Unfortunately, linguistics meets with many problems, because linguistic facts do not always coincide with chronology and historical events. The origins of the Balts and the Lithuanians can be studied profitably by using two sciences—linguistics and prehistory. Archaeology can give precision to linguistic conclusions; it can determine the pre-Baltic cultural origins and trace its evolution through time, and even place this evolution in a chronological framework. Finally, archaeology can determine the ethnic composition of any period of culture.

THE FIRST APPEARANCE OF MAN IN LITHUANIA

The appearance of human life in Lithuania depended on natural conditions. These conditions were determined by glaciers which covered Lithuania three times. When the glacial masses finally melted, conditions became conducive for human habita' tion. The first people appeared in Lithuania around 20,000 years ago. This is the start of Lithuanian pre-history and cultural history. The first man set his foot in the Vistula region. Later men spread out to the north and northeast. The earliest findings of the late glacial period are in Kulm, where a reindeer antler with carved marks was found; on the basis of geological data, this discovery dates back to about 18,000 B.C. Discoveries of later periods were found in East Prussia. Near Klaipėda was the site of bone tools dating back to 8500-8100 B.C. Flint tools dating back 10,000-8000 B.C. were found in Vilnius, Ežerynai (in Alytus county) and elsewhere. These were the remains of the Paleolithic period. Paleolithic man in Lithuania lived under harsh climactic conditions. At first, as the glaciers retreated, the climate was harsh, Arctic-like; later, it became sub-Arctic or sub-glacial. The flora was of the tundra type. The fauna consisted of the mammoth, wooly rhineoceros, reindeer, and other Arctic animals. At the end of the Paleolithic period (about 10,000 to 8000 B.C.) the climate became Atlantic and the flora was of the steppe variety: birches, willows, firs, aspens and others. Aurochs, moose, wild horses and other steppe creatures appeared. The people of this period were nomads, hunters and gatherers of plant fruits. No physical remains of man dating from this period were found in Lithuania. No one knows the ethnic composition of the first inhabitants of Lithuania.

LITHUANIA IN THE MESOLITHIC PERIOD (8000-3500 B.C.)

The climate of this period changed greatly and conditions became more tolerable. Larger groups of people kept wandering into Lithuania and formed larger settlements. We have much material about the culture and manner of living of these people. It was found in peatbogs and in ancient riverbeds and camps near lakes and rivers. The inventory of the culture consists of various flint and bone tools. Lithuania at this time had several cultures: the Swiderian (named for the stone-age camp at Świdry Wielkie near Warsaw), Maglemose (for the Maglemose peatbog in Zealand) and the Microlithic-Macrolithic culture, which used both small

21

and huge flint tools. All three of these cultures belonged to nomadic ethnic groups, whose nationality is still unknown. Physical appearances of these people can be reconstructed from skulls found in Kabeliai (southeast of Priekulė) and near Kamšai (in Kalvarija township). Racially, both skulls belong to the dolichocephalic type.

Mesolithic man in Lithuania was not sessile, but continually moved with the seasons from one camp to another, remaining at one place only when comfortable climactic and environmental conditions existed. They gathered wild fruits, hunted and fished. These Mesolithic people did not practice agriculture or animal husbandry. The only domesticated animal in their possession was the dog, necessary for the hunt.

THE NEOLITHIC CULTURES PRIOR TO THE INDOEUROPEANS

We have much more information about the cultural evolution in Neolithic times (3500-1800 B.C.). The Mesolithic culture did not suddenly break off, but was slowly replaced by the Neolithic. The Mesolithic Swiderian culture had an influence on early Neolithic culture. According to available information we can discern several cultures.

THE PROTO-FINNISH COMBED POTTERY CULTURE
(3500-2000 B.C.)

The oldest postmesolithic culture was the Combed Pottery culture, named for the decorative method of pressing indentures or comb-like impressions in the soft clay for ornamentation. Remains of these pots, moulded by hand, pointed-based, were found in Neringa, southeast Lithuania, especially near the Merkys basin and elsewhere. This culture made amber objects which were found near the Lithuanian seacoast: near Juodkrantė, Smeltė, the port of Klaipėda, Palanga and elsewhere. At Juodkrantė were found all sorts of beads, buttons and art objects. (Of singular importance are the flat human and animal figurines, most likely amulets.) The representatives of the Combed Pottery culture were the ancestors of the Baltic Finns. They were nomads, hunters and fishermen.

During the Neolithic period, agrarian cultures expanded. Around 2500 B.C. along the Baltic seacoast between the Oder and Vistula and Kulm, in Western Prussia, appeared people who belonged to the Danubian culture. The center of this culture was in Central Europe. The characteristic remains of this culture are: semi-globular clayware, decorated with spiral-meanders, lines and bands, stone semi-circular axes, and stone hoes. The people of this culture lived in villages, planted barley, wheat, and sorgum, and bred cows, sheep, goats and swine. It is not clear to which ethnic group this culture belonged.

At roughly the same time, a new culture moved into the southern and southwestern regions of the Combed Pottery culture, namely the Funnel Beaker culture. This culture is named after its characteristic form of pottery, which is similar to a funnel; the culture reached its apex in eastern Jutland, the Danish Isles, southern Sweden and northwestern Germany. From there it reached the Baltic shores. Of all of the eastern Baltic regions, the Funnel Beaker culture thrived best in East Prussia. The last wave of this culture reached the Gumbinė (Gumbinnen) region near Lithuania. Yet the Funnel Beaker culture did not exert a great influence in Lithuania. Members of this culture were farmers and husbandmen. Their nationality is unknown. One thing is certain, they merged with the Indoeuropean Corded Pottery culture.

At the end of the Neolithic period a new culture reached the eastern Baltic region, the so-called Globular Amphora culture. The name comes from the globular shaped amphorae this culture produced. The center of this culture was north-central Germany. From there, it spread in various directions, reaching the lower Vistula, the land of Kulm, East Prussia and Mazovia. Members of this culture were farmers and husbandmen. They traded amber; banded flints were received in return for amber from Poland (Krzemionki, Opatów county). The ethnic identity of this culture is not known.

23

At the end of the Neolithic period a new culture arrived which played a prominent role in Lithuania's Indoeuropeaniza-tion. In the period 2300-2000 B.C., a new culture developed rap-idly in the eastern, central and northern reaches of Europe. This culture differed from all previous cultures in its ceramics, stone and flint tools, burial customs and other idiosyncrasies. Character-istic of this culture were beakers and clay pots covered with corded ornaments in the cords of soft clay used to mould vessels. The culture used battleaxes shaped like boats, and constructed barrow mounds or flat-top graves. Because of these characteristics, this new culture was called variously the Beaker culture, the Corded Pottery culture, the Boat-axe culture, the Barrow Mound culture, etc.

The Corded Pottery culture (as it is most generally desig-nated) covered a large area from northern Holland, northwest Germany and Jutland in the west to the Volga and the Caspian Sea in the east; from Sweden, Finland, Novgorod and Viatka in the north to the Black Sea and the Balkans in the south. These expanses were settled by corded pottery groups that had some difference in material culture and burial customs. The gigantic expansion of the culture creates difficulties in pinpointing its origin and center. The question of origins is made more difficult by the fact that the majority of archaeologists and linguists con-sider this culture Indoeuropean, while the ancestral homeland of the Indoeuropeans still has to be solved. Archaeologists and lin-guists are not in accord about the source of the Indoeuropeans. Linguists familiar with Sanskrit consider this archaic language to be the mother of all Indoeuropean languages, and maintain that the ancestral homeland had to be in northern India. Since the Lithuanian language has many similarities in grammar and vocab-ulary with Sanskrit, some amateur Lithuanian historians traced the Lithuanians back to India. However, it was later learned that the Indoaryans came to the Punjab region around 1500 B.C. The Indian theory of the ancestral homeland, therefore, had to be dis-carded. Later, the Indoeuropean homeland was sought in Central Germany, Scandinavia and even along the Baltic Sea, near Lithuania. Recently, most scholars sought the Indoeuropean homeland in the region from the Ukranian Steppe to the Caspian and Urals. It was surmised that because of climactic conditions, the nomadic Indoeuropean tribes moved out of the Eurasian Steppes in various directions—some went to Asia Minor and reached India, others moved to Europe. One of the earliest Indoeuropean migrations took place around 2400-2200 B.C. to western Asia Minor, to the Aegean Sea and to the Balkans. In the period 2300-2000 B.C., Indoeuropeans broke into Central Europe, Central Russia and the eastern Baltic areas.

It is impossible to determine when the Indoeuropean Proto-Nation and Proto-Language existed. Since language develops slowly, during the Mesolith period a more or less compact linguistic unity of Indoeuropeans existed. At first they split into the Satem and Centum groups, and in the middle of the third millennium B.C., the great Indoeuropean migration began. At the time, both groups were well differentiated. As they settled in separate regions they developed independent proto-nations. This differentiation was effected by new living conditions—these were essentially geographical. The aborigines were culturally and linguistically absorbed. In those regions where the influence of previous cultures was small, the old Indoeuropean culture forms remained relatively unchanged; the small nomadic groups did not produce significant changes in the Indoeuropean languages. Densely populated areas with advanced cultures had to be taken over by force; in those regions the process of Indoeuropeanization was different: the culture and language were strongly affected by a substrata, and departed from the Indoeuropean roots. In those areas the Indoeuropeans met with dense populations, and for some inexplicable reason they were either unable to hold their own or to withdraw, as was the case in areas of southern Finland which were absorbed by the local inhabitants. By the end of the Neolithic and the beginning of the Bronze ages, we see separate Indoeuropean cultural units which can be identified as the nuclei of individual proto-nations—the Proto-Germans, Proto-Celts, Proto-Slavs, Proto-Balts, etc.

It is believed that the Indoeuropean group from which the Proto-Balts sprang left its home along the lower Dnieper and moved to the Baltic around 2300-2200 B.C., reaching southern Finland. A second, related group moved from the middle Dnieper to the upper Dnieper, upper Volga and Oka regions. In all of these areas the newcomers came into contact with members of the Combed Pottery culture (Proto-Finns), and in the Vistula Basin, with members of the Funnel-Beaker Ceramics and Globular Amphora cultures. The Indoeuropeans assimilated the local inhabitants and gradually forced their own language on them; the result of this Indoeuropeanization was the formation of a distinct Corded Pottery culture, which the archaeologists call the Rzucewo culture (after the settlement Rzucewo [in German, Rutzau] near the Bay of Danzig) and the Baltic Bays culture (in German: *die Haffküstenkultur,* after the settlements found in Aismarės and the Courish Bay). Both names designate the same culture, which is deemed Proto-Baltic—that is, related to the ancestors of the later Lithuanians, Prussians, Latvians and other Baltic nations.

Most available information deals with the Western Proto-Balts. A number of prehistoric remains of settlements running from Danzig to the port of Šventoji in Lithuania, and from Kaunas and Rumšiskės to the southeast (Nemunas, Merkys rivers) have been investigated. Many fragments were found in this area dating back to this culture. Proto-Baltic ceramics are variegated: their chief characteristics are curved goblets, bulging amphorae, round and long bowls, wide pots, etc. The chief ornamentations are corded impressions, triangular impressions on the necks of the vessels, rows of indentations, vertical and slanted bands of lines, etc. Among the stone tools are battleaxes (about 120 were found in Lithuania), broadaxes made of flint, hoes, triangular or heart-shaped arrowheads, and other small flint tools.

The settlements were often chosen near waterways, along the seacoast, rivers and lakes. The Proto-Balts who settled there were engaged in fishing and hunting; they also worked the land, sowing sorgum, barley, wheat (triticum) and perhaps even flax. They bred horses, cattle, swine, goats, dogs, and lived in small villages. Their homes, as can be reconstructed from remains found at Succase (near Elbing), were rectangular, about four to six meters wide and eight to twelve meters long. The walls, made of stockades, with brush and clay shoved between the layers, were constructed of split logs; the roof was supported on posts. The dwelling usually had one living-quarter with a stone hearth in the center.

We can learn about the religious life of the Proto-Balts from their graves. The dead were buried in deep pits, usually on the side with folded legs (in a sleeping position); rarely were the dead laid out on their backs. Clay pots were placed in the graves, especially beakers, battleaxes or plain stone axes, flint knives, bone awls and ornaments. In addition to an ancestors' cult, the Proto-Balts practiced a natural cult, with the sun, stars, thunder and other natural phenomena regarded as objects of worship.

We learn about their racial characteristics from skeletons found in graves near the Vistula and Nemunas. The average height of a man was 169.2 cm. (between 158-177 cm.); the women were 157 cm. (between 154 and 161 cm.). The dominant subrace was the Nordic.

The exact boundaries of the Proto-Balts in the transition from the Neolithic to the Bronze ages is difficult to determine. We have the most data about the area of the Western Proto-Balts near the Baltic Sea, from the Bay of Danzig to the Dauguva. Farther to the north the same culture spread in part to present-day Estonia and even touched Southwestern Finland. However, the Indoeuropeans in these areas were assimilated by the Proto-Finns. Beyond this, remnants of the Proto-Baltic culture can be found in the Dnieper, upper Volga and Oka regions. The Oka, Central Volga, Moscow, Yaroslavl, Kostroma and the Nizhni Novgorod regions contained the Fatianovo culture, which had many related characteristics with the eastern Proto-Balts. For this reason, the archaeologists are prone to consider the Fatianovo culture a Proto-Baltic one. In the south, between the Dnieper and Vistula, the Proto-Slavs developed; their heritage was the Trzciniecka culture.

Around 1800 B.C., the Proto-Balts began using metal—copper. Copper axes, spiral hairclasps and other items passed from the Unĕtice culture to the western Proto-Balts. (One flat copper axe was found near Tilsit.) In a short time the Unĕtice type of bronze axe spread in the region from Pomerania to Lithuania. Metal-hilted halberds (one was found in Veliuona, Kaunas county), swords (found in Lithuania), bracelets, pins and other ornaments made of bronze spread to Lithuania. The use of bronze for tools and weapons ushered in a new age. Bronze brought in from abroad was expensive, and could only be purchased by the well-to-do. The masses still used stone, flint, bone and even wooden tools. The forms of local tools are important in determining the continuation of the Proto-Baltic culture through the Bronze Age. This continuity can be observed in several manners: according to the evolution of material culture, burial customs, and the spread of this culture. Some Proto-Baltic cultural forms remained throughout the later material evolution; for example, the stone boat-shaped battleaxes continued to be used in a modified form. Some flint items, like the heart-shaped arrowheads, did not change their form. The same could be noticed in ceramics (e.g., beakers). Major changes did not occur in the manner of burial: the dead were still placed in barrow-mounds. The continuity is proved by the fact that throughout the Bronze Age earlier mounds were still used (viz., Wiskiauten, in Sambia; Rantau near Rauschen, in Sambia; Reznē near Salaspils (Kirchholm), Latvia, etc.). The remains of Baltic artifacts covered the same area as those of the Proto-Baltic culture (especially in the West).

As has been mentioned, the early bronze tools were imported, nonetheless, as trade increased and bronze (in tool and ore form) was introduced into the Proto-Baltic areas, the Western Proto-Balts developed a local industry producing a number of indigenous artifacts which differed from those of the neighboring cultures. Around 1300 B.C., a definite Baltic culture existed. Characteristic of this material culture was the Baltic-type bronze flanged axes with circular edges on the blades, in addition to long and narrow battleaxes with a socket for the shaft, so-called

Nortycken axes (named for Nortycken, Sambia, where twenty-four such artifacts were found), large spearheads with wide barbs, stone snakehead hoes, brushed pottery which spread throughout the eastern Baltic regions, etc. These purely Baltic-type tools spread throughout the western and eastern regions inhabited by the Proto-Balts.

The western Baltic regions (eastern Poland, East Prussia, western Lithuania and part of Latvia) were influenced by Central Europe—at first by the Unětice culture, later by the Lusatian culture—while the eastern Balts maintained their archaic cultural pattern with some southern influence. Because of the different cultural components in the west and east (based on pre-Indoeuropean substrata, differing neighboring influences, different climate and geographical conditions) the Baltic culture began to differentiate, and the Balts split into two basic groups; the Western and Eastern Balts. The linguists consider the Prussian tribes to have constituted the Western Balts, whereas the Lithuanians, Semigallians, Latvians and Selians were the Eastern Balts. Culturally speaking, it would be proper to consider the Prussians, Sudovians or Yatvingians, and Curonians as Western Balts, and those living east of present-day Lithuania as Eastern Balts. The eleventh to twelfth-century Russian chronicles mention the Galindians who lived near the Protva River, not far from Moscow, and still other Baltic tribes whose names were not recorded.

There are a number of problems regarding the boundaries of the Balts during the Bronze Age, for the Baltic regions, archaeologically speaking, have not been uniformly studied. The best-investigated areas are those from Eastern Pomerania to the Daugava. There are many Bronze Age artifacts from this region. The eastern and southern areas of the Balts have not been thoroughly investigated; therefore, in determining the southern and eastern bounds, one must utilize linguistic findings as well as hydronymic and toponymic studies. By coordinating linguistic and archaeological findings, one can draw a provisional boundary of the Balts during the Bronze Age. In the west, the Balts were few in numbers along the Persante River (Pomerania). The border then ran from Persante along the lower Vistula to Bydgoszcz (Bromberg), and from there to the confluence of the Bug and Narew.

The southern boundary ran along the Pripet River and to the south, then along the Desna to the right bank of the Seym. The eastern Balts reached the Oka Basin and upper Volga; the north-ern boundary went from the upper Volga through Tver toward the Baltic Sea (toward modern Latvia and Estonia).

The climate during the Bronze Age was not uniform: around 1500 B.C. it was very dry, but around 500 B.C. it became damp and cold. In the western settlements the mode of living did not differ from that of the Neolithic Proto-Balts. Agriculture spread slowly. The cleared field ("slash and burn") system was used—trees were chopped down and burned to make arable clearings. Bronze sickles made an appearance (e.g., near Littausdorf, Sam-bia, sixty-four bronze sickles were found). Oats were added to the crops. Cattle, sheep and horses were raised. Houses were small and quadrangular, consisting of a four-by-six-meter room and antechamber. In Eastern Lithuania (e.g., in Samantonys, Ukmergė county) remnants of rounded huts with matted walls of brush and clay were found. The hearth was made of clay.

Through the mediation of the Unětice (later Lusatian) cul-ture, trade was developed with Greece and Italy. Baltic amber played a key role in this trade. At the beginning of the Bronze Age a large amount of amber was found in the graves of the Unětice in Silesia, Bohemia. Around 1600-1500 B.C., amber beads were found in Mycenean shaft-graves in the Peloponessis, Crete, Northern Italy (Terramara) and elsewhere. The large number of bronze artifacts found near the lower Vistula, on the banks of the Notec River, Warta, etc., and the spread of amber objects to the central and southern parts of Europe, show that the amber routes went from the Baltic Coast along the Vistula, Notec, Warta and upper Oder rivers to Bohemia, Moravia, and to the Danube. From there the route spread out—one went straight to the eastern coast of the Adriatic to Greece, Crete; the second went over the Alps to Northern Italy. Relations were established with Asia Minor via the Greeks. This is proven by the discovery of a Syrian bronze statuette found in Šernai (Klai-pėda county) and of a second statue of Anatolian origin, found in Lithuania. Trade with the Caucasus was also established (am-ber items were found in Osetia). Baltic tools found in Northern

Germany, Denmark, and southern and central Sweden attest to Baltic relations with the Germanic tribes. For example, Baltic bronze axes were found in Brandenburg, Denmark (even three Baltic-type axes were found in the Smorumovre hoard). Nortycken type battle-axes were discovered in Brandenburg, Rügen Island and elsewhere. The Mälar-type axe of Central Sweden was found in the Vaškai hoard of Biržai county, Lithuania.

During the Early Bronze Age the dead were buried by the Western Balts in burial mounds erected by earth and stone. Around 1100 B.C., cremation of the dead became an established custom. Nonetheless, concentric rings of stone were still constructed at the burial mounds. The cremated remains were either buried in graves or placed in urns.

CONTINUATION OF THE BALTIC CULTURE DURING THE EARLY IRON AGE

The earliest artifacts of iron can be traced among the Western Balts (in Sambia) dating from around 700 B.C. Iron items were more frequent after 500 B.C. The use of this new metal spread very slowly. At first, iron was imported in various ingot forms; during the second century B.C., the Western Balts began to extract native bog iron. Around 100 B.C., an Iron Age culture started to evolve; not only tools and weapons, but ornaments as well were made of iron. It is probable that the use of iron was introduced into Lithuania about the same time, although we do not have any artifacts. It is only after the second century A.D. that we find an iron culture in Western and Central Lithuania. This iron was extracted from the swamps and bogs.

We do not have iron artifacts of the early period. Some of the forms and patterns employed during the Late Bronze Age were probably used during the Early Iron Age (for example, some of the bronze socketed axes, pins, stone and bone implements were found in northeast and eastern Lithuania in later mounds). New forms of tools were also found (pins with spiral heads, necklaces, spiral arm-rings, temple ornaments, etc.). Two finds are worth mentioning: the hoard at Baudėjai (Alytus county) which contained two bronze pins with large spiral heads, two flat spiral arm rings, five bronze plates and several pieces of pewter; and the hoard found in Pabaliai (Panevėžys county) which contained four bronze necklaces and two pins with spiral heads. Both hoards dated from around 500 B.C.

We can learn about the manner of life and economic system of the people from the settlements that were unearthed. In the regions of the Western Balts are many settlements of stone emplacements that have been investigated. The dwelling structures were not of uniform size: some were five-by-three meters, others eight-by-five meters. In each dwelling the hearth occupied the center. In northeast and eastern Lithuania, the people also lived in stone-enforced settlements on hillocks. The following explored settlements are worth mentioning: Petrašiūnai, Moškėnai (in Rokiškis county); Vorėnai (in Utena county); Velykuškės, Vozgėliai (Zarasai county), Dūkštas (Švenčionys county). The Sites for settlements were chosen on hills near lakes or rivers. Ramparts of earth or trenches were constructed to protect the exposed side. The Dūkštas settlement had a subterranean quarter which was 12.5 meters long, about six meters wide and about 1.5 meters deep. No major changes in agriculture are discerned for this period. The cleared field system continued to be used. In the Western Baltic lands new crops made an appearance: rye (secale cereale) and peas (pisum sativum). Eastern Lithuania still planted barley and wheat. Animal husbandry played a more important role in the eastern regions. The Petrašiūnai mound contains the bones of many animals (cattle, swine and, to a lesser extent, horses and goats). Moose, boars and bears were the animals killed during hunts.

The dead were still cremated in the western regions. In some places, the bones of the cremated were placed in cistas, formed out of flat rocks; in other places they were placed in urns. The remains of people thus buried have been found in areas Western Lithuania (viz., Egliškiai, Mišeikiai, Klaipėda county, and Kurmaičiai in Kretinga county). Only the mound at Kurmaičiai contains a skeleton dating back to 500 B.C. In the first century B.C., the Western Balts changed from cremation to the custom of burying the dead in flat graves.

All available archaeological data permits us to follow the Baltic culture from the Bronze Age to the first centuries of the

32

Christian Era. All evidence points to the natives having been of the same ethnic stock—the Balts. The Germanic Vandals, Burgundians and Goths who made an appearance in the Lower Vistula and Pomerania, did not have a great influence on the Western Balts during the first century A.D. The differentiation between the Baltic tribes continued during the Iron Age. The Western Balts formed distinct tribes. The Curonian tribe took form along the seacoast of Lithuania. This is evidenced by the simple structure of their mounds and by the adoption of burying their people in flat graves. In eastern Lithuania and the present-day territory of the Byelorussians and western Russians, the Lithuanians were forming a distinct group.

Historical evidence gives some light on the subject. For example, the Greek writer Herodotus (fifth century B.C.) spoke of the Neuri as living to the north of the Scythians. Some historians and linguists hold that they were Balts, but this hypothesis has not yet been proved. Fragments of the travel account of the Greek sailor and geographer Pytheas still remain. In 350-325 B.C. he traveled from Marseilles, France, to Britain and the Island of Thule. He also reached the amber coast, a large island called Basilia, Basilea or Balcia. Later Gaius Plinius Secundus (23-79 A.D.), in writing about amber stated, "According to Pytheas, in the ocean bay called Matuonidis, about 6000 stadions (600 geographical miles) away live a Germanic tribe, the Guiones. From this place, one day's journey by sea, is the isle of *Abalum*. There the spring waves bring in amber, which is hardened sedimentation of the sea. The natives use it in place of wood for fuel and sell it to their neighbors, the Teutons." It is not possible to determine whether Pytheas reached the coast of the eastern Baltic Sea or just the Frisian Isles, which also has amber. It is not possible to localize the islands named in the accounts, because they do not appear in later historical sources.

IV. LITHUANIANS AND THEIR KINSMEN IN THE FIRST MILLENNIUM A.D. AND IN EARLY HISTORICAL TIMES

MATERIAL CULTURE

If scholars have to utilize limited archaeological sources in order to delve into the earlier periods of Baltic and Lithuanian history, then in the era after the first millennium A.D. and later there is a wealth of material taken from the systematic research of cemeteries and burial mounds, fortified hillocks, caches and other discoveries. And the historical (and literary) sources, though not very numerous or too accurate, bring much light upon the past of the several Baltic nations and tribes.

At the beginning of the second millennium A.D., almost all of the lands inhabitated by the Balts, especially Prussia, western and central Lithuania, Courland and Semigallia, developed an extraordinarily rich and independent culture which continued without interruption until historical times. Even in the eastern Baltic lands, which had archaic cultures, the use of metal expanded, and a great deal of progress can be noted in the material culture. Iron, extracted from various ore deposits in bogs, became the main driving force of the material culture. Specialized iron implements made an appearance (axes, knives, shears, saws, sickles, awls, drills, chisels, metal chipping implements, etc.) as well as weapons (variformed spearheads, shield rims, shield bucklers, broadswords), clothes for warriors (leather belts, metal fasteners and pins, spurs), and riding gear (bits, saddle hitches, decorated bridles, etc.).

From the first century A.D. to the beginning of recorded Lithuanian history, local craftsmen created many decorative items, engraved with geometric motifs, azure patterns, and the like. Jewelers and craftsmen were acquainted with the various skills of metallurgy—moulding, smithery, silver-plating, enameling, and glass work. Bronze and silver was used for the making of decorations and jewelry. Most silver artifacts discovered come from the ninth through twelfth centuries. In the tenth century, silver cast bars were used as monetary units and they survived until the time of Vytautas the Great (fourteenth to fifteenth centuries).

COMMERCIAL RELATIONS WITH OTHER LANDS

Of great importance to the rise of material culture were the ties with the provinces of the Roman Empire, Germany, the neighboring Slavs, the Finno-Ugrians, Teutons and others. During the first centuries of the present era (first to fourth centuries

A.D.) trade relations were active with the Danubian and Rhine provinces and with the Nicaea in Bithynia, in northwest Asia Minor. The Balts exported animal hides, skins, honey, wax and the most important item, amber, which the Romans and their neighbors used for decorations, amulets and eye and throat medicines. The Roman provinces, especially the southern Rhine region, sent to the southern and eastern Baltic region various goods: bronze, silver and gold coins, bronze utensils (pitchers, ladles), glass beakers, ceramic *terra sigillata,* glass and enamel beads, bronze, silver, gold-plated and enamelled pins, Roman broadswords, etc.

With the fall of the Roman Empire, trade with the southern countries decreased, yet the "amber routes" were still used in the fifth and sixth centuries. However, with the German advance on the west and south and the expansion of western Slavs into Bohemia and Moravia, the amber trade was disrupted. Ties were then established with the northern neighbors, the Finno-Ugrians and with the ancestors of the Estonians. From the fifth century, Estonia was greatly influenced by the Lithuanian and Semigallian cultures. Around the seventh century the mid-eastern and southeastern Baltic Aistians contacted the Scandinavian Germans. These relations were of a dual nature—trade and war. Scandinavian trade centers were established at Grobina, near Libau, Latvia, which between 650 and 800 A.D. was a large Gotlander trading colony; and Viskiautai (Wiskiauten), East Prussia, which was a trading colony in the ninth and tenth centuries. Viskiautai was a Danish and Norwegian center around 800 A.D. Afterwards, it was taken over by Swedes. Truso (now Elbing) in the eighth and ninth centuries was also an important center. The English traveler Wulfstan visited it in the ninth century on a mission for Alfred the Great. Ninth-century Scandinavian sources tell of Danish and Swedish military expeditions to the eastern Baltic shores (among them to the castle of Apuolė, Skuodas township, Lithuania).

In the tenth and eleventh centuries, relations between the Scandinavians and Balts were of a commercial nature. At the same time, in relation with the trade with the Near East, the eastern Baltic was the recipient of Arabic silver coins, many of which date back to the first half of the ninth century. Beginning with the tenth century, relations were established with Bremen, Hamburg and the cities of the Rhine; silver coins from Lower Saxony, Koeln, Metz and other Rhine cities attest to this. In addition to silver from Germany, woven goods, ceramics, glassware and even broadswords with the inscription "Ulfberth" were imported. During the Middle Ages, trade relations were established with Kievan Russia; these trade relations helped raise the cultural level of the Balts in the western region. Crafts abounded and agriculture and animal husbandry was improved.

FURTHER DIFFERENTIATION OF THE BALTS

Baltic differentiation began during the Bronze Age and Early Iron Age, and continued until the first centuries after Christ. However, the weaker tribes were gradually absorbed by the stronger and crystallized into larger national units. This Baltic differentiation and later consolidation could be followed archaeologically by observing the manner of burial and the characteristic elements of individual regions (jewelry, weapons, ceramics and others). Also in answering the ethnic question, one is aided by fragmentary historical sources, which mention the individual Baltic nations and tribes which lived in certain areas, as for example the Aistians (100 A.D.), Galindians and Sudovians (second century A.D.), Semigallians (870 A.D.), Prussians (ninth century A.D.), Curonians (875 A.D.), Yatvingians (983 A.D.), Lithuanians (1009 A.D.), Latgallians (1040 A.D.), Galindians (1058 A.D.), Sambians (1075 A.D.), Selians (1208 A.D.), Skalvians (1240 A.D.), Nadrovians (1250 A.D.) and others.

Although one could notice more unifying than diversifying elements in Baltic culture, one could nevertheless discover differences among the various Baltic tribes which were caused by differing geographic conditions, the proximity of trade routes, stronger or weaker development of crafts, community organization, and so on. These differences can be noted among the Western Balts as well as in the eastern reaches. Let us pause briefly to study the cultural and ethnic differentiation in Lithuania, and attempt to establish a connection with Baltic cultures outside of present-day Lithuania.

As was mentioned earlier, in the Early Iron Age the region of the western Lithuanian seacoast (also Courland in Latvia) saw the formation of a separate cultural group which buried its dead in mounds (usually after cremation) with stone borders. In the first century A.D., the dead were still cremated, but after the second century they were buried in shallow flat graves. Stone-bordered graves were found in the seacoast areas in the following counties: Kretinga (Anštakiai, Gargždai, Kurmaičiai, Lazdinin-kai, Rūdaičiai, Senkai, Tūbausiai), Klaipėda (Plūciai, Šernai) and Šilutė (Barzdēnai). Cemeteries with stone borders existed in this region until the sixth and seventh centuries (in Lazdininkai, Plūciai and Tūbausiai), while they disappeared in other areas (and the dead were buried in ordinary graves). After 800 A.D., cremation gradually was resorted to. Graves found in the north-west corner of Lithuania and in western Latvia are designated as being part of the Curonian culture, which had reached a high cultural level and had close ties with the Prussians. The people of the Curonian culture are mentioned in historical sources (see Rimbert's *Vita Anskarii, the Henrici Chronicon Lyvoniae,* and others). In the middle of the thirteenth century, the Germans broke the resistance of the Curonians, who then merged with the Lithuanians and Latvians.

In the Nemunas delta, especially in the region of Tilsit and Ragnit and part of the right bank of the Nemunas, lived the Skalvians, who were subdued by the Teutonic Knights prior to 1281. Grand Duke Kęstutis settled some 800 Skalvians in south-eastern Lithuania between the Rodūnia and Pelesa rivers.

To the east of the Curonians, in the Samogitian highlands up to the Nevėžis River, a mingling of burial mounds and flat graves dating from the first centuries of this era can be found in the lands of the western Lithuanians who in the thirteenth cen-tury were known as the Samogitians. (This region was later set up as a separate duchy.)

In the northern part of Lithuania (in the environs of Žagarė, Joniškis and Šiauliai) and in central Latvia, burial mounds dating from the first centuries A.D. belong to the Semigallians. From the fifth to the sixth centuries, customs in this region changed to flat graves where the dead were buried uncremated. From the sixth century, Semigallia was a strong cultural center which exerted an influence on Estonia and even Finland. In the thirteenth century a Semigallian port is mentioned (portus Semigallorum), at the mouth of the Lielupē River near the Gulf of Riga. The Semigallians together with the Lithuanians often attacked the Teutonic Knights during the thirteenth century; however at the end of that century, they were conquered by the Knights. Some of the Semigallians migrated to Lithuania where they were Lithuanianized.

During the first centuries A.D. there existed in southern Lithuania a cultural group which buried its dead in burial mounds and in flat graves. These people were the Sudovians or Yatvingians. In Lithuania there are three cemeteries of this culture: the stone-piled graves at Delnica (Marijampolē) of the third and fourth centuries; the flat graves at Seiliūnai (Alytus county) of the fourth and fifth centuries; and the burial mounds at Krikštonys (Alytus county) of the fifth and sixth centuries. The best information about the Sudovians can be obtained from the data of German researchers who explored the remains at Galdapē, Ungura, Lēcius, Alēcka and Lukas (in German: Goldap, Angerap, Lötzen, Markgrabau and Lyck) and from the post-1955 investigations of Polish archaeologists in the Suvalkai region. At first, the Sudovians buried their dead in burial mounds of stone and earth, but after the fifth century they practiced cremation. Fine results were found at Szwajcaria, north of Suvalkai, where burial caches of Sudovian dukes or nobles were discovered. There is little information about the material culture of the Sudovians for the ninth through twelfth centuries. The Sudovians were one of the largest and warlike members of the Baltic family; historical sources give them various names—Western sources call their country Zudua, Sudowia, Sudoweh, terra Sudorum; the Russians and Poles call them Yatvingians (Jatviagi, Jatveze, Yaczwagy); the sources of Lithuania (beginning with Mindaugas' *Donation of 1253* and ending with the Chronicles of the Grand Duchy of Lithuania and Samogitia) call their land Dainava (Deynowe, Dainowe, Denowe, etc.). The majority of scholars feel that the names Sudovians, Yatvingians and Dainavites designate the same stock. However, since Sudovia covered a large expanse,

38

it is possible that it contained cultural and linguistic differences within its ethnic confines—the western Sudovians were closer culturally and linguistically to the Prussians, while the eastern Sudovians were closer to the Lithuanians. The Sudovians or Yatvingians, being the neighbors of the Poles and Russians, since the tenth century had clashes with the Russians and since the eleventh century with the Poles. These relations were of a war-like nature. To the end of the thirteenth century, the Sudovians waged war with their neighbors until they were subdued by the Poles, Russians and Germans. Later, the larger part of Sudovia or Yatvingia came under the rule of the Lithuanian Grand Duchy.

As was mentioned earlier, from the end of the Bronze Age we are confronted with the Brushed-Pottery culture which spread throughout all of eastern and southeastern Lithuania and even farther to the east during the first centuries of the new era. This culture should be marked as Lithuanian and is the culture of the ancestors of Lithuania and their kinsmen. This Lithuanian culture can be traced from the first century A.D. It was related to the culture of the Curonians and Samogitians, but has its own characteristics: burial in flat graves in coffins of dugout oak logs, and ornaments (spiral and flat bronze clasps with key-shaped holes, bronze bracelets, bronze necklaces with hitches and club-shaped ends, etc.). During the fifth and sixth centuries the Lithuanians began cremating their dead. In central Lithuania the dead were still buried in flat graves, while in the east and southeast, burial mounds were used up to historical times. A continuation of this Lithuanian culture can be found farther to the east in Byelorussia and Russia.

BOUNDARIES OF THE BALTS

During the first millennium after Christ great changes occurred in the regions occupied by the Balts. On the one hand, the Balts were disturbed by the Eastern (and later Western) Slavs and the expansion of the Germanic Skandinavians; on the other hand, the Balts themselves moved to the north into the lands inhabited by the Livonians and the ancestors of the Estonians. All of this movement took place with small- or large-scale warfare. This is attested to by the network of fortifications (castles) in the border regions, the graves of men have a large number of weapons. Fragments of these conflicts are recorded in the scanty literature of the period.

During the first centuries A.D. the western boundaries of the Balts shrank. Whereas, during the Bronze Age, the Balts reached the Persante River in Pomerania, during the first century A.D., when the Goths pulled out from the Lower Vistula, the Prussians spread as far as the mouth of the Vistula. The southwestern Sudovians or Yatvingians reached the confluence of the Narew and Bug. The southern Baltic boundary ran along the Berezina and Dnieper confluence; farther to the east, the Balts inhabited Sozh and the Desna and Oka basins. In the east their boundary almost reached present-day Moscow, in the north—the Upper Volga; farther on, the Eastern Balts inhabited the area where the Finno-Ugric tribes met (along the present Latvian-Estonian border).

After the fifth century, the Eastern Balts were forced to bow to the great pressure of the Slavs. Slavic expansion began about 400 A.D., and eventually forced the Eastern Balts to relinquish large areas. The eastern Baltic lands were infiltrated by the eastern Slavic tribes: the Viatichi, Krivichi, Radimichi, Dregovichi and others. In the tenth to twelfth centuries, the eastern Baltic border ran along an almost straight line from Pskov to Minsk. Farther to the east, a number of Baltic enclaves remained. For example, in the eleventh and twelfth centuries, west of Moscow, along the upper Protva, near Gzhatsk and Mozhaisk, a tribe of Eastern Balts, the Galindians remained. The Russian chronicles mention that in 1058, Iziaslav conquered the Galindians. But at the beginning of the twelfth century they were still not assimilated, for in 1147 the *Kievan Chronicle* speaks of these self-same *Goliad'*. The hydronymes of this area have the Baltic suffix -*eja*.

The Slavonization of the eastern Balts proceeded slowly. Archaeological and linguistic studies show that the ancestors of the Lithuanians and Latvians did not evacuate their inhabited lands *en masse,* as the Lithuanian linguist K. Būga asserts; the majority remained. When Slavic colonization was intensified in the ninth and eleventh centuries, part of the Lithuanian element was Slavonized. This process began slowly and then intensified. During the fourteenth and sixteenth centuries the Byelorussianization of Lithuanians began, and this process ended only at the beginning of the twentieth century!

While the process of differentiation was strong at the beginning of this era, the differences between the Balts gradually lessened. This is tied to the rise of social orders. The quick growth of crafts, trade and agriculture had a great influence on the social order, meanwhile creating great differences in wealth. This can be seen from the discoveries made in graves. A number of caches are found in graves dating from the third century A.D. For example, at Seredžius (in Kaunas county) the grave of a young woman contains a bronze collar with five glass and enamel beads, and eight bracelets. At Veršvai (near Kaunas) one grave contains, in addition to the remains of a poor man, a coffin with the remains of an exceptionally rich woman contains a necklace, chain, glass and enamel beads, six bracelets and, above the head in a birch box, five collars, seven bracelets, an ornate head or chest decoration, and a Roman bronze pitcher. In Upytė (Panevėžys county) the double-grave woman's coffin revealed a silver Lithuanian style collar with spoon-shaped fasteners, an azure pin with four chains, six bracelets and other artifacts. Rich graves were discovered in Sudovia, at the Szwajcaria cemetery: two graves of "dukes," a grave of a "duchess," a grave of a warrior, and a grave of a noble boy. These graves date back to the fifth century.

Defensive hillock castles also attest to the existence of regional centers which later grew into regional strongholds of rulers. The regional strongholds include the following large castles: Apuolė (Kretinga county), Įpiltis (Kretinga county), Aukštadvaris (Trakai county), a Gediminas mount in Vilnius, and many other castles that still need to be investigated. At the slopes of these fortified hillocks, settlements were established. Construction of these strongholds required massive labor forces, which were manipulated by powerful regional rulers. The hillocks evolved into strong castles ruled by dukes (kunigaikščiai). The more powerful regional rulers dominated the lesser dukes. A number of senior dukes arose who dominated the less powerful; for example, in

1219 a peace treaty was concluded with the widow of Roman of Volynia-Halich. Twenty-two dukes, representing five ruling Lithuanian families, signed for Lithuania. The treaty mentions that five were "senior dukes"—Mindaugas, his brother Dausprun-gas, Živinbudas, Daujotas and Viligaila. Eventually, Mindaugas emerged as the supreme ruler of the Lithuanians, the eastern part of Samogitia, and the Yatvingians by the middle of the thirteenth century.

Lithuania to World War I

by JUOZAS JAKŠTAS

The Rise of the Lithuanian Nation

Dating as far back as the second millennium B.C., tribes of the Indoeuropean proto-nations have lived in the Baltic area between the Vistula and Dauguva rivers. Referred to in the oldest sources as the Aesti, they were later given the name Balts. These Baltic tribes lived scattered over large areas divided by uninhabited forests, swamps, and large bodies of water, and were without much inter-relationship, and thus went by separate names. They can, however, be generally divided into three large groups: the Prussians, who lived in the western sector up to the Vistula; the Latvians, who stayed around the Dauguva; and the Lithuanians, who settled around the Nemunas and Neris rivers. The Prussians disappeared as an entity in the area sometime in the seventeenth century, the Latvians went on to develop into a nation, and the Lithuanians succeeded in establishing a great state—one of the oldest extant dating back to the thirteenth century.

The Lithuanians remained in the southeastern Baltic area, almost contiguous to Russian Kiev, and, as a tribe, are mentioned in early literature as dating back to 1040 A.D. However, later sources—the German Quendlinburg yearbooks—date the name "Lithuania" back to 1009 A.D. In describing the death of St. Bruno, he is mentioned as having perished as a martyr, along with eighteen followers, at the "Russian and Lithuanian border."

Whether the "Lithuanian" herein mention corresponds to that country which was later named Lithuania Proper (*Lithuania propria*) has never been fully established. The territory came to

43

be called Aukštaičiai toward the end of the thirteenth century; however, it should be remembered that Lithuania, per se, was in that territory, as the chronicler Dusburg referred to it as "the land of the Lithuanian king."

According to a treaty of 1219 between the Lithuanian Dukes and the Dukes of Volynia, the Samogitians were excluded from Lithuania as well as from the Deltuva region (the present-day Ukmergė region). Historians have concluded, on the basis of this and other evidence, that the area known as Lithuania during that period corresponded to the present-day southwestern Auk-štaitija, roughly the Vilnius region. It is from this area that the Baltic tribe flourished which developed into the modern Lithu-anian state.

The nation developed as a result of both internal and external conditions. The external factors included separation from the neighboring Balt tribes who had come under foreign rule: those around the Dauguva River, along with the Prussians, came under control of, and were shortly thereafter united into a common state under, the German Order. After this, the borders of the free Balts narrowed considerably. Remaining free, along with the Lithuanians, were their cousins the Samogitians, who occupied the area between the Nevėžis and the lower Nemunas rivers, as well as reaching as far north as the Baltic Sea. Since their land was a wedge between the two states of the Order that had been united politically as one, they were continually subjected to at-tacks on both sides. The Samogitians and Lithuanians, while living as one state geographically, did not merge, although they did draw closer together as time went on—especially when the Samogitians began moving toward the Lithuanians politically, the latter having begun to live in a more sovereign manner. (An example of the affinity between these two peoples is to be found in the famous protest publication to Emperor Sigismund, which refers to the both tribes as *"Unum idioma et uni homines."*)

The primary external factor leading to the growth of the Lithuanians as the leading nation in the community of the Balts was the formation of the state. Perhaps it was not merely by chance that the Lithuanian nation began at a time when the

44

Baltic tribes of the Vistula and Dauguva regions fell under the rule of the Order.

I. Beginning of the State

1. *Establishment of the Duchy*

As is the case with all states which were rooted in the tribal community and whose unification was the result of gradual development, it is impossible to pinpoint the exact period of geographical and political origin, let alone the exact date. Suffice it to say, the Lithuanian nation emerged as an agricultural community, divided into large estates under the control of those who had risen to the eminence of landowner and nobleman. As an ancillary factor, there were the serfs—the majority of the inhabitants of the area, none of whom had many rights, all of whom were bound to the estates. In time, with the nobles and landowners contesting for supremacy, there began to emerge those more powerful figures who eventually became the rulers—these were the dukes. It is from the Russian and German chronicles of the twelfth and thirteenth centuries that we learn of the power and influence that was beginning to be exerted by these dukes. The chronicles tell of campaigns in the Dauguva River area and in neighboring Russian lands, and describe how, by that time in history, the Lithuanians had already united politically under the dukes.

The earliest source which can be considered as "proof" of the inception of the Lithuanian state is found in the Volynia Chronicle, which tells of the aforementioned 1219 treaty. Of the twenty-one Lithuanian dukes mentioned therein, five were referred to as "elders," thus attesting to their superiority over the remaining sixteen. Prominent among the five elders was one Mindaugas, descended—as we learn from other chronicles of that era—from a powerful duke who apparently had no equal. In the Volynian Chronicles, there is mentioned Mindaugas' brother Dausprungas, along with two nephews, Erdvilas and Vykintas, identified as dukes of Samogitia.

The most powerful member of his clan, Mindaugas united the area by eliminating his relatives. According to the Volynian

Chronicle, he "began killing his brothers and nephews, expelling others from the country and ruling alone in all of Lithuania." In view of the fact that the brother and nephews are not mentioned later, we may conclude that Mindaugas was successful!

Although the means by which Mindaugas united Lithuania are unknown, the unity of the state is attested to by the successful campaign in Šiaulai (1236), as a result of which the Lithuanians succeeded in defeating the Livonian Order. Though some sources credit the Samogitian duke Vykintas with having led the victory, evidence seems to weigh heavily in favor of Mindaugas. (Thus, in addition to being considered the founder of the Lithuanian nation, Mindaugas also enjoys the distinction of being the first conqueror of the Order.)

Mindaugas was faced on all sides by enemies threatening the state he had created. His expelled relatives turned for support to the neighboring states—specifically, to the Duke of Volynia, thus succeeding in setting the Livonian Order against the Lithuanians. In 1249, the Duke of Volynia attacked the western Russian region, which Mindaugas had annexed, while from the north a large army of the Livonian Order advanced, crossing the land of Nalsa and reaching the area of Voruta (Voruta, a common name meaning "fortified place," was the seat of Mindaugas' government). Though he succeeded in repelling the Order, Mindaugas was faced with uprisings among his own people. It was at this time that his chief opponent, Vykintas, turned to the Archbishop of Riga and, in order to secure the latter's favor, had himself baptized. The Archbishop was an opponent of the Order; thus, Vykintas could not receive the support of the Order against Mindaugas, who succeeded in breaking the coalition of his enemies. The Order's Magister agreed to a reconciliation on the condition that Mindaugas submit to baptism, in return for which he was promised a king's crown (Mindaugas, in turn, presented his former opponent with some land). As a result, the coalition against Mindaugas disintegrated rapidly and completely.

Following his own baptism, as well as that of his wife, two sons, and "many pagans," Mindaugas began the baptism of his entire nation. Also, he allowed Christian, a cleric of the Order, to be ordained Bishop of Lithuania, and promised to build a cathedral. After a delay of three years, primarily because of competition between the Archbishop of Riga and the Order over who was to "Christianize" Lithuania, the Order was acknowledged as the protector of the Bishop of Lithuania (who had been given lands in Samogitia, and who, having been separated from under the authority of the Archbishop of Riga, was directly subordinated to Rome). Obviously, through the baptism of Mindaugas, the Order was attempting to win what they could not win on the battlefield—suzerainty in Lithuania.

Following presentation to the Order of various parcels of land (the six documents written during this time give evidence that the land Mindaugas awarded to the Order included some area over which he did not even rule), Mindaugas was crowned king in 1253. During the approximately eight years of stability and peace that followed, the Teutonic Knights attempted to gain a firm footing in Samogitia. The independent Samogitians resisted the Knights. The Order built three castles along the Samogitian borders: Doben, Georgenburg (Jurbarkas) and Memelburg (Klaipėda). The purpose of the last castle was to cut off the Samogitian water route across which the Lithuanians had been receiving from abroad such necessary commodities as salt, iron and clothing.

Now enjoying peace with the Order as well as with his internal enemies, Mindaugas began to direct his attentions toward annexing Russian lands contiguous to his border, and pushing back the constant Tartar incursions. It was during this period that Russian Novogrod became an important city in the Lithuanian state (some historians surmise it became Mindaugas' capital). Also coming under Lithuanian control was the Russian city of Polock, a major center of commerce in the Dauguva River basin. Mindaugas' overall design was clearly to defeat the Tartars and to organize under his control the Slavic lands, which by now were in a state of chaos.

Concurrently, the Order was attempting to enslave the Samogitians; the Prussian revolt had broken out; and the Couronians and Zemgalians were beginning to stir. The Order called on the help of the Western (i.e., European) Christians, as a result of which Pope Alexander IV called for Crusaders to go into the area. Of the many invasions by the Crusaders, the biggest was planned for 1260, for which purpose the Teutonic Knights assembled at Courland. However, before they could initiate their campaign, they were attacked near Lake Durbe (July 13) where, after a great battle lasting eight hours, the Crusaders were defeated by the pagan Samogitians. (The chronicler of the Knights blamed their defeat on the Couronians and Estonians, who allegedly not only left the battlefield but went so far as to attack the Knights from the rear.) Along with this victory, the Samogitians managed to buy a few years of peace, what with the continuing Prussian revolt against the Germans, as well as the disturbances on the part of the Estonians, Couronians and Zemgalians (the latter receiving Lithuanian support).

Obviously, Mindaugas did not remain apathetic to what was going on about him. Evidence survives that the Samogitian leader, Treniota, talked him into reverting to paganism. Mindaugas, having achieved the position of being considered the most important ruler among the Balts, appears to have accepted Treniota's advice, for the two united in battle against the Knights (1261). Also, Mindaugas went one step further by allying himself with Duke Alexander Nevsky of Novgorod, who was also an enemy of the Order. Thus, Mindaugas, with his eye on the great Dauguva basin, was repeating the policy of previous Lithuanian regional leaders who, while fighting the Germans in the Dauguva basin, sought union with the Russians.

Immediately after allying himself with Alexander Nevsky, Mindaugas, along with Treniota's forces, marched his troops into Livonia and attacked the Cesis (Wenden) castle. But the attack failed because the Russians arrived too late. Disappointed by the failure of this campaign, Mindaugas abandoned hope of uniting with the Latvians (Treniota's overall plan), and, regretting his having fallen away from the Order, turned on Treniota for having thus encouraged him. Treniota, having concluded an alliance with Duke Daumantas of the Nalsia region, succeeded in killing Mindaugas, along with his two sons, in 1263, thus averting what surely could have become a civil war. Despite the quick succession of rulers which followed Mindaugas' death, the Lithuanian state did not disintegrate, primarily because he had strengthened the government in Aukštaičiai, repelled the attacks of the alliance between the Order and the Volynians, and had expanded the boundaries to the east and the south.

Treniota held power for one year, and was succeeded by Mindauga's son Vaišvilkas, who ruled for three years (1264-67). Vaišvilkas, following his baptism, had become a monk. Now with Russian support, he not only avenged his father's murder (by overthrowing and killing Treniota)—possibly with Russian support—but expanded the Lithuanian boundaries even farther. He was succeeded by his brother-in-law, Duke Švarnas of Volynia, who was in turn succeeded after three years by Traidenis, who ruled until 1282. It is not known whether Traidenis belonged to the Mindaugas clan or whether he was merely a noble of Aukštaitija. From the rhymed Livonian Chronicles, we learn that his seat of government was at Kernavė, which was probably his native fief.

His rule was marked by the revival of paganism and an attempt to suppress Christianity in the country, thereby incurring the emnity of the Orthodox Russians. Also during his reign, the western area of Suduva-Yatvygia came under Lithuanian control. One of his main policies was to support the Zemgalians in the north, into whose area the Teutonic Knights were making incursions; thus, he was working in the best interests of the Lithuanian state. In 1274, the Germans built the Daugavpils castle on the Dauguva River as part of a campaign aimed at Traidenis' seat of government. After unsuccessfully attacking the castle, Traidenis said—as quoted in the Order's chronicles—"That castle is built in my heart and I will suffer pain from it as long as I live." It would seem that by these words, the chroniclers wanted to emphasize the danger to Lithuania inherent in the construction of the castle. Not long afterward, the Germans reached Kernava and plundered it, but while they were returning to their home base they were overtaken by the Lithuanians at Dauguva and defeated, as a result of which it was decided by the Germans that both branches of the Order should become more unified against the Lithuanians.

It was also during the reign of Traidenis that the Prussian Order began attacking the Lithuanians (they had already con-

quered the Prussians and were coming closer to Nemunas). Traidenis gave asylum to some of the Zemgalians who were defeated
by the Teutonic Knights in that area. With the close of his
reign, the first epoch in the history of the Baltic area ended.
For under Traidenis, the final development of the Lithuanian
tribes into a unified state had come about.

II.   The Development of Lithuania's Grand Duchy

1. *Beginning of the Dynasty of Gediminas*

Many legends abound concerning the rise of the Gediminas
Dynasty. One fifteenth-century chronicle mentions how the Teutonic Knights spoke of the lowly origins of Jogaila and Vytautas
as having been descended from a horse-groom (*pferdemarshalck*)
who had been a "low nobleman." A sixteenth-century story
among the Russians at the time of the Lithuanian wars with Moscow dates the rise of the clan from the flight of Duke Vytenis of
Smolensk to Samogitia following the Tartar attack on that city.
And a Lithuanian legend, dating from the sixteenth century,
credits the Gediminians as having descended from the Roman
Columnus ("Column") clan that settled originally in Samogitia;
according to the legend, Traidenis found the Gediminian Vytenis
in Ariogala and took him into his palace, and that the Gediminian inherited the throne following Traidenis' death.

Suffice it to say, historical research has all but proved that
the clan was already ruling an already strengthened state, centered in Aukštaitija, during feudal times; indeed, the first Gediminians may well have been landowners in that area who rose
to eminence. Their descent from the Aukštaičiai is reflected in
the former "kingly manors" (*königes hof*) in that region, as recorded in the chronicles of the fourteenth century. The first
Gediminian mentioned in the chronicles is Pukuveras. The first
Gediminian, the one credited as being the progenitor of the dynasty, was the Duke of Lithuania who was the father of Vytenis
and Gediminas.

50

2. Expansion of the Lithuanian State in the East

The new dynasty continued the expansion process of the pre-vious Lithuanian rulers in the south and east. In addition, they strengthened their ties to the Russians through a series of political marriages: Gediminas' daughter was married off to the Duke of Tver; his son, Algirdas, was married off to the sole inheriting Duchess of Vitebsk, which region she brought with her as a dowry; and another son, Liubartas, was married to the Duchess of Volynia, whose dowry included part of that state. In time, the influence of Gediminas reached as far as Smolensk, Pskov and Kiev (where his little-known brother Teodoras was set up as the ruler).

It was around this time that the Grand Duchy of Lithuania became a geopolitical entity. Though the surrounding Slavic lands surpassed it in area, the Grand Duchy was not "Western Russia," as some Russian histories claim; rather, the Russian states were annexed to the Lithuanian core, though they retained their own laws. The Lithuanian core was not adversely affected by the fact that the official language was Slavic, since that was the only written language in Eastern Europe at the time.

3. Lithuania's Grand Duchy—a Feudal State

From its very inception, the Grand Duchy was an aristo-cratic regional federation belonging to the clan of Gediminas, who was distinguished from the other dukes by virtue of being permanently known as Grand Duke, and having his residence at what became the nation's capital, Vilnius. Otherwise, he was more or less *primus inter pares* in his relationship with the other nobles with whose assistance he ruled. With the aid of these other dukes, he was able to organize an army, which played such an important role in the nation's history, and from which emerged an order of noblemen. The Grand Duchy was a true aristocratic state in that the land was owned by the nobility, who held in thrall the great masses of peasants—the serfs.

4. Lithuania—the Goal of the Crusades

Whereas in the eastern Slavic areas the Lithuanian rulers were able to achieve their ends more or less politically, from the

51

west (and, to a degree, from the north) the threat of the Order hung over them like the Sword of Damocles, involving the nation in a series of war that extended over 150 years. Concurrent with the rise of the Gediminian Dynasty, the Order completed the conquest of Prussia and the Dauguva basin, and was thus in a position to launch direct attacks upon Lithuania. While the Prussians and Dauguva Balts had, as one chronicler wrote, "submissively bowed to the Church of Rome," the Lithuanians had to be forced to do so by "the holy Church"—i.e., in the name of Christianity.

With the Order representing the West, it was as if the entire Christian world was allied against the Lithuanians.

As they had done in defeating the Prussians, the Order resorted mostly to the waterways in their campaigns. They chose the main artery—the Nemunas—to get at Lithuania, beginning successful attacks in 1283 when the Teutonic Knights besieged the Bisenai Castle. The second largest castle to come under attack was the Gardinas, the strongest fortress in the entire southern area of Lithuania. Although the defenders fought bravely, the castle fell and the Knights, in addition to razing the castle, murdered many people and led many others into captivity.

Despite these successes, however, the Knights, convinced that the Lithuanians could not be as easily defeated as had been the Prussians, did not organize further attacks for six years. The strong will of the Lithuanians is shown by their deciding (1291) to build a new castle at Veliuona, which had been selected as their center of defense for the entire lower Nemunas region. The success of the Lithuanians in fighting off the enemy is reflected in the fact that the Knights were not able to seize the castle until 1348—after fifty-seven years of stubborn fighting!

5. Union with Riga

The Lithuanians gained an unexpected ally against the Order of Livonia, due to internal quarrels in Livonia itself. The Archbishop of Riga came into conflict with the Order, whose sovereign he pretended to be. Concurrently, a third political power developed—the wealthy class of Riga citizens who, having been allowed by the Order to govern itself independently, allied itself with the Archbishop. (It should be noted that the important trade center at Hamsa had become important, for trading purpose, to the Lithuanians.) In 1298, the Archbishop invited the Lithuanians to join in an alliance with the City of Riga, against their common enemy, the Order. This was followed by campaigns undertaken by the Lithuanians, supported by Riga. This arrangement lasted until 1313, when the Order, forced to conclude a peace with the City of Riga, in turn forced the people to break their alliance with the Lithuanians. The alliance, which had been concluded by Vytenis, was renewed by Gediminas around 1322.

It was around this time that Gediminas, who ruled from 1316 to 1341, was becoming known abroad for his famous letters. Of special significance is his letter to the Pope, wherein he not only describes the villainous deeds of the Teutonic Knights, but avers that Lithuania would have been Christianized if not for the Order's predatory attacks, reiterating that he fought against the Order only in defense of his country, and not because of any hostility toward Christianity. (In view of his subsequent refusal to be baptized, the probity of this letter is questioned.)

Of the six letters, the most interesting are the three written in May, 1323, addressed to the Saxon province of Dominicans and Franciscans, as well as to several cities of Hansa, in which he invites monks, traders, craftsmen and farmers to come to his country, promising special privileges for permanent settlement, and guaranteeing them freedom to leave the country if they so desire. (As was the case of many Middle European rulers who invited similar colonization, Gediminas was clearly attempting to populate empty regions and otherwise raise the country in an attempt to catch up with the West.)

When Gediminas made it known that he desired peace with the Christians, representatives came from the Livonian region to Vilnius to discuss peace, trade—and baptism. Though Gediminas refused even to discuss baptism, a treaty of peace and trade was concluded (October 2, 1323). But the agreement remained meaningless, as the Order refused from the very beginning to abide by its terms. As the old quarrels rose anew, the City of Riga was thus led to renew the alliance with the Lithuanians, an alliance which was in effect until the Order abolished the city's self-government and invested it, seven years later.

6. Gediminas—the Creator of the Lithuanian Grand Duchy

After Riga lost its independence, Gediminas had to hold off the Order's severe attacks from Prussia and Livonia. Pressure came from both sides—the Prussian Order stormed the Samogitians, while the Livonian Order occupied the central areas of Lithuania, reaching as far as the Vilnius region. In addition, the Prussian Order was being aided by the Crusaders coming from Western Europe. Of the many attacks made by the Order, three are especially well remembered: that on Medvègalis in 1329, the one on Pilènai in 1336, and the attack the following year on the Romainiai Islands. The attack upon Medvègalis was eye-witnessed by the French poet, G. de Machaut, who was part of the suite of the Czech King John of Luxembourg, and who describes vividly the king's baptizing of 6,000 defeated pagans following the fall of their castle. The defense of Pilènai, one of the most heroic in history, has been a constant source of inspiration for poets and musicians (it forms the basis of a contemporary Lithuanian opera). The attack on the Romainiai Islands, in which the Emperor's relative, Duke Henry of Bavaria, participated, resulted in the building of the Bajerburg castle (near Veliuona) for the conquest of the Lithuanian central region. The fact that the resistance on the part of the defenders was equal in intensity to the attacks by the Order, attests to Lithuania being a strong and well-organized state by that time.

III. CRISIS OF THE STATE AND UNION WITH POLAND

1. The Diarchy of Lithuania

The Grand Duchy of Lithuania, being a patriarchal state, was considered the personal property of its ruling clan. Gediminas proceeded to partition the state into six regions and entrust them to his sons. (It is significant that they were given not only parts of ethnographic Lithuania, but regions of Russia, which further indicates the extent of the Lithuanian holdings. However, of the remote Russian regions, only two were involved in the partition: Vitebsk, which had come into the possession of Algirdas through marriage; and Volynia, with the city of Luck, which Gediminas had incorporated after the fall of the Halich-Volynia state.)

Vilnius itself, including large surrounding regions, remained directly under the rule of Gediminas, and after his death it came into possession of his seventh and youngest son, Jaunutis, who had not previously received any appanage. It is not clear whether Jaunutis was meant to have become the Grand Duke; though he held the throne in Vilnius, he lacked any precedence over his six brothers. Be that as it may, two of the brothers—Algirdas and Kęstutis — took possession of Vilnius and expelled Jaunutis (1345), thereby becoming the rulers of the nation.

Under this diarchy (i.e., rule by two individuals), the eastern sector, with the center at Vilnius, belonged to Algirdas, while the western sector, with the capital at Trakai, came under the control of Kęstutis (who had, of course, already been given the land by his father as part of his appanage). Since the center of government was at Vilnius, Algirdas enjoyed priority; according to contemporary chronicles, he was soon being called king (the title was also accorded to Kęstutis on occasion).

Lithuania's geographical situation complimented the diarchal system. In the east, the Slavs had to be organized and united into their own state, which Algirdas accomplished by expanding his borders to the east and south, taking over the Russian areas of Smolensk, Matislavl, Briansk, Novgorod-Seversk, Chernigov, Starodub, and Trubtsevsk, among others; and, politicking on his own eastern borders, he aided the Duke of Tver, going so far as to organize three campaigns into Moscow. In the south, he clashed with the Tartars successfully and took the large territory of Podolia. In effect, the extensive Russian holdings around Kiev came into the Grand Duchy of Lithuania.

In the west, the Lithuanians still had to defend themselves against frequent attacks by the Teutonic Knights, who were now receiving further aid from Western European knights. In addition to moving into Samogitia (where they devastated the land

and took into captivity those inhabitants they could not kill), the Knights continued to concentrate their efforts along the Nemunas. (In one campaign, that against the castle at Kaunas in 1362, the defense was led by Kęstutis' son Vaidotas; unable to resist the invaders, they set the castle afire before surrendering.)

The influx of Crusaders from Europe, along with their organized attacks upon the pagans, plus the heroic defense by the Lithuanians, made the Grand Duchy famous throughout the West. The "journey into Prussia" (i.e., the crusade to fight the pagan Lithuanians) became an enticing slogan among European knights. This would explain why Chaucer, writing his *Canterbury Tales* in the second half of the fourteenth century, idealized his Knight as having made the journey into Lithuania and Russia.

Emperor Carl IV, having been in Prussia at least twice prior to his accession, knew about the pagans and their strong resistance to Christianity, and felt compelled to suggest baptism for Algirdas and Kęstutis, With the consent of the Grand Dukes, he sent an archbishop to Vilnius toward that end. The brothers agreed to baptism on two conditions: that the Lithuanian and Prussian border be redefined to their advantage, and the Lithuanians be allowed to take the lands up to the Dauguva River; and that the Order be moved to the southern steppes to defend the Russian lands against the Tartars. Since neither the Emperor nor the Knights could agree to such conditions, the conference came to naught. Almost at the same time, while the Lithuanians and Poles were fighting over the lands of the former Halich-Volynia state, the Pope, encouraged by the Polish king, began to put pressure on the Lithuanian Dukes to baptize. (The Papal letters proved to be little more than interesting historical documents.) The confrontation between the pagans and Christians continued until the death of Algirdas in 1377, following which many internal changes brought about an altering of the Grand Duchy's relationship with the Order.

2. *Internal Struggles*

Algirdas was succeeded by his son Jogaila who, unlike his father, was unable to get along with Kęstutis. Being much younger than his uncle (he was at the time around thirty), Jogaila was intent on seeking ways to lead Lithuania out of its isolatory paganism and toward Christianity. The situation was made difficult by the uprising of his older brother, Andrew, Duke of Polotsk, who demanded the overthrow of his brother on the grounds of seniority; in addition to seeking aid in Moscow for his fight to replace Jogaila as Grand Duke, Andrew was now on the verge of turning to the Order for assistance.

Capitalizing on the internal conflict, the Order diverted their attacks in the direction of Kęstutis' region around the Bug River. For his part, Jogaila was improving his relations with the Order (he even sent his brother Skirgaila to the Order as his personal envoy). In 1379, Jogaila and Kęstutis concluded a ten-year truce with the Order at Trakai. The Order adopted an unfavorable policy toward Kęstutis, and therefore the Samogitia was not included in the truce agreement; also, Jogaila followed the signing of the truce by entering into secret negotiations with the Germans, thus attesting to his willingness to submit to the authority of the Order—he went so far as to agree to the clear separation of Kęstutis' lands, and further proved his hostility toward his uncle by secretly agreeing with the Order to withhold aid from Kęstutis during subsequent attacks on his lands.

Kęstutis retaliated by attacking Vilnius and taking Jogaila into captivity (August 10, 1381), and forcing him to be content with the regions of Vitebsk and Kreva, retaining Vilnius for himself. However, Kęstutis was not able to hold onto his gains for long. Jogaila, aided by the Order, recaptured Vilnius, and by deceitful means imprisoned Kęstutis and his son Vytautas. Five days later, Kęstutis died under mysterious circumstances, but Vytautas managed to escape the prison, and immediately fled to Prussia where he began conspiring with the Order against Jogaila. Rapidly changing its policies, the Order chose to aid Vytautas rather than remain loyal to Jogaila. After an incursion into Trakai, Vytautas was forced to retreat back into Prussia. He was entrusted by the Order with Samogitia up to the Nevėžis River—but only in the expectation that he would encourage the inhabitants to submit to Christianity. Vytautas, to all intent and purpose a prisoner of the Order, added more lands to the Order, west from the Nemunas River and up to the Russian

border in the south; thus, the Germans received much added territory from their prisoner. Their victory was a resounding one,
with Vytautas going so far as to proclaim that the territory in
question "never belonged to our forefathers, but since the oldest
times, belonged to the Order!" Having completely subjugated
himself to the Order, Vytautas was baptized, choosing the Christian name Vigandas.

Jogaila, sensing the danger from two enemies (the Order was
strengthening itself with new castles along the Nemunas River),
persuaded his cousin Vytautas to come over to his side (in exchange for which Vytautas was given rule over the Volynia region with the city of Luck). It was important to Jogaila that
Vytautas be separated from the Order (accomplished in 1384),
and that he have a relatively peaceful country, for he had already
been informed that the aristocrats of Poland desired him to become
their king.

3. *Alliance of Kreva*

Paganism in fourteenth-century Lithuania was fast becoming
an anachronism, doomed to disappear entirely. Jogaila demonstrated his intent to accept baptism, as is demonstrated by his
use of the Christian title "Dei gratia Rex Lethowye" in a document dated January 6, 1384. Ironically, it was the question of
the Polish Succession that accomplished for Lithuania what the
Order had been trying to bring about for more than a century!

When King Louis of Poland (and Hungary) died in 1382,
he was survived by only two daughters, Maria and Hedwig.
Maria's husband, Sigismund of Luxembourg, was the pretender
to the throne, but he was unacceptable to the Polish nobility
because he refused to reside permanently in Poland (Sigismund
was already the ruler of Brandenburg as well as Hungary, and
was expecting to get the Bohemian throne). The eleven-year-old
Hedwig was therefore crowned queen, despite the fact that she
was already betrothed to Prince Wilhelm of Austria, and the
Poles, who were also opposed to the Order, did not want a German on their throne. Thus, they offered Hedwig and the throne
to Jogaila, in the hopes that by having a king of Lithuanian descent they would be able to extend their borders into the eastern

58

Russian regions. (A prior relationship had been established between the Lithuanians and Poles through the marriage of Gediminas' daughter Aldona to Casimir of Piast in 1325.)

Following secret negotiations, Jogaila issued a declaration which is accepted as the Kreva Union Act (August 14, 1385) whereby Jogaila agreed to baptism and to marriage with Hedwig. Furthermore, he agreed to the baptism of his family and the nobility of Lithuania, in addition to paying 200,000 florins to Prince Wilhelm for breaking the betrothal to Hedwig; also he agreed to the return of all Polish lands taken by the enemies, the release of all Polish prisoners, and the pledge to keep the Lithuanian and Russian regions united with the Kingdom of Poland. Although this last contingency did not go down well with his subjects, Jogaila was able to have his way (he later took the Polish, i.e., Christian names of Wladyslaw and Jagiello).

4. Immediate Results of the Union

Jogaila's plan to rule Lithuania from Poland proved to be unrealistic. The dukes of Polock and Smolensk immediately revolted, and the Livonian Order plundered at the borders; Jogaila had to send Skirgaila and Vytautas (who was also baptized, and who took the Christian name of Alexander) from Cracow to restore his authority. Skirgaila defeated the Duke of Polock (Jogaila's brother Andrew), dethroning him and assuming the rule himself, at the same time retaining his control over Trakai, which was confirmed by Jogaila in 1387 when Skirgaila was named Duke of Trakai. With Jogaila in Cracow, Skirgaila was left to assume local rule in his stead.

Jogaila returned to Vilnius in 1387 with a group of Polish as well as Lithuanian noblemen, and in the rites that followed—the citizens were driven into the Neris River for their mass baptism—the Catholic Church came to Lithuania. The Bishopric of Vilnius was established, and construction was begun on the churches (the Bishop, as well as the clerics, were, of course, Polish). The growth of the Church in Lithuania was helped along —as was the spread of Christianity itself—by the fact that the government not only supported it, but it went so far as to grant land concessions and other holdings; according to one source of the times, Jogaila ceded to the Bishop a section of the capital city of Vilnius, along with "plots of land and houses, their inhabitants, and all their possessions." In addition, he issued a proclamation (1389) obligating all the Lithuanian regents to supply the priests and churches, both in the cities as well as the outlying villages, with money, acreage, and facilities for every parish priest "to build a tavern for himself." These gifts of Jogaila, as well as those of succeeding Grand Dukes, served to promote a privileged class of clergymen, concentrating large real estate holdings and other wealth in their hands. The wealthy Church extended its hierarchy throughout the country though was not able to suppress the paganism that persisted several ages.

5. *The Rise of Vytautas and the Decline of the Order*

Skirgaila, though only the nominal ruler in Jogaila's stead, sometimes made pretensions of being the real authority in Vilnius and Trakai. However, Jogaila, while heavily involved in negotiations with the Order, did not remain apathetic to these pretenses, nor did he remain apathetic to all Lithuanian affairs. His negotiations with the Order, however, were carried on largely with the assistance of his Polish advisers, as a further result of which the Poles began to exert their influence into Lithuania, going so far as to assume command of some of the major castles, and to station troops in Vilnius. Vytautas capitalized on the hatred the Lithuanians felt toward the Polish newcomers, and conspired to take over Vilnius in his own right. But when his conspiracy was uncovered, he was forced to retreat—back into the arms of the Order, who, while not trusting Vytautas, hoped that they could eventually impel Jogaila to change his tactics. Vytautas took up residence near Kaunas, where, as a result of the influence he exerted over the Samogitians, representatives of a few townships in Samogitia arrived in Koenibsger in 1390 and submitted to the protection of the Order. With this victory handed them, the Order now set about organizing repeated campaigns into the Grand Duchy (in one of which campaign they were assisted by the English Prince Henry of Derby, later King Henry IV).

The attacks of the Order, as well as the growing number of

partisans to the cause of Vytautas, threatened Jogaila's rule in Lithuania. The threat was compounded when Vytautas' daughter Sophia married Duke Vassili of Moscow, thus bringing the Russians into the fight against Jogaila. In addition, Jogaila realized that the Lithuanians were antagonistic to having Polish troops on their territory, and were thus thronging around Vytautas. Jogaila therefore negotiated a settlement with Vytautas, whereby the latter cut his relations with the Order, in return for which he was given back the patrimony of the Duchy of Trakai and was established as ruler in Vilnius. On his part, Vytautas promised to recognize Jogaila's superiority, and never to go against him again. Though Jogaila was still the Grand Duke of Lithuania, Vytautas, after a while, adopted this title, as was his right as the ruler of Vilnius, and in time became coeval with Jogaila. Thus, there was now a repetition of the diarchy system that had existed at the time of Algirdas and Kęstutis.

Vytautas strengthened the independence of the Grand Duchy of Lithuania, placing it on the same level as Poland. Through his determination and wisdom, the two states soon became united into one commonwealth. The support of the nobility enabled Vytautas to suppress some of the sons of Algirdas who were making claims to the Grand Ducal throne. Included in the group of insurgents was Švitrigaila. When the insurgents were expelled, he turned to the Order for support, and was again unsuccessful; he did not give up trying to overthrow Vytautas until the day he died.

Though Lithuania was Christianized, the Order persisted in looking on it as a pagan country, going so far as to spread the rumor that Vytautas had returned to paganism and was advocating that the entire nation follow suit. (This rumor made such an impression on the Pope, he sent an investigating body to Vilnius.)

Lithuania's Christianity notwithstanding, the Crusaders persisted in their military campaigns, going so far as to attack Vilnius (1394); the Knights were forced to retreat under the furious counterattack by the Lithuanians, and on their coming back they were, in turn, attacked by the Samogitians and suffered heavy casualties. Within a short time, relations between Lithuania and

61

the Order passed from the arena of military combat to the arena of diplomacy.

The diplomats of the Order were vitally interested in separating Lithuania from Poland and negotiating with the Grand Duchy alone; they desired to live in peace with the Poles, but not with the Lithuanians, contending—if only for their own ulterior motives—that the Grand Duchy had returned to paganism. Their efforts were frustrated when the archbishops of Riga and Tartu formed an alliance with Vytautas in 1396, promising to support him against all enemies, in return for which Vytautas promised to aid them in their missionary work. (It should be noted that the Bishop of Vilnius was also a participant in this alliance.)

With Christianity thus flourishing in Lithuania, the Order was unsuccessful in pressing its old claims to the country on the grounds of a reversion to paganism. Nor did they receive any support from Rome, convinced as the Church was that the claims of paganism were patently false. The Order even went to the extreme of propagandizing that Vytautas, supported by the Pope, was seeking to become King of Lithuania and Russia. When the Order saw that its program was all but doomed to failure, and was averse to antagonizing Poland, it agreed to reconciliation. Preliminary negotiations for "an everlasting peace" were held at Gardinas on April 23, 1398. Vytautas consigned to the Order Samogitia up to the Nevėžis River, as well as lands on the other side of the Nemunas west from Šešupė. On its part, the Order promised to aid Vytautas against Novgorod. Lithuanian traders and those of the Order were allowed free access to each other's territory. Vytautas and his subjects were obligated to remain loyal to the Roman Catholic Church as well as to the Holy Roman Emperor, and were enjoined from waging war against any Christian country in alliance with the Order. The agreement was signed on the Island of Salynas on October 12, 1398, between Vytautas and the Grand Master of the Order. The fact that Vytautas signed alone on behalf of Lithuania, showed him as being an independent ruler; this brought him into favor with the Teutonic Knights who, along with the Lithuanian nobles, honored him by calling him King of Lithuania.

Vytautas had, in the meanwhile, been politicking in the Russian territories, capturing the Duchy of Smolensk (1395) by taking advantage of civil disorder there. He even organized a campaign against the Tartars south of the Russian steppes, reaching as far as the Black Sea. (He brought back many Tartars and Karaimans, settling them in the Trakai region.) His biggest campaign was undertaken in alliance with Khan Tochtamysh of the Golden Horde when the latter, driven back by the great warrior Tamerlain, turned to Vytautas for support. Aided by a few German and Polish detachments, the two clashed with the enemy near the Vorksla River, at the base of the Don River, in August, 1399. The campaign was a disaster: many of the Lithuanians died (among them about twenty dukes), and Vytautas and Tochtamysh barely escaped death by retreating. Despite this failure, Vytautas did not desist his politicking in the east, even going so far as to wage war against Smolensk repeatedly (though avoiding any military confrontation with the Duke of Moscow).

Having delivered over the Samogitians (1401) to the Order, Vytautas continued to maintain good relations with the Germans (he even went so far as to aid the Order in capturing the Samogitians). With the Samogitians rebelling continuously against their rule by the Order—secretly supported by Vytautas!—the Order, to protect its own interests, supported Švitrigaila in a few campaigns in Lithuania against his enemy, Vytautas.

The rebelling Samogitians succeeded in expelling the Teutonic Knights, who immediately began preparing for war in order to reclaim the land—and hoping that such a war would separate Lithuania from Poland. They went to the extreme of having Emperor Sigismund offer Vytautas a crown, if he would separate from Poland, but the Lithuanians, as well as Jogaila and the Poles, persisted in maintaining their commonwealth status. Indignant, the Order began attacking Poland (1409), after which a truce was agreed upon. But it was only a temporary truce. All sides were preparing for the inevitable war.

Meeting to plan strategy, Vytautas and Jogaila, at Brasta early in November of that year, decided to destroy the Order once and for all by capturing its capital, Marienburg. War broke out the following June. On the 30th, Vytautas' army (11,000 Lithuanian and Russian troops joined up with the Poles (aided by Czech mercenaries) at Vistula, and the combined armies marched to the Drevenca River, which they found well fortified by the oncoming Teutonic Knights, and therefore decided to bypass the area, going in a northeasterly direction, until, at Tanenberg, actual hostilities began. After a fierce battle lasting ten hours, the Lithuanian and Polish forces were successful, and headed toward Marienburg, arriving there ten days later. Unable to besiege the fortress, the allies were further hampered when illness started spreading among their troops. The first to withdraw from the city of Marienburg (which had been burned by defending troops under Commander Plauen) was Vytautas (September 11th), followed eight days later by troops under command of Jogaila. Unfortunately, Plauen was able to regroup his forces (aided by additional Knights from the West), and in a short time the Order's main bastion had been reestablished.

The Lithuanians and Poles were now faced with having to negotiate with the Order. At the conference, held at Torn, Vytautas, negotiating for the allies, fiercely defended the Lithuanian claim to Samogitia. When, on February 11, 1411, the Peace of Torn was signed, a compromise was achieved whereby Samogitia would remain under Lithuanian control until the deaths of Jogaila and Vytautas, after which it would revert to the control of the Order. The Peace of Torn further served the purpose of weakening the Order's power, in addition to enhancing the prestige of the Grand Duchy of Lithuania in the eyes of the Western states. Vytautas, as the nation's ruler, could no longer be disregarded by the Pope as well as by the Holy Roman Emperor.

6. Between Independence and Union

The Order demanded written agreement that Samogitia would revert to their control following the deaths of Vytautas and Jogaila, and Emperor Sigismund's representative, Benedict Makras, was invited to settle the dispute. The long last quarrel, over which it appeared that fighting might again break out, was settled at the Peace of Melno (1422), when a disorderly and winding border line was set up between the Order and Lithuania. Lasting until 1919, it was one of the most permanent border

64

lines in all of Europe. It was organized so that thinly populated areas were evenly divided between the two states; some disputes arose, but these were quickly settled by minor alterations along the line.

Just as this agreement symbolized the strengthening of the Lithuanian nation, the Horodle Union Act of 1413 demonstrated its independence in regard to Poland. By the pact, Jogaila and the Poles agreed that after the death of Vytautas, Lithuania would be ruled by its own Grand Duke, who would be independent of the King of Poland. However, the stipulation was made that Vytautas' heirs would have to be designated by Jogaila or his heirs; thus, the pact acknowledged a separate Lithuanian state within the union with Poland.

Vytautas continued to politick, primarily in the East, achieving the payment of tribute by the independent cities of Novgorod and Pskov. He was even intent on taking Moscow, but was restrained from doing so by his daughter, who was the widow of Duke Basil of Moscow. (Vytautas became the guardian of his young grandson, Basil II, heir to the Moscow throne.) Many of the Russian dukes submitted to Vytautas, yielding him their oaths of loyalty as well as tributes, and he gained influence among the Golden Horde and even among the Tartars of Crimea (many of whom he incorporated either into his armies or into other areas of the Grand Duchy). Through these activities in the East, and because of his successes in battles and negotiations with the Order, Vytautas raised Lithuania to a position of eminence in Eastern Europe. Thus, it was quite appropriate that Emperor Sigismund selected the city of Luck, Vytautas' quandum capital, to be the site of the International Convention called in 1429 in order to solve the problem of the border between Poland and the Order, as well as the affairs of the Husits and Turks.

As soon as the various representatives (including the Emperor and Jogaila) convened, Sigismund raised the question of Vytautas' coronation. This caused the Poles (and Jogaila) to leave the conference in protest, thus cutting short the meeting. However, Vytautas nevertheless went about preparations for his coronation, supported as he was by the Lithuanian nobles.

Only his death stopped him from realizing his great ambition to have Lithuania become a kingdom.

How the Lithuanian ruling elements wavered between union and total independence is demonstrated by the events following the death of Vytautas. The nobles chose, with the approval of Jogaila, Švitrigaila to be Grand Duke. As Švitrigaila chose to follow the independent policies of Vytautas, the Poles began infiltrating his government, organizing a conspiracy against him which came to a climax in 1432 when Švitrigaila was attacked at Ašmena, whence he managed to escape to Polock. The conspira- tors then elected Vytautas' younger brother Žygimantas to be Grand Duke. Žygimantas then ruled the more or less ethnographic area of Lithuania, while Švitrigaila ruled the Russian lands.

Lithuania now found itself torn between two opposing leaders, and on the verge of civil war. Žygimantas signed an agreement by which Lithuania would revert to the control of Poland after his death. His obvious pro-Polish policies caused the Lithuanian nobles to turn against him; but on the other hand, it brought him the support of the Poles, which was important in light of the subsequent conflict which followed. At the battle of Pabaiskas (1435), Švitrigaila and the Livonian Order, with whom he had become allied, were badly defeated. The victory restored the rather unstable Lithuanian-Polish union, determining the ties between the two states which were to last until both nations lost their independence.

Žygimantas, having gone so far as to attempt an alliance with Emperor Sigismund, was now unable to disengage himself from the Poles. He had to acknowledge five times the union, promising to hold Lithuania for the Polish crown. Only his sudden death in 1440—it is assumed that his own nobles did away with him— mitigated the solidity of the union.

IV.   THE BEGINNING OF THE REPUBLIC OF THE NOBILITY

1. *The Election of Casimir and the Opposition to the Union*

At the time of Žygimantas' death, Jogaila's son Vladislaw ruled Poland, having inheriting the throne upon the death of his father in 1434. The Lithuanians could not elect their own ruler, as per the terms of the previous agreement of union, and were compelled by the agreement to acknowledge the King of Poland as their own Grand Duke. However, thanks to the atmosphere that had been created by Vytautas' independent policies, the Lithuanian nobles decided to contravene the terms of the agreement and thus elect their own ruler, independent of Polish acquiescence. It was the Poles, ironically, who gave them the ruler they wanted! When the Poles proposed Jogaila's thirteen-year-old son Casimir as a replacement for Vladislaw, the Lithuanians brought this same Casimir to be their Grand Duke. Along with their policy of independence from Poland, the Lithuanians, in the words of Dlugosz, "taught the young ruler their native language and customs." However, in 1445, union was again achieved between the two states—this time, at the instigation of Poland. King Vladislaw died in battle with the Turks at Varna, and the Poles invited Casimir to become their king. The Poles had their way—in other words, renewal of union with the Grand Duchy—against the desires of the Lithuanians. Forced to submit, the Lithuanians allowed Casimir to be taken to Poland where he was crowned King (he made his residence at Cracow and ruled the Grand Duchy from a distance—only visiting it on rare occasion).

2. Growth of the Landowning Class

The old Lithuanian state grew from the landworking communities, in which the small class of landowners prevailed. From this class, in turn, came the first dukes and noblemen (including the progenitors of Gediminas). Though the dukes had acquired great influence, the landed gentry retained its political power, as the Grand Duchy grew and thrived. With growth, there developed the influential and aristocratic Council of Nobles, whose power increased tremendously in the reign of Casimir, when the leading noble Jonas Goštautas, palatine of Vilnius and Trakai, actually ruled in place of the absentee Grand Duke.

Jogaila, Vytautas, and especially Žygimantas all had realized the power of the independently growing class of landowners-turned-nobility, and had given them certain privileges (privileges also given to other nobles, especially those performing military service). But it was Casimir who granted the most far-reaching privileges, prior to departing for Poland to become king. Casimir granted to the secular and ecclesiastical nobles the same freedoms enjoyed by the Polish nobility, such as certain immunities for the Church, a public trial for miscreants, freedom to travel abroad, the right to control one's property and to dispense with it freely, and the like. (Under Vytautas and Žygimantas, widows were allowed permission to remarry whom they chose, but with the stipulation that their possessions and those of the children of the first marriage were to revert, on the widow's death, to the children or, if there were no surviving heirs, to the relatives of the first husband.)

The most important privilege (1447) concerned the peasants. It released them from paying certain duties and performing certain labors—but prohibited them from moving from their nobles' estates and into the estates of the Grand Duke, and vice-versa. By this last regulation, the peasants were thus tied to the nobles; moreover, court trials were to be directed by the nobles, since the Grand Duke promised not to interfere. Although this privilege gave more rights to the nobility than to the peasants, it is incorrect to assume that this marked the beginning of serfdom, or that the estate peasants were separated from the state per se. Actually, serfdom had existed much earlier; and the peasants, as always, belonged not only to the nobles but to the state, as personified in the Grand Duke. They were assigned certain tasks on behalf of the state, such as the building and maintenance of castles, bridges, roads, etc.

The Lithuanian Council of Nobles became, in time, the governmental authority, assuming the rights and prerogatives of the Grand Duke (i.e., the King of Poland), who only visited the country, as has been demonstrated, on rare occasion. Led by Jonas Goštautas, the Council began their independent rule by becoming involved in a dispute with the Poles over the territory of Podolia.

A large territory in the southwestern area of the Grand Duchy, Podolia was taken by the Poles following the confusion which resulted after the death of Vytautas. When the Poles refused to return the land, the Lithuanians hoped to regain it through Casimir (this is revealed by the regulation written into the 1447 privilege, in which Casimir promised to maintain the lands of Lithuania under the boundaries "that Vytautas . . . had held and ruled"). But Casimir did not fulfill his promise, because of strong Polish opposition to such a move.

Also, when Švitrigaila died (1452), a dispute arose over Volynia, with the Poles claiming that territory despite the fact that Švitrigaila had left it to the Lithuanians. The two sides quarreled bitterly over the disputed territories from 1448 to 1458, with the Lithuanian nobles taking great pains to reiterate their independence from, as well as equality with, Poland.

Concurrently, Poland became involved in the internal conflicts of the Teutonic Order, supporting the townspeople in their opposition to the Order. Because of their own quarrel with the Poles, the Lithuanians saw no reason for becoming involved in the dispute with the Order, which lasted over a period of thirteen years. Thus, they paid scant attention to the Baltic and northeastern Prussian areas, not realizing—as is realized today—the vital importance of those territories. For this reason, they failed to take advantage of the second Peace of Torn (1466), in which the Poles received from the Order the Vistula basin with Dancig, as well as the Bishopric of Varme, in addition to large areas of western Prussia including the city of Marienburg (the Order retained only East Prussia, with its capital at Koenigsberg).

3. The Beginning of Aggression from the Duchy of Moscow

By the end of the fifteenth century, coincidental with the decline of the German Order as well as the stabilizing by the Lithuanians of their western borders, a new danger threatened from the east: the ever-expanding Duchy of Moscow.

The Duchy of Moscow evolved from among the smaller duchies established in the northeastern area of Russia, in the wake of Slavic colonists fleeing Kiev, along with the local Ugro-Finns and other Mongolian races. The first of these duchies to rise to eminence was that of Suzdal, with its capital at Vladimir; it was this state, along with contiguous ones, which soon came under the suzerainty of the expanding Duchy of Moscow. Also, the Dukes of Moscow had been successful in gaining the favor

69

of the Khans of the Golden Horde—winning the right to collect duties, which right they soon expanded to include the collecting of land (as typified by John Kalita, who ruled from 1325 to 1341, and who became known as the "land collector").

Algirdas was the first Lithuanian Grand Duke to come into real contact with the growing Duchy of Moscow—which was still comparatively weak, and thus not much of a threat to the Lithuanians. (That Russia meant little in the way of a threat may be surmised by Algirdas' remarks that "All Russia should, commonly, belong to the Lithuanians" [*Quod omnis Russia ad Litvanos deberet simpliciter pertinere*]).

But by the time of the rule of Vytautas, Lithuania had to contend with Moscow (e.g., over the Duchy of Tver). Following the reign of Vytautas, the signs were apparent that Moscow was growing in strength, was, indeed, becoming the center of the Russian Orthodox Church. And by the time of the reign of Casimir, the Tartars were oppressing Lithuanian from the south, as Moscow was doing from the east. Having attached the previously independent city republics of Novgorod and Viazma, Moscow began eyeing those regions ruled almost independently by the Russian nobles along the Oka and Ugra rivers. This was the first sign that Moscow intended to attempt eventual control of the Grand Duchy of Lithuania.

Casimir died in 1492, and was succeeded by his son Alexander, who ruled until 1506. From the start, Alexander wavered between war and peace as regarded Moscow: while preparing for war, on the one hand, he was making known his intent to marry Helen, daughter of Grand Duke Ivan III of Moscow. But before agreeing to the marriage, Ivan was demanding that an agreement of peace be signed—on his own terms. Alexander agreed, and according to the Peace Act of 1494, all Lithuanian territory either captured by Russia or surrendered peacefully to Russia was to be acknowledged as being the possession of the Moscow Duchy.

To Ivan III, accustomed as he was to taking land, the fact that Alexander became his son-in-law meant little—it would appear he had no intention of maintaining the peace even as he signed the pact!

In 1499, Ivan began open warfare against the Grand Duchy of Lithuania. The following year, the Lithuanians lost their first battle to Moscow—at Vedroša. Following that success, Moscow advanced into Lithuanian territory, closing in upon the Dnieper. The Lithuanians were forced to defend themselves without the support of the Poles—even though they had gone to the extent of electing Alexander to be their king (1501). With the attacking Russians fighting for two years in their advance on Smolensk, an area of strategic importance which they were anxious to take, Alexander attempted to negotiate a peace. He was forced to be satisfied with a six-year truce, to last until 1509. But Ivan (who ruled from 1462 to 1505) was not a man to honor even a truce pact. His position had been somewhat solidified—and his intention of aggressive imperialism revealed—when, with the collapse of the Byzantine Empire, he had, through the mediation of the Roman *curia,* married the niece of the last Byzantine emperor, thus adding immensely to his holdings as well as to Moscow's prestigious eminence as "the third Rome."

In addition to being threatened by Moscow, the Grand Duchy was also being threatened by the Turks, who had captured the Crimea in 1475. The Tartars, despite their previous friendship with Vytautas, now began—in collaboration with Moscow, and under the influence of the Turks—to plunder the southern areas of Lithuania.

The Russian border was coming closer to the Dnieper River as the Duke of Moscow broke the truce with Alexander and persisted in his attempt to capture Smolensk. The battle, interrupted by a short truce in 1508, continued until Basil III, capitalizing on the treachery of the deserting Lithuanian noble Mykolas Glinskis, captured the city in 1514. Although the Lithuanians, led by the famous leader Konstantinas Ostragiškis, won a great victory at the battle of Orša, they were unable to regain control of Smolensk—which was to remain under Russian rule for almost a hundred years.

Following the fall of Smolensk, the Russians succeeded in occupying a third of the previously Russian land which now belonged to Lithuania, and began advancing farther into the heart of the country. The gradual weakening of the Grand Duchy's resistance to Moscow was compounded by the concurrent expansion of freedom on the part of the Lithuanian nobles, thus diminishing the powers of the Grand Duke and his magistrates.

4. The Classes of Society

Lithuania was becoming more and more a republic of the nobility, with the Grand Duke as its first among equals by virtue of the fact that he was the wealthiest magistrate in the country. The noblemen on his estates scattered through the nation were, in effect, his local regents, empowered to collect duties, which went into his treasury (they were also responsible for the protection of the inhabitants of their fiefs). The rights of the nobles varied according to local customs and traditions; however, their most important right was to lead, under their own banner, regiments in case of war (hence, they were called "banner lords"). Also within this structure were the independent landowners who later became known by the Russian word *boyar,* or gentry. Although they had not, at the beginning, enjoyed the same privileges as the nobility, they soon became one class with them: having come in closer contact with the Poles, they demanded equality with the nobles, achieving this equality in the late fifteenth and early sixteenth centuries, mainly through the privileges granted by Casimir.

Whereas the nobility and landed gentry (the boyars) were the leading class, economically speaking, the lowest class was comprised of the serfs—the vast majority of the people—who were restricted in their privileges, and who, for the most part, depended upon the landowners for their very survival. The third class in the economic order were the city dwellers, who, in the beginning of the formation of the nation, lacked much influence with the nobles, primarily because the entire economy of the nation was concentrated on the large estates of these nobles. However, with the rise of two trade groups—the merchants and the craftsmen—the economic picture was changing, as a result of which the nobles supported the city dwellers (i.e., they encouraged these groups because crafts and trades encouraged the sale of their agricultural products, and thus great profits were realized in the form of taxes).

In time, the larger cities were operating under the Magdeburg Law (which originated in the German city of Magdeburg and, after union with Poland, came into Lithuania). Under this law, the cities were excluded from all taxes save those paid to the Grand Duke; also, they received autonomy in selecting their own administrators and magistrates. Also in time, with the Polish influence spreading—and bringing with it foreign merchants and traders, mainly from Germany—the city class became, in many respects, alien to the land-bound peasants in the rural areas. It was also around this time that the Jews began coming into Lithuania, mostly from German areas, and forming the basis of what became in time the greatest center of Judaism in Eastern Europe.

5. Administrative Reforms

With the Grand Duchy drawing closer to Poland, the ancient Lithuanian system was changing from a confederation, in which many different regions were under the rule of the Grand Duke, into a commonwealth of nobility with a common parliament and system of courts and laws. The reforms of 1565-66 came about because of the demands of the nobles that they be allowed to hold public trials. Three types of trials were established: the land courts, trying cases concerning land and other property; the castle courts, which tried criminal cases; and the "border" courts, which tried land border cases.

It also now became necessary to reorganize the country into new administrative units. There evolved nine counties in the Vilnius and Trakai palatinates (the Samogitians were not affected, as they were left with their own administration, which included its own balliwicks). The capital, Vilnius, and Trakai—which had seen, during the time of the Union of Horodle in 1413, the establishment of the palatinates—were made the center of the nation, administratively speaking; thus, these two palatinates, together with the Samogitian province, were the territory referred to on the maps as "Lithuania propria." (Excluded were the Russian areas, which, like the Grand Duchy, had been divided into ten palatinates, each of which was subdivided into smaller counties.)

6. Agrarian Reform

The agrarian reform, begun under the rule of Jogaila's last two descendants (especially under Sigismund August, who ruled from 1548 to 1572), was undertaken at a critical time: from the east, Lithuania was being oppressed by Moscow, and from the south by the Tartars of Crimea. The Grand Duchy needed—but lacked—funds for defense and for tributes to buy off the Tartars. The greatest source of income was the King's domains, and for this reason it was decided to survey and to mark off the boundaries of the land belonging to the Grand Duke. These lands were, in many cases, scattered among the properties of the nobles, sometimes even appropriated by them as their own. Thus, while checking the ruler's domains, the Grand Duchy was also investigating the property holdings of the nobles and confiscating land whenever the nobles were unable to produce evidence of ownership.

The western three-field farming system was used in setting up the agrarian reform. It was designed especially to accommodate the peasant serfs. The land surveyors measured off three square fields for the serfs' domain, leaving the center area of each three-field lot reserved for the village. Each of these three fields was divided into ten or eleven tracts of land (each about two-thirds of a ha). Each serf would receive such a land in each field. The total unit of land designated to the serfs of a specific village amounted to twenty-one ha—or thirty to thirty-three tracts. Each serf could take as much land as he was able to work, although the land rent, taxes and other tributes for the entire village were based on the total fifty-two acres of land.

The workers of the domain were divided into higher and lower groups. The higher group consisted of "mobile boyars," servants with horses, forest watchmen, hunters, bee-keepers, and various types of craftsmen such as builders, blacksmiths, carpenters, wheelwrights and coffin makers. Such workers usually received sixty tracts of land and were exempted from any other duties or taxes. The lower group was made up of gardeners, bond-servants and osadniks. They received small parcels of land, and had to work on the estate one day a week. During the summer, their wives also had to work on the estate, weeding gardens or harvesting the crop, but not for more than six days. The bond-servants provided the chief source of labor, for, in addition to paying tribute and monetary taxes, they had to work for the estate a few days each week. They were tied to the land and were not allowed to act freely. The majority of serfs fell into the category of bond-servants. The osadniks were those bond-servants who had bought their freedom.

The fifty-two-acre reform was first introduced in ethnographic Lithuania: in the palatinates of Vilnius and Trakai, and in the province of Samogitia. The reformation of these estates before any others may have been undertaken because of their proximity to the harbors of the Baltic Sea, by means of which the produce of the estates could be transported easily to the markets of the West.

In addition to wheat, lumber was in great demand abroad, and, during the agrarian reform, the forests were not neglected. They were measured, categorized and well guarded; the neighboring nobles were forbidden to use them for their own purposes.

The agrarian reform was also carried on—to a certain extent —in the Russian regions, and was even adopted by the nobles in marking off their own estates. However, the increasing trend towards oligarchy prevented the Grand Duke from making full use of his reformed domains. Eventually, they fell into the hands of the nobles, and the innovations of the Grand Duke began to disappear. . . .

7. Protestant Reformation

Closer ties with the West brought the teachings of the German Martin Luther into Lithuania. The new religion spread rapidly, especially among the German immigrants in the cities. A good example of this reformation occurred in East Prussia in 1525, when the former Grand Master of the Order, Albrecht Hohenzolern, became a secular duke. Albrecht's reformation in East Prussia and, in connection with it, the spread of education, had its effects upon Lithuania. Especially meaningful was the establishment of Königsberg University in 1544, which became the center of Protestantism not only for East Prussia, but also for the neighboring states. Lithuanians who planned to attend foreign universities did not remain indifferent to the University of Königsberg. In 1545, two Lithuanians who advocated Lutheranism held professorships at the university. They were Abraham Kulvietis and Stanislovas Rapolionis. Martynas Mažvydas (d. 1563), the publisher of the first Lithuanian book, studied at the university upon invitation of Albrecht himself.

Political ties with Poland bent the Lithuanian nobles toward the other branch of Protestantism, namely Calvinism. Calvinist Protestantism had greatly influenced the nobles of Poland Minor, and the Lithuanian nobles followed their example. Judging from the county of Ukmergė, where, in 1563, all the nobles were recorded as Calvinists, we may state that Calvinism had become quite common among Lithuanians during the middle of the sixteenth century. Two nobles were primarily responsible for the tremendous influence of Calvinism. They were Mikalojus Radvila the Black, palatine, marshal and chancellor of Vilnius; and his cousin, the palatine of Trakai, Mikalojus Radvila the Red. Being, in effect, the actual rulers of Lithuania, they managed to influence other nobles to follow their example in religious matters.

Once the nobles had accepted Protestantism, the common people were forced to follow their example; the economics and laws which made them dependent upon the nobles did not allow otherwise. Moreover, many common people had always considered Catholicism as more or less of a formality imposed by Poles, and had clung to their old pagan customs. Ordered to do so by the nobles, they attended Calvinist services, just as they had previously attended Catholic services. Very often the same churches were used, because the nobles, exercising their rights of patronage, frequently changed the churches that they took away from the Catholic hierarchy into Calvinist prayer houses. The Catholic priests were either removed from their posts or had to become servants of the new religion.

As it had done previously under Catholicism, the Polish influence filtered into Lithuania under Calvinism, too. The Radvilas and other nobles invited Calvinist scholars from Poland, and disseminated publications in Latin and Polish, though not in Lithuanian. (Calvinist books were printed in Radvila's Nesvyžius printing office. The Lithuanian printing office of Brasta put out a Polish translation of the Bible, dedicated to Sigismund August.) Thus, in the middle years of the sixteenth century, Lithuania was well on its way to becoming a Calvinist nation. The great influ- ence of Calvinism is revealed by the Charter of 1563, which gave equal rights and privileges to members of all religions. (It should be noted that of the twenty-one Charter signatures, only three belong to Catholic bishops and not one belongs to a Catholic noble.)

The Protestant reform had spread quickly, and just as quickly it began to wane. It did not have the support of the Grand Duke's government, which was the only body that could have been able to establish Protestantism as a state religion and to destroy the hierarchy of the Catholic Church. The decisive blow against the Protestant reformation was struck by the ar- rival, in 1569, of the Jesuits, who had been invited by the Bishop of Vilnius. The Society of Jesus helped to revive Catholicism by establishing schools, notably the Academy at Vilnius. They also disseminated Catholic publications and preached sermons in order to convert the nobles and the masses alike. The nobles did not greatly resist the Jesuits, since, like the common people, they essentially lacked deep religious conviction. (They had easily converted to Calvinism because of social and political motives, especially because of their envy of the Church hierarchy whose wealth and influence equalled that of the greatest lords.) Finally, the reformation was weakened because it had split into various western sects. In present-day Lithuania, Protestantism may be found in the form of German-descended Lutherans along the western border, and in a few Calvinists inhabiting the regions of Biržai and Kelmė. More significant to Lithuania is the fact that the Protestant Reformation was responsible for the first publica- tions written in the Lithuanian language: in other words, for the beginning of a national Lithuanian literature.

8. *The Renewed Wars with Moscow*

After the fall of Smolensk, the wars with Moscow, which had continued for several years, were ended by longer-lasting truces. The wars were renewed in 1562, but this time they were more complicated, since one of the issues was the controversy over Livonia.

Livonia had become an independent, though weak state after the secularization of the Prussian Order. The secularized Order did not have control of the entire country because the territories of the Bishops, the territory belonging to the Archbishop of Riga, and three independent cities (Riga, Tallin and Tartu) did not belong to the Order. Meanwhile, the Duchy of Moscow captured two western Russian republics: Novogrod in 1478 and Pskov in 1510. Moscow's Czar, Ivan IV, "The Terrible," declared Livonia his patrimony and began threatening to invade it. His purpose was to reach the Baltic Sea and thus obtain easier access to the West. Livonia's close trade, political and cultural ties with the Baltic countries awakened their interest in Livonia's fate. Battles for the domination of the Baltic Sea began. Sweden, Denmark, the Duke of Mecklenburg, and Albrecht of East Prussia began to interfere in the affairs of Livonia. The Lithuanian nobles, together with Grand Duke Sigismund August, did not remain apathetic.

When a quarrel arose between the Landmaster and an officer of the Archbishopric of Riga, Vilhelm Hohenzolern (Sigismund's cousin), resulting in the Landmaster's imprisonment of Hohencolern, Sigismund marched his army to the borders of Livonia and forced the Landmaster to release his cousin. Subsequently, Livonia and Lithuania signed an agreement against the Czar, thus providing Moscow with a good reason for attacking Livonia in 1558. After the Russian Asiatic soldiers had virtually devastated the country, the Order's last Landmaster, Gotard Kettler yielded to Lithuanian protection. Kettler signed the *Pacta Subjectionis* in 1561. According to this agreement, Livonia retained its German self-government, but became subject to Lithuania. Livonia's narrow southeastern strip of land, extending north from the Dauguva River, received the Polish name of Infliant and remained under the rule of the Commonwealth until 1772. The regions of Courland and Žiemgalis, along with the capital city of Mintauja, went to Kettler as a fief. (The Duchy of Courland remained until the final partition of Lithuania and Poland in 1795.)

78

With Lithuania now occupying Livonia, Moscow, which had wanted that territory all along, ended its truce with Lithuania, and the fight for the Russian lands was renewed. Lithuania now had to defend not only the upper parts of the Dauguva and Dnieper rivers, but Livonia as well. Because of the extended front, it became necessary to organize stronger defensive forces, and in order to do so, some Lithuanians urged the formation of an alliance with Poland. But the Poles, feeling safe from the threat of Moscow, were not inclined to offer aid, and plans for a closer union were discouraged. Besides, the Poles were not so interested in forming new union agreements as they were in the "execution" of previous ones, since they felt that Lithuania was already in league with them. The Lithuanians, although they did not agree, were not inclined to separate from the Poles. Excluding the matter of danger from Moscow, the Lithuanian nobility was drawn to Poland by the latter's Western culture and especially by its policy of freedom for the nobility. The Poles hastened to exploit Lithuania's situation; the war with Moscow lasted ten years, during which time the decisive union with Poland was formed.

9. The Union of Lublin

The Lithuanian nobles organized a confederation in 1562, demanded that a union with Poland be set up, and presented their plans to the Grand Duke in Vilnius. According to their program, the following points were to be agreed upon: election of a common ruler, a common parliament, similarity of structure in both states, and common defense of the borders. While making these concessions to the Poles (and probably expecting to be repaid by aid in the wars with Moscow), the Lithuanians entered an important requirement—that the Grand Duchy of Lithuania remain geographically separate. Even though the Polish agents eventually talked the Lithuanian nobles into accepting their conditions for union, the nobles were able to resist the Poles to the extent of adding the above-mentioned condition concerning separation of their state.

The act of union was hastened by further attacks from Moscow in the beginning of 1563, when the stronghold of Polock fell. Ivan IV demonstrated his cruelty here, as he had done in

Livonia: he had the Jewish population drowned in the Dauguva River, killed the Bernardine (Cistercian) monks, and sent all Lithuanian captives to Moscow. (The Polish captives he sent home.) The terror aroused by Moscow's attempts to invade Vilnius stirred a favorable feeling towards union with Poland among the Lithuanian people. Sigismund August, influenced by the nobility, sent a delegation to the Warsaw Parliament. Long negotiations were conducted because Lithuanians refused to accept the Polish demand for "executions" of the previous acts of union. While they quarreled, the danger from Moscow decreased as a result of the Lithuanian victory at the Ula River (near the Dauguva River) in 1564. Meanwhile, more reforms were undertaken whereby the nobility were given even greater rights: overwhelming influence in the newly organized county parliaments and in the three county courts. In 1566, a second statute was published, extending the rights even further.

The nobles now felt that they had no reason for seeking union with Poland. But the question of union remained, primarily because of the continued threat of Moscow and because Sigismund August had no heirs to succeed him. This last factor meant much to the Poles, since with the end of the Gediminian Dynasty that had united both states, any previous unions would cease.

It was under such circumstances that the Polish and Lithuanian representatives met in January of 1569 in Lublin. When the Poles began resisting the Lithuanian demand that Lithuania be geographically separated from Poland, the Lithuanian nobles left Lublin, and the Parliament continued without them. The King, on the side of the Poles, declared two decrees favorable to them: he renounced his rights to the Grand Duchy of Lithuania, and attached to Poland the southern palatinates of Podlachia, Volynia, Braclav and Kiev.

While the annexation of the first two palatinates, over which quarrels had risen since the fourteenth century, was slightly justifiable, occupation of the last two palatinates lacked any lawful basis. Only two alternatives were left to the Lithuanians: fight with Poland or accept the loss and negotiate further for union. The lords were inclined to fight, and called on the nobility to defend the border; but the nobility, tired of war and threatened by Russian aggression, did not show any determination to fight. Soon, representatives were returned to Lublin to continue negotiations.

A large delegation arrived in Lublin in June, 1569, and quarreled needlessly over some of the conditions of union already set down by the Poles. When the Poles refused to give in and when it became evident that they were supported by the King, the Lithuanians had no other choice but to accept the terms dictated to them. The dramatic climax of the negotiations occurred on June 28, when the chairman of the Lithuanian delegation, Jonas Katkevičius, kneeling and crying with his whole delegation, begged the King "not to wrong his fatherland." This moving scene presents clear evidence of the hopelessness of the situation which the Poles exploited by imposing the union.

The union created a commonwealth out of the Polish Kingdom and the Grand Duchy of Lithuania. The head of this commonwealth was to be commonly elected in Crakow and crowned King of Poland and Grand Duke of Lithuania. There was to be a common Parliament and Senate, and the same foreign policy was to be practiced by both states. Both had to aid each other, and the affairs of one state were to be looked upon as the affairs of the other. Poles could purchase property in Lithuania, and vice versa. However, Lithuania and Poland still retained their own forms of government, their own military forces, their own treasuries, and their own, independent laws. Thus, the union did not change the existing situation between the Grand Duchy of Lithuania and the Kingdom of Poland to any great extent. Nevertheless, its results were disastrous to the Lithuanian people and state: the union opened wide the doors for the influence of western Polish culture and the anarchy that accompanied it.

V. The Commonwealth of the Gentry

1. The Successful Resistance Against Russia During the Time of Stephen Bathory

After long battles with Moscow and after the Lublin Union, the boundaries of the Grand Duchy of Lithuania narrowed. The

81

Russians and Poles occupied large territories and effected what seemed to be the first partition of Lithuania. However, during the first decades following the Lublin Union, the state rose from its political and cultural decline because of two factors: the activities of the Jesuit Order and the election of the first liberal King and Grand Duke, Stephen Bathory.

The Hungarian Bathory, Duke of the Turkish-protected Transylvania, was elected after Prince Henry Valois deserted his post, and ruled from 1576 to 1586. At first, the Lithuanians did not want to recognize him, since he had been elected by the Poles, alone. However, when the nobility received its recognized rights, they acknowledged him as the Grand Duke.

From the beginning, Bathory served Lithuania faithfully. He resumed the unfinished war with Moscow (temporarily halted because of a truce). Conspiring with the Danish Prince Magnus, who ruled Ezel Island and part of Courland, the Czar had, in 1577, captured all of Livonia except for the cities of Riga and Tallin. Bathory not only pushed the Russians out of Livonia, which he succeeded in doing with the aid of the Swedes, but also continued to fight for the territory that the Russians had taken from the Lithuanian Grand Duchy. Inviting mercenaries from Transylvania and engaging German troops, Bathory arrived near Polock with the Lithuanians and took it away from the Russians in 1579. (In this manner, the palatinate of Polock reverted to Lithuania and remained in Lithuanian hands until the first partition in 1772.) When the Czar did not agree to peace and refused to give up his remaining holdings in Lithuania, Bathory took the important stronghold of Velikie Luki, along with many surrounding villages. This was followed by the siege of Pskov in 1582.

Pskov, a free city for many years, was an important trading center with an "invincible" fortress defended by large garrisons. Arriving with large numbers of infantry and cavalry, Bathory unsuccessfully tried to storm the city walls for three months. He was determined not to retreat. Meanwhile the Czar, by fraudulent diplomatic means, sent messengers to Vienna and Rome, offering to organize crusades against the Turks and encouraging the Pope's hope for Church unity—at the price of peace with

Bathory. The expectation of Church unity influenced the Pope to send an able diplomat, Antonio Possevini, into Pskov to act as mediator between the Czar and Bathory. Possevini found both sides inclined to make use of his mediation, but once he became convinced that the Czar was not interested in a compromise settlement, he took Bathory's side. In January, 1583, a ten-year truce was signed, awarding Polock (with Veliz) and Livonia to Bathory, thus pushing the Russians away from the Baltic coast for some 150 years. The wars with Moscow revealed Bathory to be an ingenious strategist, able diplomat and realistic politician. He was intent on regaining the lands taken over by Moscow and, to a degree, he succeeded in so doing. He also managed to influence the unruly nobles to the degree that he was able to collect their taxes and utilize their warriors to fight Moscow.

In order to ingratiate himself further with the nobles, Bathory allowed them to establish the Highest Tribunal in 1581. This was the highest court of appeal for nobles and received cases judged by the court of the Grand Duke. By means of the Tribunal, the nobles received the right to control the country's proceedings, as well as its laws. Two representatives to the Highest Tribunal were elected by the nobles in each county parliament. (Samogitia, considered as one large county, sent three representatives.) In all, the tribunal had forty-nine members, which were re-elected every year. The tribunal judged cases according to the rule of the majority, and became an important agency of the state.

Also under Bathory, preparations were made for the establishment of the third Lithuanian Statute, which was published after his death, and acknowledged by his successor in 1588. (Of the three Statutes, only this last one was printed in the Slavic language.) It remained the basic code of laws until 1840.

Bathory was the last ruler to serve Lithuania well. In addition to allowing Lithuanians to free themselves from the union to some degree, he was interested in aiding agricultural development and improving the condition of the peasants. He even planned to establish a bank in Vilnius, following the example of the banks established in the West.

Under Bathory, Lithuanians were almost completely engulfed by Western culture, as may be seen by their acceptance, in 1582, of the new calendar established by Pope Gregory XII. The Jesuits, who came to Lithuania during the reign of Bathory, were among the greatest proponents of Western Christian culture.

2. *Lithuania Becomes a Nation of Western Culture*

The pagan Lithuanian state had not been culturally attached to either East or West. Forced to fight against the West for independence, it spread to the east and south, thus coming into contact with the eastern Christian Slavic culture. However, this Slavic culture and Christianity affected Lithuania only superficially. Its limited influence extended only to the establishment of Slavic as the official language of the Grand Duchy of Lithuania (it was the only literary language in Eastern Europe), and to the Orthodox Christianity embraced by some nobles, including the Gediminians. But in ethnographic Lithuania, Orthodoxy remained meaningless even in earliest times, since it did not overcome paganism entirely.

The manifestation of Western Christianity, on the other hand, was different. After its introduction into Lithuania, it began to spread throughout the state-established and state-supported church hierarchy. Needless to say, the process did not occur immediately. Even after nearly a century, Christianity had made few inroads into paganism. Suddenly imposed, and usually taught by Polish priests in a language not understood by the peasants, it could not have been expected to flourish: the peasants remained partly pagan until the sixteenth century.

The cultural and religious change in Lithuania occurred as a result of two Western movements: the Renaissance and the Reformation. They reached Lithuania through Poland and were first felt by the aristocracy. Young nobles became attracted to Western universities. Whereas they once attended the University of Cracow (newly re-established by Jogaila), they now began to turn their attention to centers of learning such as the Universities of Bologna and Padua. (Nobles and city dwellers who intended to prepare themselves for high Church offices, however, still studied at Cracow.) A great number of students also flocked to the German universities (Heidelberg, Leipzig, Wittenberg, and even Leiden); and when the University of Königsberg was founded, at least ten Lithuanian students enrolled during its first academic year (1544-45).

Once the Lithuanian gentry had been introduced to Renaissance and Western culture, they also found it easy to accept the ideas of the Protestant Reformation, which filtered into Lithuania through Prussia and Poland. As we have already seen, the teachings of Martin Luther were first adopted by city dwellers, especially by German colonists, and the tenets of Polish Calvinism influenced the nobility to such a degree that it nearly became Lithuania's national religion. The Renaissance and the great religious movements that were part of it, gave the impetus for the development of secular as well as religious literature. The printing press, invented by Gutenberg, aided in the dissemination of such literature.

The first printer in Lithuania was a Byelorussian from Polock —Franciscus Skoryna. He belonged to a wealthy class of city dwellers, and held a doctoral degree in medicine from the University of Bologna. Influenced by the Renaissance movement, and following the example of Italian printers, he began to publish translations of religious and secular classics, first in Prague and later in Vilnius. In Prague, he translated and published the Holy Bible in Byelorussian, inserting his own instructions to the peasantry in prefaces to the chapters. In Vilnius (1525) he published "The Apostle" and "The Small Book of Travel," the latter being a collection of translated psalms and sermons meant to be read by traveling merchants.

With the Reformation well under way, Radvila established a printing office in Bresta and later in Nesvyžius, where Polish and Byelorussian books were printed for the purpose of disseminating Calvinism. Of the many publications of this office, the most famous is the Polish translation of the Holy Bible (*Biblia Brzeska*). After Radvila embraced Catholicism, he donated the Bresta printing office to the Jesuits, who moved it to Vilnius. There, the Society of Jesus printed academic books which exerted a great influence upon Lithuanian culture throughout the sixteenth century, as well as in later years. (*Katekizmas* [1595] and *Postile* [1599] by Mikalojus Daukša were among some of the works published.)

The University of Königsberg played an important role in the cultural and educational progress of Lithuania at the beginning of the sixteenth century. From Königsberg, the teachings of Luther spread into Lithuania and the first well-known advocates of humanism emerged—among them the priest Abraomas Kulvietis, who established a college—the first Lithuanian institution of higher learning—in Vilnius in 1539. Attacked by the Bishop of Vilnius for disseminating Lutheran ideas from the pulpit of Saint Ann's church, Kulvietis withdrew to Königsberg. Here he made the acquaintance of another well-known Lithuanian humanist, Stanislovas Rapolionis, and the two became professors at the University. Both men are now considered influential in the development of Lithuanian literature: both did translations of hymns, and both were assigned to prepare the first Lithuanian Catechism by the Prussian Albrecht. Unfortunately, the completion of this project was interrupted by their deaths in 1545 and had to be carried out by Martynas Mažvydas, who published the Catechism in 1547. Although this Catechism is the first book to be published in the Lithuanian language, it is believed that excerpts from the Bible, the Gospels, the Epistles of Saint Paul, and various hymns had been published in Lithuanian at an earlier date. (A few years ago, the text of a prayer published in 1503 was discovered in the library of Vilnius University, and there may have been texts reaching back as early as the first years of Lithuania's Christianization.)

The Königsberg offices printed the first Lithuanian church materials, and thus spread Protestantism throughout Lesser and Greater Lithuania.

Protestantism gradually disappeared and Catholicism once again flourished, fostered by the Counter-Reformation movement that was initiated after the Council of Trent (1545-1563). The resolutions of this council were being carried out and acknowledged by secular and ecclesiastical authorities alike. The King of Poland accepted the resolutions in 1564; the Episcopacies of the Provincial Synod, in 1577. The permanent nuncios sent by Rome encouraged Bishops to put the resolutions of the Council of Trent into practice.

Perhaps the leading champion of Catholicism was Bishop Hosius of Varmė—the son of a German immigrant from Vilnius. He invited the Jesuits to his diocese and, at the same time, into Poland. The Jesuit Order campaigned successfully against the Protestant "heretics," especially through the establishment of schools (e.g., their college at Braunsberg), and were soon known as the greatest activists of the Counter-Reformation movement.

Following the example of Hosius, Bishop Protasevičius invited the Society of Jesus to establish a college in Vilnius, which the Society did in 1570, following an endowment of property and funds on the part of the Bishop. In 1579, the college was transformed into an academy by Stephen Bathory; it remained a center of culture until the fall of the Grand Duchy.

The Jesuits founded colleges in other parts of Lithuania, too; notably in Nesvyžius, Kražiai, Gardinas, Naugardukas, and Kaunas. Such colleges attracted mainly the youth of the gentry —Catholic as well as Protestant—and in many cases succeeded in directing the latter toward the Catholic Church. The Jesuits also established a seminary in Vilnius in 1582, and another in Samogitia in 1607. The Papal Seminary of Vilnius was eventually placed into their hands, as well.

Another sphere in which the Jesuits actively participated was that of missionary activity. The first mission station was established at the Church of St. John in Vilnius. At first the missionaries preached in German, but soon they mastered the native languages of the region—including Lithuanian. Much work went into the sermons, which even non-Catholics flocked to hear. By means of these sermons, the Jesuits managed to reach a great number of people, especially because they scattered their mission centers throughout the country, neglecting not even the smallest towns.

The Jesuits also attempted to attract the people through sermons, masses, processions and various other means. These external methods had special value to the Lithuanians, whose Christianity was still weak and whose customs were still permeated by paganism. Not without reason did the Jesuits call Lithuania *India Septentrionalis* (northern India) whenever they sent reports to Rome. By gradually destroying pagan customs in their attempts to lead the population closer to the Catholic Church, the Jesuits also became the first to bring Lithuania closer to the West. The Jesuits helped open a new era, and its vivid remains may be seen in the many Baroque churches standing even to this day.

The Jesuits accomplished a great deal in the area of Lithuanian education, especially by encouraging the use of the Lithuanian tongue. Unlike their predecessors, the Jesuits did not force the Polish language upon the people, but tried to recruit clergy who could speak Lithuanian. They were also interested in the publication of works written in Lithuanian. Mikalojus Daukša's *Catechism* and his collection of sermons were printed at the academy, and such educated members of the clergy as Konstantinas Sirvydas, Jonas Jaknavičius and others later published books written in correct Lithuanian. The most important work published by the Jesuits (1629) was Konstantinas Sirvydas' Latin-Polish-Lithuanian dictionary. The Academy of Vilnius also prepared several grammar handbooks on the Lithuanian language, of which only a few have survived.

Another accomplishment attributed to the Jesuits of this period is the Lithuanian history written by the academy's Professor Vijukas Albertas Kojalavičius from 1650 to 1669 in the Latin tongue. This work was not an original, but a reworked translation of Maciej Stryjkovski's Lithuanian history, written over a hundred years previously. Kojalavičius latinized and changed the history in part, aiming to produce a good reader for his Latin students as well as to introduce them to the Lithuanian past.

The Jesuits, with their conservative church ideology, also greatly influenced the Lithuanians by establishing their monasteries and colleges contiguously in various places. These were the first schools of higher learning in Lithuania. The Jesuits were able to establish monasteries and schools by using the funds from landowners who gave them lands and resources. The nobility, during these times of Catholic revival and Jesuit influence, showed great generosity toward these matters—the building of churches and providing of funds for monasteries was a matter of honor for them.

These institutions scattered throughout the country influenced the people and became their sole educational and cultural centers. The Jesuits were the greatest transmitters of the Western Christian culture into Lithuania—which also spread the superstitions coming from the West. One of the worst superstitions was the belief in witchcraft. It was believed that some people, especially women, having sold themselves to the devil and associating with them, could accomplish various wicked deeds. For this reason, some women were persecuted, tried and punished even by being burned at the stake. Court cases and stories concerning the burn-ing of witches still exist. From these, we find that the court of Žagarė tortured and burned three women for witchcraft during the years 1691 to 1692. In their reports, the Jesuits of Pašiaušė mentioned three cases where women were burned at the stake for witchcraft in 1666, 1695, and 1716. The common error of Christians of Western Europe was not evaded in Lithuania.

3. The Beginning of the Battles for the Baltic Sea

Although the Lithuanians had lived on the shores of the Baltic Sea since prehistoric times, they had never become a mari-time people. Instead, their interests were directed toward the vast eastern Slavic areas, where they established a large land empire. The first to rule over the Baltic Sea were the Normans, but in the twelfth century the area was dominated by the Hansa of the northern German cities, and later by the cities of the Netherlands. The German Order, spreading throughout large southern Baltic regions, also took part in maritime affairs. Thus, during medieval times, the Germanic nations were the only ones with access to the Baltic Sea. As we have seen, the Duchy of Moscow became interested in the Baltic during the sixteenth cen-tury, but its movement was thwarted by Lithuania-Poland, and by Sweden as well.

The fight for the Baltic Sea was resumed shortly after Stephen Bathory's death, when Prince Sigismund of Sweden (nephew of Sigismund August and the last of Jogaila's descendants) was elected King of Poland and Grand Duke of Lithuania in 1587. (The Lithuanians recognized him only after he acknowledged the recently-published Third Statute.) Although Sigismund had been raised in a completely Protestant environment (his father was Protestant), he grew up a staunch Catholic under Jesuit guidance, at his mother's request. According to the laws of inheritance, Sigismund also ascended the throne of Sweden upon the death of his father in 1592. However, a Catholic King was not trusted in this Protestant country, even though Sigismund had sworn not to interfere in religious matters even before his corona- tion. Eventually, Sigismund's uncle, who had been appointed regent, ruled in his stead, and Sigismund returned to Poland- Lithuania. (In 1604, the Swedish Parliament acknowledged Carl IX as their rightful King.)

Even before this declaration, Sigismund had begun to wage war in Livonia, where Lithuanian troops were stationed. Under the leadership of the great captain Kristupas Radvila himself, these troops were ordered to attack Estonia, which was then held by Sweden. The attack proved unsuccessful, so much so that all of Livonia (with the exception of Riga and Daugagryva) fell into Swedish hands. In 1601, however, united Lithuanian and Polish forces, led personally by Sigismund, forced the Swedes out of Livonia. After the victory, the Polish army returned home, leaving the Lithuanians as sole protectors of Livonia. Then the Lithuanians, under the leadership of Jonas Katkevičius, again at- tacked Estonia and managed to occupy Tartu. The most famous battle of this campaign occurred near Kirchholm in 1605, when Katkevičius defeated the forces personally commanded by the Swedish king. Within four hours, the Lithuanian leader, whose troops numbered 4,500 at the most, struck down about 9,000 soldiers belonging to King Carl. At this time Livonia could easily have come under Lithuanian rule, were it not for internal strug- gles within the Lithuanian-Polish state and outside enemies such as the Russians, the Tartars and the Turks. Because of this, Lith- uania did not capitalize on its victory, and soon afterward the Swedes found themselves in a more favorable position for waging war: Gustav Adolf, the famous warrior, ascended the Swedish throne in 1611 after the death of his father, Carl IX.

Gustav arrived in Livonia in 1617 in order to continue the campaign his father had begun. For several years he fought the weakened Lithuanian forces—he captured Riga in 1621, all of Livonia and several parts of northern Lithuania, including Biržai. Then he moved against the "Polish Prussians," taking Klaipėda, Piluva, and Elbing. At the same time, the Lithuanians, led by

Kristupas Radvila, signed a truce with the Swedes in 1625, leaving the Poles to fight in Prussia alone. As a result of this act, the Lithuanians were accused of treason.

The war in Prussia coincided with the Thirty Years' War, and mainly because of this, a six-year truce was signed in 1629 in the town of Altmark, near Marienburg. According to this agreement, Sweden was to keep the three harbors (Klaipėda, Piluva, and Elbing) and to have control over Prussian sea trade. Thus, the Baltic Sea became a Swedish "lake." The Lithuanians decided to build a port on the Šventoji River so that they could conduct maritime trade independently of Sweden.

4. Renewed Wars with Moscow

Closer political and cultural ties with Poland served to separate Lithuania from Russia. Lithuania was fast becoming a Western, Catholic nation, and the differences between it and the Russian Orthodox state were becoming all the more evident. However, the influence of the Jesuits had also touched the adherents to Orthodox Christianity, especially those who had come in close contact with Roman Catholics. The exemplary Jesuit schools influenced members of other religions, including the Orthodox. The academies at Polock and Kiev were very important.

The result of Jesuit missionary work among the Orthodox was the Union of Bresta, signed in 1596, according to which the Orthodox population of the Grand Duchy of Lithuania and the Kingdom of Poland was to be brought into the Catholic Church. Such an attempt was not new: Algirdas, and, later, Vytautas, as well as Švitrigaila, had tried it. The question of union had been seriously discussed in Moscow in 1449, the same year in which the ecclesiastical synod at Florence was being held. However, it took the Jesuits and King Sigismund to transform the desire into reality. The King, as well as the Jesuits, drew up the articles of the union. The Orthodox gentry expected two things from the union: equal rights with the Catholic gentry and improved educational standards, which they expected the Jesuits to provide. The Orthodox Synod agreed to the union in 1590, and notified the King of their decision in 1591. Acceptance of unification by the Orthodox leaders came at an appropriate time, since the partriarchate of Moscow had just been established, and could have tried to influence the decision of the Orthodox hierarchy of Lithuania and Poland. However, because of the state of relations with Moscow, the interference of its church leaders would not have been accepted by the Orthodox clergy of Poland-Lithuania. With permission of the government, negotiations with the Papal nuncios were held in Cracow, and both sides agreed to accept the regulations set up at the Florence synod of 1449. Delegates were immediately dispatched to Rome, so that Pope Clement VIII could approve the regulations set up at Cracow. Then, in October of 1596, the Synod of Orthodox Bishops met at Bresta and accepted the union.

The previously unforewarned Orthodox lower clergy and peasantry did not react favorably. Even some of the Bishops were of differing opinions. Some supported the union and the government; others were against it, and sided with the peasantry. This led to religious quarrels and acts of terrorism, which influenced relations with Moscow.

At the beginning of the union, the last descendant of the Russian House of Rurik died (1598), and with his death ended a dynasty which had controlled Russia for 700 years. Stability of government was also at an end. Boris Godunov, chosen by the Parliament of nobles to be the provisional ruler, was not trusted because he had been accused of killing Dimitri, the last heir to the throne. The Poles took advantage of Godunov's unstable situation, and supported a "false Dimitri," who arrived in Poland— probably from Moscow—insisting that he was actually the Czar's son. The Jesuits supported him, and even the Polish King accepted him. After becoming a Catholic and obtaining assurances of Polish support, the "false Dimitri" hired Cossacks, marched against Moscow, and defeated Boris Godunov in 1605. The fortuitous death of Godunov made it simple for "Dimitri" to gain the throne, and the result was that Moscow had crowned a Czar who was supported and surrounded by Poles. The Pope and the Jesuits were pleased with the likely prospect of Orthodox Russia's return to Roman Catholicism.

However, the Polish hegemony in Moscow was distasteful to the Russians, and their resistance became a full-blown revolution. During this revolution, Dimitri, the imposter, was killed (1606). The Poles, together with the Lithuanians, tried to enter Moscow under the leadership of another pretender Dimitri. When this attempt proved unsuccessful, they proposed that the Russians accept King Sigismund's son, Vladislovas, as Czar. Although at first an agreement was reached enabling the Polish forces to march into Moscow, the Poles were unable to establish themselves. A massive revolt against foreigners forced them out of Moscow along with the Lithuanians. In 1613, the Parliament of nobles chose Michael Romanov as Czar, thus establishing a new Russian dynasty which was to last until 1918.

Taking advantage of the revolt in Moscow, the Lithuanians resolved to regain the lands previously occupied by Russia. After a long siege, they succeeded in regaining Smolensk (1611) and several other cities, but further fighting seemed useless, and in 1619 a truce was signed. After the truce, the Poles and Lithuanians fought only to defend the territories they had regained. Smolensk proved difficult to defend, and the Czar managed to seize and hold it for nearly a year in 1632-33. However, the defense eventually proved successful, and led to the signing of the "Everlasting Peace." This pact endured for twenty years.

The reign of the second Vasa King, Vladislovas, was peaceful. The gentry made free use of its "golden" rights and pretended to be sole rulers of the country. But the high nobles, especially the Radvilas, still played dominant roles, and the end of the peaceful era came with the emergence of the Cossacks in the southern Russian steppes.

The Grand Duchy of Lithuania did not have definite borders. Its lands merged with the vast steppes that extended to the Black Sea. People of various origins wandered through the steppes. They were primarily hunters and fishermen, but their main occupation was war and plundering, for which the Mohammedan Tartars and Turks, as well as the Christian Lithuanians, Poles and Russians provided suitable targets.

Until the time of the Lublin Union, the lands of these nomads —called Cossacks—belonged, at least nominally, to Lithuania. But the Lithuanians paid little attention to the steppes, and, as a result, refugees from Russia, Poland and Lithuania could live there freely. Their common circumstances drew them to the communities of the independent Cossacks.

The situation of the Cossacks underwent alteration when the steppes were ceded to the Poles as one of the conditions of the Lublin Union. The Polish nobility hastened to erect estates on these fertile lands. They needed serfs to farm the land, and began to enslave the Cossacks for that purpose. The Cossacks, who had long lived independently, and who were unfamiliar with agriculture, did not react favorably to the yoke of foreign rule. Neither did they like the attempts of the Jesuits to influence them to abandon Orthodoxy in favor of Church union. The Jews, who came in the wake of the Polish nobles, also angered the Cossacks, especially since they became involved in the monetary operations and trade of Cossack economic life.

New legislative policies were added to the economic restrictions. In 1590, under the rule of Sigismund Vasa, it was declared that a certain number of Cossacks were to be registered as soldiers, while the remaining, unregistered Cossacks were to be considered serfs. Since all the Cossacks were accustomed to fighting, the "serfs" were inclined to riot against the Polish landlords, forcing them to keep small armies on their estates for self-protection. Occasionally the nobles were even forced to call in government troops for support.

Several revolts which had to be put down by the government occurred under the reign of Vladislovas Vasa. The most important of these began in 1648, under the leadership of Bogdan Chmelnicki, and took place at Zaparože Žiče, near the Dnieper River. The main targets of this revolt were the Poles and the Jews. (The Jewish pogroms which resulted were surpassed only by the Nazi massacres of World War II.) Lithuania, too, became involved in putting down this revolt, and under the leadership of Jonušas Radvila, Lithuanian troops reached Kiev in 1651. When the Cossacks realized that they would be unable to withstand the combined forces of Poland and Lithuania without aid, they surrendered to Moscow (1654) after obtaining promises that their rights and freedom would be respected.

Having placed the Ukraine under his care, the Czar renewed his wars with Lithuania, and soon marched into it. The

Lithuania nobles, caught unaware, showed little resistance, and in 1655 the Russians took possession of Vilnius, plundering and devastating that city. They also entered Kaunas and Gardinas, although Samogitia and northern Lithuania remained untouched. As it turned out, these two regions were invaded by Swedes from Livonia as soon as Sweden declared war against Jonas Kazimieras, the third Vasa King, who had not renounced his claim to the Swedish throne.

Taking advantage of the situation, Jonušas Radvila (the palatine of Vilnius), who had never favored Polish-Lithuanian unification, decided to yield to Sweden in order to establish a Swedish-Lithuanian union in its stead. He summoned the Lithuanian nobility to his estate at Kėdainiai and drafted the Kėdainiai Agreement of 1656, which was signed by one thousand Lithuanian nobles. Under the terms of this agreement, the Swedish king was called upon to replace the Polish King as Grand Duke of Lithuania. However, the agreement was fundamentally meaningless, since the Swedes paid little attention to it, behaving like occupants of Lithuania rather than as allies.

The future of Sweden in Lithuania depended upon its victory over the Poles. Poland put up great resistance, nationalistic as well as religious (for example, the miraculous defense of Chenstachov forced the Swedes to retreat). Finally, according to the terms of the Oliva Agreement of 1660, the Swedes withdrew from Lithuania. Sweden retained Livonia, but returned Latgalis, which was later made into a palantinate.

Meanwhile, the wars with Moscow continued. In 1660, Lithuania regained Vilnius, Gardinas and Mohilev, and forced the Russians from Lithuanian soil. The Russians could not control the Cossacks, who constantly revolted and even tried to surrender themselves to the Turks. Since neither side seemed to be gaining the upper hand, the Russians and Lithuanians signed Andrusov's Peace in 1667, which provided that the previously Russian-occupied cities of Polock and Mohilev be returned into Lithuanian hands. The Russians kept Smolensk, which the Lithuanians had retaken several times in the fifty years that preceded the treaty. Starodub, Chernigov, and several other cities remained in Russian hands. The Poles had to give up the Ukraine, on the left bank of the Dnieper River; and Kiev, on the right. All in all, the Peace of Andrusov resulted in a great Westward advance on Moscow's part.

5. *Social Manifestations and the Unruliness of the Nobility*

During the sixteenth and seventeenth centuries, Lithuanian society was almost entirely agrarian. Medieval feudalism still flourished, as witnessed by the large numbers of serfs, and the lot of the serfs became more difficult to endure as contacts with the West increased. The growing urban communities in Western countries caused the monolithic agrarian communities to diminish, often resulting in a shortage of farm products—which had to be imported from somewhere else. Thus, the Eastern agrarian countries found ready markets for their produce in the West.

Since Lithuania had convenient access to the Baltic Sea by way of Klaipėda, Königsberg and other harbors, it came in contact with the markets of England, Holland and France. Grain, hemp, meat and other farm products were exported. The Grand Duke had ordered the superfluous produce from his estates to be shipped to Königsberg or Danzig in 1547, and the nobles followed his example. The crop surplus could be sold at high prices to the merchants arriving from the West, and the landowners, greedy for profit, began to expand their estates. They tried to increase the area of arable land and to improve agricultural methods in general. With the expansion of farm land came an extension of bondage, because many peasants, who had previously simply paid taxes for their farm lands, became serfs when the land was reabsorbed by the estate. In other instances, land-lords took fertile land away from the peasants and replaced it with land of poorer quality. Such was the case on the estates belonging to the nobility, the Church, and the Grand Duke. Some peasants, unable to bear the increased servility, fled the estates and took the moveable stock with them. Many escaped to Prussia, where they were welcomed as colonists.

In addition to increasing servility, the seventeenth-century Lithuanian peasant was also burdened by continual warfare and the plundering that accompanied it. The armies of the period resembled gangs of marauders whose livelihood seemed to be

96

obtained through robbery. After taking a stronghold, the troops more often than not descended onto the villages—stealing grain and live-stock, poaching fish from the ponds, and sacking honey from the hives. Famine and plague were among the evils which the soldiers bestowed upon the peasants.

Until the arrival of the Jesuits, spiritual life in Lithuania was in a sad state. Operating through the Academy of Vilnius, the Jesuits strived to produce secular and ecclesiastic scholars who would become supporters of the Church. For this reason, theo-logical and philosophical studies formed the core of the Acad-emy's curriculum. In general, the Academy represented the think-ing of the Jesuit order and of the Catholic Church. Conservative feudal ideology prevailed, even though some liberal trends had been allowed to filter in from the West. For instance, Marcin Smigleckis, a former Academy student who had also studied in Rome and who was later appointed professor at Vilnius Academy, protested against those who compared the serfs to Roman slaves. His views appeared in an article printed at the end of the seven-teenth century. Another Academy professor, Olizarevskis, ex-pressed similar opinions in an article published in 1651. However, these were individual views, and did not reflect nor change the essentially conservative outlook of the academy.

6. The North War and the Beginning of Russian Intervention

During the disorder among the nobles, the Žečpospolita chose the Saxon Kurfürst August as King in 1696. By bribing and by changing his Protestant religion to Catholicism, he influenced many nobles to his own side and suppressed others. His primary purpose was to establish firmly the Saxon dynasty in the Žečpos-polita. The Lithuanian nobles, enemies of the Sapiega, tended to uphold the King in this case and declared him, by a certain act, absolute ruler of the Grand Duchy of Lithuania with the right of inheritance. The common Warsaw parliament of the two states did not accept the decision of the Lithuanian nobles, and the act was revoked in 1701.

Nevertheless, August tried politicking independently of the nobility, supported by the troops brought from Saxony. At the beginning, he justified his holding the troops because of war with the Turks. After a successful victory, he declared that the troops were needed against the insurrection of the Sapiega. In reality, this adventure-seeking, unbalanced ruler sought to use the troops for some magnificent campaign which would impress the nobility. The nobles of the Žečpospolita did not forget having ruled Livonia once, which was now occupied by the Swedes. By ingratiating himself with them, August tried to regain this Baltic country. His intentions coincided with those of the young Russian Czar, Peter the Great, who planned to extend his state boundaries to the Baltic Sea, as had his predecessors. The Baltic was the window by which he hoped to close the ties between the emerging Russia and the West. As the purposes of Peter the Great and August were the same, both rulers, meeting in the Polish Rava in 1698, agreed upon sharing the Baltic basin and upon uniting their forces to overthrow the Swedes.

The war was precipitated by the intrigues of the leader Johann Reinhold Patkul, caused by the Livonian landowners' dissatisfaction of the Swedish rule. Patkul, having been expelled from the country, managed to bring himself into favor with August, who appointed him ambassador to Moscow. As a result of his effort, the Lithuanian-Polish, Russian and Danish coalition against the Swedes was agreed upon in 1699, thus bringing on the great North War.

The united forces of Žečpospolita and Russia did not match those of Sweden, a leading power at this time. Peter, first attacked, was strongly defeated near the Narva. His agreement with August to act in unison against the Swedish King Carl XII, a brilliant war leader, did not help. Carl defeated the two allies at Riga and entered Lithuania. At first the Swedes pretended to be the allies of the Sapiega, and declared that they had arrived in Lithuania not to be at war with it, but to protect Sapiega estates. Although they seemed peaceful, they did not attract the favor of the Lithuanians, who were decidedly against them. When the nobility attacked the Swedes, the latter declared war on Lithuania and nearly occupied the whole country, together with Samogitia, Vilnius, Kaunas and other areas.

The Swedish invasion meant escalation of the war. The Sapiega returned to the country and, supported by the Swedes, fought with their enemies. Oginskis and other nobles who also resisted the Swedes, went against them. Fighting went on, devastating the country. The inhabitants suffered not as much from the Swedes as they did from their own people, although the remaining legends attribute the years of torment to the Swedes. How the inhabitants suffered may clearly be realized from the reports of the Jesuits of Pašiaušė in Samogitia. For example, a 1700 report begins with the following words: "This year, nothing else was evident, than groaning and lamenting." The invaders as well as the Lithuanians burdened the people with large taxes, demanded high contributions, confiscated horses and carriages, and allowed soldiers to plunder as much as they desired. Famine and the plague spread throughout the destroyed country; famine was so widespread that some became cannibals.

When Carl XII followed August into Poland with his Saxon soldiers, Peter the Great intervened among the Lithuanian nobles. He renewed the ties with them; recovering from the Narva defeat, he overtook Ingermanland, part of Livonia, and established his Baltic harbor, Petersburg, in 1703. The Russians joined the yet unending civil war and made agreements with many Lithuanian nobles. Peter himself solemnly entered Vilnius in 1705 and was met by his loyal nobles.

Meanwhile Carl XII, fighting August for six years in Poland and Saxony, forced him to relinquish his throne and to acknowledge Stanislovas Lesčinskis as king (he had formally been chosen by the parliament, but actually endorsed by the Swedes). After concluding his affairs in Poland, Carl turned to the East in order to leave Lithuania in the charge of the new king. His general, together with the Sapiega, overtook Vilnius. His further campaign was to reach Moscow. Because of certain hindrances, he had to turn to the Ukraine, with whose hetman he entered into an alliance. But at the famed battle at Poltava his plans crumbled. Defeated and wounded, he barely escaped, retreating into Turkey.

After the battle at Poltava, the Swedes retreating from Lithuania were followed by the Russians, with the Czar himself turning to Livonia. They forced the Swedes out of Livonia, and the Baltic basin—from the Neva to the Šventoji rivers—became part of the emerging Russian Empire. August, by the grace of the Czar, was allowed to return to his throne with his Saxon troops. The King, with his troops, restricted the freedom of the nobles. Thus, the nobles demanded redress. When the King refused, they tried to revolt (1714-15). The Russians, at hand, took the opportunity to interfere, acting as the reconciliators. Their general, Grigorij Dolgoruk, dictated the following peace conditions at the Warsaw parliament in 1717: August, within twenty-five days, was to lead out the Saxon troops; the nobility was forbidden to gather into confederations; Lithuania was allowed to maintain 6,000 soldiers, Poland, 18,000; a fixed poll-tax was introduced to provide funds for the maintenance of the troops; hetmans' power was limited; the right of liberum veto was left.

The Russian general, by use of his soldiers brought to the parliament, forced the representatives to accept his dictated conditions and to disperse. For this reason, historically, the parliament was given the name of "dumb" parliament. Its silence was the first act in the long drama of the loss of freedom.

VI. Disintegration of the Commonwealth

1. Unsuccessful Efforts of Revival

The destructive war and the resulting plague and famine disrupted the country's economy. The fields remained unplowed and overgrown with weeds; the farms became disorganized, since the estates did not have a sufficient number of serfs to work them, and the poverty stricken farmers could not work their own fields because they lacked working animals.

Conditions began changing during the long years of peace following the end of the North War. They improved with the re-establishment of the serf farms and the increasing tax duties put on the peasantry. The only people able to re-establish their farms under the existing conditions were the owners of estates who managed to rebuild their own estates and to get a sufficient number of working animals, especially oxen. They rented their animals to the poor peasants in return for money or crops, though the peasants worked the estate lands with the same animals.

The estate owners, acquiring their own livestock and having many unworked lands, began establishing farms and inhabiting them with unemployed peasants. The poverty stricken peasants settled in their villages, very often under adverse conditions. Sometimes the estate owners demanded a written agreement that the peasants would not move from the given farms. At that time, the so-called Industrial Revolution began, when cities grew with the establishment of industry, and the demand for farm products increased. It was profitable for the estate owners to produce and export as great an amount of goods as possible. Because of this, it became necessary to enlarge the estate farms and those adjacent to it, and to decrease the serfs' plots. Sometimes the serfs were left a half or even a fourth of a *valakas* (fifty-two acres of land).

Corvees, violence, monetary duties, taxes and other factors now burdened the lives of the peasants. Often, because of the hardships, they secretly left the farms and sought other establishments. The estate owners tried to use various means in order to make the serfs return, and severely punished those who were caught. Some overburdened peasants revolted spontaneously (at Meškuičiai in 1707, at Skuodas in 1711, at Jurbarkas and a few other Samogitian districts from 1750 to 1760).

The state of the king's, or Grand Duke's, treasury depended in part upon the complex of estates. From several existing economies, one of the largest was at Šiauliai. Its structure maintained fifty estates, five towns, three hundred twenty villages, and had 5,536 valakas of workable land. Antanas Tiesenhausen, the descendant of German estate owners who came from Livonia, received the right to rule this large economy.

He was one of the first in Lithuania to understand the changing farming methods, and tried to lead the king's estates under his control in the direction of modern farming. He aimed at organizing industry on a wide scale. He transformed two suburbs of Gardinas into its center, where he established textile factories, candle, paper and even playing-card production. He also built manufacturing shops at Šiauliai and Joniškis. Fostering industry, he also increased the production of land goods, improving agricultural techniques and enlarging seeding areas. Tiesenhausen, by

101

his land-farming policies, affected the serfs, when their lands were taken away and decreased to a fourth of a *valakas*. But he demanded the same output and completion of other obligations and other farm work: road and bridge repairing, tree planting, trench and canal digging and so forth. The peasants of the Šiauliai economy soon demanded the abolishment of the new servile duties, and complained of them to the king. When their complaints had no reaction they revolted (1769); their revolt lasted half a year. The peasants, for some time, managed the economy themselves, removing various officials, until the troops dispersed them and the leaders were severely punished.

As the hardships of serfdom became harder to bear, disturbances of the peasants occurred as a concomitant to the increase of freedom the nobility was now enjoying. The nobles, especially those in the higher levels, having great power since the Lublin Union, now gained even more power under the reign of the Saxon kings who ruled from 1695 to 1764. To these kings, the Saxon *kurfürsts,* Lithuania and Poland were secondary states and were more or less left to themselves; their only interest lay in receiving funds from these states and using them for Saxony or their own pleasures. Under such rule, the nobles saw the advent of days of "golden freedom." They freely controlled their estates, exploiting the serfs as they pleased, and sometimes had their personal troops discipline them. They solved the affairs of state and their own counties at parliaments, which rarely ended peacefully, as they were often dissolved by the *liberum veto.*

The nobles did not feel the consequences of the existing disorder; they were not aware of the end of the state. Following the king's example, they were inclined to feast, to show off their wealth, to try to surpass one another in extravagance. They considered it an honor to have beautiful manors, to build churches, to establish monasteries and to bestow presents upon them. They paid little heed to education, which remained in the hands of the Jesuits and Piars. The former paid more attention to the schools of higher learning, while the latter paid more attention to primary schools, though later they also began establishing schools for higher learning. Because of the monastic educational system, there developed throughout the country a hatred for the members of other

religions—Calvinists, Lutherans, and even the Orthodox. Occasionally, hatred gave rise to public tactless intolerances against the
members of other religions.

Fanatical Catholics, mostly pupils, assaulted the ministers
and servants of the other churches, and scorned their prayer
houses, sometimes taking them away and converting them into
Catholic churches. The Catholic intolerance touched upon the
nobles of other faiths, when they were often rejected for state
positions and sometimes not admitted into parliaments. These
nobles complained to the foreign governments of their own religions. By this, they gave the governments a chance to butt into
the internal affairs of the Žečpospolita. Russia, which since 1717
had already intervened, now made use of the complaints of the
wronged Orthodox and began interfering even more. The complaints of the Protestants occasioned Prussian intervention. This
resulted in an agreement of the two states in 1766 to unite
against the persecution of the dissenters. This was the primary
step toward the first partition of the Žečpospolita.

2. Partitions of the Žečpospolita

With the beginning of Russian intervention into the internal
affairs of Lithuania, it became important to have a favorably disposed ruler once the Saxon dynasty ended. Since the second Saxon
did not leave a suitable heir, the throne could come into the possession of a local noble. One of the most famous line of nobles
was that of the Čartoriskis who knew how to ingratiate themselves with the Russians. One of its young members, Stanislovas
Poniatovskis (Stanislaw Poniatowsky), having served in the English and Saxon embassies at Petersburg, became the lover of
Catherine II and through her favor received the throne of the
King of Poland in 1764.

Though it was fated that Poniatovskis should be the last Polish King and Grand Duke of Lithuania, it was not through his
fault that the Commonwealth was disintegrating. He had good
intentions and tried to reorganize the state from its foundation
and to strengthen it. But he lacked the ingenuity and the will to
act. He particularly did not dare go against the Russians, through

whose favor he had received the throne. Pleasing the Russians, he was unable to restrain the members of other religions seeking equal rights with the Catholics. On the other hand, he was unable to affect the strong conservative Catholic trend to give in to the dissidents. The dissidents, supported by the Russians, aimed to seek lawful equality and organized into confederations in order to accomplish this aim. Thus, the confederation of the Grand Duchy of Lithuania was composed mainly of Orthodox nobles, but it was led by the elected Calvinist Grabauskas. (A similar Protestant confederation of Poland was established at Torn.)

The question of the dissidents raised by the Protestant and Orthodox confederations was closely associated with the family of the Čartoriskis which led the reform movement. The most important demand of the reformers was to determine economic affairs according to the majority of votes at parliaments excluding the *liberum veto*. Besides this, the reformers found the king unsuitable and demanded his removal.

In the atmosphere of the dissident confederations and the reforms of the Čartoriskis, the Radom parliament of 1767 was called. The Russians well understood the importance of the parliament to the state, and therefore took it under their control. First of all, their supported confederates chose as marshal for the parliament upon his return from exile Karolis Radvila, who favored theirs and the Russian cause and was an enemy of the Čartoriskis. The Russians gathered their forces at Radom and set them up at the parliament. Under these conditions, the members of the parliament had to accept the dictated conditions. Among them, the most important were the guarantees of religious freedom to dissidents and a request to Empress Catherine II "to accept the duty" of guarding the cardinal state laws (i.e., the constitution) and to see to it that they were not changed.

When, after some time, the same parliament met at Warsaw (1768), it had to acknowledge the conditions drawn up at Radom and to accept the Russian agreement. The Poles understood that the acceptance of such an agreement with a stronger state meant submission to it, and for this reason tried to oppose it. The Russians quickly quenched the uprising by arresting the leaders of the opposition and exiling them into Russia. The parliament,

104

overwhelmed by the arrests, accepted the conditions dictated by the Russians.

The Warsaw parliament revealed the Russian intent to control the Commonwealth according to their own desires. The country's patriots, realizing this before the parliament had ended, began organizing into a confederation in the town of Baras for the purpose of opposing the Russians and the king favoring them. Following this example, various other confederations were organized in Lithuania and Poland, forcing the Russians to conduct a widespread partisan war. The partisans retreated into neighboring countries and began attracting the attention of their governments to the disorder in the Commonwealth. The government of Austria, going against the confederates, overtook the Polish Spis (Zips) region at the border of Hungary. The region, since the earliest times, had belonged to Hungary, and since 1412, when it was turned over to Jogaila by King Sigismund, it was retained by the Poles. The Austrian government joined this region to the Hungarian kingdom in 1770, thus beginning the partition of the Lithuanian-Polish Commonwealth. The example became contagious, and the question of the partition was discussed among the higher levels in Berlin and Petersburg. The final plan of partition was worked out by Berlin and presented to the Russian government at St. Petersburg. The Prussian government, with some difficulty, talked Austria into participating in the partition also. All three tracts of the partition devised in St. Petersburg on August 5, 1772, by the three governments began with these words: "In the name of the Holy Trinity."

The occupation of the Grand Duchy of Lithuania followed. Russia annexed the lands up to the Dauguva and Dnieper rivers including the cities of Polock and Vitebsk; it also annexed Latgalis, which had belonged to Lithuania since the sixteenth century. The Prussians annexed the so-called royal Prussians with the bishopric of Varmė. Only the two cities of Danzig and Torn opposing the Russian annexation were excluded from it. Austria received a section of Poland Minor and Galicia. The occupation was accomplished without any opposition; the nobility, shocked by the occupation, did not oppose even the ambassadors of the partitioning governments, when they demanded the acknowledgment of the partitioning.

According to the demand of the Russian ambassador, Stakelberg, a small parliament convened at which the greater number of representatives were bribed. The ambassadors were not sure whether the parliament would accept their demands unanimously; for this reason, they declared it confederational, as such a parliament could accept resolutions according to the rule of the majority. So that the proceedings of the parliament could go smoothly, a commission of thirty members was assigned to prepare the resolutions and to present them for the approval of the majority. Thus, the extorted parliament calmly accepted the laws of the partition with the exception of the dramatic opposition of Tadas Reytanas, representative of Novgorodok.

Struck by the decisive blow, the government of the Žečpospolita understood the need of fundamentally reorganizing the disordered state. The King himself, loyal to the Russians, upon receiving their permission, began a reformation. He managed to receive the right to change the important rights of the dissidents even in the Russian-guaranteed cardinal laws. Their rights, though, remained hampered. They were allowed to send only three representatives to parliament but not one to the senate. There were other restrictions as well.

The most important new reform was the Permanent Council (Concilium permanens). It was the highest executive power, made up of thirty-six members, chosen in equal number from the senate and the parliament. They were elected every two years. Five departments (ministries) were under the Council's jurisdiction: those of foreign affairs, police, war, justice and treasury. The Council, just as its departments, were common for Lithuania as well as Poland, and the high Lithuanian administrators were under the jurisdiction of the corresponding department. The Council, not without the intervention of Stakelberg, was assigned the chief duty of maintaining the old system with the prescriptive rights of the aristocracy. But it also carried out significant agricultural and economic, as well as cultural and educational, reforms. Its economic reforms affected the cities most. The outdated Magdeburg system and guilds were abolished. The city dwellers were given freedom to earn their living by trade and crafts, to have possession of lands, and even to become nobles. The Council began reorganizing the fundamental rights of the state, for which purpose the new Code of Zamojiski was prepared. (The Russians, unable to tolerate greater changes, did not allow the code to be put into practice.)

The existence of the permanent Council was of great importance to education. The Educational Commission, established after the abolishment of the Jesuit Order in 1773, carried out great educational reforms. It took over the properties of the Jesuits and used the proceeds on them for the establishment and maintenance of schools. The former Jesuit Academy of Vilnius, now called the Highest School, became the modern educational center of the Commission. Twenty-five similar schools of higher learning fell under its jurisdiction. Primary schools were established close to the parishes, and the Seminary of Vilnius was established to prepare primary-school teachers.

Although the schools did not lose contact with the past, and reflected, basically, the spirit of the conservative aristocracy, they did not ignore the new ideas spreading from France. They evinced a keen interest in the more accurate studies of nature, mathematics, medicine, biology, and astronomy. In social studies, they also began paying more attention to natural phenomena, rather than to former superstitions. They began examining the past, the peoples' mode of life (even those of commoners) and their customs and folk art. The new Highest School of Vilnius, as well as the university later established there, reflected this new trend.

The new educational trend fostered a new generation which differed from the older ones; the new generation, drawn closer to the common people, realized their hardships, and was inclined toward reform. The intelligentsia, better able to understand their society, felt the hindering oppression of foreign rule and the need to free themselves from it. Reforms and the resultant struggles for independence were organized by the younger intelligentsia.

Though the matter of changing the old system was ripe, it was necessary to wait for the right opportunity to carry it out. The right opportunity seemed to present itself when Russia began fighting against Turkey in 1788, with Austria entering the war also. Prussia did not side with Russia; it was in opposition to the Czarist government, as were other European states. Under these conditions, the confederational Žečpospolita parliament convened to determine the basic state-law affairs. At that time, by the influence of the French Revolution, it was decided to fundamentally reorganize the state, drawing up plans for a constitution. The parliament met for four years from 1788 to 1792 and produced the so-called May Third Constitution, which was finally accepted May 3, 1791.

The most important issue of the constitution was the planning of a new administration, called Guards of Legislature, to be established in place of the abolished Council and to be composed of five ministries. The ministers were to be chosen by the king and responsible to the parliament. The king's rule was extended without the obligation of being responsible for his acts. His throne was to be inheritable and his heir was to be chosen from the line of the Vetin. The parliament was to remain aristocratic (the abominable *liberum veto* was abolished). The rule of the majority was to remain.

There were no major social reforms. The Commonwealth remained, as it had been, a state composed of three social classes: the nobility, city dwellers, and peasants. The complete rights of citizens were recognized only to the nobility; the extended rights of city dwellers gave them the right, under certain conditions, to become nobles. Basically, the conditions of the peasants did not change. They still remained under patrimonial rights of nobility.

According to the influence of the reforms of the French Revolution, the May Third Constitution emphasized the unity of the Commonwealth without once mentioning the name of Lithuania. But the Constitution was unable to obliterate the existence of the Grand Duchy of Lithuania, so the following decisions were made: the third consecutive parliament was to convene at Gardinas; in the common ministries, half of the officials were to be Lithuanian and the other half Polish; the Polish and Lithuanian forces were to be maintained separately; a common treasury was to exist, with a separate Lithuanian section.

When the conservative nobles now turned to the Russians for

support in opposing the realization of the new constitution they gave the latter an opportunity of interfering in the affairs of the Commonwealth. The alliance between a few nobles of the Commonwealth and the Russian government was called the Targovich Confederation. Under the pretext of supporting this confederation, the Russians once again set foot into the Commonwealth in 1792, and kept the constitution from being put into effect. They made another agreement with the Prussians and enacted a second partition in 1793: Prussia annexed Danzig, Torn and Poland Major with Poznan and part of Poland Minor. The Russians annexed the remainder of White Russia up to the Dnieper and Dauguva rivers including the city of Minsk and the Polish Ukraine.

The parliament, summoned in Gardinas, and coerced by the Russian forces, acknowledged the partition, agreeing to have the former confederate system put into practice with a revived permanent Council. But there was no time for the revived order to be put into actual practice, since the revolt of 1794 caused the complete disintegration of the Commonwealth.

Patriots, aroused by the new constitution, remained uneasy under the yoke of neighboring countries, and began preparing for a revolt. They aimed to raise an army of 300,000 men. Its leader was to be Tadas Kosciuška, an officer of Lithuanian descent who had finished his schooling in France and had gained recognition in the fight for independence by the United States of America. The nobles of Lithuania arose also, overtaken by the spirit of independence; an ardent republican officer, Jokubas Jasinskis became the leader in Vilnius, and by suddenly attacking the Russian garrison at night, he overtook the capital. At the square of the city hall, he declared the act of revolt and acknowledged Kosciuška as the revolutionary leader of the Commonwealth. Struggling with the Russians, the rebels persecuted the members of the confederation siding with them; they caught two of their leaders, the last Lithuanian hetman, Simonas Kosakowskis, and marshal Šveikovskis, and hung them in the same square.

Following the example of the French Revolution, the organizers wanted to make their revolution massive, with the inclusion of the peasants. Kosciuška himself, as well as the Highest Council, turned to the Lithuanian peasants with appeals written in the Lithuanian tongue. These appeals found response among the people and induced more people to revolt. The rebels organized more strongly in Samogitia (where they even managed to retake Liepojus).

The sudden revolt was unable to withstand the attacks of the Russian army, led by the famous General Suvorov and supported unexpectedly by the Prussians. The Prussian king, expecting a large share of the disintegrating Žečpospolita, withdrew from the alliance against France and attacked the rebels. Pressed from two sides, Kosciuška lost his last battle near Maciejovice on October 10, 1794; he was severely wounded and taken into captivity.

The victors, drawing Austria in also, decided to divide and share the remainder of the Žečpospolita. Austria annexed Poland Minor without the city of Cracow; Prussia received central Poland with Warsaw and Užnemunė, and Russia occupied Lithuania itself up to its old and new border contiguous to Prussia.

With this partition, a new era began for Lithuania. Existing for centuries as one of the largest central European states, the Grand Duchy was now reduced to a mere Russian province, even losing its name. The Lithuanian people now began their stateless history. . . .

VII.   LITHUANIA IN THE FIRST HALF OF THE 19TH CENTURY

1. The Old Society in a New State

At first neither the Prussians nor the Russians who divided Lithuania tried to change existing social conditions; both states were monarchies with the prevailing class the landowning aristocrats, thus they were reluctant to alter the former Žečpospolita society as well as its economy. However, several administrative reforms were made: Russian Lithuania was divided into governments and these, in turn, into counties (the counties retained relatively the same borders); the Prussian Užnemunė was divided into three counties which were connected to the so-called New East Prussia.

The Užnemunė area remained under Prussian rule from 1795 to 1807, during which time relatively few German colonists were admitted (most of them were craftsmen who established themselves in towns); otherwise, few changes were made. But the mode of life in Užnemunė took a different course from that of Lithuanians living elsewhere when, in 1807, it entered the newly-established Kingdom of Warsaw, where the Napoleonic Code of civil law was established. According to the Code, serfdom was abolished and the former serfs were given personal rights equal to those of the nobles. Since they did not receive any land, they were forced to remain economically dependent upon the nobles; but the path was open for them to become independent, by renting or buying land. In this way a nation of free farmers was being established in Užnemunė while bondage continued in other parts of Lithuania. This may explain the reason for the cultural lead of the people of the Užnemunė area at the time of the later national renaissance.

The rule of the nobility continued in Russian Lithuania. The nobles were allowed to hold governmental and county parliaments, where they pondered over the affairs of their social class and elected all government officials. Lithuania remained under the rule of the aristocracy, as earlier—only, this ruling class was now composed of the local as well as the newly-arrived Russian nobility.

Greater reforms were made in those cities which were transformed into governmental and county centers. Their inhabitants were given autonomy. They elected their own administrators and magistrates, and they had their own courts. The smaller cities remained, as before, dependent upon the estate owners and had to serve them and to pay taxes. Often, the city dwellers complained in vain of their oppression, asking the government to give them the rights of county cities.

The peasants were completely without rights. The Russian government did not interfere with their relations with the landowners, who held the latter in total dependency. The state burdened the peasants with hard tasks also: service in the army for twenty-five years, in addition to having to billet troops on the farms, and, most important, having to pay state taxes. According

111

to the common Russian procedure, each man not belonging to the privileged class was to pay a tax. The payments were distributed by the estates, which received a lump sum for all the serfs. Because of the inaccurate census, made every fifteen years, the amounts of the payments were not constant and equal among the estates. Thus the serfs bore the yoke of servility placed on them by the foreign government as well as their own nobles.

2. *Cultural Growth After the Partitioning*

Lithuania became part of Russia at the time of the great European cultural and social revolution. New freedoms and nationalistic ideas were widespread, influenced by the French Revolution. In Lithuania, they found response at the University of Vilnius, established in 1803. The University was actually the reorganized Highest School of Vilnius. It was not only a school of higher learning, but also a research institution. All the district schools were under its jurisdiction. It was able to attract good instructors from the former Commonwealth as well as from abroad, since its influential guardian, Adomas Čartoriskis, had provided the university with adequate funds. Many scholars arrived from the West, making the University of Vilnius one of the leading schools of Europe.

The influence of the spirit of the new era was most apparent in the humanities. The educational ideologies spreading from France caused the common people to take an interest in their mode of life as well as their past. Representatives of these studies came closer to the people and were the first to foster the nationalistic sentiments. The greatest credit for this belongs to the historians.

Jochim Lelevel (1786-1861), a Polish professor of German descent, made the history taught by him at the University the greatest single factor in the nationalist movement. To Lelevel, history was not solely the history of kings and rulers, as it was generally looked upon; he infused a spirit of new democracy and liberalism when he paid attention not so much to the political events as to society's mode of life as well as its collective actions and creativity. According to Lelevel, who joined the University

112

in 1815, history must examine "the social relationships, the attitudes and aims of people, which change." With his understanding of history, Lelevel began fostering nationalistic ideas, for which reason he gained great respect from the students and from society as a whole. The object of Lelevel's studies became the Lithuanian past. While still studying at the University of Vilnius in 1808, he wrote a study concerning the antiquity of the Lithuanian lineages. The Lithuanian Samogitian Dionyzas Poška had, it seems, this study in mind, when he urged his nationals to familiarize themselves with "books of wisdom written by the Masovian" (Lelevel).

The Lithuanians are more indebted to Žegota Ignas Onacevičius (1780-1845), though his writings do not equal those of Lelevel. Not as rational and analytical as the latter, he was far more the romantic and enthusiast. Closer to the Lithuanians by his descent (he was born and raised in Lithuania), he studied at the University of Königsberg and was a lecturer there for some time. There he became interested in Lithuania's past and began collecting archival material concerning it. From Königsberg he was invited to St. Petersburg by Count Runiancev to work at his library. Four years later he returned to Vilnius (1811), received his master's degree at the University, and taught for a time at the Balstogė high school, after which he returned to the University to teach history (1818).

Onacevičius' merit lies in his great love for the Lithuanian people and their past; he was the first to lecture in Lithuanian history (without payment). His lectures were full of love and enthusiasm, as befits a romanticist. He awakened the interest of his students to the Lithuanian past, and influenced many to devote themselves to it. Among his devoted students was Simonas Daukantas, a Samogitian, who began writing the history of Lithuania while still a student.

The third scholar worthy of the esteem of the Lithuanians was Ignas Danilavičius (1787-1843), a law historian, well known in Lithuanian law research, especially that of the Statute. In libraries and archives, everywhere, he searched for law and historic sources, and having found them, copied them and made parts of them known. He found, for example, one copy of a Lithuanian yearbook—the Chronicle of Supraslis—and published it in 1825. To the preface of the introduction, Danilavičius was the first to add a review of the Lithuanian historiography wherein he critically described several authors, especially M. Stryjkovski. Danilavičius based his criticisms on sources which he scrutinized analytically, and raised the idea that history should be based on source. In this manner, he paved the way for the scholarly writing of history void of unproven stories and legends.

The University of Vilnius surpassed all Russian universities by the number of its students and its high level of education. Russian poet A. Poližajev compared it to such famous universities as those of Goetingen and Oxford. It influenced the development of Lithuanian culture and national awareness, spreading its influence throughout the schools attended by the children of the nobility, who thus received a more sophisticated education than did the commoners. In 1809, the university organized a commission to gather information about the Lithuanian language, assembling teachers from Kėdainiai, Raseiniai, Kražiai, Padubysis and other places to gather linguistic data, old Lithuanian writings, songs, and the like.

3. Influence of the New Education upon the Samogitians

The enlightenment coming from the University of Vilnius influenced the Samogitian nobles. They were more receptive to the influence than were the other Lithuanian nobles, since they were closer to the common people. The Samogitian nobles, maintaining their self-government through long centuries, did not give in to the Polanizing influence to such a degree as did the Lithuanian nobles. They did not forget their language. Many of them were not owners of large lands and thus, agriculturally, were not far above the commoners. The Lithuanian literary historian Mykolas Biržiška correctly notes: "The Samogitian nobles were much closer to their own people, much more democratic, than were the nobles in other provinces." The Samogitian authors who studied at the University or who had contact with it were fostered under the influence of its modern enlightenment. A good example is Silvestras Valiūnas, the author of a popular song about Birutė.

Better known is Kajetonas Nezabitauskis, who published a Samogitian primer, bibliographies, dictionaries, grammars and other material. Foreigners read his valuable writings and praised him. He received a letter from the famous patron of the arts, Count Rumiancev, who congratulated him on writing in a language which was not yet rich in literary works. M. Balinskis of Vilnius also honored Nezabitauskis on his being practically the only Samogitian-Lithuanian writer in command of his native language to write so many works in it.

The Samogitian most affected by the influence of the university was Simanas Stanevičius, who studied during the University's developmental years (1822 to 1826), when the strong political movement, influenced by the new romantic trend, began. The esteem of the nation's past, its creativity and its former freedom stemming from the romantic movement, was reflected in Stanevičius' ode *The Honor of the Samogitians*. In this high hymn, as the author called it, aimed at the Samogitian students, he rejoices that "The old Lithuanian lineages, in their ruin, remained sound." He advises the students to "build up what the ages destroyed." This means, that "the honor of the fathers and the tongue" [language] must be revived.

By this noble, romantic hymn, Stanevičius outlined the aims to be reached by the Samogitian and Lithuanian students and by which he worked also. His first aim was to revive the language, and for this reason he reprinted a grammar book written by an unknown author. He took interest in Lithuanian writing, as we may see by his publication of several sermons by canon Mikalojus Daukša published in the sixteenth century, to which he added the canon's famous foreword concerning the native language. Stanevičius, influenced by romanticism, was fascinated by the Samogitian folk songs.

That Stanevičius was a noble very close to the people may be realized by the six fables he wrote. They are didactic in form, aimed at teaching the people and written in the correct language of the commoners. Among the fables, one is exceptional. It is called *The Horse and the Bear*. In it, the horse represents, allegorically, the High Lithuanians (whose symbol was the steed), meeting a bear, representing the Samogitians. The meeting takes place at the banks of the Nevėžis River, the old border between the Samogitians and the High Lithuanians. In the fable, the bear complains to the horse, saying: "Chains remain on my neck, while fetters remain on you." Some believe there is a political motif in this complaint—that of pity that Lithuania has lost her independence. But, in the case of the romantic Stanevičius, it was more fitting to have the social idea in mind. For at that time, when social and economic movements were widespread, and serfdom was abolished in the West, the bondage in Lithuania seemed a great injustice. Romantic writers, affected by the widespread radical ideas, considered serf owners the enemies of the people, their enslavers. The social motif in Stanevičius' fable is characteristic of that period of time. The ideas spreading from Europe based on political, national and social freedoms influenced the Samogitian nobles and were reflected in their writing and actions. The best example of a Samogitian noble influenced by the new ideas is Dionyzas Poška (1757-1830).

D. Poška was a self-taught intellectual who had not even finished high school. Living at his estate and working at the office of the Raseiniai city court, he devoted himself to research of his country's past. Not satisfied with written histories, he began excavating the nearby tumuli, collecting antiques and storing them inside a large hollowed oak tree. Thus he established a unique museum, the first in Lithuania.

Although Poška had never been outside of Samogitia, he was interested in all of Lithuania and the studies involving it. He followed the accomplishments of the University and corresponded with famous professors—J. Lelevel, Z. Onacevičius, Lobojko, and others. He discussed Lithuanian problems with them and gave them invaluable advice. He was interested that someone should write the history of Lithuania. Concerned that no one accepted this task, he himself wrote in Polish *The Village Ploughman's Thoughts Upon the History of the Lithuanians and Samogitians and Their Language*. He did not pretend to be an educated author, but wrote in accordance with his inborn desire "to know the history of his fatherland and of the country of his people." He went on to hope that "the enlightened University of Vilnius, existing in the capital of Lithuania, would be able to find, among

116

its numerous professors, Lithuanians or Poles just as able to write the history of Lithuania as they would be able to prepare a dictionary or a grammar." Meanwhile, he was gathering data for a future history. Excluding the historic criticism, his written article was interesting not because of the given facts but because of his aim—to show that the Lithuanians had had a large and powerful nation.

Besides the history, Poška was anxious to learn more about the Lithuanian language. He worked, as he himself states, "on the heightening of the lucidity of our tongue." In the article, he compared the history of the nation with its language, and wanted to have both revived and fostered. He paid a great deal of attention to the literary purity, so that it could be understood by the commoners. In order to enrich the language and to stabilize it, he began the Lithuanian-Polish-Latin dictionary which he did not finish. Poška's love of language and his national past show him as being similar to the common people, affected as he was by the ideals of independence. This was clearly revealed in his famous verse work, *The Samogitian and Lithuanian Rustic* in which he depicts in dark colors the hard burden placed on the serfs and expresses compassion for them. Through this truly sincere, sentimental literary piece, Poška expressed the democratic Western spirit.

Several other enlightened men such as Klemensas, Daukantas and Strazdelis, expressed similar views against serfdom. Antanas Strazdelis even dared to threaten the lords owning serfs with "forged steel." Meanwhile, the Samogitian nobles did not threaten the serf owners. The question of the abolishment of bondage was foreign to them. But once they became closer to the commoners and became interested in their lives, they began fostering nationalistic ideas.

4. Political-National Student Agitation

Since its inception, the University of Vilnius displayed an active political-patriotic spirit. It could not have been otherwise during the changing times, when the old conservative ideas were in opposition to the new progressive ones. The students began politicking in their own clubs (which were allowed to exist since the establishment of the University). It is possible that Lelevel, while still a student, had them in mind when he wrote that: "Vilnius is thundering with studies and politics."

The existing social organizations in Lithuania and Poland exerted great influence over the students. Freemasonry, directly inheriting ideas of the age of reason, influenced them the most. The Masons fostered the ideas of perfecting the individuals and society: their humanism and rationalism, together with demands for political freedom, attracted the students of the University. But the students were unable to reveal openly their progressive teaching because of the Russian reaction which had overtaken the University. Then the establishment of secret clubs began.

The best known student club was established by the Philomats in 1817—the year that the patriotic German students organized the Vartburg Holiday, which moved the European reaction forces, and established the Welfare Union in St. Petersburg. The Philomat club fostered the patriotic student movement. The movement expanded and led to the establishment of similar clubs such as those of the Filadelfists, Radiates (Towarzystwo Promenistych) and the most famous club, the Villains (Szubravcy). The Villains published a witty magazine of political satire, *Wiadomosci Brukowe*. These clubs fostered a deep patriotic spirit, love of commoners and contempt for the nobility oppressing them. Their interest lay in their native people, their lives and creativity, in other words—in Lithuanianism.

Although, for safety reasons, politics were not mentioned in the student regulations, the students took interest in them. The strong demand for absolute freedom in the neighboring Polish Duchy, to which part of Lithuania belonged, influenced the students of Vilnius. The political aims of the students were disclosed in 1823 by a pupil of the Vilnius Gymnasium, which was next to the University, who wrote "Hurray for the May 3rd Constitution" on the bulletin board. The Russian government, watchful of any revolutionary movements, reacted immediately and sent a commission led by Senator Novosilcov. The commission arrested about one hundred Philomat and Philarette students, and discharged the rector and several professors, among them the historians Lelevel and Danilavičius. Twenty students were exiled to Russia, three received short prison sentences.

The Russians raged against the University; the students as well as their professors were closely watched. The latter were required to present the outlines of their lectures to the University council for inspection and for verification by the new curator, Nikolaj Novosilcov, who took over when Čartoriski resigned. But the combined efforts of the University administration and of Novosilcov to isolate the students from public life and to change the University into a seeming monastery bore little fruit. The movement spread into other schools of higher learning; for instance, in the school maintained by the Kražiai monks, they detected the existence of a secret "Black Brother" organization, and in 1825 seven leaders were given hard sentences.

In Vilnius itself, a revolutionary spirit was fostered until it flared out in 1830 when the effects of the French Revolution overcame Lithuania. In vain, the rector tried to appease the students when the revolt began in Poland before Christmas. Ordered by the chief of the Russian army, the rector forbade the students to leave for Christmas vacation. The students did not heed the rector's orders and began disturbances. Some were accused of conspiracy and were thrown into jail. Ignas Kraševskis (Kraszewski), who later became a famous writer, was among those imprisoned. The fact that the students of Vilnius had a strong patriotic spirit and a feeling of resistance against the Russians was revealed by a group of 400 students who broke through the Russian troops and joined the rebels who had reached the outskirts of town June 29-30, 1831.

By their revolutionary activities, the students destined the sad fate of their alma mater. As soon as the revolt was quelled, by the act of Czar Nikolas I, the "revolutionary" University of Vilnius was closed (May 1, 1832). Thus the Lithuanian beacon, fostering the idea of freedom and light, was put out.

5. The 1831 Revolt

As in the past, resilient ties still bound Lithuania and Poland. Not including old political and cultural ties, the two nations were now bound by a common oppressor. The 1830-31 revolt was the first common resistance to the occupants by force. The revolt, brewing in Poland for a long time, finally occurred in the wake of the French Revolution. Within months it broke out in Lithuania when the Russians, gathering a greater army, began recruiting soldiers and demanding compulsory quotas of food to be delivered to the army. The Samogitians were especially agitated by the Russian demand to transport the food quotas to a warehouse near Gardinas. The revolt began in Samogitia after bands of armed men were organized in the districts of Salantai and Gintališkis, in February of 1831. Although the first rebels were unable to develop their activities to a greater extent and, overtaken by the Russians, were forced to retreat into Prussia, they set a good example for others. Immediately, the Samogitian and High Lithuanian centers, i.e., Raseiniai, Telšiai, Šiauliai, Panevėžys, Ukmergė, Ašmena, Trakai, Švenčionys, came into the hands of the rebels. Of the more famous cities, only Vilnius, Kaunas and Palanga remained under Russian rule. Thus, the insurrection spread throughout the country in a very short time. The Vilnius civil governor's publication in 1831 gives adequate evidence of the spreading revolt: "The city of Raseiniai began the commotion. Several evildoers, organizing a band of armed peasants, managed to overthrow the legal government . . . the example of the Raseiniai insurrectionists has been followed by the remaining districts. Now all of the governments of the Vilnius area, excluding the city itself and its suburbs, do not recognize their legal government. . . ."

The national governments, now controlling almost the entire country, were concerned with peace and order. The inhabitants congratulated their own governments, and in many places the arriving rebels were greeted with the ringing of bells. Crowds of people gathered to honor the new governments. Here they signed the so-called confederational acts, renouncing their oaths of allegiance to the Czar. The populace was in high spirits. Throughout the country, people hung flags with mottos such as: "Freedom, unity, independence"; "Freedom, or death"; "For our country's laws"; and others.

The joy of freedom was short lived. The freed towns were

able to hold out as long as the surprised troops were disorganized and not united by common leadership, but this did not last long. By April, the job of suppressing the revolt was given to the General-Governor of Latvia-Estonia (then considered a German Baltic province), Baron von Pahlen. He arrived in Samogitia with Bishop S. Giedraitis and his two aiding priests. His hope to calm the inhabitants with the help of the clergy was useless. But the rebels were unable to withstand the greater Russian pressure. The Samogitian fighting mood was rather low because of their many unsuccessful tries to regain Palanga. The Germans of the Baltic obstinately defended Palanga, since it was incorporated into the former Courland, ruled by them. At that time the rebels desired to get Palanga, hoping to be able to get arms from France or England through it. The rebels, pressured by the enemy, holding out for about two months, had to retreat from their occupied towns and hide in the forests.

The army, sent from Poland in May of 1831, led by Generals Chlapovski, Gelgaudas and Dembinski could not help the rebels. Roaming about central Lithuania for a while, the Poles tried to overtake Vilnius. After repeated attacks from the hills of the Neris basin, they came into contact with the Russian defense. After encountering great losses, the attackers retreated. Among those killed were many Lithuanians who had been drawn into the army just before the battle, lacking experience in warfare.

The rebels turned from Vilnius to Samogitia and tried to overtake Šiauliai on the way. Although Gelgaudas had stronger forces than the defending Russians, he was unable to capture the city. After the second blow, the leaders of the insurrection met at Kuršėnai and still tried to set up various plans, although they did not expect to carry them out. As usual, hopeless quarrels broke out—a Polish colonel began blaming the Lithuanians for the defeat. A Lithuanian answered him back: "The Lithuanian rebels held out with scythes until the end, which the Polish army leaders brought about."

After the meeting at Kuršėnai, the Polish leaders were solely interested in how to lead the army from the theater of war to the borders of Prussia or Poland. Dembinski alone, passing over Vilnius from the eastern side and evading the Russian troops, reached Poland. Meanwhile, Gelgaudas and Chlapovski crossed the Prussian border and disarmed. Some soldiers recognized the treachery of their leaders; thus, an officer shot Gelgaudas because of it. After the retreat of the Poles, the disappointed Lithuanian peasantry and nobility ceased fighting. Some hid in forests, others secretly returned home; some leaders, not having fallen into Russian hands, emigrated.

The Lithuanian serfs became interested in the social and national affairs during the revolt of 1831. The then widely-discussed abolishment of serfdom gave rise to their hope that together with political freedom economic freedom would also come. Thus, to them the revolt was not only political but also economic. Since its leaders, the nobles, did not mention the abolishment of serfdom, here and there the peasants displayed their agitation. A greater revolt went on at the estates of Zubovas; the peasants expelled or killed the estate administrators and elected their own to replace them. They were even prepared to go to Telšiai to overthrow the government of the nobility. Army units of nobles went against the serfs and defeated them.

The national motive was not foreign to the Lithuanians when they went against the Russians. This may be seen by the flattering proclamation written by the Poles to the Lithuanians which was published in Lithuanian as well as in Polish; the Lithuanian text appeals to the Lithuanian national feeling: "Posterity of Gediminas, Vytautas and Jogaila! All time brothers of common calling, if you have inherited the love of freedom and independence . . . gladden the immortal shadows of the warriors, let their examples reawaken you." Reawakening the patriotic spirit of the Lithuanians, the Poles were probably sure that their appeal would be understood and favorably accepted. Only by knowing the Lithuanians to have a national consciousness could they have reasoned in this manner.

6. Resistance to Oppression

The 1831 revolt occurred at the time of the reaction of the Russian Empire during the reign of Nicholas I. Nicholas' reactionary policies were based on three principles: Orthodoxy, autocracy and nationalism. According to these principles, priority in the Empire belonged to the Orthodox Russians, supported by the autocratic government. This system sorely affected Lithuania during the postwar era. It began the confiscation of lands belonging to the Church and nobility. For the first time in Lithuania, the many possessions of the churches and monasteries, gained through the centuries, were greatly reduced. They were given, in some cases, to the newly-established Orthodox Church or to the Orthodox monasteries. At that time, the Orthodox monks received the monastery of Pažaislis with a fine baroque manor. The confiscated estates were sold cheaply and given to high Russian officials and generals. The Russian colonists were being transferred into Lithuania and complete villages were given to them.

The systematic Russification of the country began. Well-known schools of higher learning were closed (only several remained open for the children of the nobility). Others were forbidden to seek knowledge, since it would "confuse their minds." They had to be satisfied with primary schools; but even these were disappearing. The Lithuanians were being more strongly Russified than the other nations of the Empire because of their unusual past. Lithuania, having once annexed large areas of western Russia, now became a small territory in the Russian Empire. In 1840, the name of Lithuania was forbidden to be used in designation of the former territory of the Grand Duchy (the name of Byelorussia was also forbidden to designate that country). Together with the abolishment of the Lithuanian name, the Lithuanian Statute, the most independent national creation of all, according to which the Lithuanians ruled themselves for centuries, was also abolished in 1840. But the common European aim for freedom and struggles against the spirit of despotism was not suppressed, as was revealed by the case of Simonas Konarskis.

Konarskis, a Lithuanian noble, was a radical fighter for freedom and democracy. He became a volunteer rebel in 1831 and fought in the army of Chlapovski near Vilnius and elsewhere. After the revolt, he crossed the Prussian border and later reached France. In 1835 he joined the Polish Democratic Society, once led by Lelevel, who persuaded him to return to Russia. Starting from Volynia he organized democratic societies everywhere—in

123

Vilnius, Minsk, Kiev and even Odessa. Konarskis established contacts with the students of the Medical Surgery Academy, which was left open after the University itself was closed, and interested them in his society. He wanted to make Vilnius the center of his movement and to set up a secret printing office for propaganda purposes. When he arrived in Vilnius, government agents recognized and arrested him. After severe questionings and punishments, he was publicly shot (1839).

The Vilnius students, having been affected by Konarskis, were uneasy after his death. The "democratic spirit" remained alive within them, despite mass arrests. When the government realized that the academy was not to be influenced, they transferred it to the University of Kiev in 1842. At the same time, the theological academy was transferred to St. Petersburg. The famous university disappeared; its buildings were now used to house political prisoners.

But the spirit of the University of Vilnius remained. The work begun was continued by its students—writers and educated people. Their themes usually dwelt upon Lithuania. Known writers such as Ignac Kraszewski, L. Kondratowicz—W. Syrokomla, J. Slowacki, and historians such as M. Balinski, J. Jaroszewicz, and especially Th. Narbutt, left well-known books on Lithuania written in Polish.

Among those writing in Polish, the Samogitian Simonas Daukantas (1793-1864) must be mentioned. He had studied at the University of Vilnius where he had been Onacevičius' student and later became his close friend until the latter's death. As a student, he was already fascinated by Lithuania's past, as may be seen by his short history of it. After the completion of his education he began writing an extensive Lithuanian history, which he was unable to complete. He also wrote a literary work, *The Character of Ancient Lithuanians and Samogitians,* wherein he used historical sources in part as well as his own imagination in recreating the mode of life of the ancient Lithuanians. Daukantas was interested in raising Lithuania and in fostering the love of his readers for their country. His works, produced from the heart, influenced the reawakening of Lithuanian national consciousness.

During the dark reactionary era under Nicholas I, there arose

King Mindaugas   *Sculpture by V. Kašuba*

Grand Duke Gediminas,
founder of the Gediminas
Dynasty.

Grand Duke Algirdas smiting the gates of Moscow with his sword
(1369). *Artist S. Ušinskis*

Seal of Grand Duke Kęstutis

Vytautas the Great, who made
Lithuania the most powerful state
in medieval Europe.

Vytautas the Great at the shores of the Black Sea.   *Artist J. Mackevičius*

King Jogaila, from a grave monument at Krakow.

Weapons and war-gear of the ancient Lithuanian army.

1475   1477—89   1480   1492   1495

Regni Poloniæ·

Ducatus Lituaniæ

B. Casimirus Regis Casimiri filius quattuor Regum 7 vnius Cardi
nalis germanus ac Ludouici Hungariæ 7 Boemiæ Regis patruue.

St. Casimir, son of King Casimir, buried in Vilnius. Picture is reproduced from the title page of the oldest extant biography of St. Casimir
by Zacharias Firreri, 1521.

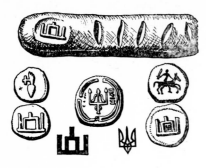

Oldest extant Lithuanian coinage.

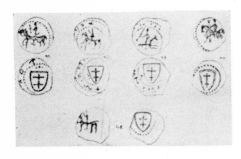

Coins from the reign of Vytautas the Great (close of 14th century).

Coins from the reign of Vytautas the Great and Zigmantas II.

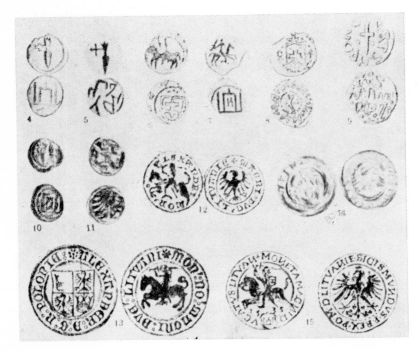

Royal burial site at the chapel of St. Casimir in the Cathedral of Vilnius.

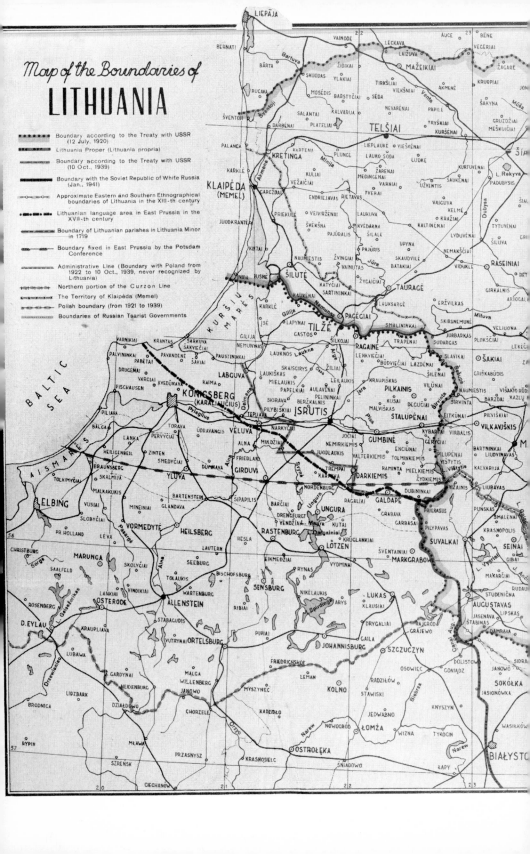

Map of the Boundaries of
LITHUANIA

Boundary according to the Treaty with USSR (12 July, 1920)

Lithuania Proper (Lithuania propria)

Boundary according to the Treaty with USSR (10 Oct., 1939)

Boundary with the Soviet Republic of White Russia (Jan., 1941)

Approximate Eastern and Southern Ethnographical boundaries of Lithuania in the XIII-th century

Lithuanian language area in East Prussia in the XVII-th century

Boundary of Lithuanian parishes in Lithuania Minor in 1719

Boundary fixed in East Prussia by the Potsdam Conference

Administrative Line (Boundary with Poland from 1922 to 10 Oct., 1939, never recognized by Lithuania)

Northern portion of the Curzon Line

The Territory of Klaipėda (Memel)

Polish boundary (from 1921 to 1939)

Boundaries of Russian Tsarist Governments

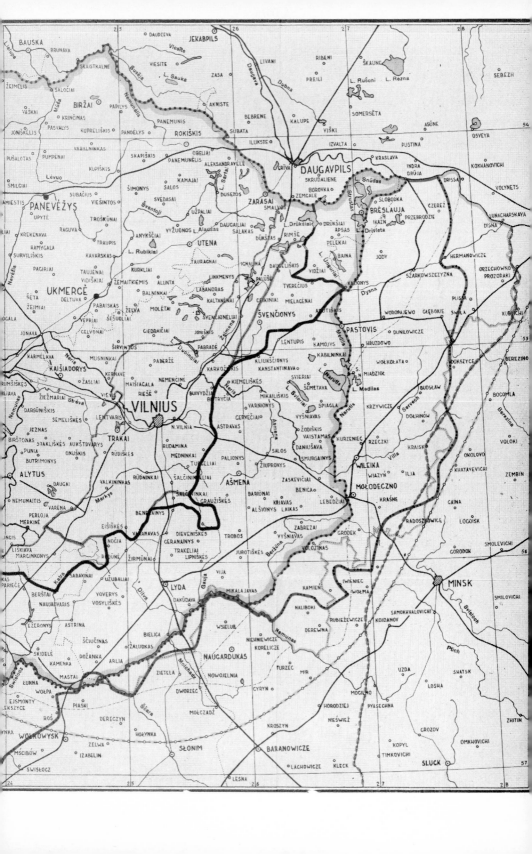

Simanas Daukantas, historian who brought to light Lithuania's past greatness and might.

Bishop Motiejus Valančius, the central figure in the rebirth of Lithuanian culture.

Dr. Jonas Basanavičius, another important contributor to the rebirth of Lithuanian culture.

Dr. Vincas Kudirka, author of Lithuania's national anthem.

PRESIDENTS OF THE
REPUBLIC OF LITHUANIA

Antanas Smetona, first and fourth
(last) president.

Aleksandras Stulginskis, second president.

Dr. Kazys Grinius, third president.

Cathedral of Vilnius, transformed into an art gallery in occupied Lithuania.   *Photo by V. Augustinas*

The Church of St. Ann in Vilnius

Kaunas

War Museum and Independence Statue at Kaunas　　　*Photo by V. Augustinas*

Rustic Lithuanian cross, at a village
wayside.   *By Vincas Svirskis*

Klaipėda (Memel)

Lithuanian Folk Dancers at the New York World's Fair (Aug. 23, 1964)

Lithuanian folk dance.
Photo by V. Maželis

Lithuanian girls in national costume.   *Photo by V. Maželis*

a great Lithuanian activist—Motiejus Valančius (1801-75), a Samogitian bishop from 1849-75. A former student of the University of Vilnius, he did not distinguish himself among the Samogitian students, but he followed in their footsteps. He was ordained a priest in Vilnius where he worked in a poor parish for a time. Later, he asked to be transferred into Samogitia where in 1834 he became chaplain of the Kražiai School and began writing the history of the Samogitian bishopric, published in 1849. The work of Valančius is the first truly scholarly achievement according to its times, a sufficiently critical investigation in Lithuanian history. By publishing a number of other religious and secular works for the common people, Bishop Valančius became not only the Good Shepherd, but also the educator of his people. He defended the people from Russification and was the first to fight for the right to print Lithuanian publications in Latin letters when this forbidden. Bishop Valančius was the greatest Lithuanian personality in the nineteenth century; he set the example for resisting Russification.

7. The 1863 Revolt

The 1863 revolt differed from that of 1831. In the earlier revolt, a political motive predominated, attempting to disband the Russian occupation and to return the former Žečpospolita. In the 1863 revolt, the socio-economic problem became evident. The reason for this is clear. The 1863 revolt began after the manifesto of the abolishment of serfdom—declared February 19, 1861—which excited the serfs, but gave them nothing. Then the peace mediators tried to separate the lands of the peasants from the estates and to clearly designate the boundaries. The peace mediators were, on the whole, local nobles and they affected everything to their own advantage. For this reason, there was great agitation among the peasantry, in all of Russia as well as in Lithuania.

Excluding the question of land, the increased recruiting of soldiers influenced the revolt a great deal. The recruits were chosen by the nobles and by the drawing of lots at community meetings, or else were caught by military policemen. The young men, sought by the military police or selected for recruitment by the community, often hid in forests. Occasionally, those caught were freed by their friends.

Under these conditions, the Lithuanian society was strongly affected by the Polish declaration to revolt, which was published in January, 1863, since it corresponded to the existing revolutionary spirit. That spirit was fostered not only by the conditions in Lithuania, but also by the growing radical-democratic movement in Russia. Especially influential was the "Land and Freedom" organization in Russia. Its demand to provide the peasants with land belonging to the estates gained favor during the time of the abolishment of serfdom.

Under the influence of the common Russian revolutionary spirit, the so-called Provincial Committee was established in Vilnius in 1862. It was led by the active leader, Kostas Kalinauskas (1838-1864), a Byelorussian who had studied in St. Petersburg and who had been active in radical-democratic circles. Arriving in Vilnius, he immediately began spreading propaganda. He also walked through Lithuanian and Byelorussian villages, fostering radical revolutionary ideas, e.g., complete freedom for peasants as well as making them owners of their own lands. He proclaimed that "A person is free when he has a portion of land!"

The Provincial Committee published an appeal on February 1, 1863, in which, among other things, it proclaimed that the property turned over to the peasants was to be "those lands which they had held." But the committee had no means of organizing a revolt according to one plan; it lacked a common leadership. Thus, disturbances began spontaneously, occurring independently in different areas and led by different leaders. The spontaneous was occurred in various places of Lithuania. The fact that the Lithuanians led in war may be revealed by the battle statistics with the rebels kept by the Russian War District. According to it, of 160 battles occurring during the year of the revolution, sixty of them took place in the Kaunas district (a purely Lithuanian-inhabited area). Second after Kaunas was the Gardinas district, where fifty battles were fought. B. Limanowski acknowledged the Lithuanian leadership in the revolt, stating: "The first provinces in historical Lithuania to answer to the freedom call were ethnographic

126

Lithuanian. . . . The peasant inhabitants actively aided them. Their leaders were such peasants as A. Bitė, Puidokas, Lukošiūnas and others." Their greatest leader was Antanas Mackevičius.

Mackevičius (1828-63), the son of Samogitian nobles, came to Vilnius while still very young, and under adverse conditions finished the Gymnasium. He later studied at the University of Kiev before returning to Samogitia to enter the seminary of Varniai. When the revolutionary movement began, he was the assigned priest in the Panevėžys district. He immediately joined the movement and began preparing the people for the revolt. As soon as the appeal of the Vilnius Committee was issued, he read it in his church and then went to the forest with a group of rebels. Not satisfied with local action, he instigated a revolution in the Kaunas, Vilnius and Gardinas districts, organizing large groups of rebels. By the beginning of March he already had 500 fighters, most of them peasants from Panevėžys and Kėdainiai. His group became the central group among others in Lithuania, and was the first to fight and to repel the attacks of the strong Russian force. Though he became the real, though unelected, commander-in-chief in Lithuania, he acknowledged the chosen leader of the Committee when he arrived in Vilnius.

The leader elected by the Provincial Committee was Zigmas Sierakauskas, a noble of Volynia. He arrived from St. Petersburg where he had served as a higher officer and had been active secretly among the revolutionary officers. It was also there that he came into closer contact with the Lithuanian revoluitonists. His aim was to unite the rebel groups and organize a common plan for battle. Soon after his arrival from Kaunas, he began assembling the rebels near Šėta. After the arrival of a group from the borders of Samogitia, they traveled to the forests of Raguva where Mackevičius' group joined them. The united rebel forces withstood the attack of a strong Russian division, and then marched on in a northeasterly direction and crossed the Šventoji River at Andrioniškis.

The Andrioniškis camp, where the rebels stayed a week, represents the most famous episode throughout the entire revolt. The unusually sincere and attractive personality of Sierakauskas charmed the rebels and their leaders, and he was especially friendly to the peasants. The peasants were taught in Lithuanian by Povilas Vivulskis, a St. Petersburg University student. Their leader, Mackevičius, admired Sierakauskas and became his "closest follower and friend." The Andrioniškis Camp, which became the nucleus of the ensuing revolt, caused volunteers from all sides to join with the rebels. It is unknown how many rebels assembled there; the number is given between 1,500 to 5,000.

After a week the rebels left the camp and marched in a northern direction, separating into three columns. They reached Courland, trying to erase their tracks so that the enemy would be unable to trace them. People everywhere gayly met the rebels, "with bread and salt," as official statements proclaimed. The revolt affected the peoples' spirits and wakened the hope of freedom. After a four-day journey, the rebels reached the Biržai district where they met with the Russian divisions which had followed them from Ukmergė. A decisive battle took place, lasting three days (April 25-27). Though the rebels defended themselves bravely, they were unable to withstand the larger and better armed enemy, and several able and experienced leaders were killed. Sierakauskas was wounded and taken prisoner; he was brought back to Vilnius, where he was tried and hung two months later.

After the battle, the remaining rebels continued their partisan war under the leadership of Mackevičius, fighting in many places, but mainly in Samogitia. The fighting lasted until the autumn, when it began diminishing because of the oncoming winter. In November, Mackevičius released a large part of the rebels to return to their homes, with the idea of assembling them in the spring and continuing the war. Mackevičius himself decided to go abroad for the purpose of buying more arms. He traveled from the Panevėžys district to Kaunas; near the border he met with the Russians, and in the ensuing battle many of his accompanying rebels were killed. Mackevičius managed to escape and make his way to the Nemunas River, but unable to cross the river, he hid in a forest hut with two of his followers, where Russian military police arrested him on December 5, 1863.

The declaration Mackevičius made during his interrogation by the Russians reveals the hopes and aims which the revolutionary Lithuanian peasants sought. Several excerpts should be noted.

> I see the people always worn out, since for a piece of bread received from the land, they must pay poll-taxes and for several decades their redemption taxes. The revolt, by its manifesto, gives the land to the people of all religions immediately and free. My brains dictated that I take action on things as they are today and not wait forty years as the Czar's manifesto stated. . . .
>
> My desire for the good of the people gave me strength and the ability to unite the people, to instill their consciousness to such a degree that they would be able to decide with whom they wanted to be allied: with Russia or with Poland. This right is established in Europe and it could not be revealed in any other way except to free ourselves, which required war. . . . Since Lithuania is lacking many of the conditions needed for an independent revolution thus, in order to acquire these, I wanted to help Poland with the peasants and then to demand its aid for the Lithuanian revolution. . . . I am the inhabitant of this country and, loving my fatherland, saw myself duty-bound to this.

The revolt in Lithuania ended with Mackevičius' arrest and death sentence, pronounced on December 28, 1863. The stifled revolt, which had not reached its direct aim, was nevertheless a meaningful period in the nation's history. The country was moved to resist its enslaver. The Lithuanians could not believe that their life, their country had become a part of Russia. Furthermore, it could be said that this spiritual separatism forced the Lithuanians to resist any and all attempts at Russification, especially the attempt to introduce the Russian alphabet. Thus, the revolt of 1863 prepared the way for a constant battle over retention of the Lithuanian free press and the Latin alphabet.

VIII. The Battle to Retain the Lithuanian Free Press and National Rebirth

1. *The Successful Resistance to Cyrilic Alphabet*

The Russian prohibition of the use of the Latin alphabet for the Lithuanian press, and in its stead the forced use of the Russian

Cyrilic alphabet, was an unprecedented event in the history of Europe. Though this prohibition did not have a direct link with the revolt of 1863, it was nevertheless an outcome. The Russians saw very well how the Poles and Lithuanians (together with the White Russians) had led the uprising. The Russians began to observe the Lithuanians more closely—the Lithuanians were, to them, too much under the influence of the Poles. The Russian concern was to separate the Lithuanians, Poles, and White Russians. The tiny country of Lithuania within the giant Russian Empire seemed to the Russians to be unimportant, and to be easily Russified. Thus, the first implement in this program of Russification was to forbid the use of the "Polish" letters—that is, the Latin alphabet. Through the use of the Cyrilic alphabet, the ultimate aim was to Russify Lithuania through prohibition of the Latin alphabet. As stated by the Vilnius' governor's statement prohibiting the use of the Latin alphabet: "The events which have come to light since the revolt in 1861 in the Northwestern part of the Empire [that is, Lithuania] has forced us to pass certain reforms . . . to return to the country its 'historical past.' [There is no doubt that this so-called "historical past" meant Lithuania, which had been referred to by certain Russian historians as Western Russia.] Now it was high time to replace the Polish influences in Lithuania, and replace those with "not only the orthodox faith, but also the Russian nation's laws . . . and at the same time . . . to retain the ancient historical ties that have existed between Lithuania and Russia."

Otherwise, the formulated control of the free press paralleled Muravjov's plans to stifle the revolt. The general-governor believed that the revolt had been inspired by the Polish landholding class, which is why he hastened to stamp out serfdom with better means than had been employed in Russia. The Lithuanian peasants were given opportunities for a more self-sufficient way of life as well as eventual separation from Polish estates and influences. According to Muravjov's plan, Polish influences would be replaced by Russian ones. Russian schools began replacing Polish institutions; the Russian language was to be spoken instead of Polish in all offices. (Parish priests were to register births, deaths and marriages in the Russian language instead of Polish.) The

prohibition of the free press had to be the implement for Russification.

The Russians thought that it would be relatively easy for the
Lithuanians to adopt the Cyrilic alphabet. The first three books
introduced into the country were a grammar, a prayer book, and
a calendar. (Even before the prohibition of the free press in 1864,
Muravjov had ordered Lithuanian grammar books to be printed
in Russian letters; these were sent to certain Russian schools
where some study of the Lithuanian language was pursued.) The
Russian grammar books meant nothing to the people, who just
read the old books. At first, even the prohibition of the free press
did not touch the average citizen, for few were schooled in recognizing Russian characters; furthermore, the awakened spirit of
anti-Russianism during the revolt helped in resisting this alphabet,
which the Lithuanians came to abhor.

Religion, as had been the case in the past, played an important
part in the lives of the people. This was especially evident concerning the new prayerbooks of Cyrilic alphabet. The Lithuanians
refused to use these missals, and naturally did not purchase them.
There was no use or profit for the Russians to continue further
publication; in fact, only fifty-four prayerbooks were published in
forty years!

Meanwhile, Lithuanian books were published in Prussia; the
first editions, printed in Königsberg in 1866, were smuggled across
the border into Lithuania by contrabandists who had engaged in
similar black market activities since ancient times.

The first united resistance against the Cyrilic alphabet began
with the peasants. At first, the relatively small educated class
did not realize the imminent danger lying in the prohibition. Some
even helped in preparing some texts for the new Russian printings.
Bishop Valančius, held under arrest, was persuaded to give his
imprimatur for the first religious writings in the Russian characters; however, he soon saw the danger and began to protest
such publications. In 1866 he wrote to Kaunas' general-governor:
"I believe it is impossible to publish the Samogitian Gospels as a
Bible in Russian letters because it is my duty to see that such a
book would not be ruined." A year later Valančius requested
permission to publish a very popular prayerbook, *Aukso Altorius,*

in the Latin alphabet. When he received no answer, Valančius realized the plan of the Russians and resolved to resist. He showed the first organized example of resistance by writing several didactic books aimed especially at the Lithuanian peasant. He also paid a goodly sum of money to a Prussian publisher for their printings.

Valančius' books became widespread and very popular among the Lithuanians. They taught the people how to resist, first of all, the Russian Orthodox religious influences, as well as all other Russian influences. He urged the people to hide old Lithuanian books from the military police; to use them in secretly studying the Lithuanian language; not only to avoid any and all Russian books, but also to burn them; and to purchase Lithuanian books published in Tilžė. Through his actions Valančius also turned the spontaneous active resistance against the prohibition into a passive though effective resistance against the Russian government.

The job of publishing and smuggling Lithuanian books became a highly organized matter, due to Valančius' efforts. At first, he alone organized and conducted this work, but a little later he had the regular parish priests join his activities. Very soon the layman also joined. The most energetic layman in this work was Jurgis Bielinis. Having started his work in 1866, he received the title of "King of books." Many people joined Valančius' activities, and there arose in Lithuania a new profession—book-smuggling. This new class of smugglers were not unlike the contrabandists except that those involved in this new profession were in much more danger than the regular contrabandists. The Lithuanian book smugglers in fact were a bother to the military police since there was no profit in their capture; it was just extra work to confiscate the books, to list them, and to send them intact to Vilnius or Kaunas, where they were burned. The military police could not stand the Lithuanian book-smugglers, and when the opportunity presented itself would either beat up, torture, or press lawsuits against them. The trials would usually end with the smugglers' convictions or deportation to Siberia.

This, however, did not stop the publications and purchasing of the forbidden books. These illegal activities were spurred on in the second half of the nineteenth century, after the abolition of serfdom. The new educated generation had arisen from the small landholders and peasants, and supported the battle against Russification. This had a strong impact on the newly-established schools in Marijampolė, Šiauliai, and Kaunas, and the teachers' institute in Veiveriai. These schools became the centers for educating a new class of people. Especially important was the Marijampolė High School, responsible for educating the youth in and around the area of Suvalkai. These students, who graduated to the universities of Moscow, Warsaw, St. Petersburg and others, began to form societies where they discussed national problems and pursued the study of Lithuanianism. A graduate of Moscow University, Jonas Basanavičius (1851-1927) began to edit a weekly newspaper *Aušra* (1883), which was published in Prussia. With the publication of *Aušra* we have the beginnings of the Lithuanian national rebirth. In 1889, *Varpas,* a monthly newspaper, was conceived and published by a graduate of Warsaw University's School of Medicine, Vincas Kudirka (1858-99). Alongside *Varpas,* with the same liberal leanings, was the newspaper *Ūkininkas,* first published in 1890. The clergy associated with *Aušra* began to publish their own newspaper with the idea of continuing Valančius' original doctrines. Their first newspaper was *Šviesa,* published in 1887. *Šviesa* was short-lived and was followed by *Žemaičiu ir Lietuvos Apžvalga* (1890), *Tėvynės Sargas* (1896), and others. Concurrently, there appeared the first Lithuanian political parties (the Social-Democrats), and various allied newspapers, most of which were short-lived.

All newspapers, magazines, and publications which were not periodicals were directed toward one purpose: to educate the rural peoples and awaken their feelings of Lithuanian nationalism. The editors and publishers attempted to circulate their publications as widely as possible, and it was toward this purpose that the book smugglers and other propagandists were of invaluable service.

The Lithuanian people struggled steadfastly and quietly for their free press, constantly attempting to circumvent the prohibitive laws. The first to succeed in this endeavor was Petras Vileišis (1851-1926), an engineer, who in his professional capacity exerted some influence in official circles. He took advantage of the Russo-Turkish War (1876-1877), when censorship was slightly relaxed, and received permission to publish five booklets. Following Vileišis' success, others made similar requests; however, the administration in Vilnius refused all such requests and even withdrew its license for publication in St. Petersburg. The only exception was the permission granted to a Vilnius publisher, Zavadskis, to publish a very popular prayerbook, *Aukso Altorius,* in 1879. Later, in Prussia, many other editions of the same prayerbook were published using the same date to confuse the authorities. Every means possible was employed to rid the country of such degrading statutes. Attempts were made to convince the Russian government that not only were the statutes failing in their purpose, but also were harmful to Russia herself. It was said that, rather than drawing away the Lithuanians from Poland, in actuality it brought them closer together. This approach was especially effective with the Russians, because the Poles, with their excessive pretenses, were rather unruly subjects. To the Russians, it seemed like a worthwhile idea to support the Lithuanians against the Poles. Thus, choosing the lesser of two evils, they allowed the Lithuanians more freedom of the press.

Finally, the Russians admitted that the suppression was a fruitless endeavor. The governor-general of Vilnius, Sviatopolk-Mirski, wrote to the Czar in 1902: "Official publications sold with no regard for their true value, and even distributed at no cost, were unpopular." About the so-called foreign (Prussian) publications, he said, "The foreign publications, regardless of their cost, irrespective of the dangers involved in their contraband distribution, and regardless of confiscations and penalties, which incur holders of Lithuanian books in Latin characters, and the arrest of distributors themselves—are spreading, spreading by the tens of thousands." Having outlined such a situation, he admitted the government's helplessness by stating that the central government, as well as individually local authorities, had no means of effectively coping with the smuggling in of Lithuanian books. Because of this, any and all efforts were totally worthless, and caused antigovernment feelings within the population. In writing so, he expressed the government's problem.

The stubborn Lithuanians had withstood oppression from the Czarist government, and had actually brought Russia to her knees. The Imperial leaders had not expected such resistance, and thus had not taken the whole matter seriously. They had failed to make it an Imperial law, and had left it merely as a local administrative decree during the war. When the war was over in 1871, this decree could not but come to naught. However, the censorship committees still held to it. Educated Lithuanian patriots whose numbers increased toward the end of the nineteenth century understood the weak legal foundations of the oppressive laws and attempted to undermine them.

The government, as though ashamed of having oppressed Lithuania with this decree, secretly lifted the restrictions on May 7, 1904. The government's central press affairs agency notified the censorship committees and local and foreign censors to abide by this decision. Thus, prohibition of the free press had gone out as quietly as it had come in.

2. The Revolt of 1905 and the Grand Vilnius Assembly

The Revolt of 1905 was more an echo of the Russian Revolution than of the political and cultural unrest in Lithuania. The revolt arose from the social and economic circumstances appearing in the Russian Empire after the abolition of serfdom and the rise of manufacturing and industry. Russian cities began to take on the semblance of Western European cities, and there now arose conditions which fostered social revolution. The straw that broke the camel's back was Russia's unsuccessful war with Japan, out of which arose widespread dissent and discontent with the government. Just as Western social revolutions were led by various radical parties, so was the Russian Revolution of 1905 guided by similar currents.

Even before the Revolution, the Social-Democratic Party had been active in Russia, having been divided into the moderates (Mensheviks) and radicals (Bolsheviks). But up to the Revolution and for some time following, the two parties worked together. Russian socialists were organizing chapters in every city, including Vilnius and Kaunas in Lithuania. Vilnius, an important railway junction, became a strong Russian socialists' center. Alongside the Russian socialists, there appeared three other national chapters: a Jewish bund, the Polish PePeSe, and the Lithuanian Social-Democrats. The Lithuanian chapter was founded in 1896, and at first worked in close contact with other national groups.

When the smoldering spark of revolution ignited in Russia following Bloody Sunday, January 9, 1905, it immediately spread through Latvia into Lithuania. In Vilnius and Kaunas, the workers were organized and led into the streets to strike for better working conditions, higher wages, and shorter working hours. The leaders of these first strikes were predominantly Jews and Russians. It was not long before the spirit of revolution reached the smaller cities and even country villages, fostered by various agitators. Most of this work was carried on by students, who had come home from the University of St. Petersburg and others, where studies were discontinued due to the Revolution. The students, believing in the liberal parties' slogans, invaded the rural districts and urged the people to resist the government. The most active student was E. Galvanauskas, who journeyed through the northeastern areas of Lithuania, informing the people about their rights, writing up their grievances and demands. The rural people were especially drawn to the speeches, known as "sermons."

These young socialistic propagandists tackled not only the socio-economic status, but also the national political, especially that concerning Lithuania's self-autonomy. The national political problems were also touched upon by Lithuania's moderate educated class and clergy, who held quite a sway over the rural citizens. Meanwhile, the Lithuanians had received certain political rights as an aftermath of the Russian Revolution. For example, the Czar decreed in April, 1905, full freedom of religion which even allowed the study of religion in the native tongue in all schools. Thus, the Lithuanian language returned to the schools, and became the official language at least in the study of religion. The next decree stated that for the first time, Catholics could freely buy land in Lithuania. And a turn for the best occurred through the Czar's manifesto of October 17, 1905, which guaranteed many political rights, including freedom to organize into political groups and freedom of convocation. Moderate Lithuanian activists decided to petition the government to grant autonomy with its own parliament in Vilnius, to join the Suvalkai area to Kaunas' and Vilnius' governments, instate the Lithuanian language in factories and offices, and to erect new Lithuanian schools.

Having sent out the memorandum and having received no answer, it was decided to call together in Vilnius an assembly composed of representatives from various districts and parishes. Though the idea for a general assembly arose during the time of the Revolution, it really was not a direct result. Actually, the idea for such an assembly arose in Vilnius among people who not only stood on the sidelines during the Revolution, but who also tried to prevent such an event. At first, these activists swarmed around during the publication of the Lithuanian newspaper *Vilniaus Žinios*, which first appeared after the declared freedom of the free press. The editor of this newspaper was Petras Vileišis, a manufacturer and engineer by profession. His ideas did not harmonize with the Revolution, and his newspaper did not write about the course of revolutionary events in Lithuania, but instead dealt with official news about the Revolution—a moderate news-paper with moderates working on it. Of course, they worried about the state of things in Lithuania; however, they did not wait for national gains resulting from the Revolution. The clergy were disgusted with the Revolution and, on the whole, all believers in the faith felt the same way even since the revolutionary leaders proclaimed it as part of the battle for atheism. The writers of *Vilniaus Žinios* were affected positively by the October 17th manifesto, and they believed that desired political rights could be accomplished through peaceful means. They conceived the idea of producing Lithuanian political demands to the government through the elected representatives to the assembly.

The man elected to convene the assembly was Dr. Jonas Basa-navičius. Having found unanimous support among the people, Basanavičius issued an appeal. Interest in this new Assembly arose as an aftermath of the Revolution. Every district's and parish's elected representatives and all educated people were in-vited to attend the Assembly. Thus, there were about 2,000 attending, half of whom were officially elected delegates. There

137

were some from Russia, Poland, and Latvia. The delegate from Prussian Lithuania was Jonas Vanagaitis.

The assembly met in two sessions, on November 21-22 and December 4-5. The chairman, Dr. Jonas Basanavičius, suggested an abstract, almost academic, schedule. After lengthy discussion, the Assembly vetoed his suggestion and adopted a new schedule. Two most important points to be decided upon were reports on Lithuania's status quo and reprints of desired political rights. Almost the entire first day was taken up with reports given by rural delegates, reports which were boring and repetitious. Although these reports did not carry much weight, the Assembly allowed these people to voice their discontent.

The main question was the question of Lithuanian autonomy. Severe disagreements ensued, the disputes concerning not the essence of self-government, but of its nature and manner of attainment. Some suggested armed resistance; others, staunchly in opposition to this, tried to show the failure of a revolt of a weak nation against a strong foe. Instead of armed revolt, it suggested conducting an unarmed resistance using other means. This latter suggestion, more befitting the peaceful and persevering character of Lithuanians, received preference, as shown in the Assembly's records.

The suggestions of means for peaceful resistance might on the whole be described as passive: refusal to pay taxes, closing out of all monopolies, not allowing children to attend Russian schools, refusing to use the district courts and services of various offices, helping the youth resist the Russian draft, and finally, "as necessary, for all workers to strike in urban and rural areas."

The Assembly also discussed the question of cultural improvement and education. Russian schools were condemned and demands were made for construction of national schools where the official language would be Lithuanian, taught by the Lithuanian teachers. The teachers would not be appointed, but elected by the populace. The question of land reform was also discussed, but was never decided. It seems that the question of land reform was the job of radicals and socialists; therefore, it did not have any weight at the Assembly, nor did it bring any results.

Even though the people in attendance at the Assembly were divided into the leftists and rightists, and the Assembly itself was held in a revolutionary atmosphere, it was nevertheless conducted in an orderly and united manner, and a general resolution was decided upon and passed: love of country and its status quo rather than political partisanship seemed to be uppermost in the minds of the Lithuanian people. All had the same goals and ideals in mind—Lithuanian autonomy.

After the Assembly, many of the representatives left for different parts of the country to continue their work actively. They urged the people to join in the battle, to refuse to pay taxes, and to close down whiskey monopolies. The Lithuanians threw out the Czar's portraits from government offices, chased out various men in charge, took away their weapons, and armed themselves with them. The offices which were closed down were reopened, and specially appointed men were installed. Even though these were revolutionary tactics, they were performed peacefully. The people did not employ violence to rid themselves of various officials, just as they made no attempt to grab any possessions from their class enemy—the landowners. Such an act was alien to them. The only portion of the landowners' property which the people wanted were the forests. They held to a tradition, dating back to the era of serfdom, that the forests belonged to the people.

This revolutionary spirit made an impression upon the Russians and forced them to make some concessions. Thus, the governor of Vilnius, Freze, immediately after the Assembly, proclaimed that the Lithuanian language could be taught in grammar schools, that Catholic teachers could be appointed, and that district secretaries could be elected by the people (those elected had to be confirmed by the government).

This decree, like others which gave special privileges to the press, was of no avail because of oncoming reaction throughout the Russian Empire. This took place after the large revolt at Moscow was quashed (December, 1905), when the government used military force against the rioters. There arose in every larger Russian city mounted armed forces specially designed to persecute the revolters. They became a horror in the minds of the people, and the appearance of these forces produced great fright. The most notorious of leaders associated with these soldiers was the executive of the district of Ukmergė, Markov, a close collaborator of Kaunas' governor, Veriovkin. Markov left a strong impression upon the people which was remembered for many decades.

The suppressed revolution left its mark upon Russia, and in turn, Lithuania. The eased restrictions of the press and other liberties guaranteed by the October 17th manifesto allowed the Lithuanians to erect their own schools, form their own cultural, political and economic organizations, print books and newspapers. The Catholic population were impressed when former restrictions were raised concerning the clergy and Church. The people were greatly conscious of the reforms instated after the Revolt of 1905, and it was often said: "It's better now than it has been before."

3. Calm Cultural-National Activities During the Prewar Decade

Though after the revolt the same government administration based on the old-fashioned rule of the aristocratic landowners remained, the old system was not used. Together with the old government, the Assembly (Duma) was also established in 1906, whose members were elected by the citizens of the Empire. The Lithuanians, from the very start, participated in the Duma elections. Among the representatives elected for the first Duma, the best man was Juozas Kubilius, who had actively participated in the Russian Workers' Party, in Trudovik, which defended the interests of the people more than any other party. When the first Duma was dismissed, Juozas Kubilius together with 200 delegates signed the so-called Vyburg Renunciation, and was arrested. During the trial, Kubilius presented a truly moving and patriotic defense, in which he outlined the wrongs committed against the Lithuanians during the years of prohibition of the free press.

In the second and third Duma the leading Lithuanian members were Petras Leonas and Andrius Bulota. The former attempted to revive the question of land reform and the latter succeeded in passing a law which allowed use of the Lithuanian language in

140

local offices in the areas of the Suvalkai government peopled by Lithuanian nationals. Martynas Yčas was the most active during the fourth Duma. He helped many Lithuanians, especially refugees in Russia during wartime. During this assembly, he joined the so-called Cadets, and raised the question of Lithuanian self-government. He received no support, and even the leader of the Cadets, Miliukov, was against him.

After the 1905 uprising there were peaceful cultural and national activities. Radical revolutionary movements did not exert much influence upon the people; they were counteracted by Russian counter-reaction. Several of the leaders had to flee the country, others who were caught were sent to Siberia. These movements also lacked money, which they had received before from supporters in Lithuania and the United States. With the ending of the Revolution, financial support seemed unnecessary. Lacking money, these various socialistic organizations were unable to continue to print their propaganda.

After the repeal of the prohibition of the free press, the newspaper *Darbininkų Balsas,* published in Prussia, had to be discontinued. *Naujoji Gadynė* (1906-07), first published in Vilnius, was often confiscated for its antigovernment writings. After *Naujoji Gadynė* was discontinued the Social-Democrats in Vilnius, who were more academically rather than politically minded, began to publish a monthly magazine *Visuomenė* (1910-11), which dealt more with cultural problems rather than with political ones. A purely radical newspaper started in Riga was *Vilnis* (1913), edited by Vincas Mickevičius-Kapsukas.

After emotions had settled down following the Revolution, the Social-Democrats began to cooperate with the Democrats and a new sphere of influence arose. The new group, known as "Pirmeiviai," encompassed Western liberals, and was later known as the Progressive Party. The "Pirmeiviai" held themselves to be the originators and messengers of the new ideas and principles, especially those based upon the sciences. They disavowed themselves from the dogma of the Church, claiming them to be superstitions inherited from the Dark Ages. The Lithuanian "Pirmeiviai" paralleling the Western Progressives considered themselves to be advancing along with education, and at times were associated with a name bearing that connotation. The "Pirmei-viai," even before the 1905 uprising, expressed their ideas in *Varpas*. During and following the uprising they employed *Vilniaus žinios* to spread their beliefs. From 1909, their philosophy was outlined in *Lietuvos Žinios* and *Lietuvos Ūkininkas*.

The "Pirmeiviai" were composed mostly from the educated class, who had attended Russian schools and universities. In the Russian schools, there was a strong spirit of anti-Catholicism, especially evident in history books. However, Western progressivism was deeply rooted in the Russian universities. It was this which greatly influenced the Lithuanian students to join the ranks of the "Pirmeiviai." These students began to work actively and became associated with *Lietuvos Žinios,* and furthermore, began to publish a supplementary newspaper, *Aušrinė* (1910).

The "Pirmeiviai" embraced only the educated, and had no influence with the masses. It was the Catholic Church, sometimes sarcastically called reactionary or clerical, which held sway over the masses. From its beginnings, the Church educated the people. After the Revolution, when more rights were secured, it was the priests who organized into publishing various literature. The priests published *Šaltinis* in Seinai, *Vienybė* in Kaunas, *Aušra* in Vilnius, and were also responsible for spreading these newspapers among peasants. In 1907, Rev. Adomas Dambrauskas-Jakštas founded an association "St. Casmiz" dealing with publication and spreading of the books. This work played an important part in the education of the people and the country's political maturation. Dambrauskas-Jakštas (1860-1938) became the most prominent religious leader in Lithuania. His influence reached the educated Catholics through his monthly magazine *Draugija*. Dambrauskas-Jakštas was a highly educated, erudite man, with a mathematically inclined mind, well acquainted with the pitfalls of arguments, and was able to refute the arguments of the "Pirmeiviai." He expressed his philosophy and support of the Christian-Democrats (which he helped establish in 1906) through carefully written articles in *Draugija*. The Catholics were responsible for having many Lithuanian schools built. In Kaunas the "Saulė" association was led by the energetic Rev. Konstantinas Olšauskas. Within a few years, he had established several Lithuanian schools and

142

opened the first teachers' seminary in Kaunas. The "Žiburys" association, founded in Seinai, also established many schools, including the all-girls' junior high school in Marijampolė, headed by the well-known authoress Marija Pečkauskaitė-Šatrijos Ragana. The "Rytas" association worked in and around the districts of Vilnius. Prior to World War I, this association had twenty chapters and about 1,300 members. Though the Lithuanian schools had to hold to the government's established rules concerning use of the Russian language, the study of Lithuanian was nevertheless pursued to a high degree.

The spirit in which "Pirmeiviai" worked with students was emulated by the conservative Christian element working with the students who were "Ateitininkai." "Ateitininkai" received their name from the publication *Ateitis,* just as "Aušrininkai" derived their name from their publication *Aušrinė.* The "Ateitininkai" were a very active organization. They united Catholicism with Lithuanian patriotism, worked for the good of the country during the war, helped the many Lithuanian refugees in Russia, and fought for Lithuania's freedom.

In between these two influences, there appeared a third element which tried to bring together the "Pirmeiviai" and the Christians to work toward a common goal—Lithuania's freedom. Not only did they want to unite the masses, but also the educated class and the clergy. Its first leader was Antanas Smetona (1874-1944), the first and last President of Lithuania. At first, Smetona had leanings toward the "Pirmeiviai," but later began changing from this socialistic view. As a law student, he was interested in Marxism, but did not embrace this philosophy because he believed it unsuitable for Lithuania. Unsatisfied with Marxism and socialism, Smetona began to doubt the fruitfulness of the 1905 Revolution. He joined the Democratic faction, and having graduated, established his residence in Vilnius and worked on *Vilniaus Žinios.* After the Revolution there arose within the Democratic party the question of whether revolutionary tactics or peaceful resistance should be continued. Smetona finally decided to adhere to the latter. Following this decision, he moved further away from the left, and with others who thought alike, began to print the

143

weekly publication *Viltis* (1907). Thus, the third stream of influence received the title of "Viltininkai."

The "Viltininkai" began to bring closer together the progressives and conservatives. Smetona's paper set the tone for their organizational work. The Lithuanian population was appeased, having experienced easier times following the October 17th Manifesto, and having been urged on by the clergy. The "Viltininkai" and the clergy, not allowing too much politics, dealt with mostly cultural and national problems, which helped to keep alive the nonviolent spirit of the people. New organizations and associations were formed, among which were the Catholic youths' "Pavasaris." However, with the oncoming World War I, the Lithuanian people abandoned all nonviolent activities and turned to opposite tactics. An entirely different age began to dawn for the country.

Independent Lithuania

by ALBERTAS GERUTIS

THE GERMAN OCCUPATION

When World War I began, it was not possible to speculate how Lithuania would be affected; but based upon past experi-ence, the prewar status of Lithuania would be altered. In the wake of the Crimean War, serfdom collapsed in Russia. The unsuccessful war with Japan shook the foundations of the Russian government, and brought certain easing of tensions not only in Russia, but also in Lithuania. Thus, it was believed that World War I would leave a marked imprint upon Lithuania. This was further testified to when Lithuania became a battlefield of the war. The eastern borders of Russia were separated from Ger-many's by Lithuania, and naturally any movements either army made were carried through Lithuania. This presented many prob-lems to the Lithuanians, but it also focused the world's attention upon this small country.

At the beginning of the war, Russia invaded eastern Prussia. Among the Russian troops which began the attack in the German territory, there was a high percentage of Lithuanians.

The Russian army forcing itself into East Prussia was severely beaten in August, 1914. Associated with that battle were two German war leaders who were destined to play an important part in the close to four-year period which ensued in the life of the Lithuanian people: Paul von Hindenburg and Erich Ludendorff. The battle itself was called the Battle of Tannenberg. Ludendorff, in his memoirs, writes concerning the battle: "Die Schlacht wurde auf meinen Vorschlag die Schlacht von Tannenberg genannt, als Erinnerung an jenen Kampf, in den der Deutsche Ritterorden den vereinigten litauischen und polnischen Armeen unterlag." (The battle was, upon my suggestion, called the Battle of Tannenberg, in memory of that fight in which the German Order of Knights was vanquished by the combined Lithuanian and Polish Armies.)

As leader of the German eastern army, Hindenburg, with his chief of staff Ludendorff, lived in Kaunas (until the summer of 1916), from where they were better able to acquaint themselves with the problems of East Europe as a whole and with the problems of Lithuania in particular. As the so-called specialists from the German side of these matters, they, especially General Ludendorff, influenced the decisive policies of eastern Germany.

Nevertheless, after the disastrous battle, the Russian army remained for a few months at the borders of East Prussia, where natives of Lithuania were thickly settled. Thus, the Lithuanian Prussians were burdened with the load of the war. In February, 1915, the German army advanced into the Russian-ruled Lithuanian territory called Lithuania Proper, and on February 18th captured the Lithuanian-inhabited border area of Taurage (whose name has been connected with the Napoleonic wars). In March, 1915, the Russian army, for the last time, advanced into the former Prussian territory and occupied Klaipėda (Memel) and Tilžė, cities which had been the active centers of the Lithuanians of Lithuania Minor and from where the Russians had deported many local inhabitants, who were kept in the heart of Russia throughout the war. But this did not change the outcome of the rest of the war. The German army kept advancing farther into Lithuanian territory, and severe battles were fought. On April 30, 1915, the German Army came for the first time into Šiauliai, an important railroad and manufacturing center. On August 17, they occupied Kaunas and on September 18, 1915, the Germans arrived in Vilnius, the ancient capital of Lithuania. In September, 1915, practically all of the ethnographic territory of Lithuania had fallen into the hands of the German army. Thus, for eight months, war was waged in the Lithuanian-inhabited areas belonging to Russia; previously, war had been waged in Prussian Lithuania.

In various places of Lithuania battles were furiously fought; the country was devastated, with many areas either destroyed or going up in flames. (The same doom overtook many single farms.) The Russian government evacuated the governmental offices and industries into the heart of Russia. Very often the inhabitants, either forced by the Russian government or by their own desire, left their homes and fled west. The Russian agencies purposely spread rumors concerning the "furor teutonicus," which caused an increase in the number of refugees. High schools with their personnel and students were evacuated from the cities. Total mobilization was declared. The flight of the refugees from the war-scarred area resulted in farms losing their owners, crops being unharvested, and fields being left unsowed. Great numbers of the evacuees settled in the cities, especially in Vilnius since it was the largest center in eastern Lithuania. The people were poverty stricken. It was necessary to quickly organize aid for them.

Such an organization was established at the beginning of the war in Vilnius and was called The Central Committee to Aid War Victims. Various well-known Lithuanian organizations helped the committee, whose chairman was the Russian representative of the Duma, Martynas Yčas, who belonged to the Cadet Party and had made use of the influence of the Grand Duchess Tatiana's Relief Fund. It was the first time that the Russian government supported activities of the Lithuanian society by submitting large sums of money. The same committee in Vilnius was soon called to play an important role in the Lithuanian nation's march down the road to freedom.

The progressing war gave a chance to bring to light the injustices Lithuania had suffered. Even before the war, the Lithuanian representatives in the Russian Duma, on a few occasions, had demanded that they be given some cultural and political autonomy. The representatives in the Duma stipulated the desire that in the wake of the war the Lithuanian people would regain both Lithuania Minor and Major, joined by the boundaries of the Russian Empire. At the same time, the Russian government was given "the amber declaration," in which the Lithuanian activists of Vilnius formulated the injustices done their nation.

147

Inspired by Lithuanians living in America, who had more favorable conditions for activities, they also led some political action. Even during the war, the American Lithuanians had organized parliaments (September and October of 1914, in Chicago and Brooklyn, New York) where they demanded political autonomy and the right of free choice for the Lithuanian people. They also demanded that Prussian Lithuania be connected to Lithuania Proper.

As the German army advanced farther into Lithuanian territory, a great number of the refugees fled into the heart of Russia and scattered in its vast areas. Someone had to provide for them. Keeping this in mind, the Central Committee Aiding War Victims separated into two branches. Some of its members left for Russia, while others remained in Vilnius and waited the arrival of the Germans. Finally, important centers were developed abroad —in countries where there were large concentrations of Lithuanians, as in the United States, or in places where small but active groups lived (in Switzerland and in the Scandinavian countries).

When the Germans had succeeded in occupying almost all of the existing ethnographic area of Lithuania Proper (September, 1915), the Russian government removed itself, and in its place the Germans established a military administration called Oberbefehlshaber Ost. Its ruling area was divided into the following Verwaltungsbezirke: Courland, Lithuania, Suvalkai, Vilnius, Gardinas and Balstogė. Soon they began changing these divisions; the region of Vilnius and Suvalkai became one, Verwaltung Litauen. Later, the administrative units of Gardinas and Balstogė were united, and in the autumn of 1917 they were connected under one administration, which was called by the name of Lithuania. In this manner, the areas which had previously made up the basis of Lithuania's ethnographic territory became united under one Lithuanian administrative unit.

At the head of the German administration was Lieutenant Colonel Duke Franz-Joseph Isenburg-Birstein. In the memory of the inhabitants of his ruling territory, the duke has remained a representative of German militarism who closely followed the Pangermanic annexational plans and tried to get hold of as many goods of the country as possible.

148

The occupying German government introduced a system of relentless requisition of food products. Quite often, the food was taken away without any consideration to the basic needs of the inhabitants. There was nowhere the people could complain about the arbitrary actions of the local administration. There was no transportation to the larger cities. Even communication among the inhabitants themselves was greatly restricted. For example, letters written in the Lithuanian language were prohibited. The people were troubled by severe punishments inflicted for the violation of various rules. Men were often forced to work at the war fronts or in Germany. The one and only newspaper allowed to be printed in the Lithuanian language was *Dabartis,* which reflected the interests of the German administration only. In many places, during the beginning of the occupation, many schools were established in which students were being Germanized.

Even under these conditions, the Lithuanian activists did not give up. In the cities as well as in the provinces, proclamations were circulated in which the people were urged not to lose hope that Lithuania might yet regain freedom, but to organize secretly. At the end of 1915, an Executive Council of five people from various Lithuanian political groups was organized in Vilnius whose duty it became to defend the interests of the inhabitants in the occupied areas. They began presenting the German occupational government with many memorandums, revealing the conditions of the inhabitants in the country, and the injustices being done to them. In the same manner, they started to express the political expectations of the Lithuanian nation.

For the Lithuanians living in Russia, favorable conditions developed, not only for their aiding the refugees but also for their wide educational work. Aided by funds received from the Refugee Aiding treasury, and because of the efforts of Martynas Yčas, chairman of the Central Committee to Aid War Victims, they built a high school and dormitories for students in Voronezh. Scholarships were organized to enable the Lithuanians scattered throughout Russia to continue their education.

If the Lithuanians living in Russia and under German occupation were restricted to act freely, the Lithuanians living in the United States of America and in neutral Switzerland had no such problems. At the beginning of the war, in Chicago, Illinois and Brooklyn, N. Y., Lithuanian parliaments established the organization to aid refugees in the Lithuanian colonies and prepare them for political work. Money was provided for financing not only activity in the United States, but also in other countries, those in Switzerland being the first to receive such aid. The work of those in Switzerland was invaluable in the field of information. This work was performed in association with the Lithuanian Bureau of Information, which the political emigrant Juozas Gabrys-Paršaitis had founded in Paris in 1911, but which was transferred to Lausanne, Switzerland in 1915. Gabrys also worked with the Paris "Union des Nationalités," which prior to World War I convoked several so-called "congresses of nations," where suppressed countries' cries for freedom were heard.

In 1915, in Berne, a joint conference of Lithuania and Latvia was called, since both were seeking total autonomy. In March, 1916, in Berne, a conference of only Lithuanians was called demanding "absolute autonomy . . ." A short time later a conference was held in Lausanne, which also was attended by Lithuanian representatives from Russia and the United States. (Realizing that there were Lithuanians from Russia, the delegates did not condemn the Russian government, officially, but transferred their attentions to the status quo of occupied Lithuania.) The participants condemned the German system in Lithuania which oppressed the people and robbed the country of its wealth. It was decided to form some sort of commission, which would be responsible for "closely following all further steps taken by the German government and informing the world of the wrongs committed against Lithuania and her people."

In Lausanne that same year, on June 27-30, a "Conference of Nations" was held, attended by delegates from thirty countries, which passed a resolution demanding that each nation be given the right of free political choice. After the arrival of the Lithuanian delegates from Vilnius, a new Lithuanian conference of broader scope was held during which the ultimate ideal was proclaimed: the cry for independence.

The Lithuanian activists used every means possible to have the German government ease up on the occupational regime. In

November, 1916, the Lithuanian representative from Prussia (Prussian Abgeordnetenhaus), Rev. Dr. Vilius Gaigalaitis, having been furnished with the necessary information, presented a memorandum to the German Chancellor, von Bethmann-Hollweg, which turned the Reich's attention to the occupational government's arbitrary rule. That memorandum raised the question of having some degree of autonomy (Selbstverwaltung) brought into Lithuania. On their return trip from the Conference, the Lithuanian delegates stopped in Berlin and visited with Dr. Zimmermann, the Secretary of State, to whom they explained the situation in Lithuania.

FORMATION OF A COUNCIL

At that time, two factors in particular had a direct influence upon the question of self-rule:

1. A declaration from the German and Austro-Hungarian monarchies on November 5, 1916, establishing a Polish state.

2. A continuingly greater demand for national self-determination.

Having decided on the rebirth of the Polish state, the German political and military leaders were confronted by the question of Lithuania. In the spring and summer of 1917, intensive discussions were conducted between the Reich's hierarchy and the top military leaders pertaining to the German policies in Eastern Europe. The German military and Pangermanic elements still fostered policies of annexation.

However, at that time, when in Berlin it was being planned to annex Eastern countries, new factors kept influencing the political scene. Even though the Revolution in Russia strengthened the German militarists' and annexationists' hopes, yet on the other hand, the cries for self-determination were taking on a particular type of reality the longer the war continued, and more and more democratic ideas were spreading throughout all the warring nations, notwithstanding Germany and Prussia. In such circumstances, neither Berlin nor other capitals could any longer ignore the cry for freedom. Naturally, without forsaking annexationistic plans, the idea to have in Lithuania a certain type of

151

council (Vertrauensrat) comprised of the trustworthy, which would represent the Lithuanian populace, began to take shape in the minds of the German civilian and military leaders. It was in Germany's own interests to ascertain that the Lithuanians would neither be pushed aside nor identified with the Poles, who also favored annexation as it pertained to Lithuania.

At the beginning, the Germans attempted to form a rubber-stamp type *Vertrauensrat*. With this purpose in mind, the Germans invited several prominent Lithuanians (Bishop Pranciškus Karevičius, Dr. Jonas Basanavičius, Antanas Smetona) to form this type of institution. However, none assented. The Lithuanians demanded that the representatives would be elected by the people themselves. After long and involved negotiations, the German occupational government agreed that a national conference be held, and that an "organizational committee" (Ausschuss) be formed. This Ausschuss met in Vilnius from August 1-4, 1917. At the start of the meeting, the German government presented the term that "ohne Ansschluss an Deutschland," "keine weiteren Verhandlungen gepflogen werden konnten." The Lithuanian activists, not wishing to bypass the opportunity to push along the question of Lithuania's status, agreed after lengthy discussions, that it was necessary to accept this ultimatum.

Since the Germans forbade elections, the delegates from each district were appointed by the Lithuanians, who wanted to reach and inform the people living in other countries, but did not receive permission to do so from the Germans. The conference was in session in Vilnius from September 18-22, 1917, with 214 representatives in attendance. The meetings were held behind closed doors, "without any representative of the occupational government being present."

At the conference, twenty people were elected to form a Council. Thus, the first governmental body was formed which carried a large load of responsibilities in reviving Lithuanian state.

On the other hand, the Council attempted to strengthen its authority by various means. It was successful in getting in touch with Lithuanians living abroad, and in sending representatives to the Lithuanian conferences held in Stockholm (October 18-20, 1917) and Switzerland (November 6, 1917). It was decided at these conferences that the Council was the highest governmental body.

The Council's delegation visited Berlin and was received by the German Reich, to whom they expressed complaints about the military's arbitrary authority. Of especial importance, the delegates were able to make personal contact with individual members of the Reich, who were informed in detail about the country's status quo, and were provided with material. In consequence, the commander-in-chief of the military government, Count Isenburg-Birstein, was recalled. Though practically nothing had been charged, it was nevertheless a blow to the occupational government's prestige.

The longer the war continued, the more problems Germany encountered. The Council was successful in gaining power, even though the occupational government practically denied the Council's existence, and for the longest time did not grant it a place for establishing headquarters. Notwithstanding this, the Council was successful in gaining access through personal contact to high personages in the German government. In the autumn of 1917, the status of Lithuania improved when the new Chancellor, Graf Hertling, explicitly expressed that Lithuania, together with other German-occupied countries, should have self-government. The cry for freedom of self-determination spread from Western Europe from the United States, and from revolutionary Russia. Even though slowly, the consequence of all this began to alter the atmosphere to Lithuania's advantage. The question of Lithuania was becoming actually heard.

In December, 1917, there occurred negotiations for a free Lithuania, attended by delegates of the Council and the German government. But the Germans stated as a necessary condition that the new state of Lithuania would form "an eternal union" with Germany. The Lithuanian delegation's arguments that this point should be decided by the future Constitutional Assembly did not change the German's decision. Such "eternal unions" were demanded not only by the military, but also by the civilian German governments. Only certain individual members of the Reichstag criticized the German policy on the grounds that the Entente could criticize Germany as having ideas of annexation.

The Council delegates gave in and accepted the German demands, and because of this, there came about the formula of December 11, 1917, which later brought forth bitter arguments between the Lithuanians and the Germans. This declaration, adopted by the Council, was as follows:

"I. The Lithuanian National Council, recognized by Lithuanians within the country and abroad as the only authorized representative of the Lithuanian people; on the strength of the acknowledged right to self-determination of nations and in accordance with resolutions passed by the Lithuanian conference held in Vilnius on the 18th and 23rd of September, 1917, proclaims the re-establishment of an independent Lithuanian State, with Vilnius as capital; and announces the severance of all previous connections the State had maintained with any other nations."

"II. In the formation of this state and for representation of its interests at the peace talks, the National Council requests the protection and help of the German Empire. Since the vital interests of Lithuania require a prompt establishment of lasting and close relations with the German Empire, the National Council advocates close, permanent ties between the Lithuanian State and the German Empire, by way of a treaty implemented mainly in the form of a military and a traffic convention, and a customs and mint community."

In analyzing this document, we must bear in mind the international situation at that time, especially from a military viewpoint. Russia had been overtaken by the Bolshevik Revolution, and was floundering in anarchy. It was the eve of negotiations between Russia and Germany at Brest-Litovsk. It was therefore important to have a statement from the Germans that Lithuania had exercised its right of self-determination. But Lithuanian interests demanded a declaration that the nation sever its relations with Russia and declare itself to be an independent state, in accordance with the accepted question of national self-determination. With the Russians out of the way, the German military strength improved considerably. Within Germany itself, the idea of annexa-

154

tion gained popularity. Even after Lithuania made maximum concessions, the situation in Vilnius worsened. Lithuanian delegates were not allowed to participate in Brest-Litovsk negotiations, and it was forbidden to make public the Formula of December 11.

The Council itself weathered a crisis at that time: claims were heard that it had been too condescending to the Germans. The pressure built up to the point of division—four of its members representing leftist groups withdrew. On the other hand, from discussions in Berlin, it was evident that without a promise to unite with Germany, the Lithuanian cause was not supported by even the leftist groups in the Reichstag.

DECLARATION OF LITHUANIAN INDEPENDENCE

Nevertheless, the Council did not fall apart, but continued intensively to search for a solution. This solution was manifested in a move which went down in Lithuanian history as the Declaration of February 16. In essence, it was decided to ignore German demands and to declare the Lithuanian Republic independent unconditionally, and with no treaties with Germany. This decision, which became regarded as the Lithuanian Declaration of Independence, was worded as follows:

> The Council of Lithuania, during its meeting, February 16, 1918, unanimously decided to address Russia, Germany and other nations with the following declaration:
> The Council of Lithuania, as the only representative of the Lithuanian people, basing itself on the recognized principle of self-determination, and the decision of the Lithuanian conference in Vilnius September 18-23, 1917, proclaims restoration of an independent Lithuanian nation based on democratic foundations with its capital in Vilnius; and, furthermore, this nation is to be freed from any unions with other nations which previously had existed.
> The Council of Lithuania also proclaims that the foundations of the Lithuanian nation and its relations with other nations will be finally decided by the Constitutional Assem-

155

bly to be convened as soon as possible, its delegates to be elected democratically by all the people.

The Council informing the government of ———— ———— requests recognition of an independent Lithuania.

An important difference between this and the Formula of December 11th is that in the new declaration, the determination of relations with foreign countries was left to the upcoming Constitutional Assembly. There were no promises made to Germans, and thus was avoided the vassal state, which Lithuania would have been made into based on the resolutions of December 11.

The Declaration of February 16 once again reunited all the Lithuanian functions represented at the Council; the Act was adopted unanimously, and signed by all members.

As was to be expected, the Council's decision prompted strong reaction from the Germans. By February 21, the German Chancellor, Hertling, wrote "Verwaltungschef in Oberost" Freiherr von Falkenhausen that the German government had been prepared to acknowledge Lithuanian independence based on the decisions made December 11. However, the Declaration of February 16 "destroyed the basis for this measure of the Imperial Government. Therefore, the latter is momentarily not able to pronounce the recognition of Lithuania under these changed circumstances." As if leaving a door open for further bargaining and renewed pressure, the Chancellor said that the Council should return to "the premises," return to "ensuring a prosperous neighborly relationship to the German Empire, for the future."

There soon started hard behind-the-scenes bargaining for interpretation of semantics. The Council attempted to reconcile the acts of December 11 and February 16, and affirmed that between these two were no differences. Again, it explicitly affirmed that the Formula of December 11 remained in effect— but did not revoke the Act of February 16. This type of sophistic interpretation, reaching to unite diverse statements and leaving the question of opposition for the future, finally brought it to the point where a special three-man delegation was sent to Berlin, where they received from Kaiser Wilhelm II recognition of Lithuania's independence, except that this recognition was tied in with the decisions of December 11.

After lengthy and difficult negotiations, it was agreed that Germany, whose army at that time was occupying Lithuania, recognize the state's independence. However, with the act of recognition, all the liabilities which the new nation had to redeem were accounted for, and the traps by which the Lithuanian republic was to be tied to the Kaiser's Germany were sprung. But even such a problematical admission was not a spontaneous act of the Berlin government, but was caused by German internal and political problems. The Reich's government more and more had to accept the cry for self-determination, especially because in the Reichstag some influential groups demanded a condition for satisfying the Brest Treaty (recognition of the Lithuanian republic).

The Council's members fully realized the severe liabilities they had incurred. However, a majority of the members firmly believed that recognition by Germany was well worth the risks involved. The Lithuanians made a *reservatio mentalis* that further events would render meaningless promises made to the Germans. This premonition, in fact, prevailed. The Council's indebtedness toward the Germans could be explained by the circumstance that, up until that time, there had been no gesture of approval from the Entente toward Lithuania. The nations of the Entente dared not draw any conclusions from their own adopted principle of free national self-determination, and still regarded Lithuania as a part of Russia. Russia, though submerged in Bolshevist anarchy, nevertheless was formally still a member of the Entente. This feeling among the member nations was known to the Germans, and they used this argument constantly during the negotiations with Lithuanian delegates, trying to make them less steadfast.

The most regrettable part of the entire situation was that after the Kaiser's recognition, nothing in essence changed either in Lithuania's or in the Council's status. It still had not been granted any prerogatives; its efforts continued to be hindered. It was evident that the military government in Lithuania did not intend to let anything slip out of its hands, and had not forsaken its old ideas of annexation. To all these burdens was added a new complication regarding the format of the Lithuanian republic. Monarchial Germany could not envision a Lithuania other than as a monarchy. There were thoughts of uniting Lithuania

157

in a personal union with the Reich or Prussia. There were also other ideas. Pretenses were raised by Saxony. But a large number of Council's members, excepting the left wing, at that time were not unfavorable to a monarchy, especially because alongside the German monarchy, there was no hope of initiating in Lithuania a republican government.

Under these circumstances, there started a fierce rivalry among certain German pretenders for the coveted Lithuania crown. The Lithuania Council, in the summer of 1918, named itself "the Council of State" (Litauscher Staatsrat), even though the German occupational government steadfastly refused to recognize this change, once again disregarding Berlin and going its own way. The majority, hoping to rid itself of candidates pressed upon it, decided to choose as a king for Lithuania Wilhelm Herzog von Urach, Graf von Wurttemberg. This candidate was palmed off on the Council by a member of the Reichstag "Zentrum," Catholic party, M. Erzberger, who continuously showed a special interest in the fate of Lithuania. On June 4, 1918, the Council voted upon the conditions by which the Duke of Urach was to assume the Lithuanian throne as King Mindaugas II, and on July 1, Urach agreed to these conditions. He even started studying the Lithuanian language.

The election of a king brought about new complications as much in relations with German officials as in the Council itself. *Norddeutsche Allgemeine Zeitung,* a newspaper close to the Reich's Chancellor, published a communique stating that the election of Urach as the Lithuanian king was an arbitrary act by the Council without consultations with the German government.

Within the Council itself, new divisions arose. The leftwing delegates no longer participated because of the election of Urach as King. In July the Council incorporated six new members. Among them were professor Augustinas Voldemaras and attorney Martynas Yčas, who with many other emigrants had been allowed to return from Russia after the signing of the Treaty of Brest-Litovsk. There now appeared in Lithuania new factions, which soon came to play an important part in the early days of the republic.

Despite the fact that the war was coming to an end, the German occupational government refused to relinquish its hold, even though the Council constantly raised this question in its memorandums. It was only in September that the occupational government alloted a small amount of funds to cover the expenses of the Council.

On October 3, 1918, Reich Chancellor Graf von Hertling was replaced by Prince Max von Baden, who was determined to coop- erate with the Reichstag's majority parties. Also, into the new government came Reichstag members Erzberger and Scheidemann as Secretaries of State (they had always supported Lithuania's aspirations) and as another cabinet member, von Payer, left over from the old government (he also quietly sympathized with the Lithuanian cause). The mood in Berlin quickly changed in Lith- uania's favor. This new mood was expressed by Chancellor von Baden in a declaration to the Reichstag by which the German government allowed Lithuania to determine its relations with Germany. In other words, Germany disavowed itself from the idea that the Lithuanian republic had to be united to Germany by far-reaching agreements which actually meant that Lithuania was to be a German satellite.

Of no less importance was another concession made by the Chancellor to a delegation from the Council, which visited with him on October 20. Berlin decided to leave Lithuania to the Lithuanians; that which the Council had for long months de- manded was to be allowed: Lithuanians could choose their own government.

However, Prince von Baden had no time to conscientiously implement his directives. Events moved faster than his govern- ment's attempts to carry out his policies. In the early days of November, the Reich government appointed a high official of Reichs-Justizamt, Dr. Zimmerle, to be General Commisar of Lithuania, granting him special powers to change the military government to a civilian one, and to establish a government. How- ever, the Commisar had little time to implement his powers. He arrived in Vilnius on November 9—on the eve of the German revolution.

The Council took the initiative: on November 2nd, it adopted

159

a resolution withdrawing its previous decision regarding the election of Urach as the king of Lithuania. With this resolution, the Council removed the sources of discontent which had led the left-wing delegates to refrain from recent Council's activities. This unification of all political factions occurred at exactly the right time: The Lithuanians themselves could now assume the government of their new republic, even though there was still some token resistance from the occupational forces.

FORMATION OF THE LITHUANIAN GOVERNMENT

The November revolution in Germany had an immediate effect on Lithuania. According to the armistice signed November 11, the German army in previously Russian territories had to be returned to Germany—not at once, but only when the command was given by the Entente; they would review German-occupied territories' conditions. The reason for this decision was, by avoiding a sudden evacuation by the German armies, to check any infiltration by the Bolsheviks of those territories. This danger was more than theoretical. In the wake of the Russian Revolution, it was most difficult for the military and civilian leaders to maintain discipline and order in occupied nations, something which Lithuania felt. In certain places, the German army dispersed and on its own began to head home. In certain places, there occurred fraternization between Germans' "Soldatenrate" and the Bolsheviks. On the heels of the German army came the Red army, poorly equipped, but led by Bolshevik leaders bent on overrunning as many countries as possible. This is what happened to Lithuania.

A few minutes before midnight on the eve of the German revolution the Reich government, led by the Duke of Baden, accepted the decision to destroy the occupational army's military government, which in more than three years had tortured its inhabitants, and to install a civilian government. The Council made plans at once for forming the government. On November 2, a temporary Lithuanian constitution had been accepted, according to which the Council was given the power to pass laws, and, together with the cabinet, to perform government duties.

On November 5, 1918, the Council asked professor Augustinas Voldemaras to form the first cabinet (three days earlier, it had been decided to repeal the resolution electing Duke Urach to be king of Lithuania). On November 11, the Lithuanian government was formed.

The new administration had neither working personnel, nor housing, nor funds. And the military occupational government continued to pose various problems, such as imposing wartime demands. But notwithstanding these difficulties, an important job was done during those fateful days and weeks—the laying down of foundations for the new state of Lithuania. Cheerful initiative was exhibited by people from various parts of the country, who founded area and district municipalities, supporting already existing schools or erecting new ones, organizing a newlife according to financial capabilities, forming police staffs, taking over the railroads, postal duties, the telegraph and telephone, and using other means to reorganize public utilities. Negotiations were started with the military government and with Berlin itself to borrow money because the state's treasury was empty. It was of extreme importance that a loan of a hundred million in German *marks* be made, which was done so by the Darlehenskasse-Ost in Berlin. This loan helped make it possible for the administration's organizational work to be given impetus during those highly critical months. And the status of Lithuania was critical. The German military, even bearing good will, had many difficulties in trying to control its disbanded army (which was now moving toward Germany). In the "Soldatenrat," places were predominated by a revolutionary element, which did not resist the Bolshevik invasion. Information was had that the "Soldatenrat" intended to relinquish Vilnius to the Bolsheviks. In the same manner, there became apparent the Polish element, which not only wanted to annex Vilnius, but the entire Lithuanian state as well.

Even before the formation of the new administration, efforts were put forth to form the country's system of self-defense. However, difficulties were encountered from the occupational government, which looked askance at the appearance of armed forces in a country still ruled by them. There was better success with the

161

civilian organizations for public safety. The Council had formed, in January, 1918, a commission whose job it was to organize a militia. It was desired that, in the first place, this militia would protect the people against bandits who roamed the countryside. (These were for the most part men who had escaped from captivity or forced labor, and who were hiding in the forests, living from the fruits of robbery.) The Germans hesitated to supply arms to the militia. However, toward the end of 1918, in October, the Commission of Defense was formed, which attended to preparatory work or laid the foundation for organized armament. At that time, the administration headed by Professor Voldemaras verbalized some rather unrealistic ideas. In their Declaration it was resolved that "We are not at war with anyone, and not one of our neighbors—Germany, Poland, the Ukraine, Russia or Latvia—has any grounds to attack us. Thus, it is not necessary for us to guard our borders." The Premier soon realized that actually there were many dangers surrounding Lithuania. On November 28, in an address to the Council, Voldemaras pointed out the growing danger from Russia and Poland. Although the Germans, according to the truce, had to defend the Lithuanian territories, they were planning to retreat from Vilnius. All hope was now placed with the nations of the Entente. Attempts were made to ask the American and Swedish armies to come to Lithuania. But foreign help never arrived. On November 23, 1918, the first directives were published toward the formation of an army.

SOVIET INVASION AND PEACE TREATY

The situation was getting more and more dangerous. The Red Army had invaded Lithuania. On January 5, 1919, Vilnius was already in the hands of the Bolsheviks. Prior to this (December 30-31), the Council and other high administrations had transferred to Kaunas. The Prime Minister himself, of the opinion that it was his duty to confer with the heads of the Entente, and to defend Lithuania's position during the conferences, left for abroad. The adminsistration addressed itself to the Allied Powers conference, being held in Spaa, requesting help against the Bolshevik invasion.

162

The republic was faced with utmost danger. In such circumstances the Minister of Internal Affairs, V. Stašinskas, having taken Voldemaras' place while he was abroad, made known the administration's withdrawal. The formation of a new government was charged to Mykolas Sleževičius, a lawyer and leader of the Peoples' Socialist party (the leftists' central wing).

The new coalition government, headed by an energetic premier, presented an emotional appeal to its inhabitants, inviting the men to join the army and help defend their country.

This appeal resounded through the land, and further encouraged the people to a fierce defense of their motherland. Men began to gather in large numbers, and strengthened the battalions and regiments. There was a shortage of arms, uniforms, and even food. The first volunteers usually arrived with their own weapons, which they acquired from the Germans in exchange for food (the Germans were retreating from Lithuania). When a loan was received from Germany, the situation improved markedly.

The Red Army, having occupied Vilnius, continued to advance slowly. All of eastern Lithuania fell under its sway. There were no doubts that the Bolsheviks were planning not only to occupy the territories ruled by the Czars, but also to carry the Revolution westward. The first such victim was to have been Germany, which at that time seemed ripe for a Communist takeover. At the end of January the Bolsheviks took over Šiauliai, in February reached Telšiai, and were approaching Kaunas and Alytus.

Though the resistance forces were now composed more of partisans, the Lithuanian army, having been strengthened, began organized warfare against the Reds. At Kėdainiai on February 7-8 a serious encounter occurred between the Lithuanians and Bolsheviks, and it was here that the first soldier of free Lithuania, Povilas Lukšys, died in combat. The Soviets were pressing from the south. At Alytus, Lithuania's first infantry division encountered strong Soviet forces. At this encounter the first officer, Antanas Juozapavičius, was killed. It was here that the Lithuanians received help from the Germans, who had to protect Kaunas since most of its administration was still there. The Lithuanian army was successful, and in the middle of April it was headed toward Vilnius.

In the summer of 1919, the Germans began evacuating Lithuania, and in July left Kaunas, their last big stronghold. The battle against the Reds continued. The army pushed the Red invaders from its territories, and by the end of August had pushed them to Dauguva. In the first days in October the Lithuanian army approached Daugavpils, an important Latvian junction, where Lithuanian-populated territory crosses with Latvia. It was here that the Lithuanian army stopped, and the war between the Lithuanians and the Communists was practically over.

The Baltic coastline was now free of the Bolsheviks. The Russian government expressed a desire for an agreement to end aggression. Peaceful negotiations were started, at first between Russia and Estonia, and shortly thereafter between Lithuania and Moscow, though between Poland and Russia armed conflict still continued. The Lithuanian-Russian negotiations ended with favorable results, and July 12, 1920, a peace treaty was signed in Moscow.

The first article of this treaty held great importance. It was as follows: "Basing itself upon the declaration of the USSR's Assembly that each nation has the right of self-determination, and becoming entirely independent from the state which it is now part of, without any reservations Russia recognizes Lithuania's independence and self-government with all its due jurisdictional rights, and with good will renounces for all times, all rights of Russian sovereignty which she had had over the Lithuanian nation and its territories."

In the second article, the boundary between Russia and Lithuania is defined in great detail. The boundary was as follows: beginning in the North at the Dauguva River and extending West from Druja, and making a sudden sharp turn westward at Breslauja (leaving this area under Lithuania's jurisdiction) incorporating the lakes, the boundary, in a rather straight line, following a southerly direction along Kazėnai, crosses the Dysna River; further, it continues through Pastoviai and turns in an easterly direction from Lake Narutis, which for some length makes up the boundary; it continues toward the Molodečna railroad junction, leaving the Vilnius-Molodečna-Lyda railroad junction within the Lithuanian territory; from there through Voložinas it turns in a southwesterly direction, reaching the Nemunas River to the mouth of the Berezina River. Later, the boundary was made up where the Nemunas met the Svisloce River, then through the Indura to Sydra where the Gorodnianka River empties into the Bobro River.

Russia also promised to return to Lithuania public and private wealth which she had taken during the war, i.e., libraries, archives, museums, and the like. It was also agreed that Lithuania could chop down all the trees from 100,000 hectars in the Russian forests for the purpose of rebuilding. (This however, never came to pass.) Finally, Moscow gave to Lithuania three million *rubles* in gold.

The signing of the treaty with Soviet Russia strengthened Lithuania's position in the international arena. Besides Germany, Russia was the second largest state, which recognized an autonomous Lithuania, and which freely acknowledged Lithuania's separation from Russia. However, the boundary set between Lithuania and Russia was never used, since in October, 1920, Poland occupied Vilnius, and Lithuania was separated from Soviet Russia until World War II.

THE POLISH INTENTIONS TOWARDS LITHUANIA

During the years of German occupation, when the idea of self-determination was beginning to ripen, the Poles began to express pretenses toward Lithuania. These pretenses caused conflict, which very shortly turned into aggressive warlike actions between the two states. The Lithuanian state, having to resist the Bolshevik invasion, could not afford to wage an unequal war against its southern neighbor, Poland, which resorted to every means possible against the new state. The Entente tried to draw demarcation lines between the two nations, which the Poles continually transgressed. The League of Nations intervened several times, but was unable to solve the dispute, because its sanctions were disregarded. Lithuania suggested that this be solved by the International Court at Hague, but this suggestion was also rejected.

165

When the Polish state was rising, its administration sought historic boundaries, and attempted to annex many Lithuanian, Ukranian, and Byelorussian territories. Lithuania and Poland were far from being equal. Poland's rebirth represented an entirely separate point in Wilson's Fourteen Points, the state's reconstruc- tion having been projected by the Allies as one of the goals of the first World War. Poland was recognized by all the nations of the Entente, and was officially invited to the Paris peace nego- tiations. Poland exploited France's special protection, since France saw in Poland a new ally to compensate for the loss of Russia. Also, Poland used its prestige as a "nation martyred," though Lithuania was part of this sacrifice. Western Europe seldom men- tioned or even remembered this. Lithuania enjoyed none of these privileges when she entered the international arena of nations. That was not enough. The Poles formed a huge propaganda ma- chine which they used against Lithuania, stating that Lithuania was a product of German intrigues; also, that Lithuania was more than sympathetic with the Bolsheviks. Thus, Lithuania had to as- sume the burden of entering an unequal war in which Poland used every means available to them to further their own cause. Pro- fessor Voldermaras, free Lithuania's first minister of foreign af- fairs, led a delegation to Paris to defend his nation.

While the German army was evacuating Vilnius because of the rising revolution in Germany, the Polish element was secretly readying itself to take over this city's government. But the Bol- sheviks beat the Poles in their game by invading Vilnius with the Red Army on January 5, 1919, in order to establish a soviet state. The Lithuanian Government moved all its records to Kaunas (December 30-31, 1918), and put forth all efforts to establish and organize armed resistance. At the same time, well-equipped Polish units began to push out the Red army from territories which had always belonged to Lithuania. Lithuania was unable to resist the Bolsheviks as well as the Poles, who entered Vilnius in April of 1919. The Allies, taking a definite interest in this conflict, suggested that a line of demarcation be established be- tween the two armies, which was accomplished in June. But the Polish army commanders refused to adhere to this boundary, and several times infiltrated into Lithuania. Then in November, the

Allied Armies' commander, Marshall Foch, determined a new boundary which, like the previous one determined by the French Army Commission, catered to the interests of the Poles, at the expense of the Lithuanians. But the Polish army did not even regard this one as acceptable. At this time, Lithuania, still directing its effort against the Bolsheviks, tried to avoid open warfare with the Poles, though several scattered skirmishes were fought. Such uncertain circumstances prevailed until the spring of 1920.

The Polish civil and military administrations not only used military might to reach its goal—unification with Lithuania—but also planned to create chaos from within. For intelligence purposes, there was created in Lithuania a military organization P.O.W. (Polska Organizacja Wojskowa), which depended upon local Polish sympathizers, and which infiltrated all areas as yet free from foreign occupation. The organization's purpose was to overthrow the Lithuanian administration, and to take power, if only for a short time, and to hold on to it until the Polish armed forces could come to its aid. The revolt was to have taken place the night of August 27, 1919. However, the Lithuanians got wind of this and were successful in containing it.

The war between Russia and Poland continued. The Polish army, following the directives of its administration to restore Poland to its former historical borders ("from sea to sea"), had reached Kiev in May, 1920. From this moment on, however, the good luck which the Poles had enjoyed went to the Bolsheviks, and the Poles quickly retreated. The fighting between Lithuania and Russia was almost at an end, and the government had begun to negotiate for peace with Moscow. (Estonia had already signed a treaty with the Soviets.) Such a treaty was signed July 20, 1920, in Moscow; according to this treaty, Vilnius was returned to Lithuania.

Meanwhile, the Polish army was retreating from the entire Russian front. The Lithuanians received the command to march into Vilnius, but the Polish army thwarted the way. When the Lithuanian army finally reached Vilnius on July 15, the city was in the hands of the Bolsheviks. The Poles would rather have seen Vilnius in the hands of the Soviets. Once the Reds evacuated the capitol the Lithuanian Government returned there from Kaunas.

167

Finally the Reds were defeated near Warsaw and had to retreat, with the Polish army in pursuit. The question arose as to how the Poles would act in regard to Lithuanian sovereignty. Although Lithuania proclaimed itself neutral during the Russia-Polish war, the first encounters between the Poles and Lithuanians began shortly. The Poles invaded various Lithuania's areas, and began propagandizing to the effect that Lithuania had broken its neutrality during the Russian-Polish war, and was actually fraternizing with the Bolsheviks. In the peace treaty signed with Moscow, the boundary between Russia and Lithuania had been agreed upon, but the boundary between Lithuania and Poland had not been settled. The Lithuanian Government suggested several times that negotiations be held, and in a telegram sent to Warsaw on August 27, 1920, suggested that the line of demarcation be drawn extending through Gardinas, Augustavas and Stabin. However, the Poles demanded that the Lithuanian army retreat to the demarcation line established by Marshall Foch in July, 1919. During the exchange of telegrams the situation was becoming more and more dangerous—wherever the two armies met in territories held by their respective governments, there would occur skirmishes or incidents. Now the demarcation line suggested by Lord Curzon (December 8, 1919,) came into being. The Lithuanian Government held to the opinion that this boundary was illegal, on the grounds that when it was made, there were no Lithuanian representatives present, nor was Lithuania informed of the proceedings leading to this decision. As far as Lithuania was concerned, this boundary could not be accepted.

The government then suggested that negotiations be held for a new boundary, in Marijampolė. The Polish minister of foreign affairs demanded that negotiations be held in Kalvarija. This suggestion was accepted, and negotiations were held September 15-19, but were not fruitful. Between September 21 and 23, the Poles attacked and severely defeated the Lithuanian army at Druskininkai, taking many prisoners.

But direct diplomatic contact was not broken, and it was

agreed to meet in Suvalkai on September 29, and to arrive at a line of demarcation between the armies. The negotiations were attended by the League of Nations commission for military control, headed by a French colonel, Chardigny, and were successful. An agreement was signed on October 7. In the history of Lithuania and Poland, this event goes down as one of the saddest.

The Suvalkai agreement's importance lies in the fact that it decided the line of demarcation and thus precluded further involvements between the two armies, as Vilnius officially came under the jurisdiction of Lithuania. The line was drawn to Bastūnai, and both parties agreed that the boundary would be continued eastward, "as soon as the Soviet forces retreat from this area." The League of Nations would be consulted again if an agreement could not be reached. The agreement was to become effective midnight October 19, 1920, and was not to expire "until each and every dispute between the Poles and Lithuanians would be settled."

Soon, it became evident that the Poles were planning to invade Lithuania, even during the Suvalkai negotiations. In Lyda, close to the line of demarcation, the Poles were preparing to attack with all their might, with the intention of occupying as much Lithuanian territory as possible. In command of these forces was General L. Zeligowski, whose mission it was to play a "rebel"—i.e., without the consent or knowledge of the Polish government. His well-equipped troops surprised the Lithuanian army, and began to head toward Vilnius, occupying the city on October 9, and then began marching in a northwesterly direction. In November they were approaching Ukmergė. Lithuania was in great peril. At this critical moment, the Lithuanians exhibited valiant courage in the face of a much stronger enemy, almost without exception, the entire nation joined in the battle; defense committees were set up in various areas, and writers, musicians, educators, students—all carried arms.

The results were quickly evident. On November 19 near Širvintai, and on November 21 near Giedraičiai, the Lithuanian army defeated the Polish forces and headed for Vilnius. But at this time, the commission of the League of Nations entered the scene, and through its efforts a neutral zone was established be-

tween the "rebel" Poles and Lithuanians on November 29. Vilnius and its environs remained in Polish hands.

THE INTERVENTION OF THE LEAGUE OF NATIONS

On September 5, 1920, the League of Nations sent a telegram
stating that Lithuania had to accept the Curzon line as its boundary, and Poland had to respect Lithuania's neutrality. Moreover,
a special commission was set up to see that both countries upheld
these conditions. On September 28, Russia's minister of foreign
affairs affirmed that the USSR was resolved to honor Lithuania's
territorial integrity.

Because Poland had no intentions of withdrawing General
Zeligowski's "rebels," the League of Nations began discussing the
problem on October 26, 1920, in Brussels. During the debates,
Polish delegate Askhenazy claimed that within Vilnius a Lithuanian government had been established; thus, the Poles dared not
call General Zeligowski's conquered territories anything but Lithuanian. The Lithuanian delegate demanded that a full session of
the General Assembly be called to impose sanctions against Poland. However, in ensuing discussions, there arose a new idea,
proposed by the Italian delegate, namely that of a plebiscite. The
Belgian delegate, Hymans, expressed the opinion that *le fond
même de la question* should be discussed foremost, and a plebiscite was the best means of carrying this out. This idea was accepted on October 25, 1920. The plebiscite was to be supervised
by a five-member commission, and an "international force" was
to be sent to the occupied territory. This force was to be made up
of Belgian, Danish, Dutch, British, Norwegian, Swedish, French,
and Spanish troops—approximately 1,500 men, under the command of the French colonel, Chardigny.

In the meantime, Lithuanian and Polish representatives, under
the auspices of a League of Nations military commission, signed
a truce (to be effective November 29, 1920), and a demilitarized
zone was set up between the two armies. Before the plebiscite,
General Zeligowski's army was to be demobilized or withdrawn.

The proposed plebiscite never took place. The dispatching of
an international military force to Vilnius was opposed by the

170

Russian government, which saw some danger to its own security in such a move. The Poles, in the meantime, not only postponed withdrawing Zeligowski's army from Vilnius, but increased it from 20,000 to 50,000 men. The Lithuanian Government argued that the results of a plebiscite could hardly be construed as the will of the people when the territory in question was under occupation, and the Polish-appointed civilian administration, which was harassing the people, had not yet been removed. During an Assembly meeting on March 1, 1921, the British delegate, Lord Balfour, suggested that the two nations begin direct negotiations in Brussels under the direction of Mr. Hymans.

During the negotiations, Hymans, on May 13, 1921, stated the following: "The resistance of Lithuania is not the main argument that prompted the Council to refrain from a plebiscite. In the view of the Council, the plebiscite was to have been completely free. It was to have been honestly and rapidly conducted. But now this has become impossible because of General Zeligowski's seizure by force. The League of Nations did not want a camouflaged plebiscite, nor did it want to keep those troops in the Vilnius region. Since the region was occupied by military force, a long preparation would have been necessary, requiring the presence of an international expeditionary force for many months. In view of these difficulties, the Council thought that, since negotiations to settle their relations had previously taken place between the two countries, it would be best to invite them to resume these negotiations under the chairmanship of a Council member." These negotiations began on April 20, in Brussels, and the first session lasted until June 3.

As Hymans summarized in his report of June 10th: "We have been informed . . . of ideas coming from several directions suggesting a federalist solution, in which event the region of Vilnius should be constituted as an autonomous unit, bound by a federal tie to the Lithuanian State, the latter itself being federated with Poland, with certain joint executive bodies."

On May 20, Hymans submitted his *Avant-projet,* the most important point of this being that Vilnius was to be recognized as the capital of Lithuania. The country itself was to be divided, following the Swiss example, into two cantons—Kaunas and

171

Vilnius, with the federal capital remaining at Vilnius. According to Section VIII of this plan, "All troops presently occupying the territory of Vilnius, as well as those officials who were not natives of the territory of Vilnius, would be removed as soon as the agreement was concluded." A "Conseil commun des Affaires étrangères" was set up to coordinate Lithuanian and Polish foreign policies. Both nations were to make up delegations of equal numbers, to sanction all foreign policy decisions of common interest. A military commission was also set up to insure cooperation between the two armies and their general staffs. A close-knit economic treaty was to follow.

Hymans' first project was intended to rebuild federal ties, which for several centuries had kept Lithuania and Poland together. But it did not take into consideration the changing time not only throughout the whole world, but also within the two nations involved. Lithuania, having regained its independent national status, held that the previous alliance with Poland would be fatal to its sovereignty. Therefore, there was a great resistance among the Lithuanian people toward the new alliance.

Notwithstanding severe pressure from the people, and many other doubts which were raised, Lithuania still agreed to accept Hymans' project as a basis for negotiations. On its part, Lithuania made two proposals by which, in her opinion, it would be possible to maintain relations between the two countries. In the meantime, the Poles made known as a precondition for further negotiations that representatives of the people in the occupied territory were to be present at the negotiations.

The League of Nations General Assembly, in its June 28, 1921, session, decided that negotiations were to be renewed in Brussels on July 15, once again under the leadership of Hymans, and based on the latter's proposals. The Assembly demanded that before its next session (September 1), Zeligowski's army was to have vacated the disputed territory, along with its civilian administrators.

From the new negotiations which lasted for over a month, Hymans drew up a new proposal (September 3), which the Poles claimed was not based on the new negotiations, but was drafted

172

arbitrarily by Hymans. The plan differed greatly from the previous one in that it was more favorable to Lithuania. The nation was not to be divided into two cantons; only the territory of Vilnius would become an autonomous district within Lithuania's borders; the canton of Vilnius was to be organized similarly to the Swiss cantons; the Lithuanian Assembly and government was to be headquartered in Vilnius. On September 12, the Lithuanian delegation agreed to principle to Hymans' project, while at the same time offering a counter-proposal. Within this proposal, the principle of a canton was changed to that of an autonomous district based on the Czechoslovakian system, as outlined in the treaty of St. Germain-en-Laye, September 10, 1919. With several other changes, Lithuania tried to disentangle herself from long-term unions with Poland.

The Polish government rejected the terms of the second project, apparently feeling that Hymans had made too many concessions to the Lithuanians.

The League tried very hard to resolve the conflict; however, it did not resort to all of the methods allowed by its charter to punish flagrant transgressions committed by the Polish government under the guise of General Zeligowski's "rebellion." The League proved powerless in restoring peace; thus, in its early years the prestige of the League suffered a severe setback. Undoubtedly, this inaction helped lead to its ultimate failure.

Unable to resolve the conflict, the League concluded that its efforts were in vain, and the Council, in its session of September 20, decided to allow Hymans to inform the Assembly of the situation. On January 13, 1922, the Council adopted a resolution which stated that the League's conciliatory procedures were ended and the military control commission was withdrawn. According to this same resolution, the previous line of neutrality became the line of demarcation.

Even while the League was arbitrating the Lithuanian conflict, the Poles perpetrated a new farce within the occupied territory. On November 10, the Warsaw Assembly decided that an Assembly should be called in Vilnius to determine the fate of that territory. The rebel general announced elections on January 6-8. As the League military commission chairman noted in his report

173

of March 20, 1922: "The Lithuanian Committee, different Jew' ish associations, and the national White Russian Committee, pur' suant to their former statements, have not taken part in the elections and consequently have not presented any list of candi' dates." According to this commission report, "the Vilnius Diet is composed exclusively of Polish members despite the mixed character of the region's population."

The commission also said, "1) The commissions in charge of the direction and execution of the electoral operations were com' posed almost exclusively of Poles. 2) The voters came to the polls without identity cards or other evidence. Thus the control of the elections was entirely in the hands of the interested party."

Finally, in its conclusion, the commission stated: "Since the Lithuanians, the Jews and a large portion of the White Russians completely abstained from taking part in the elections, and since the elections were held under a system of military occupation, in which the Polish element disposed of all means of exerting pres' sure on the governmental apparatus, it does not seem that one can consider the present Vilnius Diet as being the true and sin' cere expression of the whole population of the consulted terri' tory." So wrote Colonel Chardigny, chairman of the military control commission, who could not be accused of being anti' Polish.

Even under such circumstances the official statistics show that only 63 percent of the electorate voted.

This Assembly, as could be expected, voted unanimously to annex Vilnius to Poland. The Lithuanian Government protested not only this action but also the legality of the elections.

With the League having stopped its intervention, the Lithu' anian-Polish conflict entered a new phase. On February 20, 1922, the Lithuanian government suggested to Poland that the Suvalkiai treaty be turned over to the International Court at Hague. However, the Poles turned this down.

ABSENCE OF DIPLOMATIC RELATIONS BETWEEN LITHUANIA AND POLAND

Meanwhile, the League wanted to erase one of the conse' quences of its intervention. When the Lithuanian army, having recovered from Zeligowski's surprise attack, had begun to push the Poles back, a truce had been signed ending the war, and creating a neutral zone between the two armies. The League now wished to divide this zone between Lithuania and Poland, and in its place create a line of demarcation. Lithuania objected. To resolve this, the League created a commission, headed by the Spaniard Saura.

Notwithstanding the Lithuanian protests, it was decided (February 3, 1923) to establish the line of demarcation. The Lithuanian government, holding this decision to be illegal and in violation of the League of Nations pact, demanded that the decision be brought before the International Tribunal in Hague. However, the Council on April 21 decided that its action had been justified, and thus it was unnecessary to take the matter before the international tribunal.

Protesting this outrage, Lithuania refused to maintain diplomatic or any other relations with Poland. For eighteen years there was no direct rail connection, mail, or any other form of communication. There existed between the two nations a state the consequences of which reached further than the situation itself, and which later gave birth to the expression "Iron Curtain." On the other hand, Poland's outrageous act toward Lithuania, and occupation of its capital, so infuriated the Lithuanian people that no government would have been able to reverse the universal feeling of distrust toward Poland, and to reestablish normal relations. The government's decision to avoid relations with Poland was agreeable to the entire nation.

Relations between the two countries were further strained by Poland's attitude toward the Lithuanian inhabitants of Vilnius. From the first days of the occupation, Polish agencies persecuted Lithuanians and their organizations. Especially hard hit were educational organizations; also, newspapers were banned, libraries closed. The industry was heavily taxed. The Poles systematically persecuted the Lithuanians, while at the same time encouraging the Polish element. Complaints of this persecution reached the League of Nations and figured in its agenda for a number of years. An event causing great uproar was the deportation of thirty-three leading Lithuanian citizens on February 5, 1922. The

Polish government, on the other hand, repeatedly complained that Lithuania was persecuting the Polish minority living in free Lithuania. Under these circumstances, the climate between the two countries was constantly strained.

THE BOUNDARIES OF LITHUANIA

After World War I, the boundary between Latvia and Lithuania ran along the borders of the Kaunas and Kurland governments, as it had in Czarist times. Yet these boundaries were not always precise and did not follow ethnographic lines. On September 28, 1920, both governments signed a treaty, according to which both states formed boundary commissions. Since neither commission could reach an agreement, the final decision had to be made by the neutral chairman, the British observer, professor J. Y. Simpson.

Even though Lithuania had to turn more territory over to Latvia than she received in return, the chief gain was the receiving of the historical Lithuanian coastal center Palanga and the mouth of the Šventoji River. Palanga is surrounded by historic legends tied to the historic personage of Duchess Birutė, who had once been a vestal virgin at Palanga. In this manner, Lithuania received access to the sea—its only access until the acquisition of Klaipėda (Memel). During the period of independence, Palanga became the most frequented sea resort in the republic. At Šventoji, a fishing center was established. Lithuanian society often raised the question of converting Šventoji into a commercial port. During the independence period, it became an improved and important fishing center. Plans were drawn up to convert this port into a commercial center. On May 14, 1921, a convention was signed between Latvia and Lithuania designating the state borders between the two countries. This convention was quickly implemented; pennants were set up along the frontier.

Although Lithuania was not a new state, it went into the international arena for the first time (in the declaration of independence, it was specifically pointed out that the state was being reestablished). It now had to face more problems than other states before it received international recognition. Neighboring Poland posed the most problems by using its influence to obstruct recognition of Lithuania, concerned as it was with forcing Lithuania to enter into a federation with Poland. On the other hand, all three Baltic States were faced with the expressed views of some Western nations that all should be done to prevent injury to Russia, as the former sovereign of the Baltic territory. These Western nations did not have Bolshevik Russia in mind; they were concerned with the vested interests of the Czarist and democratic interests of a future Russia. The former Czarist diplomatic corps in the West continued its work with these aims in mind. Such views also influenced Washington for a while.

This Russian policy faced a blow when all three Baltic States signed peace treaties with Soviet Russia, according to which the Soviet government renounced all claims to sovereign rights. In addition to Germany, which gave a reserved recognition to the Lithuanian State on March 23, 1918, Soviet Russia, on July 12, 1920 signed a peace treaty with Lithuania.

It was important for the Lithuanian Government to be recognized by the victorious Western Allied powers. The new prime minister and foreign minister, professor Augustinas Voldemaras, devoted his energies to obtaining international recognition and good relations with the Western powers. This can be seen by the fact that immediately after his appointment he went to the West while leaving the defenses of the country and the organization of the state to his other ministers.

In spite of all his efforts, the Lithuanian delegation was not officially admitted to the Paris Peace Conference. The delegation prepared a great number of memoranda calling for recognition of Lithuania. The fact that she did not receive it was a hard blow, especially when the Versailles Peace Treaty was signed. According to Article 99 of the Treaty, the Klaipėda-Memel territory was separated from Germany but was not given unconditionally to Lithuania. The Klaipėda District was for the time being to remain in the hands of the Allies, for "the status of the Lithuanian territory has not yet been determined."

When the plenum of the League of Nations met in November, 1920, the requests of Lithuania, Latvia and Estonia to be admitted as full-fledged members of the League were turned down. It was decided to postpone final decision until the situation in the Baltic

177

became clearer. In the meantime, the Baltic States were admitted into technical commissions of the League of Nations. Only Colombia, Italy, Paraguay, Persia and Portugal had voted for Lithuania's admission into the League. As the Portuguese representative in his speech pointed out, one neighbor (he had in mind Russia) could create a danger to the Baltic States; the argument was extended to the point that the same danger could arise to other states from their stronger neighbors. However, the arguments of Portugal and the other backers did not sway the majority of the League Members.

The question was again brought up at the plenary meeting of September 5, 1921. The Lithuanian Government, as did the Estonian and Latvian governments, again submitted its request for admission. This time the whole matter went along more smoothly, but Lithuania again met with problems initiated by the Poles, who accused Lithuania of persecuting the Polish minority in Lithuania and who intrigued against the republic. These same tactics were used when the League plenum considered the Lithuanian-Polish conflict which arose when General Zeligowski seized Lithuania's capital, Vilnius. On September 22, Lithuania was, nonetheless, admitted as a full-fledged member of the League of Nations. No one voted against admission. Twelve members either abstained or did not take part in the meeting; they included Poland, France and the three states of the "Little Entente" (Czechoslovakia, Rumania and Yugoslavia).

DE JURE RECOGNITION

The *de jure* recognition became a vital issue, when the Ambassadors Conference of July 13, 1922, informed the Lithuanian representative in Paris O. Milašius-Milosz about the decision of four great states (France, Great Britain, Italy and Japan) to grant Lithuania *de jure* recognition, but with the proviso: (62, 63) "that the latter agree, purely and simply, to approve and to obey the provisions of the Versailles Treaty insofar as they concern the system of navigation on the Nemunas." Recognition itself, as stated in the note, "will become effective on the date that receipt of the above-mentioned terms is acknowledged."

The proviso presented the country with a dilemma. The Lith-uanian government, according to the Versailles Treaty, was to permit free transit on the Nemunas River. This freedom could only be used in practice by one country, Poland. But Lithuania was in a state of war with that country. The Ambassadors Con-ference wanted to exact as its price for the *de jure* recognition of Lithuania the settlement of differences between Lithuania and Poland in the light of the Zeligowski aggression and the recogni-tion of that aggression. The price of recognition was rather high.

On December 20, 1922, the four great powers informed the Lithuanian government that from that day hence they had decided to recognize Lithuania *de jure*. In this manner, the Lithuanian Government received the recognition of the great powers and at the same time shunted aside a direct promise to open uncondition-ally the Nemunas River to Polish traffic and to establish some sort of relations with Poland and thereby recognize the Polish occupa-tion of Vilnius.

The Lithuanian Government in its note made two further observations. First, it repeated its earlier desire that after *de jure* recognition the Klaipėda District was to be joined with Lithuania. (That same year, the Ambassadors Conference authorized a com-mission to study the Klaipėda-Memel question. Whereas the Con-ference did not succeed in forcing Lithuania to open river com-merce to the Poles by dangling *de jure* recognition, the Confer-ence, in which the Poles' allies the French had an important voice, sought to place a new noose on Lithuania by trying to satisfy Polish interested during the Klaipėda controversy. However, at the same time that the Conference was trying to give Poland a privileged position in Klaipėda and to normalize Lithuania's rela-tions with Poland *vis-a-vis* Vilnius, plans were in preparation for a revolt in Klaipėda which would upset all Polish machinations.)

The second observation of the November 18th note had harm-ful results for Lithuania. The Lithuanian Government asked the Conference to determine Poland's eastern boundaries according to the provisions of the Versailles Treaty.

On March 15, 1923, the Ambassadors Conference made the decision by which it defined Poland's eastern boundaries. The demarcation line with Poland was accepted on February 3, 1923, as the border between Poland and Lithuania by the League Council over the protests of Lithuania. In this manner, the Ambassadors Conference maintained that it had the right to sanction the situation created by Zeligowski's aggression. The Conference based its decision on the right given by Article 87 of the Versailles Treaty; it also mentioned the Polish request of February 15, 1923, and finally, the November 22, 1922, note of the Lithuanian Government. It also complied with the February 3, 1923, resolution of the League Council on the substitution of the demarcation line for the neutral zone between the two states.

This decision caused a furor in Lithuania. The April 16th note to the Ambassadors Conference declared that under no circumstances would such a decision be accepted, and under no conditions would it be held binding.

It was not surprising that on the same day that the Ambassadors Conference made its decision, the Polish Government hurried to accept it. By the same token, the Lithuanian Government, like the entire nation, felt deeply injured by this sanctioning of the Zeligowski aggression. The decision of the Ambassadors Conference strengthened the resistance of the Lithuanians to this injury. October 9th, the day when the Polish Army under Zeligowski treacherously seized Vilnius, became a universal day of mourning and protest throughout the country. The poet Petras Vaičiūnas' verse about Vilnius: "Hark, world, we will not rest without Vilnius!" (Ei, pasauli, mes be Vilniaus nenurimsim) became the rallying cry of the nation. In 1925, the Society to Liberate Vilnius (Vilniui Vaduoti Sąjunga) was formally established, though it had existed earlier under another name. It became one of the most popular organizations in Lithuania, drawing all segments of society. Its journal *Mūsų Vilnius* was widely read both at home and abroad, especially by the Lithuanian Americans who also had numerous chapters of the Society.

The decision of the Ambassadors Conference was a painful blow to Lithuania. The Government was accused of having acted without foresight, asking the Conference to determine Poland's eastern borders. In view of the fact that Poland's ally France exerted great influence in the Ambassadors Conference, it would have been almost impossible for Lithuania to win a favorable decision in spite of the moral and legal arguments it could muster against the Polish seizure of Vilnius. However, the decision of the Conference did not quash the nation's aspirations to continue the fight to regain its capitol. From a moral point of view, Lithuania's position was strengthened by three renowned jurists: A. de Lapradelle, professor of international law at the University of Paris, member of the International Law Institute in Paris and former vice president of that Institute; L. le Fur, professor of international law at the University of Paris, and member of the International Law Institute in Paris; and A. N. Mandelstam, doctor of international law (St. Petersburg University) and member of the International Law Institute. In 1928, the three declared in answer to Minister Petras Klimas' query of May 1, 1928, which was as follows: "In law and in equity, is the Government of the Lithuanian Republic bound or not bound by the decision of the Ambassadors' Conference of March 15, 1923, concerning the boundaries between Poland and Lithuania?"

In answer to this question, all three international lawyers, after an exhaustive analysis, answered: No.

EFFECTS OF THE VILNIUS CONFLICT

Relations with Poland were attempted on many occasions. Occasions offered themselves when the questions of transit and the floating of timber down the Nemunas were raised by Poland, the Ambassadors Conference, or the League of Nations which sought to force Lithuania to normalize relations with Poland by not touching on the essential question, namely that of Vilnius. In 1924, the Lithuanian Government suggested calling a conference of the major powers to deal with the Vilnius Question. This suggestion was rejected.

The following year the Polish government, on the basis of the Lithuanian Government's promise, in signing the Memel Convention, to open the Nemunas to the floating of timber, offered to negotiate. *Volens nolens,* the Lithuanian Government had to accept the offer. The negotiations took place in Copenhagen and were later moved to Lugano. They ended without any results, for it was clear that the Polish Government was seeking far-reaching political goals which were not limited to technical questions such as the floating of timber.

The Polish demanded that railway communications and consular relations be opened. The Lithuanians rejected these demands, and as a result, the negotiations were broken off. Wishing to fulfill its promise to settle the matter of floating the timber, the Lithuanian Government (January 27, 1926) published regulations for timber transit on the Nemunas. Poland, however, did not avail itself—it was more concerned with breaking Lithuania's resistance to establishing normal diplomatic relations. The Lithuanian public reacted sharply to the negotiations with Poland, and this precipitated a crisis in the government. The question of relations with Poland always affected Lithuanian society, and this gave the Lithuanian Government limited freedom of maneuvering, because each measure could be interpreted as a concession to Poland which would result in violent public reaction. Each government had to reckon with this circumstance. The extent of the anti-Polish sentiment in Lithuanian society can be seen from the fact that during the negotiations on the Hymans Project, an assassination attempt was made on the life of Ernestas Galvanauskas who headed the Lithuanian group during the negotiations. Some extremists felt that he would make far-reaching political concessions to the Poles.

The situation worsened after the December 17, 1926, *coup d'état* when professor Augustinas Voldemaras' new government tried to activize the Vilnius Question on the international level. On the other hand, the Polish Government intensified its persecution of Lithuanians in the Vilnius territory, even resorting to out-and-out provocative measures. It was apparent that the dictator of Poland, Marshal Jozef Pilsudski, a Lithuanian by descent who went completely over to the Poles, was the engineer of Zeligowski's *coup*. Pilsudski hated the Lithuanian state with the passion of a renegade. He wanted to force Lithuania to accept the situation in Vilnius. The Polish Government began to concentrate troops along the demarcation line, and in Lyda the Poles organized and armed Lithuanian political exiles who had fled abroad because of illegal activities. Marshal Pilsudski declared in public that he could not sleep nights pondering whether or not to order mobilization against Lithuania.

In the light of the provocative Polish behavior the Lithuanian Government approached the Council of the League of Nations, requesting the inclusion of the Lithuanian-Polish tension in the agenda of the Council's work. The Council meetings took place under rather dramatic circumstances, when the Polish dictator Pilsudski arrived in Geneva and presented Prime Minister Volde-maras with a provocative question: "Peace or war?" When the prime minister answered "paix," there was a moment of relaxa-tion in the Council. After further discussion in the Council, a resolution was adopted on December 10, 1927, which suggested that both parties begin direct negotiations. This resolution took into consideration the Lithuanian prime minister's declaration that "Lithuania does not consider itself in a state of war with Poland, and, consequently, peace exists between the two Countries." On the other hand, the resolution maintained that "the Polish Repub-lic acknowledges that it will fully respect the political independ-ence and territorial integrity of the Lithuanian Republic."

The last article of the resolution, which alleviated Lithuanian fears, stated that the intervention of the League of Nations should not be construed as forcing the Government of Lithuania to accept the present situation in the Vilnius territory.

The case raised at Geneva renewed the Vilnius Question on the international level, which was what Lithuania had wanted in the first place. Although the question itself was not moved one iota forward, the discussion and echoes resulting from the debate in the Council of the League of Nations, which were followed by the Lithuanian-Polish negotiations, produced international public opinion and clearly demonstrated that the Vilnius wound was not healed and that the Vilnius case was not solved—though the Warsaw Government wanted it to be closed. When he returned from Geneva, Prime Minister Voldemaras was enthusiastically met by part of the public and feted for masterfully defending Lithuania's rights.

Nonetheless, in the League of Nations apparatus there was a tendency, especially in the communications and transit commis-sion, to force Lithuania to open communications on the Nemunas

River and to open the railroad line between Lithuania and Poland. In 1927, at the Third Conference of Communications and Transit, the Latvian delegate intervened because of so-called difficulties at the Latvian port of Liepaja due to the nonexistence of railway communications between Lithuania and Poland, due to the Lithuanian-Polish conflict. The Conference declared its concern over the freedom of international communications and transit. In September, 1928, the Plenum of the League of Nations adopted this resolution, while the Latvian foreign minister once more drew attention to the interruption of railway travel between Poland and Lithuania. The Council in its December 14, 1928, resolution directed the consultative and technical communications and transit commission to concern itself with the freedom of communications and transit. The Commission formed a subcommission, comprised of two sections (economic and juridical), and in September, 1930, suggested that the Lentvaris-Kaišiadorys railroad line be opened to international communications. The Lithuanian delegate, the then foreign minister, Dr. Dovas Zaunius, rejected this offer, especially the part which mentioned transit on the Lentvaris-Kaišiadorys railroad. Under the circumstances, the Council of the League of Nations, in its January 24, 1931, resolution, decided to ask the International Court of Justice at The Hague whether existing international promises under the present circumstances were binding on Lithuania, and, in the event of a positive answer, what provisions should be taken to open communications or the railroad line. The organs of the League of Nations, which had begun with the question of flotation of timber, now went into a different level, namely, the opening of a strip of railway closed until then because of the conflict with Poland and because of the nonexistence of diplomatic relations between the two countries.

On October 15, 1931, the Court reached the unanimous decision that existing international commitments were not binding on Lithuania under existing circumstances, and it did not have to take measures to open traffic or other categories of communications. The decision was a great victory for Lithuania. As a result, the right not to establish relations with Poland was recognized. The decision strengthened Lithuania's position vis-a-vis Poland.

By the same token, it confirmed Lithuania's moral international situation and destroyed the machinations of Poland's friends in the League to force Lithuania to establish relations with Warsaw. Vaclovas Sidzikauskas, who defended Lithuania's position at the Hague Court, declared: "The absence of any relations with Poland is considered by Lithuania to be the highest protest against injustice, whose victim Lithuania is." The decision of the Hague Court justified Lithuania's position.

At this time, the 1930's, conditions in Eastern Europe took a turn for the worse. In Germany revanchist nationalist tendencies grew. These tendencies, later taken over by the National Socialist movement, came to be a threat to both Lithuania and Poland. Under the circumstances, Lithuanian circles began to realize that some sort of *modus vivendi* must be found with Poland. A number of private soundings were made, and in the summer of 1935 Lithuanian Foreign Minister Stasys Lozoraitis met *incognito* in Geneva with Polish Foreign Minister Jozef Beck. These moves, however, did not produce any new prospects. Poland was ruled by the Pilsudskite regime, led by a colonels' clique which pursued a policy of *Grossmacht*. This group for a while cooperated very closely with Nazi Germany. It did not seem possible to straighten out matters with Poland. Both states exchanged newspaper correspondents, yet, nothing essential changed. The only difference was in the psychological mood. "The blind wall" between Lithuania and Poland was not as hermetical as previously.

Then occurred a major incident on March 7, 1938. A Lithuanian guard shot a Polish soldier who had been sneaking across the border, believing that the Pole was a smuggler. In spite of medical assistance, the soldier died after a few hours. Appropriate official Lithuanian organs made an inquiry, and the incident was considered closed. However, it soon became apparent that the Polish Government wanted to exploit the incident. The Polish press exaggerated the facts and threatened Lithuania. The Poles began to organize provocative demonstrations which demanded that there be a "march on Kaunas."

The purpose of this artificial clamor soon became known when, on March 17, the Lithuanian Minister in Tallinn, Estonia, received an ultimatum which demanded that Lithuania establish diplomatic relations with Poland. Lithuania had until March 31 to set up railroad, highway, telegraph and telephone communica' tions with Poland, and to exchange diplomatic representatives. The ultimatum had to be answered in forty-eight hours.

The Lithuanian Government accepted the ultimatum, declar' ing that it was not bowing to law but to force. On March 30, 1938, an agreement was signed at Augustavas renewing commu' nications between the two states. On the following day the Polish diplomatic representative arrived in Kaunas. The Lithuanian rep' resentative to Warsaw was Colonel Kazys Škirpa who had been a permanent delegate to the League of Nations. After eighteen years, diplomatic relations were established between Poland and Lithuania. It was, however, a result of Polish force, as was the long state of war which had existed until then. As that conflict was not settled, this did not provide for the creation of mutual understanding. Dr. Antanas Trimakas was appointed Lithuanian Consul General in Vilnius.

FORM OF GOVERNMENT

During the World War I German occupation, the State Council began to deliberate the legal foundations of the emerging postwar state. The monarchical form of government was foisted upon the Council by the German authorities, who would not per' mit any other order. When the revolutionary movement gained momentum in Germany, and the founders of the Lithuanian state freed themselves from the pressures of Berlin, the State Council, on November 2, 1918, unanimously revoked its decision of June 4, 1918, whereby the Prince of Wuerttemberg Urach had been elected king of Lithuania.

It was quite natural that when foreign pressures were allevi' ated, the Council chose a republican form of government. This decision was influenced by the spirit of the times. It was also un' derstandable that Lithuania, having declared her independence on the basis of the democratic idea of national self-determination, would choose a democratic foundation for her state organization. As a third principle, the founders of the Lithuanian republic chose the parliamentary system of government which was copied

186

after the continental, or French form, of parliamentarianism. The legislative branch of government was to have the dominant powers in the relationship between the executive and lawmaking bodies. The choice of parliamentarianism was in a way a reaction against the former autocratic regimes of the Russian, German and Austro-Hungarian empires. The Lithuanians also rejected the Soviet dictatorship emerging in Russia.

Revoking the decision to invite a monarch to the throne of Lithuania, the State Council, on November 2, 1918, passed the "The Basic Law of the Provisional Constitution of the Lithuanian State" (Lietuvos Valstybės laikinosios konstitucijos pagrindiniai dėsniai), which determined the functions of the highest state organs. These were the State Council and the Presidium of the State Council, with a cabinet of ministers. The State Council was given the power of legislation, while the Presidium of the Council became the executive body, which set up a cabinet of ministers responsible to the State Council. Until the election of the State President, his functions were to be performed by the Presidium, comprised of the chairman and two vice-chairmen. A collective institution of the state executive was set up, based on the parliamentary system, which was later more clearly defined. In addition, according to this provisional constitution, the provisional government was to pass a law for the election of the Constituent Assembly (Steigiamasis Seimas). The calling of the Constituent Assembly was uppermost in the political thinking of the day.

The President of the Presidium of the Council was Antanas Smetona. His two vice-presidents were Rev. Justinas Staugaitis and Stasys Šilingas. This system soon proved impractical. On April 4, 1919, the system was changed and Antanas Smetona was elected the first State President. (At the end of 1918 when the Bolsheviks and Poles were moving on Vilnius, there was talk of concentrating the state power in the hands of a dictator at this critical moment. This suggestion was rejected.)

The State Council, which had been formed during the German occupation, lived through several crises. The first arose over the election of Urach as king of Lithuania. Because of it the Council split, but was later reunited on the common principle of the February 16th Act. The Council itself was dominated by the conservative element. Refugees returning from Russia brought back radical, revolutionary ideas. When the leftists pulled out of the Council they were replaced by new members, also back home from Russia. The left wing of the Council was weakened. For this reason, there was criticism that the Council did not represent the entire nation. Under these circumstances, it was decided to strengthen ties with the public at large and to call a conference before the convocation of the Constituent Assembly, to be attended by all leaders. This conference met in Kaunas at the beginning of 1919. Reports were made about the situation in the country and about the work of the Council and its provisional government. The question of the Constituent Assembly was discussed and the question of land reform was raised.

Just before the Kaunas conference, there was a change in government. Professor Voldemaras, the first prime minister and foreign minister, had announced optimistic views to the effect that no one would hinder a peaceful Lithuania. Voldemaras placed his hopes on the victorious Western allies, and expressed the opinion that the fate of Lithuania would be decided at the negotiation tables of the Paris Peace Conference. For this reason, he hurried to the West to defend Lithuania's interests.

In the meantime, the young Lithuanian state was threatened with mortal danger by revolutionary Russia and Poland, which sought to revive the old union. With the absence of both the prime minister and the president of state, who was in Berlin negotiating a large loan from the Germans, new factors and new people emerged. In the face of danger, during the last days of 1918, a new government was formed in Vilnius, headed by Mykolas Sleževičius. He formed a coalition cabinet. It included three Social-Democrats (Mykolas Biržiška, Augustinas Janulaitis, Juozas Paknys), two Socialist Populists (Mykolas Sleževičius, Jonas Vileišis), two Christian Democrats (Voldemaras Čarneckis, Aleksandras Stulginskis), one Santarininkas (Petras Leonas), one Jewish representative (Jokubas Vygodskis), one Byelorussian Socialist (Juozas Voronko), one representative of the Nation's Progress (Juozas Tūbelis) and three independents (Mykolas Velykis, Jonas Šimoliūnas, Jonas Šimkus).

In its declaration, the new government outlined its plans as follows:

> The most important task of the provisional government is to lead the country to the Constituent Assembly, which will determine Lithuania's form of government and will promulgate a number of social reforms. "In the first instance we are faced with the problem of land reform and the protection of the workers. [From this declaration one could see that the government caught the pulse of the country and understood what the country wanted.] The German occupational authorities, declared the government, were disorganized, while "from the East a new invader, the Russian, is forcing his way into our country." "We will defend ourselves from anarchy, by constructing the state on democratic foundations. We will organize an army to defend the borders of Lithuania.
>
> The provisional government will use all means to support our demands at the Peace Conference and will demand the unification of all Lithuanian lands with the capital Vilnius and with an exit to the sea.

In addition to the State Council, which declared the restoration of Lithuania and which formed the first government, a new element took the initiative. This new element was political parties. Even though the State Council had representatives of political parties, their participation in this institution was of an academic nature. The political leaders returning from Russia were men of party convictions, and they introduced a new dynamism into the Lithuanian state. They introduced a careful formulation of problems, but they also brought with them factional particularism which had an effect on the country's political evolution.

The government considered as its immediate goal the gathering of volunteers and the formation of an army. Its appeals met with positive response. The young Lithuanian Army soon went to battle the foreign enemies.

At the same time, the creation and perfection of a state apparatus was undertaken with great energy and speed. The government was forced to evacuate Vilnius and set up a provisional capital in Kaunas because of the invasion of the Red Army and Polish forces. Recruits were called to the colors, a mobilization

189

of officers took place. A military school was established to train cadres. Laws regarding citizenship, the establishment of local administrations and county apparatus and the creation of a court system were promulgated. County doctors were appointed. A health service was set up. The new state had to quickly organize all spheres of public life. The structure of the State Council was too complex; therefore, on January 24, 1919, the Provisional Constitution was amended and the cabinet of ministers was authorized to promulgate laws between the sessions of the State Council, which had to be ratified by the succeeding session of the State Council. Among the many laws promulgated were decrees dealing with tariffs, taxes, a detailed law on cooperatives, etc. The cooperative was to assume an important role in the economic life of the country. Russian money was taken out of circulation, and the acceptance of Russian currency was prohibited. German *marks* remained in circulation. In the summer of 1919, the first internal loan of 30 million auksinas (*marks*) was floated and a State Savings Depository Law was promulgated. A great deal of attention was paid to the creation of a network of schools. It is interesting to note that one of the first laws passed by the State Council (December 5, 1918) dealt with the creation of the Vilnius University. This law declared the newly established university to be the successor to the Vilnius University, closed by the Russians in 1832. When the Poles seized Vilnius, the first university of Independent Lithuania began its existence in 1922 in Kaunas. From this condensed list we can see that the State Council had a gigantic task to perform during the first year of independence. The State Council also had to defend the new state on several fronts from external enemies.

Establishment of the new state took place under trying conditions. Lithuania was in a poorer situation than most states which emerged after the first World War. Lithuania was deprived of its capital. The state had to be coordinated from Kaunas, which became the provisional capital but which was not prepared at the time to assume such a role. The city lacked appropriate buildings. During Czarist times, the city did not have water pipelines and lacked a sewage system; transportation was primitive (horse-drawn tramways). All of these shortcomings were surmounted

190

during this period. Nevertheless, during the first years of inde- pendence much energy and material had to be expended to catch up to the level of other new states. Construction was undertaken by young people, men and women, who compensated for their lack of experience by their enthusiasm and hard work.

The general mood prevailing in Lithuania can be drawn from the following: At the end of 1919, the treasury was empty and neither the army nor the civil servants had received their wages for close to four months. In the words of Martynas Yčas, who was finance minister at the time, "In spite of the fact that they were not paid, they did not desert their offices, they did not leave the army. On the contrary, they experienced great patriotism, suffered patiently and performed their duties with great sacrifice and conscientiousness . . . [they] are working not so much for money as from a sense of duty to their nation."

In March 1919, a government crisis developed and the new Christian Democratic Prime Minister, professor Pranas Dovy- daitis, formed a rightist coalition cabinet. This cabinet lasted for one month, after which Mykolas Sleževičius again took up the portfolio of prime minister. He formed a cabinet based on a wider coalition. Applying his method of "people's tribune," Sleževičius repeatedly appealed to the public, urging the people to help in the construction of the state. In the appeal of July 12, 1919, he declared: "The Germans have left our country. The time has come when the Lithuanian public will be able to demonstrate in its entirety its creative power. It must demonstrate to all that Lithuania does not need any guardians, that Lithuania on her own could maintain order and justice in the country. Now, when all means of communications—the railroads, the telephone, the telegraph—are in our hands and when there are no foreign forces in the interior which would hinder us in our work, we must utilize all energies in order to heal the wounds caused by war, in order to follow the example of cultural states and in order to establish law and justice."

The line set in the declaration was implemented by the hard- working prime minister and his government. The state apparatus was improved and new laws were passed, among them laws on the State Archeology Commission, high schools and teachers seminaries, scholarships, court-martials, commerce, etc. (According to the latter bill, internal commerce was to be free, and licenses were to be issued for exports and imports during the postwar period.)

On October 7, 1919, Ernestas Galvanauskas formed a new cabinet; he was the leader of a rightwing Christian Democratic and National Progress coalition. During this period, each cabinet had ministers for Jewish and Byelorussian affairs. (There was no minister for Polish affairs, which Sleževičius bemoaned in public during his first government.) Ernestas Galvanauskas was a new personality in the political arena. As a representative of radical democratic views while still a student, he participated in the Great Vilnius Assembly of 1905. He was active in the revolutionary movement of the time, having had to emigrate to study engineer-ing in Belgium. After the first World War, Galvanauskas par-ticipated in the Lithuanian delegation sent to the Paris Peace Conference. He later returned to Lithuania where he rose quickly. During the long period of emigration he had broken off relations with the homeland and did not really fit into any political party, though he was considered a follower of democratic views. For several years Galvanauskas played a key role in the foreign policy of Lithuania, being, in addition to prime minister, the foreign minister. For a while, he was communications minister, and later played an important role as finance minister.

Galvanauskas' first cabinet was at the helm of state from October 7, 1919, to June 19, 1920. While he headed the govern-ment, the country was still engaged in war with foreign enemies; except for the Polish front the enemies were pushed to the fron-tiers. The military situation in Lithuania began to stabilize. Gal-vanauskas' government continued the task of improving the governmental apparatus. First, the work of the several ministries was rationalized; three ministries were liquidated and their func-tions taken over by other ministries. The Supply and Food Min-istry was joined to the Ministry of Defense, the Commerce and Industries Ministry was joined to the Finance Ministry, and the Work and Social Security Ministry became part of the Ministry of the Interior. Until the convocation of the Constituent As-sembly the State Council performed the functions of a legislature.

192

It ratified a number of laws decreed during Galvanauskas' first cabinet. The Local Administration Law was an important piece of Galvanauskas' legislation, for it provided the legal basis for the established or emerging local governments. On November 30, 1919, a law was passed fixing the length of the work day to eight hours.

The most important work of the 1919-20 period was the preparation for the Constituent Assembly and land reform. The Declaration of Independence specifically called for a Constituent Assembly; according to the declaration, it was to be "called as soon as possible" and "elected by all inhabitants by democratic means." Since the territory of Lithuania had not yet been cleared of foreign enemies, elections were not possible. Nevertheless, during the independence wars preparatory work was carried on. On September 30, 1919, the State Council passed a comprehensive Constituent Assembly Electoral Law. The first article of this law stated: "The representatives to the Constituent Assembly of Lithuania are elected universally, by lawful, equal and secret ballot, safeguarding the proportional system." The voter's age was set at twenty-one years. There was to be one representative for every 15,000 inhabitants. The law provided that soldiers would receive a passive, not an active vote; however, just before the elections this provision was changed and the soldiers were given an active voting right. (Soldiers as young as seventeen years were given the franchise.)

At the same time a "Law to Protect Electoral Freedom" was promulgated. Laws providing for freedom of assembly and the press were passed. The state of siege was lifted. In this manner, all measures were taken to create free and unrestricted electoral conditions. The elections took place on April 14-15, 1920, without any untoward incidents. The Constituent Assembly was comprised of 112 deputies. The Christian Democratic Bloc received an absolute majority, receiving fifty-nine mandates; the other representatives were distributed as follows: Peasant Union and Socialist Populists' Bloc—28; Social-Democrats—12; independents—2; Jewish Minority—7; Poles—3; and Germans—1 representative.

The composition of the Constituent Assembly demonstrated

the political climate of the Lithuanian nation. The Christian Democratic Bloc, divided into three parts (Christian Democrats, Farmers Union and Labor Federation), emerged as the strongest political group and held for the next few years the dominant political position in the country. An important role in this Bloc was played by the Catholic clergy, many of which used their influence to sway the voters to the Christian Democratic Bloc. This caused a reaction in the opposition circles and press. Second place was taken by the Peasant Populist Union, as the coalition of Peasant Union and Socialist Populist Democratic Party came to be known in 1922, after it discarded the "socialist" label. In reality, it was never a socialist party. The populists were left-of-center liberals. The Peasant Populists were representatives of the liberal elements of the villages and cities. The third position was taken by the Social-Democratic Party. The National Progress Party, whose most prominent representative was Antanas Smetona, Chairman of the State Council and the first President of the Republic, and which had the first prime minister, Augustinas Voldemaras, did not return a single deputy to the Constituent Assembly. (Santara, which had many intellectuals, experienced the same fate.) The National Progress Party was later reorganized into the Tautininkai Union (i.e., Nationalist Union). The Santarininkai merged with the Farmers Party.

A second task which the State Council and government had to perform was to pave the way for land reform. Volunteer soldiers were promised land. In order to implement this promise, a number of laws were passed. On June 20, 1919, a special "Law to Provide Soldiers with Land" was promulgated. Its first article read: "Lithuanian soldiers, citizens, landless ones and smallholders, who volunteered or who answered the Lithuanian Government's appeal and joined the Lithuanian Army to defend Lithuania's independence, and while defending her from enemies, were not court-martialed and who served with distinction until the end of the war and until demobilization, have the first priority to receive land from the state."

On January 8, 1920, the government passed "Regulations for the Work of the Land Reform Commission." According to these regulations the commission was being formed under the aegis of the Ministry of Agriculture and State Resources. "The duty of the Land Reform Commission is to collect and organize materials, necessary for the Constituent Assembly to make a decision on the question of land reform in Lithuania, and to prepare a project of the land reform law."

Even during the wars against the foreign aggressors, the government did not forget cultural matters. In the first place, the government was concerned with the creation of a network of schools and their functioning. The establishment of primary schools was undertaken with great energy. The number of secondary and higher schools was also increased. The first gymnasia offering courses in Lithuanian had been created during the first World War. With the restoration of independence and after the foreign invasions were repulsed, the creation of high schools was resumed with intensity. On August 22, 1919, two important laws were passed, namely the law on higher general education schools (junior high schools and gymnasia) and the law on teachers' seminaries. The law on higher schools stated that schools could be established not only by the state, but also by civic organizations and individuals. Public organizations received aid from the state. On December 20, 1919, the government passed a decree on "the Central State Library." The decree spelled out its purpose to concern itself with getting at least one copy of all old books printed in Lithuania and at least four copies of every new book being published in Lithuania; to collect scientific and other books published abroad; to take over the old archives of the Russian State libraries in Lithuania; to register and preserve private collections of book, left in Lithuania by absentee owners, and to compile a catalogue of all books in the libraries of Lithuania.

In January, 1920, higher courses were inaugurated in Kaunas. In 1922, these courses evolved into the first university of independent Lithuania. On December 31, 1920, an opera house was opened in Kaunas. In 1921, the theater began which grew into the State Theater. On January 27, 1920, regulations were passed to set up the State Archeology Commission. This Commission was authorized to handle all matters connected with the cataloguing of all archaeological monuments and their preservation. When the Lithuanian language became a state language, a number of terms were necessary, which did not exist or which were not in popular use. On March 14, 1922, a terminology commission was created under the aegis of the Ministry of Education. Its purpose was to form and standardize terminologies for the state administration and various scientific fields. The commission's works were published in the Education Ministry's periodical *Švietimo Darbas*.

A new step was begun in the life of the Lithuanian state when on May 15, 1920, the Constituent Assembly was convened. The period of parliamentary life was ushered in. (Until then, of course, the nation had been led by the State Council, which had passed the Act of February 16, 1918, which declared Lithuania an independent state.)

The Constituent Assembly, meeting on May 15, 1920, was presided over during its first meeting by the oldest deputy, the writer Miss Gabrielė Petkevičaitė. The Assembly chose as its chairman Aleksandras Stulginskis, who also replaced Antanas Smetona as President of the Republic. Stulginskis remained the President for six years because the Christian Democratic bloc held the parliamentary majority during that period.

The Constituent Assembly ratified the Declaration of Independence: "The Constituent Assembly of Lithuania, expressing the will of the people of Lithuania, proclaims the restored independent Lithuanian State, as a democratic republic, with ethnographic boundaries and free of any state ties which had previously bound it with other states."

One of the most important tasks of the Constituent Assembly was the drafting and ratification of the state constitution. Since this task required long and careful preparation, the Constituent Assembly, on June 10, adopted an eighteen-article "Provisional Lithuanian State Constitution," which briefly enumerated the functions and relations of the state organs. The first article confirmed that "the Lithuanian State is a democratic republic." As was the case with the provisional constitution of the State Council, the Assembly's provisional fundamental law introduced the parliamentary system, declaring that the government rested on the confidence of the Constituent Assembly. The election of the President of the Republic was within the competence of the Constituent Assembly, until his election his duties were to be assumed by the Chairman of the Assembly. (This situation existed through-out the entire period of the Constituent Assembly.) All citizens of Lithuania, regardless of sex, nationality or religion, were declared to have equal rights before the law; all orders and titles were abolished. The final drafting of the constitution was to take some time.

During the summer of 1920, a peace treaty was signed with Soviet Russia; the Lithuanian Army marched into Vilnius. In September, 1920, Lithuanian state agencies began to move into the capital. However, not long after, on October 9th, the Polish army led by the "mutineer" General Zeligowski again seized Vilnius and military engagements were fought with the Poles. The fate of Lithuania hung in balance. These events had an effect on the Constituent Assembly. It terminated its meetings; a number of deputies went to the front. On October 25, 1920, a law was passed setting up the "Small Seimas" which included the Chairman of the Constituent Assembly and six members. The Small Seimas was authorized to perform the duties of the Constituent Assembly; that is, to pass laws and review the work of the executive organs.

Although the Christian Democratic Bloc had the majority in the constituent body, it was agreed to form a coalition govern-ment, which was formed by a Peasant Populist leader Dr. Kazys Grinius. The cabinet was formed on June 19, 1920. The former premier, Ernestas Galvanauskas, remained as minister of finance and as the communications minister. Dr. Juozas Purickis took over the functions of foreign minister. Dr. Grinius' cabinet continued until January 1922, when the Christian Democratic-Peasant Pop-ulist coalition fell apart. On February 2, 1922, Ernestas Galva-nauskas formed a new cabinet. Dr. Vladas Jurgutis took the foreign minister's portfolio.

After repulsing the Polish invasion, though Vilnius remained in Polish hands until World War Two, the Constituent Assembly renewed its work and promulgated many important laws. Kaunas once again became the administrative center of the state and was considered the provisional capital. It quickly grew into a modern city, its construction expanding so rapidly that the provisional

197

capital became a peculiar mixture of old and new structures, a cross between a modern city and a provincial town.

Editing and polishing of the Constitution took over two years of work. The Constitution was passed on August 1, 1922, and announced in the August 6, 1922, issue of *Vyriausybės Žinios,* the state gazette. It was a comprehensive document of 108 articles, containing the dominant democratic ideas of the continent at that time. The first article declared that the "government of the sovereign state belonged to the nation." Article 14 defined the rights of citizens (equality before the law, inviolability of person and property, freedom of religion and conscience, freedom of correspondence, word and press, etc.). The right to property was defended. Citizens received the right to submit petitions and propose legislation. Legislation was delegated to the Seimas (Diet) which was elected every three years by universal, equal and direct suffrage. The government consisted of the President of the Republic and the Cabinet of Ministers. The President of the Republic was chosen for three years by the Seimas and could be removed from office by two-thirds majority vote in the Seimas; he could not be elected for more than two terms. The President of the Republic, according to the constitution, "invites" the Prime Minister and authorizes him to form a cabinet of ministers. The President confirms the cabinet and can receive its abdication. All acts of the President of the Republic must be countersigned by the appropriate minister. The President has the right to send a law passed by the Seimas back to that body; but his veto power is not absolute. When the absolute majority of the Seimas passes a law, the President must promulgate it. The President of the Republic can dissolve the Seimas, in which case new elections must be held within 60 days; when the new Seimas meets, the President must be reelected. According to the Constitution, the President is the chief of all armed forces. The Cabinet of Ministers is responsible to the Seimas and must resign if the Seimas declares nonconfidence. The Constitution guarantees national minorities the right to handle the cultural affairs of the group. The freedom of religion is also guaranteed.

In a word, the Constitution adopted by the Constituent Assembly introduced a continental type of parliamentary regime, in vogue after World War I. The Constitution in its adopted form was still not democratic enough to the center and socialist parties, but was passed by the Christian Democratic Bloc which had the necessary majority. This fact was characteristic of the mood of the times. The leftwing and center parties felt that the civil rights guaranteed by the Constitution did not protect the citizen enough and that the government, especially the President of the Republic, had too many powers.

Shortly before the Constitution was adopted the Constituent Assembly promulgated the Seimas Election Law (July 19, 1922). The right to vote was given to all citizens over the age of twenty-one. Candidates to the Seimas had to be over twenty-four years of age. Also, after promulgating the constitution, the Constituent Assembly passed an amnesty act for all prisoners, including political prisoners. Having adopted the Constitution, the Assembly felt that it had accomplished its most important task and dissolved itself after setting October 10-11, 1922 as election day to the first Seimas.

The second most important task which the Constituent Assembly had to perform was the adoption of land reform. The agrarian question was an old one in Lithuania. The Russian government did not take radical measures to solve the land problem before the war. The question had complex economic, social, national and political aspects. Although agriculture was the occupation of three-fourths of the population, production was rather meager, and agricultural methods were primitive, to say the least. Apart from a few progressive districts, the majority of people lived in villages, the land was divided into strips. Various grains and flax were grown; horses were also bred. Yet, the productivity of the land was not very high. Radical measures had to be taken not only to increase productivity, but also to improve agricultural methods.

On the other hand, the land question also had social, national and political aspects. As statistics show, half of the arable land belonged to large estates. The majority of landowners were non-Lithuanians or Polonized natives, who had lost touch with the indigenous peasants. From a national point of view, there was a huge gap between the estate and village—and even profound antagonism. For these reasons, since the very start of the national renaissance the land reform question was discussed in the sense that the land had to fall into the hands of the native Lithuanians. At the same time, social issues arose. The village proletariat and the small-holders had to be satisfied. The so-called land famine was acutely felt.

Therefore, when the Lithuanian state was being set up, the land reform question had matured and the public wanted solutions. Political motives also came into play. The land question in Russia at the time was being solved by revolutionary means. In 1918-1919, the Bolsheviks invaded Lithuania and propagated agrarian revolution. They started to implement the land revolution in the areas that they seized. During the war, many estates were left without owners, because they had evacuated Lithuania. Some of them were opposed to the national interests and political aspirations of the Lithuanians. Some of them actively joined the enemies of the Lithuanian state. On the other hand, the Lithuanian authorities, wishing to enroll volunteers in the newly created army, offered land first to the volunteers and then to other soldiers. During the first months of independence, a number of decrees were passed which were an introduction to the land reform.

However, the actual drafting of the land reform law was left to the Constituent Assembly. On August 14, 1920, the "Introductory Land Reform Law" was promulgated. It was called the "Small Land Reform." According to this law, forests and timber stands of over sixty-seven acres were nationalized; swamps and peatbogs, rivers and lakes, natural resources and mineral water sources were also nationalized. Entailed estates, the Russian Czar's personal gifts, and the property of the former Russian state were nationalized without any compensation. Estates given to absentee landlords by the Russian government were also nationalized. In addition to legislative norms, the practical aspects of the reform were also worked upon.

After many heated debates the Constituent Assembly on February 15, 1922, passed the land reform law on the eve of the Independence Holiday. This legislation, consisting of seventy-seven articles, was one of the major laws passed by the young republic; it laid the legal foundations for all subsequent land reform measures. This monumental law was a manifestation of the dictate of the Lithuanian nation's evolution and also a consequence of postwar needs in Eastern Europe. Lithuania, like her northern neighbors Estonia and Latvia, solved this economic and social problem by radical means.

The financial situation of the new republic was rather hard. Sufficient tax revenues could not be raised from the devastated country. There was a great shortage of all sorts of necessities. These goods could only be brought in from abroad, primarily from Germany, in return for local wares. According to available statistics, during the war 1,200 villages with 14,270 dwelling units were destroyed, and 2,000 homesteads and fifty towns were ruined. Altogether, 57,000 dwelling units were destroyed. At the same time, war operations still continued because of foreign invasions. The state treasury was at times completely empty during 1919. By the end of 1919 the state lacked the wherewithal to pay its army and civil service.

During these trying times the inhabitants displayed a great deal of patriotism and solid determination to restore the economic life of the country. Within a short time, the war wounds were healed, and agriculture recovered and began to produce for the market. Foreign trade developed; it was not hard to find markets for agricultural products because of the shortages in Europe. Germany became Lithuania's chief customer.

In spite of the financial situation, the government did not use deficit measures; on the contrary, it followed the difficult but solvent course of saving and moderating government expenditures, a policy characteristic of the entire period of independence. Expenses were made in close conformity with available revenues. Even when the economy recovered, this policy was adhered to. By these means, the welfare of the country grew, not by spectacular leaps, but organically.

On August 16, 1922, a law was passed establishing a national currency. The law declared that "the money of the Republic of Lithuania will be based on gold." The monetary unit was the *litas,* worth 0.150462 grams of pure gold and divided into 100 *centai.* The American dollar was taken as the standard: The value of the *litas* was one-tenth of a U.S. dollar. In 1934, when the dollar was

201

devaluated, the value of the *litas* remained untouched and its value was equivalent to 0.693 dollars (one dollar was equal to about six litai). The new currency became effective on October 1, 1922, although the money was put into circulation on October 2. The existing currency was exchanged for *litai* until the end of 1922.

At the same time, the right to issue currency was given to the Bank of Lithuania (Lietuvos Bankas). On August 11, 1922, the Constituent Assembly passed a banking law which defined, among other things, the regulation of monetary circulation, the simplification payments at home and abroad, and the introduction of a stable monetary system to encourage agricultural, industrial and commercial growth. The stock of the Bank of Lithuania was capitalized at 12 million *litai;* most of the shares were owned by the government. In order to establish the Bank, permission was given to use the credit of the state gold fund. The Bank was given the right to issue banknotes for twenty years. No less than one-third of the banknotes issued were to be covered by gold, the remaining sum to be covered securities (based on gold). The Bank was permitted to buy state bonds and other state securities, but it could not obtain more shares than one-third of the value of its capital. Also, the Bank was authorized to handle state treasury and savings operations. The Bank President was appointed by the President of the Republic upon the recommendation of the Cabinet of Ministers. Coins were to be minted by the state treasury.

The introduction of a national currency was an important moment in the life of the Lithuanian state. Thanks to the foresight of the Bank of Lithuania and the state financial authorities, and the policy of thrift, the *litas* kept its value until the Communist occupation and was considered one of the most stable currencies of the world. No economic crisis could shake its base. Much larger financial powers were forced to devaluate. (On October 1, 1935, a control was set up to handle foreign drafts.) On December 31, 1931, the amount of litai in circulation reached 166 million *litai* in banknotes. At the same time, there was 40 million *litai* in silver and copper coin.

The Constituent Assembly also passed a number of other important laws dealing with the administration of the country, the economy and cultural fields. These laws strengthened still further the basis of the state.

THE QUESTION OF KLAIPEDA

At the same time that Lithuania lost Vilnius to Polish aggression, its position on another front weakened: attempts to join the Klaipėda-Memel district to Lithuania did not meet with success.

The Lithuanian delegation, unofficially attending the Paris Peace Conference, undertood action to reunite Lithuania Minor, part of Prussia, with Lithuania Proper. On March 24, 1919, the delegation submitted a memorandum to the members of the Entente calling for the revendication of Lithuania, which would include the incorporation of "Prusse orientale lithuanienne." When the revolution broke out in Germany, the Lithuanians of Lithuania Minor met at Tilsit, which was an old cultural center, and organized the National Council of Lithuanian Prussia. On November 30, they expressed the desire that the Lithuanian-inhabited districts be separated from Germany and reunited with Lithuania Proper. On various occasions the Prussian Lithuanians in various notes and resolutions raised the question of uniting both parts of the Lithuanian nation into one state.

The Lithuanians met with difficulties for two reasons: 1) the influential powers at the Paris Peace Conference did not have sufficient data on the actual situation, and 2) the Poles engaged in counteractivities. The Poles, of course, wanted to see the Lithuanians break away from Germany—they had designs of their own on all the Lithuanian lands.

Seeking to unite Lithuania Minor with Lithuania, the Lithuanians argued on the basis of national self-determination which had been enunciated in Wilson's Fourteen Points. In practice, it was difficult to define the ethnographic boundaries of the Lithuanian lands, because the process of Germanization over the years had made great inroads: The cities were Germanized to a great extent, although the villages retained their Lithuanian character.

203

Even the national consciousness of the Lithuanian-speaking peoples was often stifled.

The Paris Peace Conference took Lithuanian aspirations into consideration only to a degree, and detached from Germany the part of Lithuania Minor situated on the right bank of the Nemunas. This district received the name of the port of Klaipėda (in German: Memel). In this manner, a new geographic and political concept was created. In addition to ethnographic arguments, the Paris Peace Conference took into consideration economic arguments: the Lithuanian state was to be granted access to the sea.

According to Article 99 of the Versailles Treaty, the territory of Germany (Prussia), situated on the right bank of the Nemunas River, was to be detached. The provison itself stated:

> Germany renounces, in favor of the Principal Allied and Associated Powers, all rights and title over the Territories included between the Baltic Sea, the Northeastern frontier of East Prussia as defined in Article 28 of Part II of the present Treaty and the former frontier between Germany and Russia. Germany agrees to accept the settlement made by the Principal Allied and Associated Powers in regard to these territories, particularly in so far as concerns the nationality of the inhabitants.

When the German government tried to defend its position in the Klaipėda district, the Entente used the following argument to detach the District: "The allied and associated Powers refuse to admit that the cession of the Klaipėda region might be contrary to the principle of nationality. The region in question has always been Lithuanian, the majority of the population is Lithuanian in regard to origin and language; the fact that a large part of the city of Klaipėda itself is German would not justify the maintenance of all that region under German sovereignty, particularly in view of the fact that the port of Klaipėda is Lithuania's only exit to the sea. It has been decided that Klaipėda and the adjoining region be entrusted to the allied and associated Powers, because the status of the Lithuanian territory has not been determined as yet."

This note is characteristic. First, it shows that the Entente had utilized the information submitted by the Lithuanian delegation of the organizations of Prussian Lithuanians about the Lithuanianism of the inhabitants of the Klaipėda district. This permitted the separation of the district from Germany, to be based on the principle of nationality. On the other hand, the Entente did not hasten to turn the district over to Lithuania, because the status of the Lithuanian territory has not been yet determined. This shows that the Entente did not completely trust or accept the views of small nations like Lithuania. The later turn of events confirmed the premise that this district should be used as a means of pressure on Lithuania to make that country normalize relations with Poland.

The small district (it had only 140,000 inhabitants) became a political instrument by which Poland (and through it Poland's ally, France) tried to implement a grand plan against Germany, namely, that East Prussia was to be surrounded by Polish pincers. The so-called Polish Corridor separated East Prussia from Germany. The free port of Danzig was to fall under Polish influence —Lithuania with Klaipėda were to fall to Poland. East Prussia was to be separated from Germany and possibly joined to Poland.

In February, 1920, the German Army was withdrawn from Klaipėda, and the Entente gave France a mandate to govern the district. On February 15, the German Reich Commissar, Graf Lambsdorff, turned the district over to the French General Dominique Joseph Odry, who was chief of the Entente Military Commission. When General Odry arrived in Klaipėda on February 17 he appointed a six-man directory which administered the district. (He arrived in the port with a battalion of *Chasseurs alpins*.) In May, 1921, the Military Mission was recalled and the former prefect, Gabriel Jean Petisné, who had worked under the Military Commission, was appointed to head the Civilian Occupation Administration.

After Klaipėda was detached from Germany, the Prussian Lithuanian organizations moved from Tilsit to Klaipėda. On February 21, 1920, the National Council of Lithuanian Minor demanded that the Klaipėda district be joined to Lithuania. On March 20, 1920, a ceremonious meeting of the State Council took place in Kaunas during which the members of the National Council of Lithuania Minor were accepted as full-fledged members. This act symbolized the union of the two parts of the Lithuanian Nation into a single state. On November 11, 1921, the Constituent Assembly of Lithuania took the initiative and demanded that Klaipėda be united with Lithuania, declaring at the same time that the government would give full autonomy to the district.

The French occupational regime in Klaipėda lasted for three years. This regime was set up on the grounds that the international status of Lithuania had not yet been clarified. Thus, the regime was a means of coercing Lithuania into reaching an accord with France's ally Poland. Lithuania was being prodded to renounce the Vilnius area in order to get Klaipėda and to form a federation with Poland. Such, in effect, was the policy of the French occupational regime when the civilian Commissar Petisné took over.

It was obvious that autonomy would have to be granted because historical circumstances had created differences between the *Grosslittauer* and the *Kleinlittauer* of East Prussia. The Government and the Constituent Assembly on many occasions made this clear in public statements. The local Lithuanian patriots also worked in this direction. They also wanted local autonomy as a condition for union. On the other hand, it is not surprising that the German element sought to reunite the district with Germany. When circumstances showed that there was no chance for this, then the Germans wanted at least to keep the dominant position at any cost and to continue the Germanization of the area. As a transitional phase, they dreamed of setting up a *freistaat* on the model of Danzig, which might at a future date join with Germany.

There was an odd agreement of interests: the idea of "a free state" met with the approval of Germany's antagonists, the Poles, especially after it became clear to them that Lithuania would not be joined to Poland. The Poles wanted to establish themselves in Klaipėda by any means. The creation of a dwarf state, Klaipėda, would serve their interests. The Polish Consulate set up in Klaipėda began action in that direction, and found supporters among the timber interests in the port. French policy, personified in the ambitious Commissar Petisné, began to identify itself with the idea of a free state.

As a result, there developed a peculiar situation: French and Polish interests in Klaipèda coincided with those of the Germans! All of these developments bode evil for the Lithuanian nation as well as the Lithuanians of Klaipèda: the French authorities sup' ported the German element, the Lithuanians, as in the days of the Kaiser, felt that they were second-class citizens in the District. The administration remained in the hands of the Pan-Germans. The Germanization of the local inhabitants continued, as before, through the schools and church.

In addition to the political intrigues, there were economic in' terests agitating in Klaipèda. The district, which used German *marks,* was drawn into the vortex of the inflation. The long, poorly guarded frontier with Lithuania, and the situation along the coast, facilitated smuggling. The government was forced to use harsh measures and to strengthen the border guard. An eco' nomic crisis developed in the district. Unemployment was on the rise. Pessimism prevailed.

At the same time, the political situation became strained. In the fall of 1922 an Entente commission was set up in Paris to study the situation in Klaipèda (Commission chargée d'étudier le statut de Memel). The commission was headed by the French diplomat Laroche. During the early days of November the rep' resentatives of the organizations and institutions of the Klaipèda District were invited to Paris, where they were questioned. The first question dealt with the eventuality of the "free state" and its consequences. The question of union with Lithuania was rele' gated to second place. The effect that the Polish-Lithuanian con' troversy over Vilnius would have on the District of Klaipèda, and the question of Polish participation in the administration of the port of Klaipèda were two important questions. The Klaipèda Lithuanians left the Paris meeting with the premonition that the Entente decision would not be favorable to them. The Lithuanians feared that the Entente would back the idea of a *freistaat.*

Under these conditions, the Lithuanians began to formulate the opinion that they themselves would have to resort to drastic measures. The idea arose to overthrow the German Directory and to take the local administration into their own hands. The Lithuanian authorities thus had to create a *fait accompli* and to take the district into their own hands as a guarantee that the Entente would make a decision in their favor, at the same time wrecking Polish and Pan-German plans to create a "free state." Giving its blessing and support to a planned uprising, the Lithuanian government had the example of the Zeligowski "mutiny" in Vilnius to go by. A secret plan was conceived to stage a revolt. The plans were drawn up by the chief of Lithuanian Military Intelligence, Jonas Polovinskas, who assumed leadership of the rebel forces. During this mission he called himself Jonas Budrys (this surname was used by him when he became the governor of the district and, still later, Consul General in New York).

At the same time, the parimilitary Šaulių Sąjunga, or Riflemen's Association, played an important role in the military preparations. Work was also undertaken in the civilian sector. A Supreme Committee to Help Lithuania Minor (Mažosios Lietuvos Vyriausias Gelbėjimo Komitetas) was set up under the chairmanship of the noted Prussian Lithuanian civic leader Martynas Jankus. On January 9, 1923, this Committee issued a manifesto in Šilutė, which among other things complained about the persecution of Lithuanians: "As a result of the Versailles Peace Treaty we were separated from Germany, as an old Lithuanian district. But even today we are oppressed by foreigners not only because we were born Lithuanians, but also because we want to remain as such. The rulers of our district, ignoring the needs of our land and opposing our desires, are working with full energy in order to make a *freistaat* of our land and to keep us enslaved."

The first four points of the manifesto were most significant:

1) As of this day, we take power in this district into our own hands and take over the government.

2) The Directory existing until now under Steputaitis and the Staatsrat is considered dismissed and removed, and no one has to obey their dictates.

3) As of this day, the Klaipėda Director will have a new chairman, an inhabitant of Klaipėda and a member of the former Directory, Erdmonas Simonaitis. He is authorized to form a new five-man directory within three days.

4) As of this day, both languages of our district will have equal rights.

The rebels took over Šilutė, Pagėgiai, Lauksargiai and other southern towns of the district without meeting with any resistance. Only the city of Klaipėda remained in the hands of its French garrison. The rebels issued an appeal to the French soldiers, declaring that the rebels would not fight against the French, but only against the Pan-Germans. Nonetheless, skirmishes took place with the French garrison, both sides suffering light casualties. On January 15, the city of Klaipėda was taken. The prefecture or office of the French civilian commissar was seized. Resistance was broken.

The military seizure of Klaipėda by the Lithuanians did not solve the problem. The severing of the Gordian knot had hurt the interests of several states so that they could not easily acquiesce in the fact of the revolt. The Polish government sent a warship to Klaipėda, but it was quickly recalled without incident. Germany maintained itself with relative calm, because it was involved with problems in the West: The Klaipėda events took place at the same time that the French Army was occupying the Ruhr District to force war reparations from the Germans. Also, economic life within Germany became rather chaotic.

As could be expected, the Entente nations presented Lithuania with notes of protest. The Lithuanian Government in its replies repeatedly argued that the revolt was not directed against the Entente, but was "directed only against the policies of the regime established by the Directorship, which, for three years, had governed the District of Klaipėda contrary to the best and most vital interests of the majority of its inhabitants." In its January 11th note, the government stated that it "does not intend to solve the Memel question by force." Both the Lithuanian Government and the Entente declared their desire to avoid larger complications (the Entente sent warships to Klaipėda—one English and two French ships, but they did not force an armed intervention), and began to prepare the ground for negotiations.

On January 17, the chairman of the Ambassadors Conference, Poincaré, informed the Lithuanians that the Conference was sending to Klaipėda an extraordinary commission. The Entente countries wanted to restore their authority. For this purpose, the Entente had to sacrifice the rebel directory, and to do this they asked the commission to form a new provisional government, which would represent the principal elements of the population. When authority and order was restored, the Entente could make a decision on the future of the Klaipėda district. Erdmonas Simonaitis, chairman of the rebel directory, in his January 17, 1923, note to the foreign ministers of France, Great Britain and Italy, once more showed that the revolt had a purpose in removing the German directory. Petisné was accused of being the cause of bloodshed when Klaipėda was taken.

On January 19, representatives of Lithuanian organizations met at Šilutė and passed a declaration. Its five points dealt with the most pressing questions of the day. The first point stated that "it had been unanimously decided for union with Lithuania while retaining the right of autonomy." Another point appealed to the Lithuanian Government asking it to "support by all means the expression of our territory's will, in the first place by military and financial assistance." The Lithuanian Seimas in its January 24th meeting took note of the Šilutė Declaration and confirmed the November 11, 1921, statement of the Constituent Assembly guaranteeing autonomy to the Klaipėda district. The government sent its special representative, Antanas Smetona, to Klaipėda. At the same time, the commission of the Ambassadors Conference, headed by the Frenchman Clinchant, arrived in Klaipėda. A provisional directory was set up in the district, headed by the native Lithuanian Viktoras Gailius, who had formerly been a member of the Diplomatic Service.

Satisfying the minimal conditions of the Entente, and having formally restored its authority, the Ambassadors Conference, on February 16, decided to relinquish the right given to it by the Versailles Peace Treaty in Klaipėda and to turn the district over to Lithuania. This decision reflected the reasons for having taken the territory away from Germany: "Because Klaipėda and the regions adjoining it were more closely linked to Lithuania—both ethnically and economically—than they were to Germany." It recognized that there were no obstacles to uniting the Klaipėda district with Lithuania, especially when the great powers recognized the Lithuanian republic *de jure* on December 20, 1922. The decision went on to state that, in view of the differences between Lithuania and Klaipėda, the latter should be given autonomy.

If these conditions were self-evident, then the Ambassadors Conference in its further deliberations, which dragged in the decision to transfer sovereignty, paid tribute to its recent policy of trying to force Lithuania to reach an agreement with Poland. The Conference in its decision sententiously requested that the administration of the port take into consideration the interests of both Lithuania and Poland. The decision stated furthermore that when Lithuania agreed to take over the sovereignty, a formal treaty would have to be signed in Paris for the administration of the district.

In its February 19th note, the Lithuanian government dourly reported that it was taking into view the decision of the Ambassadors Conference. Thus ended the first stage of Lithuania's efforts to unite Klaipėda with the Lithuanian state. Ahead lay the negotiations with the Entente; negotiations which were especially hard, for France was demanding that Poland be given special rights in the administration of the port. After the *freistaat* plans collapsed, the Poles tried to have a regime created during the negotiations that would give that nation a voice in the administration of the port, and as a consequence be able to exert pressure on Lithuania.

After some more efforts had failed to solve the Klaipėda problems on the Entente's terms, the Ambassadors Conference decided to appeal for intervention to the Council of the League of Nations, on the basis of Article 11 of the League's charter. The Council began its deliberations on December 15, 1923; on December 17 it authorized a three-man commission to study the question and to prepare a report for the following Council session. This commission was headed by Norman Davis, a former American Undersecretary of State.

The Commission traveled to Kaunas and Klaipėda; it also visited Warsaw. It decided to draw up a convention between the Allies and Lithuania, by which the sovereignty of Klaipėda would

211

be transferred to Lithuania. The autonomy of the District would be determined, the administration of the port of Klaipėda would set up, and the freedom of transit would be declared.

The commission, in its report to the Council of the League of Nations, decided that Lithuania was to receive the sovereignty of Klaipėda without any provisos.

The Allies turned the sovereignty of the Klaipėda district over to Lithuania, including the right to legislation, administration, courts, and financial autonomy within the bounds set by the "Statute for the Memel Territory" which was an added stipulation. The introduction declared that the purpose of autonomy was to "insure the traditional rights and culture of the inhabitants of the territory."

The district was to have a democratic parliamentarian regime. The legislature, elected through universal suffrage by equal and direct ballot, was to have autonomy in local legislation. The executive branch was to be comprised of the directory, which rested on the confidence of the Legislature. The president of the directory was to be appointed by the governor, who was to represent the central government and supervise the preservation of autonomy. The governor was to be appointed by the President of the Republic, and could call special sessions of the legislature; he enjoyed a limited veto power; upon agreement with the directory, the governor could dissolve the Legislature. All special privileges provided for by the proposal of the Ambassadors Conference were deleted. This could be considered a great victory for the Lithuanian government, for no mention was made of concession to the Poles.

According to the statute for Klaipėda prepared by the commission, the administration of the port was delegated to a Directory, composed of three members, one of whom was appointed by the Lithuanian government, the second by the Directory of the District, and the third by the chairman of the Consultative and Technical Communications and Transit Commission of the League of Nations. These appointments were to show the "international character" of the port of Klaipėda. The representative of the League of Nations was charged with the following task: "He shall give special attention to international economic interests served by the port and particularly to those of the districts for which the port of Memel is the natural outlet."

The third codicil to the statute defined questions of transit. The Lithuanian Government, in this instance, agreed to follow the Barcelona convention on freedom of transit (April 20, 1921): "transit by sea, by water and by rail . . . traffic coming from or destined for the Memel Territory or in transit through said Territory." It also declared that "the same freedom of transit shall also be ensured in respect of postal consignments and postal and telegraphic communications."

Unforeseen future complications were inherent in Article 17, which stated: "The High Contracting Parties declare that any member of the Council of the League of Nations shall be entitled to draw the attention of the Council to any infraction of the provisions of the present convention."

This provision was systematically employed against Lithuania the moment Germany was admitted into the League of Nations and became a permanent member of the Council. The Berlin government thus received an instrument by which it could create difficulties for Lithuania in the Klaipėda district. The Germans used every pretext to dramatize events in the district and to raise cases against Lithuania in the Council of the League of Nations. In this manner, Berlin became the protector of the Pan-German and nationalistic elements in Klaipėda who were disloyal to Lithuania. The Consulate General of the German Republic in Klaipėda became a secret central institution which protected, led and even incited the restless element and used it for German interests which aimed at overthrowing the limitations imposed by the Versailles Treaty and reannexing territories lost by Germany as a result of World War I.

POLITICAL TRIBULATIONS

On October 10-11, 1922, elections to the first Seimas took place. Of the 78 deputies elected, the Christian Democratic Bloc won thirty-eight seats, the Peasant Populist Union won twenty seats, the Social Democrats, ten, the pro-Communist "Work Companies," five, the Jewish minority, three, and the Polish minority, two.

213

From the first, difficulties developed, due to the absence of a parliamentary majority. Aleksandras Stulginskis was elected President of the Republic. The opposition, however, raised objections to the interpretation of the voting results. It was not easy to form a government. In February, Ernestas Galvanauskas was called upon to form a cabinet, but when a vote of confidence was taken in the Seimas, the votes were split down the middle. Under these circumstances, the Seimas was unproductive and in March, 1923, it was dissolved. This sudden dissolution did not help the prestige of this institution. New elections were called for May 12 and 13. This meant that the country had to experience the fever of electioneering once again after a very brief interval.

The elections to the second Seimas gave the Christian Democrats an absolute majority; but the margin was very slight; of the seventy-eight seats, the Bloc received forty. The Peasant Populists received sixteen and the Social Democrats eight. A greater change occurred in the representation of the national minorities. The Communist Workers Companies could not return candidates, and it is assumed that they gave their votes to some of the national minority representatives. The minorities had fourteen deputies in the second Seimas. At the beginning of June, the new Seimas reelected Aleksandras Stulginskis to the Presidency. Ernestas Galvanauskas formed a cabinet, keeping for himself, in addition to the premiership, the portfolio of foreign minister. The cabinet was comprised of Christian Democrats and Peasant Populists, a coalition that lasted for only a year, dissolving in June, 1924. From then on, the Seimas formed cabinets from Christian Democrats exclusively. However, although the Bloc had an absolute majority in the Seimas, during a comparatively short period of two years there were three governments: that of Antanas Tumėnas, Vytautas Petrulis and Dr. Leonas Bistras.

Although the coalition split up during the second Seimas, that body was able to pass important legislation. In spite of the difficult diplomatic battles which were being waged for the Klaipėda district, and in spite of international complications over Vilnius, which required the expenditure of great energy by the government, the nation was becoming stabilized. Land reform was tackled with great energy; two ministers of agriculture distin-

214

guished themselves during this period: Jonas Aleksa and Rev. Mykolas Krupavičius. (The latter was minister of agriculture in several cabinets.) Lithuania recovered from the ravages of the war; and in addition to land reform, efforts were made to improve agricultural methods and to adjust the economy to the require' ments of the world market.

Creative work was undertaken in various fields: roads were improved, bridges were built, a new railway line was begun unit' ing Klaipėda with the Lithuanian network. A great deal of atten' tion was paid to the expansion of the network of schools. At the end of 1922, a "Primary Schools Law" was passed making pri' mary education compulsory for children between the ages of seven and fourteen. In the 1923-24 period, the tax system was normalized, and three important laws were passed dealing with land tax—trade, industry, credit and crafts were taxed; there were also local taxes. Health protection was improved. A number of hospitals were established. After the introduction of a national currency, a number of central banks were set up, which lasted throughout the independence period. In addition to the Bank of Lithuania, which had the right of emission, an important role was played by the Land Bank set up in 1924 to extend credit to farmers. In that year, a tariff law comprising 216 articles was promulgated. The basis was laid for social legislation. The eight' hour day had been introduced earlier. Work and industrial in' spection laws were promulgated; their purpose was to "protect the life and health of hired laborers." In 1925, a stock company law was introduced. That same year, the Chamber of Trade and Industry was set up to improve and foster trade and industry. In May, 1926, a law setting up a social insurance administration was passed. This institution regulated and supervised social security and insurance matters. Also, a comprehensive Workmen's Com' pensation Law was passed. In this period also, an Academy of Ag' riculture was established, which trained agricultural specialists (a large number of its students were women); a Chamber of Agricul' ture Law was promulgated, entrusted with the improvement of agriculture and representing the professional interests of farmers; a state servants pension and welfare law was passed. At the same time, legislation established the institution of the state comptroller.

Although this institution had existed earlier, its functions were more clearly defined. The comptroller's office was to supervise state incomes, expenditures, loans and disbursements. A number of special agencies were established, such as the meteorological station, the natural research station, the central statistical bureau, the central state archieve, and other offices necessary to a modern state, modeled after the progressive states of Europe. To this end, a number of specialists had to be prepared; scholarships were given to study abroad and to specialize in those fields which the Lithuanian schools could not train.

However, in addition to positive developments, several negative manifestations occurred. During the second Seimas relations between the political parties became strained, causing tension in the country. The opposition accused the Christian Democratic Bloc of clericalism. Tensions developed because relations with the Vatican were not defined. The unresolved conflict with Poland over Vilnius also contributed to this strain. In the *concordat* with Poland, the Holy See recognized Vilnius as an ecclesiastical province of Poland. In April, 1926, the Vatican unilaterally created the Church province of Lithuania. This antagonized Lithuanian society, even the supporters of the Christian Democrats were angered. In the hostile atmosphere of ideological controversy, the second Seimas ended its term, and in May, 1926, elections to the third Seimas were held.

In the third Seimas the Christian Democratic Bloc lost its absolute majority, receiving only thirty out of the eighty-one seats. The Peasant Populist Union won twenty-two seats, the Social Democrats, fifteen, the national minorities, six. Three deputies came from the Klaipėda district, which was participating in the Seimas elections for the first time. This Seimas, also for the first time, returned three Nationalists (Tautininkai) and two deputies of the liberal Farmers Party. The elections, on the one hand, demonstrated a radicalization, because the Work Federation of the Christian Bloc lost seven seats which were seized by the Social Democrats. On the other hand, two new groups came to the Seimas, one of which—the Nationalists—was to play a major role in the life of the nation.

The country wanted a new political line and a new govern-

ment. Since the Christian Democratic Bloc had ideological differences with the Peasant Populist Union, a coalition between
these two groups was impossible. A coalition was thus formed between the Peasant Populists and Social Democrats; some national
minorities also supported this coalition. The new President of the
Republic was Dr. Kazys Grinius, a leader of the Peasant Populists. The cabinet was formed by Mykolas Sleževičius, also a
Peasant Populist leader. The Social Democrats received the ministries of the interior and of education. The behavior of these two
ministers soon precipitated sharp polemics and public indignation.

CREATION OF THE LITHUANIAN CHURCH PROVINCE

Although the vast majority of the Lithuanian nation professed
Roman Catholicism, the Lithuanians during their national renaissance of the nineteenth century experienced great hardships because of the pro-Polish tendency of a segment of the clergy. The
Catholic cleric in the course of history was the most ardent and
consistent Polonizing factor in the nation. When Lithuania regained its national consciousness, an unavoidable conflict between
the Polonizing clergy and patriots developed. Conversely, among
the clergy a national consciousness was also developing. These
were clergymen who not only sympathized with the aspirations
of the awakening nation, but who also joined the Lithuanian national movement and even assumed its leadership. The great bard
of the Lithuanian national renaissance, Maironis, was a priest.
One of the staunchest opponents of Russification in the nineteenth
century was Bishop Motiejus Valančius. One of the most prominent of Lithuanian poets was Bishop Antanas Baranauskas. At
the same time, when Lithuanian patriots appeared at the head of
the Church hierarchy of the bishoprics of Samogitia and Seinai,
the diocese of Vilnius fell into the hands of ardent Polonophiles.

This situation existed when, during the first World War, the
idea of Lithuanian statehood was realized in Vilnius. The activists
were interested in improving conditions for the Catholics. During
the war, the Bishop of Vilnius was deported by the Russians to
Russia. In August, 1917, a group of Lithuanian civic leaders submitted a memorandum, addressed to the Holy Father, through

the Papal Nuncio in Bavaria, Pacelli, detailing the situation in the diocese of Vilnius. The memorandum asked that the new bishop for Vilnius be a Lithuanian.

The State Council formed in 1917 worked in the same direction. The German administration was not opposed to the appointment of a Lithuanian bishop and for its part supported the Lithuanian efforts. In 1918, the general of the Marion Order, Jurgis Matulaitis, was appointed bishop of Vilnius. However, conditions for his national activities were rather difficult, as Vilnius was changing hands in the course of the wars for independence. Conditions became even worse when the Polish General Zeligowski seized Vilnius.

When the Lithuanian state was established and unofficial relations with the Vatican were set up, the government raised the question of the creation of the Lithuanian Church Province. Formally a large part of Lithuania belonged to the Archdiocese of Mohilev, while southern Lithuania was part of the Archdiocese of Warsaw. When the Poles seized Vilnius, the Lithuanian government was worried that the Vilnius diocese not be joined to Poland, and thus preferred to have the diocese administered directly by Rome. When the Vatican recognized the Vilnius area as part of the Polish Church province, the Lithuanian Government submitted a firm protest to the Holy See and recalled its representative. The Vatican retaliated in kind, and relations were severed. The recognition of Vilnius as part of the Polish Church Province caused a storm, and many Lithuanian voices were heard crying "Los von Rom!" After Poland signed the concordat with the Vatican, Bishop Matulaitis left his see. A fierce Polonizer was put in his place and during the period of the Polish occupation, the Church in Vilnius was engaged in an intensive Polonizing campaign.

On April 4, 1926, the Pope issued his *Lituanorum gente,* which created the Lithuanian Church Province; it was a unilateral move on the part of the Pope. The head of the new province was Archbishop Juozas Skvireckas. The territory of Lithuania was divided into five bishoprics: Kaunas, Vilkaviškis, Telšiai (with a prelature in Klaipėda), Panevėžys and Kaišiadorys. The Lithuanians, however, were not satisfied with this. On the contrary, the public showed its disapproval by not backing the Christian Democratic Bloc during the May, 1926, elections to the Seimas. The government fell into the hands of a leftwing coalition. The new government did not recognize the reorganization of the Church in Lithuania. In addition to ideological differences, their position was also swayed by the Vatican's behavior in the Vilnius controversy, that is, by the Vatican's recognition of Polish rights to the diocese.

COUP D'ETAT OF THE 17TH OF DECEMBER, 1926

The leftwing coalition formed by the Peasant Populists and the Social Democrats could not form a majority. Thus, the majority could only be formed with the help of the national minorities, a cooperation which had to be purchased by concessions. The Polish minority demanded national schools. The conflict over the Vilnius area set the public against the Poles. When the Social Democrat minister of education, professor Vincas Čepinskis, permitted them to open a number of Polish-speaking schools in the country, this action gave the opposition a reason to maintain that at this critical juncture in the country's history, the liberal regime was aiding and abetting the spread of Polonism in Lithuania. The public was incensed—the Poles were systemmatically closing Lithuanian schools in Vilnius and persecuting Lithuanian cultural leaders. The nationalistic student body and youth were aroused against the government's pro-Polish policy.

The new government refused to recognize the reorganization of the Church in the country, and did not want to pay salaries to the new Church dignitaries. Leftist circles began to discuss the question of separating the Church from the state, which incited the Catholic opposition. The Sleževičius government, in executing the leftwing coalition program, opened the door to civil rights which had been curtailed by the Christian Democratic governments. In the cities, especially in Kaunas, political meetings and marches were organized. The workers' professional unions demonstrated. Mass meetings were used by Communist agitators to incite the workers. During one parade in Kaunas an incident occurred which involved a well-known army officer while the demonstrators sang the *Internationale*. The opposition in the Sei-

219

mas made an interpelation which demonstrated the "Threat of Bolshevization." After this incident, the Catholic and Nationalist students tried to organize a demonstration without permission from the government. The participants were scattered by the police, a clash occurred, and the opposition expressed its dissatisfaction over the prejudice of the police. The minister of the interior, a Social Democrat, Vladas Požėla, became the target of sharp criticism. The government was accused of partiality to left-wing elements, to Kerenskyism.

During its brief existence, the government tried to retrench in various fields. An army reform was undertaken. This reform was associated with the name of the Chief of Staff, Colonel Kazys Škirpa. This officer who had recently completed the Belgian Military Academy was full of ideas; however, his schemes covered by the government met with opposition from the officers corps.

All of these events aroused opposition against the liberal regime. The opposition was led by the Christian Democrats and the Nationalists. The leaders of the Nationalists in the Seimas, Antanas Smetona and professor Augustinas Voldemaras, used their influence in the nationalistic opposition.

The government was preparing to celebrate the sixtieth birthday of President Grinius on December 17. During the night of December 16, a group of officers led by colonel Povilas Plechavičius staged a *coup d'état*. Important government buildings were occupied. The government was taken by surprise and could not organize any resistance. This 1926 *coup* took place without a single drop of blood being shed. The organizers of the *coup* planned to turn the government over to Antanas Smetona, the first President of the Republic and leader of the Nationalists. They tried to legalize the *coup* and follow constitutional patterns. After a brief parley, the Sleževičius government resigned and President Grinius called upon Voldemaras, one of the Nationalists leaders, to form a new cabinet. On December 17, a new government of Nationalists, Christian Democrats and members of the Farmers Party was formed. Professor Voldemaras became premier and foreign minister.

After confirming the new cabinet, President Grinius resigned. On December 19, a special meeting of the Seimas was held despite the absence of Peasant Populist and Social Democratic deputies. President Grinius' and Sleževičius' cabinet's resignations were acknowledged and Antanas Smetona was elected the new President of the Republic. The Seimas gave Voldemaras cabinet a vote of confidence. Thus, constitutional formalities were observed.

The December 17th *coup d'état* was a drastic turn in the life of the Lithuanian State. It ended the period of parliamentarianism, which had been introduced by the Constituent Assembly. The *coup* created a split in the society, which divided itself into irreconcilable factions. This situation lasted through the remainder of the independence period. The repercussions of the *coup* were even felt in the Lithuanian emigration. A new era was begun, ushering in an authoritarian regime. Lithuania, in other words, was following the between-wars trend in Eastern Europe.

THE BROADENING OF THE PRESIDENT'S POWERS

The new government showed in its declaration that its program foresaw a change in the state constitution and in the Seimas electoral law. It was to create conditions for a stable and strong government by means of these changes. Constitutional change became a topic of political discussion. Opinions were expressed that the powers of the executive branch should be strengthened, especially the powers of the head of state, and that the powers of the Seimas should be curbed. On the other hand, the leftist opposition, removed from the helm of government by the *coup d'état,* began to form secret committees "to defend the constitution."

At first, the government handled state matters in a formal manner in conformity with the norms of the existing constitution. The situation changed when the security organs arrested a member of the Peasant Populist faction of the Seimas. He was accused of conspiring against the government. The matter was submitted to the Seimas, as a result of which the Seimas voted a no-confidence to the government. The President reacted dissolving the Seimas on April 12, 1927. After the dissolution, however, new elections were not called for, which was not in keeping with the constitution. (In the act dissolving the Seimas was a clause which stated that "new Seimas elections will be called by a separate act.") The Christian Democratic Bloc and Peasant Party decided to withdraw from the government.

The President accepted the resignation of the cabinet and appointed a new one, keeping closely to the provisions of the constitution. He named as finance minister, Juozas Tūbelis, a well-known Tautininkas (Nationalist) and agronomist, who was destined to remain in the government a long time. The President continued to promulgate acts according to the provisions of the constitution. Later, however, he began to promulgate laws without even mentioning the constitution. After the *coup d'état* it was apparent that the regime intended to follow an independent course, yet this course was not determined for a while. Since the regime came into existence as a result of a military *coup*, the army was to become an important political factor. Though the President constantly reiterated the importance of the army in the life of the state, there were no tendencies among the army officers to take a direct hand in the affairs of state. The officers' group which organized the *coup* turned the government over to civilians, and reiterated their faith in Antanas Smetona. In speaking about the December 17th *coup* in one of his speeches, Smetona declared: "The President took it upon himself to reorganize the form of government along national lines. However, he was opposed to introducing a foreign state program or ideology into Lithuania. "The Lithuanians," he said, "must form their own system of government that is national, in other words, which comes from the life of the nation." The President, however, never clarified what he meant by "an indigenous form of government."

One thing was certain: the new regime would rest on the authority of the President of the Republic, and the principle of a strong and stable government would be introduced. After dissolving the Seimas, Smetona turned to the nation in 1927, declaring his political goals: "A strong government will exist when the president is elected not by the parties of the Seimas, but by the whole country, and when the president will have more power than he has under the present constitution." All of these tendencies became clear when, on May 25, 1928, a new Constitution was

222

promulgated. In the preamble, it was stated that the Constitution was being promulgated "by the President of the Republic with the approval of the Cabinet of Ministers." The decision on the new Constitution was made on May 15, "the holiday of the army." This was a hint of new trends.

The new Constitution placed the President of the Republic as the central organ of the state. His election was taken out of the hands of the Seimas and turned over to "special electors of the nation." He was to be elected for seven years and could be reelected. He designated the government and was empowered to dissolve the Seimas. In the absence of a Seimas, he could promulgate laws. The rights of the Seimas were curbed: It still had the legislative function, but it no longer had a basic right of parliamentary regimes; it could no longer practice closure. The government was freed from parliamentary restrictions. The Seimas could "oversee" the work of the government and ask "questions and interpellate." Since the following Seimas was elected in 1936, the President of the Republic had in his hands not only the executive, but also the legislative powers. He was even called the Leader of the Nation or State.

It is difficult to place President Smetona's regime in any specific framework. On the one hand, he had accepted the idea of being the "leader of the nation" as his vocation; this idea was realized in both constitutions that were promulgated during his administration, which gave the President many powers. On the other hand, his regime did not go as far as fascism or nationalsocialism. Smetona, in his many speeches and published writings, advocated the idea of concensus and unity, by pursuing an indigenous path of government which followed a more or less pragmatic line. The nation was advised to trust in the wisdom of an autoritarian leadership. The President himself identified his prior activities with liberalism and with the writings of the Greek philosopher Plato (which he had translated into Lithuanian). The ideas of the writings of Smetona had an influence on his ideology and on his regime.

PROFESSOR VOLDEMARAS' DISMISSAL AND TUBELIS' APPOINTMENT

President Smetona's moderate policies began to clash with the line of Prime Minister Voldemaras. At the start of the new regime a sort of Smetona-Voldemaras duumvirate reigned, but as time went by, their views and methods of government began to differ. Voldemaras was a proponent of sterner policies, he was prone to dictatorial methods. As a result, a sharp cleavage of views developed between the President and the Prime Minister. In September, 1929, Smetona dismissed Voldemaras from the post of prime minister and called upon Finance Minister Juozas Tūbelis to form a new cabinet. Mr. Tūbelis stayed at the head of government until 1938. Dr. Dovas Zaunius, a native of Lithuania Minor, was designated foreign minister.

With the change of government, a slackening took place, for a new manner was introduced into the government by the new Premier. Juozas Tūbelis was an accomplished economist and one of the original organizers of the cooperative movement. He was a sort of antithesis to his predecessor, who had focused most of his attention on foreign policy and diplomatic matters. Juozas Tūbelis did not seek personal glory. He had a sober view of state problems, devoting his attention to the economic and internal problems of the country, governing as a proprietor. He kept the finance minister's portfolio as well as that of premier. His first concern was financial equilibrium. While he was the head of government, Lithuania experienced progress, in spite of the international economic crisis which also touched Lithuania. The President of the Republic valued the services of this close collaborator. They cooperated sincerely during the 1929-38 period. On the other hand, Tūbelis' extra-careful policies, according to critics, did not facilitate rapid economic development. As finance minister, he did not bring about any spectacular victories in this transitional period. In short, Antanas Smetona and Juozas Tūbelis formed a patriarchical regime, wherein the Prime Minister put into practice the ideas of the President of the Republic.

As a result of the ouster of Voldemaras, a split took place in the ranks of the Tautininkai. The leaders of the Tautininkai Union remained loyal to Smetona, while the less numerous followers of Voldemaras showed great persistence and often caused the regime headaches by trying to restore their leader to the helm of state.

The 1928 Constitution introduced a new institution—the

Council of State, entrusted with the preparation and codification of laws.

With the introduction of the new Constitution, on December 11, 1931 Antanas Smetona was reelected for seven years as President of the Republic. According to the new Constitution, an electoral college was set up, which also chose municipal and county councils.

During Tūbelis' administration the government concentrated its energy, first of all, on economic matters and on the improvement of living standards. Bearing in mind that agriculture was the chief occupation of the majority of the citizens, the government devoted a great deal of attention to modernizing farming methods and to increasing production. During this period, a great deal of work was devoted to the amelioration of conditions, to the raising of the educational level of the country, to the establishment of a network of special schools, and to the proliferation of the press and similar projects. "The Young Farmers Circles" exerted a positive influence on village youth, because they fostered new agricultural methods and encouraged innovations in farming. Since the regime pursued a regulatory policy, a law "to regulate agriculture" was passed, the object being to influence careless and unproductive farmers. A village construction law was also passed. The question of creating "mason-work villages," i.e., of propagating the construction of brick dwellings, was discussed. Detailed regulations on seed improvement and control were passed. Attention was devoted to the improvement of animal stockbreeding and to the elimination of animal diseases; a cattle tuberculosis fund was created.

Similar measures were applied to social security. During the same period, legislation accounted for a new industrial workers hiring law, improved industrial health and safety regulations, and accident insurance laws and social welfare for injured agrarian workers. Hospitalization provisions were improved with the passage of a comprehensive hospital fund law, a special village health improvement law was passed and a new hospital law was promulgated to regulate public hospitals.

A 1935 law established the Chamber of Labor whose purpose was to safeguard the cultural, economic and social matters of hired workers and laborers in the fields of industry, commerce, construction and transportation. In this manner, in addition to the state-sponsored Chamber of Agriculture and Chamber of Commerce and Industry, a new chamber was set up to represent and protect the interests of the workers and laborers. Since the country lacked natural oil and coal resources, a new source of energy had to be developed. The question of the electrification of Lithuania was seriously considered; an Energy Committee was formed to study indigenous resources and to search for mineral deposits.

The question of improvement of highways and communications was a touchy one. A new law established a systematic plan for expanding the network of highways; a special fund was set up for this purpose. The system of roads inherited from the Russian government had been poor, and the first World War had led to the decline and ruin of many public roads. In 1937-39, the Samogitian Highway was laid from Kaunas to Klaipėda and the highway from Kaunas to Biržai was extended. In 1940, construction on the Kaunas-Vilnius autostrada was begun. Excluding the Klaipėda region, Lithuania in 1935 had 1,222 km. of turnpike; in 1940, 1,600 km. According to the government plan for 1938-48, an additional 2,600 kilometers of turnpike were to be laid.

Lithuania lacked private capital; therefore, the state was forced to utilize its meagre resources for various investments and support projects.

During this period with the passage of laws the basis of the state was strengthened and modernized. The Council of State, in addition to matters of public legislation, began to prepare a series of bills of capital importance, among which the most serious consideration was given to a new civil statute, a statute of civil procedure and a criminal code. These projects sought to codify the existing laws in these areas and to eliminate the shortcomings of the past when Lithuania had several codes forced on her territory.

The 1930 world depression hit Lithuania somewhat late. The catastrophic collapse of prices in the world market of Lithuania's chief products caused severe hardships for the farmers. This was coupled with foreign trade restrictions on exports. Budget revenues also decreased, while the government stuck to its tried policy of keeping the budget in line with actual revenues and by its avoidance of deficit spending. This conservative policy helped keep the currency from devaluation; the government, however, was forced to pass laws regulating foreign currency operations. In 1935, a price control law was passed and a price regulator set up. With the fall in prices the farmers were unable to pay loans. The discontent of the Suvalkai farmers in 1935-36 was fanned into strikes and disorders. The strikes at first were of an economic nature, but later they assumed a political hue when the opposition parties began to direct them.

THE PROMULGATION OF A NEW CONSTITUTION

After the December 17, 1926, *coup d'état* the opposition was gradually restricted. As time went on, the restrictions increased, the regime took the stand that the parties represented segments of the society and therefore were a divisive element in the nation and that the state represented the unifying element. In a sense, there was no official party in Lithuania because the Tautininkai (Nationalist Union), though it supported the regime and tried to assume the role of the state party, was only considered a handmaiden and helper of the regime by President Smetona, who considered it to be a link between the state and society.

Opposition to the regime took various forms. While Voldemaras was at the head of the government, the leftist groups were the most active oppositionists. They tried to stir up trouble (the Taurage putsch of 1927) and tried to assassinate Voldemaras (1929). After these attempts, they formed a small political emigration which at one time were supported by the Polish government.

The most difficulties came from the Christian Democratic Bloc, which was supported by the Catholic organizations influential in the country. A difference of views regarding the provisions of the concordat arose. Likewise, the regime and Christian Democrats did not see eye-to-eye on the activities of the Catholic youth organizations' opposition, especially in the schools. The press had been censored even earlier, and in 1936, a Social Works Committee was set up to create a better public image of the regime.

227

The government itself never rejected the idea of calling together the Seimas as an institution of national representation. But its views of the Seimas differed from the practices of the old body. It had to be formed on a different basis now. Before implementing Seimas elections, however, the regime set out to eliminate the old political parties. The Organizations Law passed in 1936 was to take care of that. On the basis of the new law, the minister of internal affairs abolished all of the active political parties with the one exception of the Nationalist Union.

The government decided to hold the elections on the basis of local administration instead of on a party basis. In May, 1936, a new electoral Seimas law was passed which put the selection of the candidates into the hands of the municipal and county councils. Lithuanian citizens over the age of twenty-four were permitted to vote; the candidates had to be over thirty years of age. The elections took place on June 9-10, 1936. Forty-nine representatives were elected, the majority Tautininkai or their sympathizers. As a result, the Seimas did not gain stature and lacked public support.

The Seimas was authorized to prepare a new Constitution. A project was prepared together with the Council of State, and the new Constitution was adopted on February 11, 1938; it was announced in the *Vyriausybės Žinios* on February 18. This was a document of 156 articles which, according to the ideology of the regime, declared the supremacy of the state in all public life. "The state is the foundation of the very existence of the citizen."

The President of the Republic was to be elected by special "national electors" (*tautos atstovai*) whose designation was to be established by law. The elected President was to "assume the leadership of the state." The decrees of the President were to be countersigned by the prime minister or appropriate minister. The decree appointing or dismissing the prime minister did not need a countersignature. Also the cabinet of ministers was to be called the Council of Ministers.

The new Constitution did not bring any innovations into the existing order. As in the 1928 Constitution, the President of the Republic was to remain the central government figure in whose hands were the most important prerogatives and who now was authorized to head the "leadership of the state." In this manner the leader-principle (*vadizmas*) was institutionalized by the Constitution, which was itself promulgated on the eve of the twentieth anniversary of Lithuania's independence—a good point for us to take a balance score of the accomplishments of the state.

This balance score showed many credits. During the twenty years since independence, progress was made in many fields. Creative energies had been used for the elevation of the commonwealth. The state had been used to direct and purposefully channel the creative energies of the nation on such public works projects as the construction of railways and highways, the construction of new schools, the organization of agricultural life, the improvement of educational and cultural standards. Hundreds of projects were conceived and given a place on a priority list of government endeavors. While Lithuania was celebrating her twentieth anniversary, the evils of the world depression were being eradicated and the way was paved for further material and cultural progress. During this period a new generation was formed which was attending or finishing its schooling in national schools and which was joining the many activities of the nation. New initiative and creative force was manifested in all areas.

STRAINED RELATIONS WITH NEIGHBORS ON THE EVE OF WAR

As the country was celebrating its anniversary of freedom, its relations with its neighbors were becoming strained. In March, 1938, the Polish government presented Lithuania with an ultimatum demanding that diplomatic ties be established with it and that the *status quo* be recognized for the Vilnius region, which the Poles had seized by deceit under General Zeligowski. The ultimatum came while Prime Minister Tūbelis was convalescing in Switzerland. Since there was no hope that he would get better, President Smetona called upon Rev. Vladas Mironas, a prominent Tautininkas, to form a new government. Several changes were made in the cabinet. Foreign Minister Stasys Lozoraitis, who had held the post since 1934, agreed to stay on for just a short while. The head of the army, General Stasys Raštikis, became defense minister. He had performed a capable job in modernizing the army;

however, after a while, friction developed between him and the President because General Raštikis spent too much time trying to attain public recognition. In 1940, he was replaced by General Vladas Vitkauskas.

On November 14, 1938, in accordance with the new Constitution, a special body, the national electors, reelected President Antanas Smetona for another seven year period.

During the 1938-39 period, the European political situation became very strained. One year after the Polish ultimatum, Lithuania was shocked by a new one—this time from Nazi Germany. The Lithuanian Government bowed to the Berlin ultimatum and let Hitler take over the Klaipėda region.

One after another, ultimatums struck at Lithuania's vital interests. Voices were raised suggesting that the basis of government be expanded to include members of the opposition. Although the opposition parties were formally closed, yet they continued to function in one way or another. The abolished parties coordinated their leadership and worked out a common plan of action. After the Berlin ultimatum, Rev. Mironas' cabinet resigned and Brigadier-General Jonas Černius was called upon to form a new government. This was the first time in Lithuanian history that an officer on active duty headed the government. The new prime minister invited several other high officers to join his cabinet. More changes took place in the civilian sector. The deputy prime minister was Kazys Bizauskas, an active Christian Democrat. His fellow partyman became minister of education. The cabinet also included peasant populists and other opposition representatives. The government did not include a single Tautininkas. Juozas Urbšys, a nonparty man, remained as foreign minister.

The new prime minister was determined to adhere to the 1938 Constitution and to follow faithfully the directives of the President of the Republic. In spite of the good intentions of the prime minister, action was directed outside of the government by opposition parties to hinder the regime and to even remove it.

In the meantime, the danger of war in Europe was growing imminent. On January 25, 1939, a neutrality act was passed whereby the President of the Republic was authorized, if necessary, to declare Lithuania's neutrality. When, on September 1,

1939, the German Wehrmacht attacked Poland, President Smetona declared Lithuania's neutrality. The war caused many problems for Lithuania. The Lithuanian government did not succumb to Berlin's guiles and threats and declined to use force to retake Vilnius from Poland. With the collapse of Poland, her soldiers and civilians began to flow into Lithuania. The soldiers were interned, as required by international law. The Lithuanian nation did not take advantage of Poland's debacle to take revenge against the Poles for having seized her capital. The Lithuanians offered aid to the interned Polish soldiers and to the refugees. In December, 1939, a "Law to Regulate War Refugees" was promulgated which established a commissariat to handle the refugee problem. In spite of trying conditions, provisions were made for the refugees to leave Lithuania.

In the meantime, the Soviet army took over the eastern part of Poland. The Vilnius region fell into Soviet hands. On October 10, 1939, a "Treaty to Turn over the City of Vilnius and Its Environs to Lithuania and the Lithuanian-Soviet Mutual Assistance Treaty" was signed. The Soviet Union turned over Vilnius and part of the territory to Lithuania in return for the right to station Soviet garrisons in Lithuania. The general enthusiasm and joy over the return of the historic capital blinded many to the veiled threat to the state's further existence. The government organs began to make preparations for the actual takeover of Vilnius. This was to take place when the Lithuanian army marched into the city. For this purpose, a special army command was created, headed by general Vladas Vitkauskas. This command marched into Vilnius on October 28, and was met enthusiastically by the inhabitants of the city. The Lithuanian flag was unfurled over the historic Tower of Grand Duke Gediminas, the first time since January 1, 1919, that the Lithuanian flag flew over the city. This ceremony was followed by *Te deums* in all the churches of the land.

The Lithuanian government appointed a special emissary to administer the city and district. His tasks included the coordination of the transitional organs of administration and paving the way for the Vilnius district to be reintegrated into Lithuania.

Antanas Markys was appointed emissary. He had been the long-time governor of Klaipėda.

The return of Vilnius raised new problems, especially financial ones. At the end of October, a special "Vilnius City and District Supervision Law" was passed which temporarily permitted the use of Polish zloty in addition to the litas. Later, a regulation was passed requiring the deposition of the Zloty. Only the deposited zloty were to be converted into litai. The Lithuanian state undertook a great responsibility by permitting the zloty, which no longer had any real value, to be converted into litai. The new projects devoted to the reintegration of the Vilnius district into Lithuania required special funds. On October 20, 1939, the Seimas passed a law authorizing a 50-million litai "Vilnius Loan." At the same time, intensive work was undertaken to take over the administration of the district. New officials had to be appointed. Konstantinas Stašys, a Lithuanian activist of long standing in Vilnius during the period of Polish occupation, was appointed mayor.

When the Soviet Union forced Lithuania to accept the Mutual Assistance Treaty, many demanded that the Černius' government resign in protest against the Soviet coercion. After careful deliberation, General Černius' government stepped down and on November 21, 1939, a new cabinet was formed. Antanas Merkys was appointed prime minister, Juozas Urbšys remained as foreign minister.

The new government, like its predecessor, contained representatives of the important political groupings in Lithuania. In his inaugural declaration, the prime minister stated that "the government has chosen the path of national unity and consolidation." The prime minister Merkys was a Tautininkas, and he declared that he would follow the guidelines of the President of the Republic. He also pointed out the hardships that "were affecting our country adversely." The government was prepared to regulate its relations with foreign states "by resting on the right to firmly defend the rights which belong to our country and by following the requirements imposed by international law and by holding to the obligations which Lithuania incurred in her treaties with other states." Mentioned for the first time was the conclusion of the Treaty of Mutual Assistance with the Soviet Union. Within six months, the treaty ended in the Soviet occupation of the Lithuanian state. Antanas Merkys' cabinet was the very last of independent Lithuania.

THE BALTIC STATES ENTENTE

Bearing in mind the geopolitical position of Lithuania and her immediate neighbors Estonia and Latvia, it was no wonder that an idea to bring about a union was conceived quite early. These states had many things in common with Finland and Poland. Buffered between two great powers—Russia and Germany—the five states of Eastern Europe, Finland, Estonia, Latvia, Lithuania and Poland, by necessity had many common interests and were influenced by the same geopolitical factors. Therefore, at the beginning of their independent existence attempts were made to coordinate their policies and to form a federation to insure their external security.

In the course of the independence wars and the work of reconstruction, initiative was taken to call the first conference. At that time, the idea was to form the so-called Great Baltic Union which would encompass all five states, but this project was never finalized. The question of a union including Scandinavia and the Ukraine was also discussed. In the summer of 1920, in Riga and Bulduri, a conference of the five Baltic nations took place which prepared a number of projects for conventions. At that time, however, Poland's aggressive policy toward Lithuania hindered any collaboration. Poland's military forces were invading Lithuanian territory. These conditions hindered any genuine understanding. This was especially apparent after Poland seized the Lithuanian capital Vilnius, when it was impossible for both Poland and Lithuania to be members of a common federation. Under those conditions, Lithuania did not participate in Baltic deliberations. The remaining four Baltic states signed a so-called *accord politique* in Warsaw on March 12, 1922. But this federation was still-born. The Finnish Parliament did not ratify this agreement. As a result, the idea of the Great Baltic Union was buried. The idea of a small Baltic Union was then raised, to include Lithuania, Latvia and Estonia.

Much time elapsed before this idea received any concrete form. Although in many fields the three Baltic States cooperated, a real Baltic Union did not materialize until September 12, 1934, when Lithuania, Latvia and Estonia signed in Geneva a "Treaty of Baltic Entente and Cooperation." Its purpose was "to coordinate the foreign policy of the Baltic States and to cooperate in international relations." The treaty also declared that the Baltic States were determined to coordinate their policies to conform to the spirit of the League of Nations and to work for peace. The organ of the union was the periodic conference of Baltic foreign ministers.

Between the creation of the Baltic Union and the Soviet occupation of the Baltic States, nine conferences of foreign ministers were held (by rotation in each of the three capitals). The Union did not limit itself to coordinating foreign policy. In a short time, it spread into other areas, starting with common standards and ending with intellectual cooperation. A number of commissions and committees were created to coordinate and even make uniform various aspects of public life. A press *entente* was signed. Intensive exchanges of ideas took place in the fields of art, theater, and literature; mutual societies were very active. In other words, the three Baltic States were on the road to closer and wider regional cooperation, which might have eventually led to the integration of Europe.

THE KLAIPEDA REGION AS AN AUTONOMOUS UNIT
OF LITHUANIA

After the signing of the Klaipėda Statute the territory of Memel-Klaipėda was organized. From the start, there were differences of opinion as to the interpretation of the provisions of the Statute, according to which the Klaipėda district was to have wide autonomy. There were grounds for believing that the Klaipėda region was a state within the state. The circles dedicated to German political ambitions did everything to preserve the particularism of the region as well as to increase differences. This was not all. There was a systematic attempt to apply wide meaning to the provisions of the Statute which would be in the interest

of strengthening the German position at the expense of the Lithuanians.

One must bear in mind that the administration of the region
was in German hands, for the most part. Such were conditions
during the German rule and they continued during the brief
French occupation. *Freistaat* tendencies were manifested; new
officials were invited from Germany. When German citizenship
was operative in Klaipėda, the question of citizenship was no
problem for the new arrivals. Unfortunately, the Lithuanian inhabitants of the region had fewer candidates to hold office than
did the Germans; there were not many pro-Lithuanian pastors or
judges; the Germans dominated the professions (the bar, the
medical field, pharmacy); big business, large estates and industry
were almost entirely in German hands. Finally a tendency manifested itself which was no phenomenon to nations without a developed national consciousness, namely, "converting" to Germanism in the eyes of many was considered a step up the social ladder.
A number of educated and established Lithuanians became dena-
tionalized or identified themselves with German interests. This
phenomenon, together with German colonization, explains why
the German element predominated in the port city. Nevertheless,
many of these so-called Germans were people with Lithuanian
names; they were autochtons of the region and of Lithuanian
Prussia. The villages in the countryside were less affected by
Germanization. Frequently, even ethnic Germans who settled
there became Lithuanianized, which explains the reason for many
pro-Lithuanian persons having obvious German names.

As in Lithuania Minor, so in the Klaipėda region, one could
discern a peculiar phenomenon that one could not determine nationality on the basis of the language used at home. This was so
in spite of the fact that most autochtons spoke Lithuanian in the
villages. When the Klaipėda region was joined to Lithuania, many
of the people doggedly sought to preserve the particularism of the
region, and fought for autonomy. The German elements skillfully
exploited these sentiments for their own benefit. Even the autochtons who did not have a clearly developed national consciousness
were fired by the notion of "defending autonomy." A new category of inhabitants in Klaipėda was developing, the so-called

235

"Memellanders," who were neither pro-German, nor pro-Lithuanian, but who were for "autonomy." Even the statistics contained a category called "Memellanders." This psychological phenomenon took the concrete social form of support for the local "Memellander parties." This was very conducive for the German politicians who formed such parties. Among such parties were the agrarian *Memellaendische Landwirtschaftspartei* and the bourgeois middle-class *Memellaendische Volkspartei*. Similar Lithuanian parties were nicknamed *Grosslitauisch* parties.

There was another group which was not so particulartistic as the others, this was the Social Democrats and their Communist rivals, or the *Arbeiterpartei*. They appealed to the proletariat and village laborers. In addition to *Memellaenderismus,* they appealed to class solidarity. This slogan drew to their ranks a number of people from Lithuania Proper who were for class solidarity before national solidarity. One must keep these factors in mind when one analyzes the results of the elections to the Klaipėda legislature and to the local councils.

The election to the first legislature took place on October 19, 1925. The United Memellaender Front got twenty-seven mandates out of the twenty-nine. Thus, the pro-Lithuanians won only two seats. It would be a mistake to determine nationality from these results. Of the twenty-nine elected legislators, clearly half were Lithuanians who spoke the language at home. If the German propaganda tried to portray the election results as proof of the Germanism of the region, the best proof to the contrary is the fact that during this period the German publishing house in Klaipėda which printed the rabid Pan-German and later National-socialist *Memeler Dampfboot,* also published the Lithuanian daily *Lietuviška Ceitunga*. The latter paper was archconservative, it was edited in a barbarized Lithuanian language, and specialized in capitalizing on scandals in Lithuania. Yet it was a Lithuanian paper. It was unprofitable for its publishers; it was financed by a secret fund in Berlin. The Germans felt that such a paper was necessary.

To influence the mood of the inhabitants of the Klaipėda region, finances were to play a key role. It was no secret that a number of banks in Klaipėda were funded by Berlin. These firms

236

gave loans at such rates that they were able to hinder their competitors, the banks of Lithuania. It was often the case that persons who tried to break away from the pro-German policies of the banks would have their loans called in and thus would fall into hard times. A number of other economic organizations played a role in pro-German politics.

The Klaipėda region is a border area with a peculiar mentality. Part of the population, possessing a national consciousness formed by German influences, looked about at the two opponents —the Lithuanians and Germans—and shrewdly chose the one who gave them the most material returns. The Lithuanians had a hard time with their meager economic resources in competing with the German money flowing in from Berlin. In addition, Lithuania was economically tied to Germany, her chief export consumer.

The number of Lithuanian representatives in the Klaipėda legislature, nonetheless, increased. During the August 30, 1927, elections Lithuanian representation doubled. During the 1930 elections, the Lithuanians received five out of twenty-nine seats. Pro-Lithuanians brought in 19 percent of the vote. During the last election (December, 1938), the Lithuanians had only four seats. These elections, however, were not typical, because they took place in an atmosphere of National-socialist terror and pressure from Germany. Under normal circumstances it would have only been a question of time until the Lithuanians would have gained an absolute majority. This could be seen from the increasing Lithuanian representation in the municipal council. In 1924, the Lithuanians won two seats out of forty in the municipal elections; in 1930, six; in 1933, nine; and in 1936, the Lithuanians had fifteen representatives. Although Klaipėda was Germanized, and the process of Lithuanianization was fraught with economic and social difficulties, an important role in the Lithuanization was played by the increase of the Lithuanian element in the city. During the last elections the Jewish minority was frightened by the National-socialist agitation, and turned away from the pro-German parties. In spite of all attempts to block the registration of Lithuanians in the district, the Lithuanian influence was steadily growing. This normal process was disrupted by the National-socialists.

In 1925, a treaty was signed between Germany and Lithuania regarding the option of citizenship for the inhabitants of the Klai-pėda district. According to this treaty, the inhabitants could freely option one or the other citizenship. Later it became known that the agencies of the Reich coaxed officials and other categories of Germans not to opt for German citizenship by promising to pay the difference in pay.

Great difficulties were encountered regarding language. According to the Statute, the Lithuanian and German languages enjoyed equal status. The autonomous organs for interpreting the Statute were in German hands, and the Germans argued that civil servants did not have to know both languages. As a result, there was constant friction between the governor and the autonomous organs on this matter.

Differences of opinion were also voiced on the language for schools. The autonomous organs, as was verified later by the school comptrollers, purposely tried to sabotage the Lithuanian-language policy of the administration. The Lithuanians were left with no alternative but to form private schools to be taught in Lithuanian. The high schools were also private institutions. They were rather successful. The Lithuanian Vytautas the Great Gymnasium in the city of Klaipėda had, in 1937, 491 students, while the German Louise Gymnasium had 301 students.

The agencies of the republic had difficulties with teachers, some of whom opted for Germany, but remained to work in Klaipėda. They, together with a percentage of native teachers, engaged in Germanizing work and fostering anti-Lithuanianism. There were difficulties in the financial field between the agencies of the republic and those of the autonomous district. According to the Statute, some of the state income was to be given to the autonomous agencies. Since no agreement was reached on accountability, the intervention of the League of Nations was called for.

During the first years of Lithuanian rule, the interpretation of the Klaipėda Statute passed without greater incidents. The problems of Klaipėda had no direct bearing on Lithuanian-German diplomatic relations. When Professor Voldemaras headed Lithuania's foreign policy, relations with Germany became an important factor. His withdrawal from foreign affairs coincided with Gustav Stresemann's death, which meant a break in German foreign policy. After Stresemann's death, militant nationalistic tendencies grew in Germany, which sought to free Germany from the restraints of the Versailles Treaty. This also had an effect on relations with Lithuania.

The source of growing friction between Lithuania and Germany grew from the Klaipėda region. Germany, as a member of the League, began to intervene demonstratively in the district. The Germans used the League every time that difficulties arose between the governor (Lithuanian central government) and the pro-German parties, especially regarding the interpretation of the Statute. Views differed on the role of the Directory as the executive organ in the district. According to the Statute, the governor was to choose the president of the Directory. The Klaipėda district had a parliamentary order, for the Directory had to get a vote of confidence from the legislature. The governor held to a policy whereby at least the president of the Directory would be a man whom he could control. The Statute gave the governor the right to appoint the president, therefore he felt that he had the right, as did the Legislature, to grant or withdraw confidence from the president. This led to differences of opinion. In August, 1930, the governor appointed a pro-Lithuanian Martynas Reisgys as president of the Directory. In his declaration, he stated that he was opposed to appointing judges who had studied abroad. The new president also pointed out the discrimination against the Lithuanian language in the public schools. He demanded that disloyal teachers be dismissed.

The Legislature returned a vote of no-confidence. The president, in return, read the governor's decree dissolving the legislature and calling for new elections. The German government submitted a protest to the League against the dissolution of the Legislature and the composition of the Directory. The Lithuanian government, wishing to avoid discussion in the League of Nations forum, made a concession to Germany, negotiating with Berlin about the elections and the composition of the Directory. The negotiations drew sharp reaction in Lithuanian society and the Lithuanian Government was accused of capitulating to Germany.

The prestige of the central government was weakened after the appeasement made in Geneva. The Lithuanians had promised in Geneva to appoint as president of the Directory the candidate who had received a majority in the legislature, Otto Boettcher, a political nonentity who was under the influence of the pro-German parties. Boettcher soon proved to be a lackey of German interests who betrayed the trust confided in him by the governor.

In December, 1931, Lithuanian agencies discovered that the president of the Directory went to Berlin with a member of the legislature where they were met by another member of the legislature. This "delegation" overstepped its legal bounds by negotiating in Berlin for exports with several German ministries. These negotiations had been arranged by the German General Consul in Klaipėda, who had even given an official pass to enter Germany to a legislator who lacked a passport. This document vouched for the bearer as "a person important to German national interests." The treasury of the Klaipėda paid for the trip of this "delegation." In January, 1932, another member of the Directory went secretly to Koenigsberg where he conducted negotiations with German agencies. Both delegations acted without the knowledge of the governor.

Governor Merkys found it intolerable that the Directory, on its own and without the knowledge of the central government, had made secret negotiations with foreign agencies. He informed the legislature about these trips, awaiting its action against the Directory. But the legislature, after hearing from the president of the Directory that the trip had been a private one (which the facts clearly disproved), returned a vote of confidence. The governor, acting on a cabinet decision on February 6, 1932, dismissed Boettcher from the presidency. A wave of protest arose in Lithuania against the interference of German governmental agencies in the affairs of the Klaipėda region. Meetings were held throughout the country which passed resolutions against the pro-Germans and against the activities of the German government agencies. But Germany also reacted with a campaign against Lithuania in the press and organizations. The German government supported this anti-Lithuanian campaign. Voices rose in Germany demanding that force be used to seize Klaipėda from Lithuania. The campaign against the Versailles Treaty was at its height in Germany at the time, events in Klaipėda were exploited by the nationalist elements. Incidents occurred in Berlin University against Lithuanian students. As a result, the Lithuanian government recalled most of the students who were in Germany on scholarships.

The German government protested to the League of Nations against the so-called violation of the Statute of Memel. The Council met on February 13 and appointed the Norwegian Colban to prepare a report. Colban suggested that the signatories of the Klaipėda Convention appear before the Hague Tribunal.

Governor Merkys did his utmost to solve the Directory crisis. When the only member of the Directory not involved in the secret journeys to Germany, Szygaudas, declined to become president, the governor temporarily appointed Jonas Tolišius. Negotiations to form a parliamentary directory were bogged down. Although Boettcher himself resigned from the presidency on February 23, the majority in the legislature did not show any interest in trying to find a compromise replacement. Therefore, on February 27, the governor appointed Eduardas Simaitis to the presidency and entrusted him with negotiating with the legislature on the composition of the new Directory. The negotiations with majority parties in the legislature were fruitless. On March 14, Simaitis appointed three directors, but the legislature, on March 22, returned a vote of no-confidence and the governor had to dissolve the legislature.

At the same time, negotiations took place between Lithuania and the signatories of the Statute. The German government interfered with attempts to form a new Directory by backing and provoking the majority in the legislature. The Lithuanian government on several occasions protested to Berlin against this interference; it also protested the German Chancellor's threat to take reprisals against Lithuania. The situation became more and more complicated. The Lithuanian government reconsidered the League's suggestion to appear before the Hague Tribunal. On

April 11, 1932, the signator states submitted six questions to the Tribunal.

The cardinal question was whether the governor had the right to recall the president of the Directory. After recognizing this right, the International Court stated that it could only be exercised on certain occasions. The other questions touched directly upon the Boettcher recall, the creation of a new Directory, and the legality of the dissolution of the legislature. The Court gave its decision on August 11, 1932, agreeing with the theses of the Lithuanian Government on the major issues, and recognizing the governor's right of recalling the president under certain circumstances.

The decision of the Hague Court was a great victory for the Lithuanian government. It confirmed the governor's just interpretation of the Statute in the matter of the disloyalty of the Directory. The interference of the German government in the internal affairs of the Klaipėda district was condemned. The Hague Tribunal's decision strengthened the authority of the central government and the governor in the Klaipėda region. It gave a guideline for subsequent laws which were promulgated to strengthen the central government's position. Everything that was not expressly placed in the jurisdiction of the Klaipėda district by the Statute was to pass over to the jurisdiction of the central authorities.

THE LITIGATION AGAINST NATIONAL-SOCIALISM

The May, 1932, elections gave the pro-Lithuanians 19.2 percent of the votes, but the composition of the legislature did not change much. The pro-Lithuanians, as before, received five mandates. The pro-Communist workers party got from two to three seats. A number of Lithuanian workers voted for them in keeping with class solidarity. Lithuanian society, however, was disappointed in the fact that after the governor's stern measures, the pro-German parties maintained their former position. An appeasing trend appeared in the Lithuanian Government: Governor Juozas Merkys, who was smeared by German propaganda, was replaced by Vytautas Gylys, a career diplomat. The government wanted to emphasize by this appointment its desire for a more moderate policy.

242

In June, 1932, in keeping with the election results, the governor appointed Dr. Schreiber, a syndic of the Chamber of Industry and Commerce, to the post of president of the Directory. This was done to show that the affairs of the autonomous regime were to be freed from demagogical politics and elevated to the realm of economic order, especially since the country was in the throes of the world depression. Dr. Schreiber belonged to the Memel Lodge of Freemasons.

Unfortunately, the calculated rewards did not materialize. The Klaipėda district fell under the shadow of the growing aggressive National-socialist movement of Germany. In the spring and summer of 1933, the followers of National-socialism began to organize formal groups. The initiative was taken by Pastor von Sass, who organized the *Christlich-Sozialistische Arbeitsgemeinschaft* (CSA). This organization was violently opposed to the old German parties, and gained a tremendous vote during the elections to the Klaipėda municipal council. The group, however, did not satisfy the desires of the Nationalists in Germany and of the German Consul General in Klaipėda, and soon fell into disfavor. A new Nazi organization, calling itself the *Sozialistische Volksgemeinschaft* (SOVOG), was formed in Klaipėda. Its leader was a veterinarian, Dr. Ernst Neumann, who received the blessings of the National-socialists of Germany and the German government. For a while, there was competition between these two Nazi groups for first position. There were even bloody clashes between the factions. In a short while, von Sass' Party was overwhelmed by Dr. Neumann.

With the appearance of the Nazi Party in Klaipėda, relations became quite strained. High officials in Kaunas felt that the educational system had to be put in line. Dr. Jonas Navakas was appointed governor at the end of 1933. He was a capable administrator and an advocate of the hard line. A sharp conflict resulted with Schreiber's Directory over the state prosecutor, teachers and officials, be they German or Lithuanian citizens, who were not loyal to the state. A number of German citizens were dismissed outright or given a period wherein they must leave their posts. The governor repeatedly demanded that the Directory dismiss officials who belonged to anti-state parties. The Directory did not

243

comply. The conflict went even deeper over the question of school supervision. A number of schools had been infected with an anti-state spirit. The school adviser was being hindered in his inspection work. Since the president of the Directory did not go against the anti-state element, and even tolerated its excesses, his resignation was demanded by the governor in June, 1934. When he refused, the governor dismissed him. The new president of the Directory was the Klaipėda Lithuanian Martynas Reisgys.

At the same time, the Gauleiter of East Prussia, Koch, and the Nazi Party of Germany as well as the German Consul General in Klaipėda, put pressure on Pastor von Sass and his party to merge with Dr. Neumann. Although von Sass was opposed for a while to the merger, his movement collapsed and a number of his followers joined the ranks of Sovog. Sovog became the spokesman of National-socalism in Klaipėda. The existing pro-German parties either officially joined Neumann's movement or were absorbed by it. Sovog came out in the open with its Nazi activities, and did not conceal its aim: to tear Klaipėda from Lithuania and to join it with Germany.

Under the circumstances, Lithuanian security organs had no alternative but to close all the National-socialist organizations and to arrest their leaders and prosecute them. Enough evidence was accumulated on the Nazi organizations to have their leaders indicted. It was determined that the Nazi and German newspapers had been inspired and financed by Berlin. The German banks in Klaipėda had operated according to directives from Germany and were financed for political purposes by Osthilfe, a fund established to strengthen agriculture in East Prussia. The indictment also showed that there had to be a systematic attempt through the district agencies to have the schools Germanized and to have the Lithuanian element stultified. Nazi pamphlets had been introduced into the school system as textbooks. It was determined that Dr. Neuman, who was not a member, had been invited to the meetings of the commissions of the legislature and that he had had access to all administrative acts. It was determined that the pro-German parties had followed directives originating with the German Consul General and in Germany. The indictment stated that Sovog was a paramilitary organization which had units

244

drilling and preparing for an armed insurrection at the beginning of 1934, and that its documents were stored in safekeeping in the German Consulate General.

All of the incriminating proof formed the basis of a court-martial which was initiated in Kaunas on December 14, 1934. One hundred twenty-six persons were arraigned; ninety-three belonged to Sovog, thirty-three to CSA. Sentence was passed on April, 1935. Four received the death penalty for having committed political murder; two were sentenced to life terms at hard labor. The Sovog leader, Dr. Neumann, and his aide, Bertuleit, received twelve years at hard labor, CSA leader Pastor von Sass received eight years at hard labor. Thirty-seven accused were exculpated. The President of the Republic commuted the death sentences to life sentences, and the Lithuanian Government strove to ease tensions by eventually granting amnesty to all of those sentenced. In the summer of 1938, even the murderers were amnestied.

Of course, Reisgys' Directory had to work under difficult conditions, but it performed a number of tasks which quashed the pro-German action and reinstated Lithuanian justice. On December 1, 1934, Reisgys resigned and was succeeded by Jurgis Bruvelaitis. Cooperation with the legislature was made more difficult because the members of the Nazi Parties had their mandates annuled. Bruvelaitis' Directory sought to quash the activities of the Nazis. Even his Directory had difficulties in working with the majority in the legislature.

Germany at the time was conducting a rabid campaign against Lithuania, whose government was accused of trammeling the autonomy of Klaipėda. Actually, this was all part of Hitler's scheme against the Versailles Treaty. Since Germany had withdrawn from the League of Nations in October, 1933, it could no longer use that body to raise complaints against Lithuania. Germany put pressure on the signatory countries of the Klaipėda Statute to intervene in Kaunas. In 1934-35, the signatory countries asked the Kaunas government to appoint a Directory in Klaipėda which would cooperate with the legislature and which would have its confidence.

After the legislature was dissolved in September, 1935, new

elections were held. The united Lithuanian lists could not break the united pro-German front, which went under the name of *Memellaendische Einheitsliste*. The pro-Lithuanian lists got 18.8 percent of the votes, the *Einheitsliste* got 81.2 percent of the votes. The elections took place under strained conditions. After Lithuania dared to try the Nazis of Klaipėda, Hitler on several occasions declared openly that he was willing to sign nonaggression pacts with all neighbors except Lithuania. Only later, after the economic crisis abated, did Hitler, in March, 1936, declare in the Reichstag that he was willing to sign nonaggression pacts with all Eastern states including Lithuania.

The fifth election to the legislature did not bring any favorable changes to the Klaipėda Lithuanians. On the other hand, the Lithuanian Government, wanting to please the signatories of the Statute and to improve economic relations with Nazi Germany, changed its policy in Klaipėda. Governor Navakas, the hard-liner, was recalled. In November, 1935, a Klaipėda Lithuanian, Augustas Baldžius, was appointed president of the Directory. Baldžius was one Lithuanian who was acceptable to the German majority in the legislature. He remained at his post until January, 1939.

THE NAZI ULTIMATUM AND THE SEIZURE OF KLAIPEDA

This period was fraught with tension and incidents. Under the cover of defending the autonomy of the district, the new Directory, step by step, rescinded the decrees of the Reisgys and Bruvelaitis directories. The old school curriculum was reintroduced which sought to eliminate the Lithuanian language. The administration was again imbued with a pro-Nazi spirit. National-socialist ideology spread in the Klaipėda district. During the summer of 1938, a number of incidents took place in the port when German tourist ships appeared. Fanatical youths organized repeated demonstrations shouting "Ein Volk—Ein Reich—Ein Fuehrer." A number of clashes with the Lithuanian security police took place. Arrests were made. These demonstrations were manifestations of the Nazi spirit that ran rampant among native German youths.

The general situation in Europe, as a whole, grew worse.

Hitler went unpunished for breaking a number of provisions of the Versailles Treaty. Soon a number of territorial violations began. After the Austrian *Anschluss,* Hitler began a campaign against Czechoslovakia. After the capitulation at Munich, Germany partitioned Czechoslovakia, annexing the Sudetenland.

It became extremely difficult for the Lithuanian Government to hold its position. During the last session of the fifth legislature of Klaipėda, a representative of the majority spoke frankly on behalf of National-socialism and demanded that it be legalized in the district. In February, 1938, Dr. Neumann was released from prison. He became the *fuehrer* of the Klaipėda Nazi movement, following the directives of Berlin. Neumann demanded that racist laws be introduced into the district. Following Berlin's orders, a new election list was created which threw aside the cover of *Memellaendisch* and called itself *Memeldeutsch.* Under these conditions, the December 11, 1938, elections to the legislature returned a *Memeldeutsche Liste* majority of twenty-five representatives. The pro-Lithuanians received four seats. On December 12 the President of the Republic appointed Viktoras Gailius as governor. He was the first Klaipėda Lithuanian to hold the post.

As later uncovered in official German *Auswaertiges Amt* documents, in December, 1938, Dr. Neumann was received by Adolf Hitler who promised to "straighten out" the Memel matter in 1939. The deadline for Klaipėda was March or April 1939. Neumann agreed to arrange it so that the new legislature would never convene. In March, 1939, he called together the pro-German members of the legislature who empowered him to speak and act in their behalf. The Directory also agreed to this authorization. Its new president was Bertuleit, who was Dr. Neumann's aid.

The Lithuanian Government was powerless in the light of these developments. With each passing day it became more and more apparent that Nazi Germany was preparing to deal Lithuania a blow. On March 17, Bertuleit told British reporters that the inhabitants of Klaipėda were awaiting *Anschluss* with Germany.

The fateful hour struck on March 19, 1939, when Lithuanian Foreign Minister Juozas Urbšys, returning from the coronation of Pope Pius XII, stopped at Berlin. The following day, he met with German Foreign Minister von Ribbentrop, who categorically declared that the Klaipėda district desires "to return" to Germany. If a "peaceful solution" of the problem with Lithuania could be reached, then "friendly relations" with Lithuania would be reestablished and Germany would be "magnanimous" as far as economic matters were concerned. On the other hand, if Lithuania did not agree to such a solution, then the problem would be solved by the military. Ribbentrop warned Urbšys not to seek help elsewhere.

Ribbentrop demanded that Urbšys immediately telephone Kaunas. Urbšys replied that he alone was not competent to make the decision, that it would require a cabinet decision. Ribbentrop, in unequivocal terms, then declared that "time is running short." If incidents and armed clashes were to take place "then it would be too late .Fuehrer would not stand for that."

Later German publications tried to refute the fact that Ribbentrop had confronted Urbšys with an ultimatum. Keeping in mind the circumstances, however, under which Ribbentrop and Urbšys met, by analyzing the German foreign minister's declaration that unrest would occur in Klaipėda (which was easy for Berlin to provoke), and considering the fact that a few days earlier Hitler's divisions had rolled into Czechoslovakia, there could be no doubt as to the nature of Ribbentrop's "declaration." All subsequent attempts to soften the character of Ribbentrop's demands cannot change the obvious fact that the Lithuanian Government was confronted with a real ultimatum. To refute the Ribbentrop ultimatum would be tantamount to refuting the territorial designs of the Nazi government. Hitler knew only one method to employ threats—blackmail and ultimatums. The German state secretary, von Weizaecker, led the negotiations with Lithuanian delegation which came to Berlin on March 22. On March 21, he had urged the German envoy to Kaunas to inform the Lithuanian Government that there was not much time, for in the event of reversals, things could take "a dangerous turn." Weizaecker repeated that if disorders arose, the German government "would resort to force."

The dictated treaty whereby Klaipėda was to be turned over

to Germany was signed in Berlin on March 23, 1939. As Weizs-aecker notes in his memoirs, the Lithuanian foreign minister, Urb-šys, placed his signature half-heartedly. It is difficult to imagine a Lithuanian statesman who would place his signature voluntarily on such an act whereby a part of her territory was being taken away.

If there are still doubts on the Berlin ultimatum, then all of them are shattered by the capital fact that six hours before the signing of the treaty the German battleship *Deutschland* steamed out of Swinemuende with Hitler and his escort, enroute to Klai-pėda. The armada sailing with the *Deutschland* included the battleship *Graf Spee,* the cruisers *Nuernberg, Leipzig,* and *Koeln,* as well as a number of destroyers, torpedo boats and lesser craft.

According to the dictated treaty Lithuania would be ac-corded a free zone in the port of Klaipėda. With this promise, Nazi Germany had to recognize that Klaipėda's natural hinterland was Litsuania and that the port was vitally necessary for it and vice-versa. In a supplement to the treaty, it was stated that Lithu-ania had a ninety-nine-year lease on the free zone and that Lith-uanian investments in improvements in the port would be consid-ered in lieu of the rental. On May 20, 1939, a special agreement was concluded by the two states concerning the free port. A simi-lar special agreement was reached on the actual administration of the port, and in May, 1939, a new agreement on trade, commer-cial payments and adjustments and frontier communications was concluded between Lithuania and Germany.

SOVIET AGGRESSION AGAINST LITHUANIA

Having fought back the Red Army invasion of 1919-20 and having concluded a peace treaty with Moscow on July 12, 1920, Lithuania had a common frontier with Soviet Russia for only a short time. Because, in October, 1920, the so-called Polish "free-booter" General Zeligowski seized Vilnius and its region, Lithu-ania was not a direct neighbor of the Soviet Union until the beginning of the Second World War.

The conflict between Lithuania and Poland over Vilnius, and the uneasy relations between Moscow and Warsaw which was at times antagonistic, created possibilities for closer relations between Lithuania and the Soviet Union. A common interest developed between the two states. The Soviet government on several occasions through its declarations and notes created the impression that it would back Lithuania in her quarrel with Poland.

In essence, however, Moscow assumed an equivocal position regarding Vilnius. On the one hand, in her peace treaty with Lithuania Soviet Russia recognized Vilnius and its territory as part of Lithuania. Later, however, in her peace treaty with Poland, concluded in Riga, Soviet Russia turned the same area with additional territory over to Poland. The boundary between Poland and Lithuania was left to the two states to determine. It was apparent that the Lithuanian-Polish conflict served Moscow's interests, for it not only prevented agreement between the two neighbors, but also hindered the formation of a common front among the states between the Soviet Union and Germany. On September 28, 1926, Lithuanian Prime Minister Mykolas Sleževičius signed a nonaggression pact in Moscow. The importance of this treaty to Lithuania was twofold: the opening article declared that the provisions of the treaty "are supported by all the power and inviolability" and that the two contracting parties hold the treaty to be the "basis of relations." The Moscow government was more explicit in the note that G. Chicherin sent to Mykolas Sleževičius and which declared that "the *de facto* violation of Lithuanian frontiers had been done against the will of the Lithuanian nation and did not change its [USSR] position on Lithuanian territorial sovereignty." In other words, the treaty recognized Lithuania's prior rights to the Vilnius region.

This declaration by the Soviet government was of no small importance to the Lithuanians politically. Lithuanian society had the impression that the Soviets backed the republic in her quarrel with Poland. There was information that when, in 1927, Pilsudski supported the conspiracy of a group of Lithuanian political emigrants against the then existing government under Voldemaras, the Soviets in the adjacent Minsk region began to regroup military forces in order to cool the bellicose ardor of the Polish dictator.

In addition to the nonaggression pact which was extended on

two occasions, and was to be in force until 1945, Lithuania and the Soviet Union signed (July 5, 1933) a convention to "Define Aggression." By this treaty, which was based on the 1926 treaty and the Kellog-Briand Pact, which both states had signed, Soviet Russia and Lithuania declared to renounce war and gave a detailed definition of all interpretations of aggression. A number of conditions were spelled out condemning aggression. Among them was the condition "of the internal situation of a state, i.e. its political, economic or social structure, so-called blunders of its administration, unrest rising from strikes, revolution, counter-revolution or civil war." Moscow was concerned about the ascendency of National-socialism in Germany. As a result, it stressed its peaceful intentions, and sought to insure itself against possible Nazi aggression or intervention.

Lithuania's relations with the Soviet Union were limited almost exclusively to the diplomatic field. By the same token, cultural relations with Russia were rather weak because of that country's self-isolation from the rest of the world. In 1929, a Society to Understand the Culture of Soviet Nations was formed in Kaunas. Its purpose was to foster cultural cooperation between Lithuania and the USSR. Among its members were a number of renown Lithuanian cultural leaders who joined without any ulterior motives. The Society was sponsored by the Soviet Legation, which sought to disseminate among leftist intellectuals the idea of a "popular front." This Society provided Moscow with a number of ready-made collaborators when the Red Army invaded Lithuania in 1940.

The public felt that the Soviet Union did not foster any dangerous designs against the state. The notion was prevalent that Moscow, as far as Lithuania was concerned, was friendly. The internal threat of Communism was considered to be insignificant. (The Lithuanian Communist Party was banned, though it continued to function clandestinely.)

Relations with the Soviet Union were not complicated by special problems. Moscow protected a group of fugitive Lithuanian Communists, whose ranks were periodically weeded out during purges, and helped the clandestine party in the country. Yet Communism, according to the prevalent view, was not a threat

251

to the Lithuanian state. With the rise of aggressive National-socialism in Germany, discussions in Lithuania sometimes centered around the question of the "popular front." Such discussions, however, never had wide circulation. The Communist party remained an isolated underground whose influence was minimal. The nation felt a real danger from Naziism. The threat of Russian Bolshevism seemed theoretical at most.

THE STALIN-HITLER PACT AND ITS RESULTS

In 1939, when Nazi Germany broke the Munich Agreement by seizing Czechoslovakia and forming a "protectorate," the Western democracies became concerned with forming a common front against Hitler. Attempts were made to draw the Soviet into that front. Negotiations between England and France on the one hand, and the Soviet Union, commenced in Moscow. These negotiations disclosed the Soviet Union's aggressive designs against Poland and the Baltic States. The West did not accept Soviet plans for this zone.

While the negotiations were still in progress, a rumor spread to the effect that Moscow was negotiating with Berlin. It soon became known that the former antagonists had reached an agreement. On August 23, 1939, in Moscow, a treaty of friendship and nonaggression was concluded between the Soviet Union and Nazi Germany. It was not known at the time that the two totalitarian powers had also reached an agreement on the grand style of nineteenth-century colonialism. Eastern Europe was to be divided into spheres of influence. According to the secret agreement reached the same day as the open treaty, Lithuania was to be placed in the German orbit, while Latvia and Estonia were to be placed in the Soviet sphere of influence. According to a subsequent protocol, reached on September 28, Lithuania also was to be turned over to the Soviet sphere.

Later events elucidated that the Kremlin, not finding support and consent from the Western democracies for its designs, chose instead as its partner the German Nazis who offered more. The Baltic buffer states became objects of desire for the two dictators, who in reality suspected one another and waited for a more

252

favorable political constellation to seize even more territory regardless of morality and rights. Cynicism and brute force were the order of the day.

After reaching an agreement with Moscow, Hitler, on September 1, began war against Poland. Lithuania, like her Baltic neighbors, proclaimed her neutrality in the conflict. On September 17, the Soviet Union attacked Poland and seized its eastern regions, among them the Vilnius region. The German government exerted pressure on Kaunas to mobilize its army and take Vilnius from the Poles. The Lithuanian Government was faced with a dilemma. Some felt that if Vilnius were taken, Lithuania would not violate her neutrality. Nevertheless, the government decided to remain neutral. On September 17, Prime Minister Jonas Černius publically announced that Lithuania would regain Vilnius by peaceful means. Lithuania resisted the temptation and did not attack crumbling Poland.

This behavior by Kaunas antagonized Berlin. The German government, not being able to make Lithuania its ally against Poland, turned Lithuania over to the Soviet sphere of influence on September 28. According to the secret supplementary protocol, Moscow received all of Lithuania in return for Lublin province in Poland. The Soviets also paid $7.5 million in gold for Lithuania.

While refusing to take back Vilnius, Lithuania herself now had to seek the USSR's favor. "The key to Vilnius" was now in Moscow's hands. In addition, Moscow, receiving the go-ahead from Berlin, decided to act and without hesitation use the favorable situation to decide the fate of the Lithuanian state. Starting with Estonia, Moscow demanded that the Baltic States sign with her "treaties of mutual assistance" whereby Red Army garrisons would be admitted into the Baltic States. Foreign Minister Juozas Urbšys was faced with this demand on the first day of his arrival in Moscow in October. The Lithuanian delegation nevertheless rejected the demand for garrisons; Urbšys noted that the demand for garrisons would be nothing more than the occupation of Lithuania.

The negotiations were temporarily broken off. The government, pondering the situation, decided to accept the mutual assistance treaty, but to reject the garrison clause and substitute in its place changes in the military missions. But Moscow relentlessly demanded garrisons. It was clear to the Lithuanians that if they did not accept the "mutual assistance" treaty and did not admit a limited Soviet garrison, the Red Army would march into Lithuania without a treaty. The choice was the lesser of the two evils. In the first treaty project, the Soviets foresaw garrisons only in the event of war. The final draft did not contain this provision.

The government realized that Soviet garrisons violate Lithuania's sovereignty, but it was hopeful that after the war and with a change in the international situation, the Soviets would have to recall their garrisons. The government was influenced by still another consideration: If the Soviet demands were resisted, then Lithuania would lose her chance of getting back Vilnius. After sounding out the political climate in other capitals, the government was convinced that Lithuania could await aid from no quarter.

Under the circumstances the Lithuanian government authorized Urbšys to sign the treaty, which was done in Moscow on October 10, 1939. The Kremlin tied the question of Vilnius to the treaty on purpose. In addition to a solemn promise to grant mutual aid in the event of attack, the treaty stipulated that Lithuania allow the entry on her territory of a "strictly limited number of Soviet ground and air forces." The seventh article was of special importance; it stated: "The execution of this treaty in no way should be an interference in the internal affairs of the contracting parties, especially in the economic and social system by military means, and generally means the principle of noninterference in internal matters. The areas reserved for Soviet military forces by all means remain the integral part of the Republic of Lithuania." The treaty was to be in force for fifteen years.

The Lithuanian Government was hopeful that Moscow, after forcing it to sign the treaty, would nonetheless abide by its provisions and would not interfere in Lithuania's internal order. During the negotiations in Moscow and thereafter, Stalin and Molotov repeatedly tried to convince the Lithuania delegates that the Soviet government did not have any aggressive designs against Lithuania and the other Baltic states. Molotov declared

254

the same in public on October 31, 1939, in the Supreme Soviet, announcing that "gossip about the Sovietization of the Baltic countries could only be useful to the enemies of the Soviet Union and to provocateurs."

THE MOSCOW ULTIMATUM AND LITHUANIA'S OCCUPATION

Yet six months later, the Soviets violated all of the treaties concluded by the two states and used force against Lithuania and against the other neighboring states, starting with Finland and ending with Rumania. The events in Finland demonstrated the fate that would have fallen upon Lithuania had she rejected the treaty. Finland ultimately was forced to bow to Soviet demands when it did not receive aid from the Western democracies. For its aggression against Finland, the Soviet Union was expelled from the League of Nations.

Moscow decided to use force against Lithuania at that moment when the Germans struck on the Western front. In May, 1940, Lithuania was startled when the Soviet government hurled accusations against the government of Lithuania to the effect that they were spying and seizing Soviet garrison soldiers. The accusations were fantastic and absurd. Yet, the Lithuanian Government could not ignore the accusations and designated a special commission to investigate. The results of the investigation proved that the accusations were baseless. The so-called kidnapped Soviet soldiers in truth had either deserted or were hiding after a drinking spree in a Vilnius district of ill-repute.

One could see from Moscow's daily behavior that she was preparing to deal Lithuania a blow. The Lithuanian delegation tried in vain to prove that the accusations were without foundation. The Kremlin was not amenable to any arguments, but rather, was predisposed to make use of the situation in accordance with the Moscow-Berlin agreement. Soviet Russia was convinced that the hour had struck when Nazi Germany was engaged in the West. Moscow was ready to harvest the seed sown by the Hitler-Stalin Pact.

The Lithuanian cabinet was in continuous session when, on the night of June 15, 1940, a telegram was received from Urbšys in Moscow conveying the Soviet government's demands. The Soviets couched their demands in fantastic assertions to the effect that the Lithuanian government organs had "kidnapped" Soviet soldiers to obtain "military secrets" from them. The Soviets used these "facts" in their fantastic accusation that the Lithuanian Government "is preparing to attack the Soviet garrison." Molotov added that the Lithuanian Government had concluded with Latvia and Estonia a "military alliance." The Kremlin concluded that these "actions" by the Lithuanians had "insulted" the Soviet Union and violated the mutual assistance pact. Such a situation could not be tolerated much longer, therefore the Soviet Government considered that it "was absolutely necessary and urgent" that the following three demands be fulfilled:

"1. that the Minister of the Interior and the Director of the Department of Security be turned over for trial as authors of the provocative actions against the Soviet Army garrisons in Lithuania;

"2. that a government be formed in Lithuania which would be prepared and able to guarantee the honorable Soviet-Lithuanian Mutual Assistance Treaty and to take to task the enemies of the treaty;

"3. that free entry be guaranteed into Lithuanian territory to an unlimited number of Soviet Army units to insure the execution of the Soviet-Lithuanian Mutual Assistance Treaty and to thwart provocative actions against the Soviet garrisons in Lithuania.

"The Soviet Government considers the satisfaction of these demands to be the basic condition for the conscientious and honorable execution of the Mutual Assistance Treaty. The Soviet Government awaits the answer of the Lithuanian Government until June 15, 10:00 a.m."

When Molotov gave Urbšys his three demands, he added: "Regardless of the answer given, the Soviet Army will march into Lithuania."

The Lithuanian Government received the text of the Soviet demands at 2 A.M. Thus, the ultimatum had only eight hours to run before expiration. The cabinet met without any hope.

The question arose, how to react to the ultimatum. The opinions of those assembled were divided. The President of the Republic, together with several ministers, expressed the opinion that the Soviet ultimatum could not be accepted. Resistance had to be offered, even though under the circumstances and in view of the numerical superiority of the enemy such resistance would be token. Several ministers offered to accept the ultimatum, for this would avoid misfortunes and would alleviate the situation. Both the then commander-in-chief of the army, General Vincas Vitkauskas, and the former chief, General Stasys Raštikis, came out in favor of acceptance. Similar views were held by Prime Minister Antanas Merkys and his deputy, Kazys Bizauskas.

Since the cabinet could not reach a unanimous decision, the meeting continued in disordered fashion. Several hours remained before the deadline. The President maintained that there would not be sufficient time to change the government and army command, even though the discussions centered around the formation of a government by general Raštikis, for some cabinet members felt that his candidacy would satisfy the demands of Moscow. But the President as a sign of protest decided to go abroad and formally passed his duties to Premier Merkys as a temporary measure.

The reason why the cabinet could not reach a unanimous decision was due, in part, to the fact that the cabinet of ministers was heterogeneous. The cabinet was comprised of Tautininkai and opposition members. They did not form a working unit. The opposition felt that the times were in their favor and that in a short time it would be possible to alter the existing regime. At this critical time, the political higher circles lacked determination.

After the President announced that he was going abroad in protest to the ultimatum and was leaving as his deputy the Prime Minister Antanas Merkys, further initiative in the cabinet was taken by those who felt that resistance was futile. General Vitkauskas, who favored accepting the Soviet ultimatum, exercised an influence on the cabinet. Vitkauskas was known as a leftist officer who maintained ties with so-called progressive elements.

257

On June 15, at 3 P.M., the Red Army crossed the Lithuanian frontier and began the country's occupation. Soviet tanks that were already stationed in Lithuania moved on Kaunas, the center of government. The President of the Republic left the capital in the afternoon of June 15 and headed for the German-Lithuanian frontier. Although he met with obstacles, he succeeded in crossing into East Prussia.

On June 2, 1940, Foreign Minister Juozas Urbšys sent a telegram to the Lithuanian diplomatic representatives abroad which directed that the former foreign minister and the then minister to the Quirinal, Stasys Lozoraitis, was designated to be chief of the Lithuanian diplomatic service "if Lithuania should meet with a catastrophe." In this manner, the diplomatic service was to maintain the continuity of the independent Lithuanian state.

THE EDUCATIONAL AND CULTURAL LIFE OF INDEPENDENT LITHUANIA

When, in 1918-19, Lithuania began creating its modern state, only fourteen years had passed since the forty-year ban on Lithuanian literature had been lifted. No other European nation had been so trammeled and hindered culturally. It had done inestimable harm on the national culture. At the time when other European nations were finding their identity through ideas of national renaissance, and were enthusiastically developing their national cultures, the Lithuanian nation was denied any sort of literature. For possession of prayerbooks with Latin characters, the penalty was prison and even deportation. The few schools in the country served Russification. Organizations were prohibited. For twenty years, a secret Lithuanian press, centered in East Prussia, was smuggled into the country with hardships and tribulations. This clandestine literature aroused national consciousness and steeled the nation in its struggles against Russian oppression. But this press, because of its illegality, could not be widely circulated, yet was considered to be a conscientious factor against the Russian oppression.

The Russo-Japanese War abolished the ban and brought some improvements to Lithuania. During the decade before the first

World War a great step forward was made in education and in the development of a national culture, yet Russia remained in the mind of non-Russian nationalities the "prison of nations." The first World War brought the Lithuanian nation hardships and woe, but it also stirred hopes for a brighter future. The idea of national awareness had taken deep roots. Thus, it is no wonder that the nation demanded the right to self-determination at the same time that other nations were making similar demands against foreign rule.

When Lithuanians began taking over the administration of their country, the young state was faced with tremendous tasks in the fields of education and culture. For the first time in its history, the nation could develop its own culture without foreign interference. The quest for knowledge was especially strong in the young generation. The sad legacy of the Russian regime had to be liquidated in a short time. Both the state and local administrations devoted a great deal of attention to the establishment of a network of primary and secondary schools and to the regulation of a new curriculum. (During the Russian rule primary education was not compulsory. As a result, the percentage of illiteracy was rather high.)

In 1918, the ministry of education started eight gymnasia and eleven progymnasia. In 1939 there were fifty-six high schools and twenty-seven progymnasia. When the city and district of Vilnius was reunited with the country, the number of gymnasia was increased by fifteen. Gradually, compulsory primary education was introduced and the curriculum was expanded from four to six years.

Characteristic of the enthusiasm in Lithuania at that time, in spite of a multitude of other pressing problems, is the fact that one month after the formation of the first cabinet, on December 5, 1918, a forty-one-point comprehensive "Statute of the University of Vilnius" was promulgated. According to this statute, the University of Vilnius, which the Russian authorities had closed in 1832, was to be restored on January 1, 1919. Conditions were such, however, that the first university of independent Lithuania could only start functioning at the beginning of 1922 and it was based not in Vilnius, which had been seized by the Poles, but in Kaunas, the provisional capital. Kaunas became the educational and cultural center of Lithuania.

Since a university could not be set up immediately in Kaunas, special higher courses were instituted in 1920. (The university itself was opened on February 16, 1922.) In 1930, in conjunction with the observance of the 500ts anniversary of the death of Vytautas the Great, the university was designated by his name. At first it had great difficulties with quarters, but it gradually grew and spread as special buildings were constructed. The number of students soon reached the 4,000 mark.

At first, the Mathematics-Natural Sciences Department of the Kaunas University also covered the studies in agriculture and forestry. But later, a special higher school the Agriculture Academy was formed (in Dotnuva, in October, 1924). This higher school prepared agriculturists. In addition, it had a home economics section which prepared specialists in that field. The number of students in the Academy fluctuated between 200 and 300. In September, 1936, in the Kaunas suburb of Vilijampolė, an Academy of Veterinary Sciences was established. In October 1934, in Klaipėda, an Institute of Commerce was established which had as its goal the preparation of commercial specialists. Ernestas Galvanauskas, several times prime minister and foreign minister, was responsible in no small degree for the establishment of the Institute, of which he was the rector. When the Germans took over Klaipėda in 1939, the Institute was moved to Šiauliai. In August, 1935, a Pedagogical Institute was created in Klaipėda which trained highly qualified teachers and school inspectors. About 80 percent of the students of this Institute were women. In 1939, the Institute was moved to Panevėžys. In 1931, the Vytautas the Great Staff School was founded. Until then qualified army officers were sent abroad to acquire additional skills and military knowledge. With the establishment of this war school, Lithuanian officers could study in their own country in order to qualify for a general staff or quartermaster's academic diploma.

In 1938, the "Antanas Smetona Lituanistics Institute" Statute was promulgated which provided for "research of the Lithuanian language, folklore and past." The Institute took into its

hands the preparation of the material for the definitive Lithuanian dictionary, land directory, the works of the commission on
surnames and place names, and the university phonetic laboratory.

A private music school had been established in Kaunas in
1919. The following year it was nationalized, and in 1933, it
was classified as a conservatory and received the rights of a
higher school. Another music school was established in 1923 in
Klaipėda. Later it was granted the rights of a higher school
(however, in 1930, it again became just a music school).

The Kaunas Art School grew out of private courses which
trained teachers. The school, established by the Constituent Assembly in 1922, was reorganized on several occasions and in
1935 was called the Fine Arts School. It taught painting, sculpture, graphics, decorative art, weaving and ceramics.

Since 1922 Kaunas, had had a Lithuanian Catholic Academy
of Sciences which, enjoying the rights of a private institution,
united Catholic scholars and helped prepare the Catholic youth.

With the establishment of an independent state, the idea arose
that a permanent opera and drama theater should be created. In
January, 1920, a private institution, the Creative Artists Society,
was formed by prominent figures in the arts. It divided its work
into four sections: theater, music, art and litearture. The Society
took the initiative in all of these fields and could be considered the
forerunner of all similar societies and institutions in the country.
On December 31, 1920, the state opera came into existence,
producing as its first work Verdi's La Traviata with Kipras Pet-
rauskas in one of the leading roles. (He was called the father of
the Lithuanian opera.) The tradition emerged that every year
on December 31 the Kaunas opera would perform La Traviata.
The opera company, having first-rate performers, soon evolved
into a strong ensemble, with seventy operas in its repertory.
(Ballet was also performed.) The drama theater began in the
Kaunas state theater on December 19, 1920. Both the opera and
the drama theater performed native works as well as foreign ones.

Since olden times, Lithuanians loved to sing. Its folksongs
helped make the country famous, and a number of foreign scholars, poets and musicians became interested in them. Church
choirs were always active. During the independence era the

number of provincial choirs grew. The Riflemen's Association (Šaulių Sąjunga) was very active in this field; it was a paramilitary organization, but it also formed large choirs. The Riflemen's Association, as a nonpartisan national guard, played an important role in the cultural life of the country. Many other organizations also had their choirs.

Because of the general prohibition against organized social activity until 1904, nationwide song festivals were first organized rather late in Lithuania. The first song festival took place in Kaunas during the summer of 1924 with eighty choirs (3,000 voices) participating. Later song festivals had twice as many participants. Song festivals were also organized by youth organizations. In 1933, a women's song festival with 3,000 participants took place in Kaunas.

The state theater did not confine itself to performances in Kaunas, but also visited various provincial centers. In 1931, a branch was formed in Šiauliai, a city which soon became an important cultural center. (A new Lithuanian opera was to develop from this theater, but the second World War interrupted the plans.)

In 1933-34 Kaunas had a "Youth Theater" which attracted young thespians. Although this private theater, because of lack of funds could not hold out long, it played a vital role in the theater life of Lithuania, for it was a proving ground for future directors and actors. In 1937-39, an academic theater studio was organized which was to form a theater nucleus, but its evolution was very slow.

The independence period also witnessed great literary activity in Lithuania. In addition to the old writers, a new generation sprang up which wrote without ideological undertones. A number of new talents in poetry, drama and the novel appeared during this period. Of course, because of the small circulation of books, very few writers could afford to live by writing alone. Together with the general rise in the cultural level, the number of literate people also increased. In 1935, the state literary prize was established which was presented every year on February 16. Also, the Lithuanian Red Cross gave a prize for the best children's literature. Publishing houses, the Catholic Action Center and the Ukmergé municipality (beginning in 1937) gave annual awards, all of which helped intensify literary activity during the last years of independence and encouraged talented writers.

In 1925, a law was passed granting pensions to distinguished civic leaders and people active in the national cultural fields. At the beginning of 1940, this law was expanded. In addition to distinguished public and cultural figures, pensions were granted to the so-called bookleggers (*knygnešiai*), that is, to persons who during the Russian ban on literature risked their lives and health to smuggle books into Lithuania. They were considered important in having helped develop the national culture.

A number of museums were opened during the independence period. In Kaunas, a special chamber was opened which housed the artistic works of the illustrious Lithuanian painter Mykolas Čiurlionis, called the Čiurlionis Gallery. A special role was played by the Kaunas War Museum, whose founder and director, General Vladas Nagevičius-Nagys, made it into a national shrine. A modest monument to Lithuania's Unknown Soldier was set up in the park of the museum, and the flag-lowering ceremony at the monument every evening drew large crowds of viewers. These moving ceremonies played an important role in inculcating patriotic and civic duty; no public organization could refrain from taking part at some time in the ceremonies at the Unknown Soldier's Monument. The museum itself was opened on February 16, 1921. In 1922, a "liberty bell" was installed in the museum tower, a gift of the Lithuanian-Americans. In 1934, a new building was constructed and the museum was rechristened the Vytautas the Great Cultural Museum. Also, several museums were set up in the provinces. The Aušra Museum in Šiauliai and the Alka Museum in Telšiai were important centers for ethnographical collections.

In 1923, Lithuania began a commission consisting of intellectuals headed by the law professor Mykolas Roemeris which was part of the International Committee for Intellectual Cooperation set up in Paris under the auspices of the League of Nations.

In 1934, in Kaunas, the Chamber of Physical Culture was set up to foster an interest in sports. A first, the Chamber prepared sports instructors, but in 1938 this work was taken over by a special department of physical culture associated with the university.

In 1926 the Kaunas radio station came into existence with several orchestras, among them a symphonic orchestra. A second station was opened in 1936 in Klaipėda, and in Vilnius in 1939. In 1940, Lithuania had 90,000 registered radio sets—a large number considering the conditions of the times. Radio broadcasts helped raise the cultural level of the nation.

In 1931, a multivolume *Lithuanian Encyclopedia* was begun, and by 1940, nine volumes were completed. This was a monument in the publication of Lithuanian language books. (Because of the war and the subsequent Soviet occupation, this encyclopedia was discontinued and a new one, consisting of thirty-five volumes, was produced in the United States between 1954 and 1968.)

In 1931, in Kaunas, a special committee to support overseas Lithuanians was created. This society supported Lithuanian schools abroad, prepared teachers, and helped foster Lithuanianism among those living abroad. In 1935, a World Lithuanian Congress was organized in Kaunas which drew cultural leaders from major colonies abroad.

Bonds between the homeland and those who had emigrated were strengthened by the flight of two Lithuanian-Americans (Steponas Darius and Stasys Girėnas) in 1933 from New York to Kaunas, Lithuania. Having flown across the Atlantic, these two pilots crashed in Germany. Though they did not reach their objective, Darius and Girėnas by conquering the Atlantic raised the enthusiasm of the Lithuanian nation.

During the summer of 1938, in Kaunas, the first Olympics took place, with famous Lithuanian athletes from all over the world taking part. It was decided to hold national olympics every five years. The olympics gave Lithuanian sports a new impulse and helped strengthen the bonds of all Lithuanian youth with their homeland.

Many Lithuanian students went to universities and special schools in Western Europe. The government in many cases provided them with scholarships. (Most of the students went to Germany, France or Switzerland.)

After Vilnius was reclaimed, the Lithuanian University began functioning on December 15, 1939, in place of the Polish university. The Vytautas the Great University was reorganized in order to avoid parallelisms. Part of the Kaunas faculty was moved to Vilnius, where an attempt was made to concentrate liberal arts, leaving Kaunas with technology and medicine. The art studios were also reorganized. Kaunas was to concentrate on applied art studios, while Vilnius was to develop the pure arts. The Kaunas Fine Arts School was converted into the Applied Arts Institute. Vilnius also established a fine arts school, later named the Fine Arts Academy. The Vilnius opera was organized during the German occupation, when the Vilnius Philharmonic was closed. The philharmonic orchestra and choir formed the nucleus of the Vilnius opera. In 1940, a state drama theater was set up in Vilnius.

The question of a special cultural fund was also discussed, to foster and encourage cultural activities, and in March, 1939, the Černius government announced that it would support the cultural fund if the public would organize it. However, this fund was not realized before the Soviet occupation.

Although financial resources were limited, the state maintained all of the larger educational, science and art institutions aiding them with public funds.

THE FORMATION OF A SOVIET GOVERNMENT

On June 15, 1940, a message was received from Moscow that Deputy Commissar for Foreign Affairs Dekanozov was coming to Kaunas to supervise the formation of a new government. Although Moscow went through the formalities of pretending that everything was going according to the provisions of the Lithuanian Constitution, in reality the situation had been drastically changed. The country was under military occupation. Further events were no longer dictated by the state interests of Lithuania but by Moscow. The events after June 15, 1940, no longer reflected the will of the Lithuanian state. Merkys government, which had resigned, was merely fulfilling the functions of government, but could no longer make independent decisions. The emissary of Moscow dictated terms.

Antanas Smetona's flight abroad created an unpleasant surprise for Dekanozov when he arrived in Kaunas. Due to his
efforts, a special delegation was sent to the Prussian border town
of Eitkūnai (Eitkuhnen) where President Smetona had temporarily stopped, to persuade Smetona to return to Kaunas, because,
it was stated, constitutional difficulties had developed in forming
a new government. But the President categorically refused to
return in order to legalize the occupation.

On June 16, it was announced that President Smetona's
flight abroad was to be considered his resignation; until the election of a new president, his duties were to be performed by Prime
Minister Antanas Merkys. At the same time, in the Soviet Legation in Kaunas, intense discussions were going on concerning
the formation of a new government. The meeting in the Legation
decided on Justas Paleckas' candidacy for the duties of prime
minister. Paleckis had been an insignificant journalist who had
done hack writing for the "yellow press." He was a leftist of
uncertain principles, not really able to fit in the framework of
any political party, though he had been close to the circles of the
liberal Peasant Populist Union (Valstiečių Liaudininkų Sąjunga).
Never having played any political role in the country until then,
he had the reputation of having been a paid agent of the Communist Party, under the protection of the Soviet Legation. Paleckis officially joined the Communist party after the Soviets
occupied Lithuania.

On June 17, the composition of the new government was
announced. Prime Minister Paleckis' deputy was to be the foreign
affairs minister and minister of education, Professor Vincas
Krėvė-Mickevičius; General Vincas Vitkauskas was to be defense
minister; minister of finance and temporary minister of communications Ernestas Galvanauskas and three inactive pro-Commu-
nists were to form the cabinet. After placing his signature on
Paleckis' appointment Antanas Merkys was forced to resign.
Paleckis, as prime minister, performed the duties of the President
of the Republic. His place as prime minister was taken by Professor Krėvė-Mickevičius.

The composition of the new government temporarily dispelled
initial fears among the populace caused by the military occupa-

tion. Galvanauskas, Krėvė-Mickevičius and General Vitkauskas were well-known public figures, there were no hardened Communists in the government; the impression was that the end had not yet come. . . .

But soon it became apparent that the government had been formed merely to lull the public into a sense of false security. On June 19, Mečys Gedvilas, a Communist party member, was appointed minister of the interior. Other Communists were appointed to the positions being vacated, in addition to which the number of ministers was purposely being increased in order to allow Communists to form the overwhelming majority in the cabinet. The leading role was taken over by Gedvilas and his duly appointed director of the security department, Antanas Sniečkus, who was the general secretary of the Lithuanian Communist party. They formed a government within the government, and executed decisions independent of the other cabinet members. They followed the directive of the special Moscow emissary Dekanozov and Soviet Minister to Kaunas Pozdniakov.

On June 25, the Communist party was legalized. Prior to that, political prisoners were released. According to available facts, 245 prisoners took advantage of the amnesty (they were Communists, for the most part). At the time of the Soviet invasion, the Lithuanian Communist party had 1,741 members who comprised .06 percent of the population. During the first year of Soviet occupation, the membership rose to 3,138 or .10 percent of the population of Lithuania.

When the government fell into the Communists' hands, purges took place in the army (now called the "Peoples Army"), police and administration. Communists or opportunists were appointed to responsible posts. All societies were closed, permits to publish newspapers were revoked. Local Communists or Russian emissaries from Moscow were appointed controllers of local institutions and agencies. The Communists also took over all propaganda apparatus.

But the real aims were still concealed from the nation, and even from the members of the government who were not informed of Moscow's designs. There are even grounds to believe that President Justas Paleckis was not fully informed of all of the

267

details of Moscow's plans. He and the other members of the Peoples' Government took the first few days to try to calm the fears of the populace by stating that the Red Army did not come to occupy the country, but to "protect it from the threat of war and to help maintain its independence." The changes were rationalized as necessary measures to insure the functioning of the mutual assistance pact to the liking of Moscow.

At the same time, the Soviet Legation, which was continually being enlarged, became the true government of Lithuania. It gave orders to the cabinet of ministers. Ernestas Galvanauskas soon became convinced that his good name was being misused by the Soviets. Under the circumstances, he secretly crossed into Germany and dropped his duties as finance minister of the "Peoples' Government."

Professor Krėvė-Mickevičius, a renowned Lithuanian writer, also quickly realized that he was premier in name only. Wanting to clarify the matter with Moscow, and still having illusions about Lithuania's future, he announced his desire to see Molotov. Received by Molotov in Moscow on June 30, he demanded that the interference in Lithuania's internal affairs by the Soviet Legation and the Red Army cease. He argued that not only was the Lithuanian state apparatus being disorganized, but the economy was being ruined as well. Molotov at first tried to dodge the issue by using meaningless phrases, but then suddenly changed his tone and declared that he "has to state frankly what will be clear to all tomorrow. If, during the Czarist period starting with Ivan the Terrible, the Russians pushed to the Baltic Sea, then it must be realized today that this was due as a necessary requirement of the development of the Soviet Russian state and nation. It would be an unforgiveable thing if the Soviet Union did not make use of the opportunity, which might not rise again. The government of the Soviet Union has decided to incorporate the Baltic States into the family of Soviet republics, of course, as separate union republics while guaranteeing full rights and possibilities to develop and flourish in the interests of the national culture, national economy and well-being." In continuing his discourse, Molotov declared that "in the future small states would have to disappear." Regarding the form of annexation, Molotov said that the "people" will be asked in the manner "set up in the Soviet Republics." When Krėvė-Mickevičius said that the Lithuanian nation would give a negative answer to such a referendum, Molotov interrupted categorically: "We'll know how to teach the Lithuanian people." After the conversation with Molotov, Krėvė-Mickevičius reported that "it became clear to me that the USSR will incorporate Lithuania into the Soviet Union with veiled force."

Returning to Kaunas, Professor Krėvė-Mickevičius informed not only the non-Communist members of the cabinet but also his close acquaintances about his conversation with Molotov. He even told Paleckis and Gedvillas, the minister of the interior. Paleckis admitted that in accepting the invitation to form a government "he had been fooled, for G. Dekanozov guaranteed him that Lithuania's independence was not in danger." It was hard for him to realize that there was no other alternative to following Moscow's demands. Gedvilas declared that he had been guaranteed that when the Red Army came, internal order would not be changed. Only later did he learn "the direction that the course of events in Lithuania were taking." But as a Communist, he had to follow party decisions, and did not have the right to quit: "The party discipline would be strict and consider such a resignation as the act of a traitor and would take proper measures."

Having his eyes opened for the first time, Krėvė-Mickevičius decided to resign from his post, but his resignation was not accepted. After several days it was announced that because of ill health he would be granted a vacation. Mečys Gedvilas was authorized to perform the functions of the prime minister, keeping the portfolio of the minister of the interior as well. In this manner, the government fell into Communist hands completely.

With the withdrawal of Krėvė-Mickevičius and the flight abroad of Galvanauskas, the few remaining non-Communists who had wavered now obeyed the Soviet Legation, and did not resist the cabinet members who belonged to the Communist party. General Vitkauskas remained as minister of defense, but he was replaced as commander of the army by Soviet General Feliksas Baltušis-Žemaitis, who had been a Red Army career officer and spoke Lithuanian very poorly. General Vitkauskas accommodated himself to the Soviets and later served in their army.

With the regrouping of the government, an electoral law was quickly passed calling for elections to the "Peoples' Diet" on July 14. Events moved rather rapidly. On July 7, the newspapers announced that a new organization, the "Union of Labor Lithuania," had been formed. Who its members were and what were its principles, was not announced. That same day, this fictitious organization announced its program, which was coached in vague phrases. In the field of foreign affairs, it emphasized the "fraternity of nation" that existed between the Soviet Union and Lithuania, and the "firm and unbreakable union" of the two states. The program did not mention a single word about plans for the future of the Lithuanian state, or, for that matter, of plans to incorporate Lithuania into the Soviet Union. Affixed to the text was a list of several hundred signatures—some of whom had not even given their consent. The signature of the Lithuanian Communist party was modestly put in last place. After the elections, the "Union of Labor Lithuania" quietly disappeared and nothing was heard about it thereafter.

The only purpose for the "Union" was to offer candidates to the "Peoples' Diet." Among the candidates were a number of prominent persons whose consent was not even asked. They learned about their candidacy from the press. Some candidates were threatened with reprisals if they tried to remove their candidacy. As the period between the announcement of the elections and the election was a mere week, the choice of candidates had to be made rather quickly. The list was read at a mass meeting and quickly accepted with enthusiasm. The candidates were divided into three categories: 1) ordinary citizens who were not known to anyone. Some of them might have been Communists, but they never played any important role in the party and their candidacy was being used to create the impression that "new people from the masses were being elevated"; 2) the largest group consisted of party members who took their orders from Moscow; 3) ten Lithuanian intellectuals who were not Communists and whose candidacy was used to dupe the public.

At the same time that emissary Dekanozov arrived in Kaunas,

270

a high Soviet security official was also sent to Lithuania. This secret police official called himself Gladkov. He did not appear in public, and only after five months was he officially appointed to the post of Commissar for state security in Lithuania. Actually, he held these duties from the start and exercised great powers. In a formal sense, at the beginning of the occupation, the post of director of security was held by Antanas Sniečkus, first secretary of the Lithuanian Communist Party.

On the same day the election campaign began, July 7, Sniečkus signed a "strictly secret" instruction which provided for the arrest, on the night of July 11-12, of the so-called "anti-state parties"—the Tautininkai, Voldemarists, populists, Christian Democrats, Young-Lithuanians, Trotskyites, Social-Democrats, Esers, Riflemen and others, "according to the list of preparatory work regarding liquidations and the operative liquidation plan." According to this detailed instruction, during the given period about 2,000 political and civic leaders were to be arrested throughout Lithuania. This wave of terror swept through the country two days before the elections to the "Peoples' Diet." Prior to that, a purge of the army, police and agencies had been undertaken, which affected a large number of people. Thus, a reign of terror was inaugurated.

At the same time, an intense pre-election campaign was instituted. These pseudo-elections were called the "most democratic in the whole world." The electors were told that voting was mandatory, that whosoever did not participate in them would be placed in the category of "peoples' enemies." Although the Communist party called endless meetings and organized demonstrations, its influence on the public was minimal. On July 10, the minister of education issued an appeal which stated: "It is noticed that the educated are not taking part in the pre-election campaign." On July 9, *Vilniaus Balsas* carried this item: "Whosoever does not vote will be a peoples' enemy. There will be no place in Lithuania for such persons."

"President" Justas Paleckis, on the morning of the elections, announced over the radio: "Only the enemies of the people, only the enemies of the new Lithuania's future can stay home today and not participate in this victorious campaign of the Lithuanian

271

people." The minister of agriculture called together his officials and civil servants and warned them: "Whosoever does not participate in the voting will by this act aid the enemies of the people." In addition to these warnings, a more effective method of coercion was introduced—voting was to be registered in passports. In this manner, it would not be hard to determine who had not voted and who was to be placed in the category of "peoples' enemies."

One could raise the question: Why did Moscow devote so much attention to getting more people to participate in the sham elections if the results were to be a foregone conclusion? The answer is obvious: as Molotov declared to Krėvė-Mickevičius, the Lithuanian nations had to be asked "in the form which was followed by the Soviet Republics"; that is, in the form practiced by a foreign state. Lithuania was to hold the same sort of pseudo-elections that were practiced in the Soviet Union where, according to official statistics, 99 percent of the electorate gave its votes to the government candidates. Moscow wanted to demonstrate that the Lithuanian nation, of its own accord, approved the candidates chosen by the Soviet Legation in Kaunas. Although the electors had no other choice, the fact was hidden from them that the "Peoples' Diet" was designated to play the role of the liquidator of the Lithuanian state.

According to official statistics, the number of voters who participated in the elections numbered 95.5 percent of the electorate, and the candidates of the Union of Labor Lithuania, which was the only group permitted to submit candidates, received 99.19 percent of all the votes. These results conformed with the results obtained in the Soviet Union. The announced results were so transparently fictitious that no one believed them.

First of all, it must be pointed out that no list of voters was kept. It was impossible to determine how many people even had the right to vote. Under the circumstances, one must dismiss the announcements made by the Soviet press as utter prefabrications with no basis in reality. For example, *Vilniaus Balsas,* on July 17, announced that in some of the precincts of Vilnius the returns were 133 percent! *Darbo Lietuva,* on July 16, broke the record by writing that "There are many places where 138 percent of the persons having the right to vote took part in the elections." The newspaper, however, did not state how one determined how many people in the precinct had the right to vote, since no prior list existed. The city and district of Vilnius had many refugees from Poland; so did other parts of Lithuania. These refugees also were permitted to vote!

The elections themselves were to take place on July 14. As the day drew to a close, voting officials noticed that there was a poor turnout, that it was an obvious reproach. The government then extended the elections another day. On July 17, *Vilniaus Balsas* announced that a flying commission had been formed to visit people in their homes and urge them to place their votes in the portable urns. According to the paper, the commission collected 21,581 votes in Vilnius on the second day of elections, which constituted a fifth of the votes in the city.

On July 16, *Vilniaus Balsas* acknowledged that the true number of persons having the right to vote in the Vilnius district was hard to determine because the census had been taken during the Polish occupation. It was impossible to use these figures because they included Polish citizens of voting age. Now, only those born in Vilnius or having long residence could vote. But despite all of these uncertainties, it was announced that 200,232 persons in the Vilnius electoral district cast their votes and that they constituted 95.95 percent of "those having the right to vote," although, of course, no lists were kept and it was not known how many people resided in the district. In the Kaunas electoral district, according to the commission report, 106.18 percent of the people who had the right to vote had cast their ballots!

The electoral commissions were made up of Communist party members or of people appointed by the party. For purposes of illustration, let us note that the chairman of the Kaunas commission was Antanas Guzevičius, who at the time was vice-minister of internal affairs. He was later appointed commissar for internal affairs. The chairman of the supreme commission was V. Niunka, an old Communist, who was later appointed Prosecutor of the Supreme Court.

Under these circumstances, it is not possible to talk about control of elections. The supreme electoral commission announced that there "were no complaints about irregularities in voting."

It remains a secret by which means the supreme electoral commission was able to establish with such precision, that 95.51 percent voted of those who held the right to vote.

On July 17, *Darbo Lietuva* announced that "in the city of Vilnius 124,382 envelopes with 733,219 votes were submitted in two days. In the townships of Vilnius county, about 54,000 envelopes with 262,000 votes were collected." Keeping in mind that in the Vilnius district there were ten candidates, it would seem that the city of Vilnius had to submit 1,243,820 votes and that the county had to submit 540,000 votes. In truth, the city submitted 510,601 and the county itself 278,000 votes less than the number required by the number of envelopes, if one maintains that each voter had to cast votes for ten candidates. The individual votes received by candidates are interesting. The most votes received in Vilnius were 97,547 and the least were 25,825. According to *Darbo Lietuva,* Vilnius submitted 214,388 envelopes. Therefore, the candidate who received the least votes got only twenty percent of the votes.

All of these disclosures of the official organ did not hinder the falsification commission from announcing that the Vilnius district returned 95.95 percent of the votes and that the candidates of the Union of Labor Lithuania received 99.85 percent. Regardless of the actual number of votes cast, the results were predetermined by the Communists. All of the candidates were declared elected.

In 1953, the United States House of Representatives' "Select Committee to Investigate the 'Incorporation' of the Baltic States into the USSR," in its findings stated that it is clear and proven beyond doubt that Estonia, Latvia and Lithuania were taken over by force and illegally incorporated into the Soviet Union. Every Soviet assertion that the July, 1940, elections were free and voluntary or that the parliament assembled as a result of these "elections" legitimately appealed for admission into the Soviet Union as a Soviet Republic is an unfounded lie.

After the "Peoples' Diets' " resolution calling for Lithuania's admission into the USSR was accepted, the diplomatic representatives of Lithuania abroad presented their solemn protest against

the falsification of the will of the Lithuanian people to the governments to which they were accredited, and unanimously condemned the Soviet aggression and the seizure of their state. A
number of Western democratic states declined to recognize the
incorporation and endorsed the continued activities of the Lithuanian diplomatic and consular representatives.

LITHUANIA'S ANNEXATION

Only after the elections did the Communist party dare come
out in the open and demand that Lithuania join the Soviet Union.
Moscow, which had until then contented itself with a military
occupation, through it satellite Lithuanian Communist party came
out in the open with its second phase, to wit, the annexation of
Lithuania. This goal was to be achieved through the newly constituted Peoples' Diet, which was to declare Lithuania a Soviet
Republic and then ask for its admittance into the Soviet Union.

The Communist party began to organize meetings which
passed resolutions toward that end. These resolutions were sent
to the "Peoples' Government" and to the "Peoples' Diet," as the
so-called voice of the nation. Everything was prefabricated. The
meeting was opened by "President" Justas Paleckis. After slan-
dering the independence period, he dwelt on the so-called desire
of the Lithuanian nation to introduce into the republic a soviet
system. But in his argumentation, Paleckis had to recognize that
all of the struggles and sacrifices would have remained fruitless
for a long time if it had not been for the "fraternal help" received from the "fraternal and friendly nations of the Soviet
Union which sent to us the liberator of nations, the Red Army."
Paleckis' public admission that the "help" of the Soviet Union
and the occupation of Lithuania by the Red Army was necessary
illustrates the only manner in which the situation could have
arisen. Prime Minister Mečys Gedvilas was authorized to present
the following resolution: "The Peoples' Diet, expressing the
united will of the free-working people of Lithuania, announce
the introduction of the soviet system into Lithuania." Afterward,
Minister of Justice Povilas Pakarklis publicly admitted that the
people had overthrown the former regime with the aid of the

"mighty Red Army," and then presented the following resolution: "To ask the Supreme Soviet of the Union of Soviet Socialist Republics to admit the Lithuanian Soviet Socialist Republic into the Union of Soviet Socialist Republics."

There were a number of accounts given by former members of the Diet about the manner in which Moscow executed its plans of annexation. These witnesses broke away from the Soviets in 1941, when the war between Germany and Russia started. Some even escaped to the West. It would be a mistake to think that the fateful meeting of the Diet took place in a Western parliamentary manner. The meeting itself was called in the municipal theater of Kaunas. The members of the Diet were seated among Red Army soldiers and members of the Soviet Legation as well as Moscow emissaries who directed the Sovietization of Lithuania. Dr. Antanas Garmus, who was elected against his will, testifies that "we, the members of the Diet, were surrounded on all sides by the secret police." The Diet formed a minority of those assembled. During the meeting, a few members of the government spoke, performing roles that had previously been assigned to them. "No one was given the right to vote," states Dr. Garmus; the "voting took place amid great noise which was artificially created by the Communist party members and Soviet agents in the hall. From all sides, from the balcony, loges, lobby and the hall came shouts and yells." During the voting, "not only the members of the Diet raised their hands. How many actually voted, how many remained silent, in spite of threats and terror, cannot be determined." According to the official communique, the resolutions were unanimously adopted.

The Diet formed a special delegation under Paleckis' chairmanship, which went to Moscow to give the request to the Supreme Soviet that Lithuania be admitted into the Soviet Union. On August 3, Moscow satisfied the request and executed the act of annexation. Prior to this, the Supreme Soviet had decided to annex Moldavia; after Lithuania came Latvia's and Estonia's turn.

THE SOVIETIZATION OF THE LITHUANIAN STATE

After Lithuania was incorporated into the Soviet Union, the country experienced Sovietization in all fields. On August 24,

the "Peoples' Diet" became the "Supreme Soviet of the Lithuanian Soviet Socialist Republic." The following day a new state
constitution was adopted, which in fact was copied from the
texts of the other soviet republics. In the words of the chairman
of the constitutional committee, Povilas Pakarklis, "The constitutional commission followed the principles of the Stalin constitution, and took examples from the functioning constitutions of
the other brotherly union republics." The new constitution was
presented as the "most democratic in the world," which shone
from the sun of "Stalin's genius." "The Peoples Government"
called itself the council of commissars and its prime minister remained Mečys Gedvilas. Justas Paleckis received the title of
Chairman of the Presidium of the Supreme Soviet of the Lithuanian Soviet Socialist Republic. Other institutions were pat-
terned after Soviet models.

With one stroke of the pen, Russian laws became effective
immediately in Lithuania. Soviet norms for civil and criminal
codes, procedure, system of courts, and norms of family, property, hiring, commerce, crafts, taxes and other were applied.
Each of these affected the situation of every individual in his
relations with the state and with other people, and in essence
these changes differed from all previous norms.

On July 1, 1940, it was announced that the government had
decided to sever relations with the Vatican, which had been
established in the concordat of September 27, 1927. After the
incorporation of Lithuania into the USSR, the Apostolic Nuncio
as well as other diplomats and consuls had to leave the country.
An iron curtain descended on Lithuania's western border.

At the end of June and the beginning of July it was announced
that the teaching of religion would be stricken from the school
curriculum and that chaplains would be dismissed from the army
and the prisons. On June 25, it was announced that the faculty
of theology-philosophy of Kaunas University would be closed.
All monasteries were closed and the monks expelled. Three of the
four seminaries were immediately shut down. (The Kaunas seminary was at first tolerated, but its quarters were soon turned
over to the Red Army.) All of the bishops' residences and their
curia were sequestrated; in many places, church rectories were

turned over to the Red Army. The religious press and organizations were shut down, religious books were destroyed. The clergy, in the eyes of the regime, was an enemy of the people and had to be persecuted. On October 2, 1940, the head of the NKVD, Gladkov, issued an instruction "for the organized struggle against the enemy clergy" to take the clergy to "task formally," (that is, to keep dossiers on them and to follow their moves). The first article of this instruction read: "Discern the places where the priests meet with students to perpetrate their hostile work. Enlist senior gymnasium students to divide the enemy." On January 21, 1941, the commissar of internal affairs, Guzevičius, issued a new detailed instruction aimed against the clergy, according to which the tailing of priests and the work of tearing down churches had to be strengthened. The clergy were cut off from all salaries, and had to pay higher special taxes.

Bearing in mind the methods which were passed by decree against the clergy and the church, the provision of the state constitution about "freedom for religious cults" was an empty phrase like the other declared "freedoms" under the constitution. During one year of Soviet rule, the balance of religious and clerical persecution was as follows: fifteen priests were shot, eighteen priests were jailed and nine priests were deported to the USSR. In December, 1940, it was decided that the Church of the Garrison in Kaunas be turned into a revolutionary museum. Two Lutheran churches were turned into warehouses.

Declaring for the Soviet system, the "Peoples' Diet" passed a number of decisions regarding property. On July 22, all of the privately owned land was declared state property; one farm could not comprise more than thirty hectares. The remaining land was turned over to the land fund "in order to permit the landless and small-holders to get more land." A land reform was instituted which led to the introduction of the same system that existed in the Soviet Union, namely, the establishment of *kolkhozes* and *sovkhozes*. The land reform was to take place at "Soviet tempo." It was to be accomplished by September 1. According to official statistics, the land reform touched 385,000 hectares, which was taken from 27,000 holders. Of this nationalized land, 56,500 hectares were kept to form new estates, namely, *sovkhozes;* 98,000 hectares of private forest became state property; 384,000 hectares were parceled out for the use of 71,000 landless and small-holders. About 30,000 hectares were kept for airfields, barracks, military camps, dumps, etc. An average 5.4 hectares were parceled out per person. If one considers the fact that many small-holders had some land, then each farmer was to have six to eight hectares.

The Soviet land reform was promulgated for purely political reasons, ignoring economic considerations. If the land reform of the independence period had led to the creation of small holding, which in some cases could not be justified by economic considerations, then the Soviet reform led to the complete pauperization of the farmers. During the period of Soviet rule, agriculture was so disorganized that in October, 1940, a communique was published to the effect that the Lithuanian government had to appeal to Moscow for bread—despite the fact that during the independence period Lithuania never had to import any grain.

The nationalized land was turned over to farmers for temporary exploitation. Although little time had elapsed until the summer of 1941, several *kolkhozes* were established. When the Communist regime began to execute its land reform, "group settlements" were formed; the village system facilitated the formation of *kolkhozes* in the future. The Soviets pursued a policy diametrically opposed to the policy of the independence period. After nineteenth-century serfdom had been abolished, the Lithuanians had parceled the remaining villages into homesteads. The Soviets now began to huddle the farmers into villages similar to the ones that had existed during the Czarist era. Following the Soviet model, the agrarian producers of Lithuania were forced to fulfill government norms. Those so-called "harvests" depressed the farmers. The "harvests" were progressively determined by the size of the agrarian unit. In practice, this pace was so rapid that it served to liquidate individual farming and prepare the way for universal collectivization, which was accomplished during the second Soviet occupation.

Lithuanian industry in the independence era was relatively small. The number of establishments having more than five workers totaled 1,500, and 40,000 workers were employed in these shops. Lithuanian industry was geared to the home market, it was provided as it was with local raw materials. Although industry grew in independent Lithuania, it did not form large industrial complexes that existed in industrial countries.

On July 23, 1940, a "declaration" (public law) was promulgated regarding the nationalization of banks and industries. According to the declaration, all establishments that had more than twenty workers were to be nationalized; in addition, shops driven by mechanized power and employing more than ten workers were also to be confiscated by the state. In practice, all shops were nationalized regardless of the number of workers. Trusts and combines were set up for the purpose of industrial concentration. Approximately 902 of the 1,500 shops were nationalized; the remaining ones, however, during the first year of Soviet occupation, almost disappeared. This was a measure to liquidate the small industrialists and craftsmen, who were to form production cooperations. The craftsmen were joined to cartels. Even barbers could not work at their trade privately; they too had to join cartels.

As in the Soviet Union, so-called "work norms" were introduced into Lithuania. If they were not fulfilled, the worker received a cut in his salary. Propaganda and work norms were used to increase production. Often, "socialist competition" was applied. The workers were denied the right to change their place of employment. So-called "work-books" were issued to laborers, without which they could not get employment. These booklets had infringements of work discipline entered in them.

From the start of the occupation the banks were faced with a rush by the people attempting to convert their deposits into goods. Withdrawal of deposits was blocked.

On November 25, 1940, a decree was passed incorporating the Lithuanian economy into that of the USSR. The Soviet *ruble* was introduced, though for the time being the old Lithuanian currency continued to circulate. An arbitrary rate of exchange was set up: one *litas* was to equal ninety *kopecks*. Actually, the purchasing power of the *litas* was three or four times greater than that of the ruble. On March 25, 1941, it was announced that the *litas* was no longer legal tender and that the

280

ruble was to be the only currency. On the same date, the banks were informed that depositors were entitled to only 1,000 *rubles'* worth of their original deposits. The remainder of the deposits were placed in a special fund. The inhabitants of Lithuania never again saw their savings.

A similar expropriation occurred regarding securities, which had been ordered to be deposited in the banks. Actually, these securities were confiscated; they were never reimbursed. It is estimated that the confiscation of deposits, securities, the arbitrary rate of exchange and other measures cost the inhabitants of Lithuania about 1 billion *litai,* which was equivalent to 150 million U.S. dollars (1940).

Expropriations also touched on other forms of property. Real property was confiscated, although the owners were permitted to keep small homes or apartments. Commercial establishments, hotels, hospitals, drugstores, motion picture theaters, ships, buses, trucks, and the like were nationalized. The state also nationalized credits, leaving the debits to the original owners.

ARRESTS AND MASS DEPORTATIONS

While Lithuania was still independent, and had not experienced Russian Communism, all talk of terror in the Soviet Union was considered exaggerated stories. Those Lithuanians who during the first World War and in 1918-20 lived in Russia, felt that civil war and Cheka terror was a thing of the past. And Soviet agents announced that the Communist regime had become democratic and humane.

During the one year of Soviet occupation the Lithuanian nation experienced all of the horrors of Soviet terror. When the Red Army occupied Lithuania, Moscow sent NKVD agents to the country, along with special emissaries. The Russians applied the same terror techniques in Lithuania that they had developed in the Soviet Union.

Due to the sudden outbreak of war between Germany and Russia in June, 1941, which caught the USSR off guard, the Lithuanians were able to get a large number of Soviet documents into their hands. At the same time, many people were able to liberate themselves from Soviet prisons. All of these circumstances provide us with living witnesses of Soviet terror. The extent of terror that had fallen upon Lithuania can be surmised from the appeal of Archbishop Juozapas Skvireckas, Metropolitan of Lithuania, who, at the start of the war, declared: "People said that it would be much better to await a terrible and devastating war on the open field rather than live passively in Bolshevik slavery."

During the first days of the Soviet occupation a number of high Lithuanian officials were arrested, including former Minister of the Interior Kazys Skučas, Director of Security Augustinas Povilaitis, and Colonel Kostas Dulksnys, head of the military intelligence. Two days before the elections to the "Peoples' Diet," acting on the orders of the NKVD commissar Gladkov, security director Antanas Sniečkus issued an instruction calling for arrests of "anti-state party leaders," which was executed on a wide scale. While Lithuania was still formally an independent state, Mečys Gedvilas, as minister of the interior, had suggested in writing to "President" Paleckis that he arrest the last prime minister, Antanas Merkys, and the foreign minister, Juozas Urbšys, together with their families. The letter stated: "send them out of Lithuania's territory as persons dangerous to the Lithuanian state and settle them in the Soviet Union." Paleckis added a resolution to the note: "I confirm this and agree to the suggestion." Therefore, two Lithuanian statesmen were sent to the Soviet Union although the Lithuanian state still existed as an independent entity. (There are grounds for assuming that Skučas, Povilaitis and Dulksnys were sent to the Soviet Union earlier.) Later, scores of thousands of Lithuanians were deported under the most frightful conditions to the depths of Russia.

With the establishment of the Soviet regime, one of the first moves was to isolate Lithuania from the West. For this reason, all of the people living along the western border were relocated, especially those under suspect. A zone several kilometers wide was declared a death zone. No unauthorized person was permitted to travel across it. On November 28, 1940, Commissar of Internal Affairs Guzevičius issued a decree about "the anti-Soviet and socially undesirable element." This "element" included not only the political leaders, officials, officers, police and priests of the independence period, but also persons "who maintain personal correspondence with the outside, foreign state legations and consulates, esperantists and philatelists," also "former Red Cross workers." Since the prisons of Lithuania could not hold all of the arrestees, cells which normally held four to five persons were now crowded with twenty and more prisoners. When a Soviet inspector visited the Kaunas prison, which was by no means modern, he said that it was like a "sanatorium." Wooden boxes were nailed to the windows from the outside through which only a slender ray of light pierced the cells. The prisoners were subjected to all of the terrorist methods of interrogation and torture that were a hallmark of the Stalin era. They were accused of being counterrevolutionaries "who were active against the Soviet state and government." In reply to protests that in independent Lithuania Soviet law had never applied, and that *ex post facto* laws were not practiced in civilized society, the Soviets rebutted that according to Soviet law each person is punished for having worked against the "interests of the working masses" and for having hindered the revolutionary activities "of the working people," and that "the Soviet Union solidifies the worldwide struggle of all working peoples who strive to overthrow the bourgeois order and to establish a Soviet regime." Those found guilty of such violations were given stiff sentences—to be carried out in the depths of Russia.

As it was later learned, terrible coercion was to prepare the way for the mass deportation of Lithuania's inhabitants, drawn up according to the instruction of Serov, the deputy Soviet commissar of state security for the USSR. An original of these instructions was later found in Lithuania after the Soviets had retreated. This mass deportation was to be carried out simultaneously in Estonia, Latvia and Lithuania. The instructions stated that "the deportation of the anti-Soviet element from the Baltic State is a task of great political importance." The instructions went on in great detail, which attests to Moscow's careful preparations, to explain how and when the deportations were to be carried out.

The first mass deportation, which began on June 14, 1941, has subsequently gone down in Lithuanian history as one of the most tragic episodes the nation had ever experienced. The "operation" began at 4 A.M. and was nationwide. The people to be deported were given a brief interval to gather their belongings; often this interval lasted only fifteen minutes. Entire families were taken to railway depots where boxcars stood waiting. As a rule, families were separated, crowded into the cars and shopped to the north and east. The "operation" in many places lasted until June 16. News of the "manhunt" spread throughout Lithuania. People began to hide. A reign of terror descended upon the Lithuanian nation.

Moscow had reached a decision to deport one-third of the Lithuanian nation toward the end of May, 1941. Preparation of the lists of persons to be deported was begun on November 28, according to commissar Guzevičius' instruction. Moscow handled the whole operation in such a manner that the responsibility was to fall on the puppet Lithuanian government. It is known that on June 10, 1941, Moscow recommended to the Lithuanian government that it decide to ask for permission to deport the "anti-Soviet element" from Lithuania. Due to Moscow's pressure, the Lithuanian Communist regime made such a decision, although a number of commissars did refuse to sign the document.

A special section of the Serov instructions states the manner in which families and their heads are to be treated. After making a search, it was to be announced that the deportees were to be transported to other Soviet regions on the basis of the decision of the government. Another section of the infamous instruction was as follows:

> In view of the fact that a large number of deportees must be arrested and distributed in special camps and that their families must proceed to special settlements in distant regions, it is essential that the operation of removal of both the members of the deportee's family and its head should be carried out simultaneously, without notifying them of the separation confronting them. After the domiciliary search has been carried out and the appropriate identification documents have been drawn up in the deportee's home, the operative worker should complete the documents for the head of the family and deposit them in the latter's personal file,

but the documents drawn up for members of his family shall be deposited in the personal file of the deportee's family.

The convoy of the entire family to the station shall, however, be effected in one vehicle and only at the station of departure shall the head of the family be placed separately from his family in a car specially intended for heads of families. During the assembling (of the family) in the home of the deportee the head of the family shall be warned that personal male effects must be packed in a separate suitcase, as a sanitary inspection of the deported men will be made separately from the women and children. At the stations of entrainment heads of families subject to arrest shall be loaded into cars specially allotted for them, which shall be indicated by operative workers appointed for that purpose.

We do not have precise information as to how many persons were arrested and deported on that terrible night. Lists were found in the NKVD offices but they cover only a part of the deported mass. However, these lists mention other documents regarding the deportations. The main station through which the trains were to pass was Naujoji Vilnia near Vilnius. Five hundred thirty-one cars were registered there as having human cargoes. It has been established that 340 cars took other routes. Although the instructions said that twenty-five persons were to be placed in one boxcar, in actuality the number of persons packed in exceeded fifty per car. Taking into consideration all of the documents regarding deportations, between 30,000 and 40,000 persons were deported in several days. The NKVD documents show that most of the deportees were sent to Siberia, Karelia, the Russian North, Kazakhstan and other remote places. The documents also show that similar deportations were planned for the future. The second "operation" was to take place on June 24, but the Russo-German War disrupted the plan.

This war, however, is the reason why we have so many documents about the Soviet terror. When the Soviets returned in 1944, they began a new terror against the Lithuanian nation. We do not have genuine documentary evidence about the subsequent deportations, as we do about the first ones. Yet it is not difficult by analogy to show the manner in which Soviet terror was reinstituted, and its form until the death of Stalin (afterward, the Soviets gradually applied new forms).

The instructions pointed out that the deportations were to be executed with the active participation of local Communist party committees. Therefore, the party was dragged into the deportations, starting with the leadership and going down to the local officials.

The deportations were to destroy, or in the language of the instructions, to "liquidate" a large part of the Lithuanian nation without specifying the reason why. According to the instructions, the deportations could be applied to an undetermined number of people. Some experts estimate that 700,000 people were to be "liquidated." The deportations were executed for purely political reasons, as stated in the Serov instructions. Moscow perpetrated an act of criminal genocide against the Lithuanian nation.

When the Russo-German war broke out, the Lithuanian Communist party leadership and the cabinet members retreated into Russia. Before evacuating the country, Soviet security personnel, party officials and Red Army units in a number of locales massacred political prisoners.

LITHUANIA UNDER NAZI OCCUPATION (1941-44)

When, on June 22, 1941, Nazi Germany began its war against the Soviet Union, the Lithuanian nation greeted the news with unconcealed feelings of relief. The Soviet regime of terror, which had raged until a week before the war, raised such a feeling of hostility against the oppressed Lithuanians that any power which would have struck a blow against Moscow would have been greeted as a liberator. The Nazis, however, made sure that the feeling of liberation would not last long in Lithuania.

The start of the war had not caught the Lithuanians by surprise, although the conditions of Soviet terror did not allow systematic preparations for it. Nonetheless, the war permitted the Lithuanians an opportunity to rise against the Soviet regime. On June 23, the rebels, taking over the Kaunas radio station, declared restoration of the independent Lithuanian state. When the Germans marched into Kaunas on June 24, the city had already been cleared of Red Army elements by the Lithuanians themselves.

On June 23, in Kaunas, a provisional government of Lithuania was formed with the following: Colonel Kazys Škirpa, prime minister; deputy prime minister and minister of education, Dr. Juozas Ambrazevičius; foreign minister, Rapolas Skipitis; defense minister, General Stasys Raštikis. The government, whose nucleus was formed by the Lithuanian Activist Front, was formed by Peasant Populists and people close to the Christian Democrats, and had a coalition cabinet.

When the revolt erupted and spread throughout all of Lithuania, and when the provisional government was proclaimed, the question arose as to how the Germans would react. Prior to the revolt, Colonel Škirpa, who had been Lithuanian Minister to Berlin, approached several German government officials to sound them out on their views; he learned that the Germans were extremely opposed to the restoration of an independent Lithuanian state. Nevertheless, the Lithuanian activists decided to ignore this, and declared independence on the second day of the war. This move conflicted with the plans of the Nazis, who wanted to conquer the country as they had done others. The Lithuanians did not have to wait long for Nazi reactions. Neither Škirpa nor Skipitis, who also lived in Berlin at the time, were permitted by German offices to return home. This alone gave a clue to German motives.

The provisional government, war conditions permitting, took the first steps to eliminate the horrors of the Soviet regime, especially in the field of economics. In July, private property was restored and Soviet confiscations were abolished. During the first days of its existence, the provisional government had many matters to take up with the German military agencies, which of course ignored the Lithuanian government, or at least remained aloof. It became known that the German Fuehrer had on July 17 appointed Heinrich Lohse, the Gauleiter of Schleswig-Holstein, to be the Reichskommissar for a newly created "Ostland." Ostland was to encompass Lithuania, Latvia, Estonia and Byelorussia, and general commissars were appointed for each of these countries. Theodor Adrian von Renteln, a German born in Russia and a leader of the Hitler *Jugend,* was named to be the "General Commissioner for the district formerly known as Independent Lithuania."

On July 28, Reichskommissar Lohse issued a declaration to the Lithuanian nation which contained the following: "Those, who during the last twenty years had promised you much freedom, thought that they can base their politics on the differences between the Soviet Union and the German Reich. But the moment when the German Reich had ceased to hold certain territories in its sphere of influence in view of the English aggression, this misfortunate moment was immediately felt. The Soviet Union was able to attack you without any resistance from your government."

The declaration went on to state that Germany had now taken over Lithuania from the Soviet Union with all rights. The result of this did not take long to become apparent. The declaration also demonstrated the views of the National-socialists toward the countries that would form "Ostland." This concept had no place for an independent Lithuanian state. Germany planned to take Ostland under its direct rule. This also sealed the fate of the Lithuanian provisional government.

Even earlier, during private talks with members of the Lithuanian Government, the idea was offered that it could continue to function as a German military occupation auxiliary committee or council. The government did not agree to such combinations, and in spite of obstacles it continued its work as best it could. On July 25, the new Ostland administration began its work, taking over areas that had been within the jurisdiction of the Lithuanian Government. The work of the provisional government was no longer feasible materially. On August 5, Generalkommissar von Renteln invited members of the provisional government to his office and told them the government could no longer operate; all of its functions had passed to the General Commissariat. The Commissar would choose Lithuanian trustees at his own pleasure. The provisional government told von Renteln that it protested this decision, but, since it had no alterantive, it would have to disband. Prior to this, the government members gathered at the monument of the unknown soldier and placed a wreath there.

NAZI GERMANY—SOVIET RUSSIA'S HEIR

One of the first acts of the Ostland administration was to declare by decree that Germany was the legal heir to the Soviet Union. On August 8, 1941, the Reichskommissar issued a decree whereby the Ostland German civilian administration (Zivilver-waltung) would take over all of the real property and chattels of the Soviet Union according to the *status quo* of June 20, 1941. This, of course, included all property that had been nationalized by the Soviets. All of the nationalized land, realty, industry and commerce now fell into German hands. The Soviet land reform had theoretically been repealed, but the land was not returned to the original owners. The farmers were given the right to administer their own land. Legally the situation of the farmers was even worse, because under the Soviets, farmers held the use of the land "in perpetuity," while now they were mere administrators-users (Bewirtschafter). It was apparent that to the Nazis the Soviet nationalization law was acceptable, for now the Reich could "inherit" the nationalized property.

Of course, it would have been a simple matter to return the land to the true owners because only three *kolkhozes* had been set up during the Soviet occupation. But the German occupational agencies began to justify their position by stating that the return of property would require much transitional work. Even the *sovkhozes* were kept. A number of small farms had been joined to the *sovkhozes;* their owners remained now as the hired workers of the Nazis.

In February, 1942, Berlin formed a special company, the *Landbewirtschaftungsgesellschaft Ostland,* which was to take over all of the *sovkhozes.* In similar manner, it took over farms whose owners had been either arrested or deported during the Soviet occupation, as well as the farms of Germans repatriated to Germany. In addition, this company took over the property of Jews and Communists, for they were denied the right to own property. After this company was formed, commentaries were published to the effect that all of the land of Ostland belonged to it, since the region was now part of the Reich's property. The news about the enforcement of the Soviet nationalization took not only the inhabitants, but the other occupied peoples, aback. This measure served to isolate the inhabitants from the Germans and helped strengthen the resistance against the new occupation.

Swiss publicist Jean Martin, chief editor of *Journal de Genève,* an expert on soviet national politics, studied the policies of the National-socialists regarding the non-Russian nations of the Soviet Union, and came to the conclusion that this policy did not offer anything to those nations, but meant in reality that one occupation was merely being replaced by another. The author wrote further: "When the war arose between Germany and the USSR and when the German army crossed the border, the greatest enthusiasm was generated among the countries along Moscow's borders, starting in the north (the Baltic States), and continuing to the south (the Ukraine and the Caucasus). The Lithuanians did not even wait for the Germans, they repealed the Soviet laws, returned the lands to their rightful owners. In this manner, the German army marched across Lithuania almost without a shot, then across Latvia, which had similar developments. Soon they reached Estonia where only the Soviet garrisons offered resistance." Jean Martin went on to express the opinion that the behavior of the Hitlerites in the Baltic States repelled the other non-Russian nations: "The conquerers did not recognize *de facto* or *de jure* Lithuania's provisional government; they announced that the land, which had become Soviet state property, automatically becomes the property of the conquerors, they restored the *kolkhozes* temporarily. The disillusionment in Lithuania and the neighboring countries was great; this news spread like lightning throughout the Soviet empire." Martin reached the conclusion that this blind policy of the National-socialists best served the Kremlin.

The Germans attempted to enlist the assistance of the other Germanic nations, like the Danes, Dutch, Norwegians, etc. In 1942, an Eastern Company was formed in Holland, which enlisted Dutchmen to go to the conquered countries and to administer the nationalized property. In the summer of 1942, those Germans who had been repatriated to the Reich began returning to Lithuania. The Lithuanian nation felt that Nazi Germany was pursuing the policies of the medieval Teutonic Knights, when all of Western Europe helped the Teutonic Knights against Lithuania.

The enrollment of latter-day Teutonic Knights aroused anxiety in Lithuania and in the other Baltic countries, so that the occupation government found it necessary to calm them. The *Kauener Zeitung,* an organ of the General Commissariat of Lithuania, on July 6, 1942, wrote that "the German administration is concerned so that the interests of the inhabitants of the Eastern spaces not be violated." The German administration demonstratively called the inhabitants of the eastern countries "locals," as during the period of colonialism, while the Baltic States even in official acts were called *"ehemalige Freistaaten"* (former free states). The National-socialist racist policy was expressed to the extent that special restaurants and other public places and stores were set up for the Germans. (They received more for their ration cards than did the "natives.") The German Red Cross in Kaunas announced that it would transport patients, but only German patients. Regardless of the status alloted by the Nazi racist categories to captured nations, they would have to be either deported or Germanized (*eingedeutscht*).

The return to private ownership took place slowly in small trade, crafts and shops. The larger concerns were taken over by German administrators (*Treuhaender*) or special organizations created for that purpose: *Landbewirtschaftungsgesellschaft* which took over realty, *Grundstückgesellschaft* which took over homes or lots, *Ostland-Fasergesellschaft* which united all of the nationalized textile industries, *Zentralhandelsgesellschaft Ostland* which took over the larger commercial concerns, etc.

Reminiscent of colonial times, special "capitulation courts" were introduced into Lithuania; that is, cases having a German as a party were taken out of local courts and given to these special courts. Decisions could be made only by special "German courts."

As was the case during the rule of the Communists, the farmers were now required to give large norms in kind. They also had to perform a number of mandatory tasks (such as clear-

291

ing snow away from airfields, providing fuel for various institutions, etc.). Each township had a "head farmer" appointed, who was charged with seeing to it that the farmers provided their norms of grain, meat, eggs and other products.

The country was burdened with the enlistment of workers for labor in Germany. In similar manner, youths were recruited for the "Work Service" (*Arbeitsdienst*) which had to be performed in Germany. As had been the case under the Soviets, all political parties and organizations were forbidden. The Lithuanian Activist Front, which had played a major role in the revolt, was to close in September when it presented the occupational regime a memorandum. For a while, a single Lithuanian political organization, the Lithuanian Nationalist Party (*Lietuvių Nacionalistų Partija*) was permitted. This organization cooperated with the occupational authorities for a brief while, but in December, 1941, even this group was forced to close down. As a result, no legal political group remained. Even the Lithuanian Red Cross was closed at the end of 1941. Its place was taken by the *Savitarpinės Pagalbos Draugija*.

A cruel fate met the Jews of Lithuania. From the outset of the German occupation they were killed wholesale and destroyed in every manner. The survivors were driven into ghettoes. It is estimated that of the 250,000 persons whom the Nazis either killed or deported from Lithuania, 200,000 were Jews. A number of Lithuanians were punished for harboring fugitive Jews.

Draconic punishment was meted out for crimes against Germans. When, on May 19, 1942, near Lentupiai (Švenčionys county), two German officials were killed, it was announced that 400 would be shot in reprisal. Actually, many more were executed. Other terrible massacres took place on June 3, 1944, just before the German retreat. When several Germans were ambushed near Pirčiupis, a village near Valkininkai, all of the inhabitants, women and children included, were burned alive; 119 perished in this bestial massacre.

After eliminating the provisional government, Reichkommissar Heinrich Lohse, in his July 28, 1941, declaration mentioned that "if necessary, trustees were to be enlisted who would be able to convey the wishes of the Lithuanian nation to the German organs." In August, 1941, a special institution of "Lithuanian General Advisers" was created with General Petras Kubiliūnas as First General Adviser. He was a former Lithuanian chief of staff who had been forced to resign for having participated in a putsch against President Antanas Smetona. A number of prominent persons were enlisted as advisers. The General Advisers were not granted wide jurisdiction. It remained essentially a German administrative organ even after Rosenberg's decree to the effect that Lithuania, Latvia and Estonia, for propaganda purposes, were to be allowed self-government (*Selbstverwaltung*). German propaganda explained this in the following manner: The German General Commissariats would supervise things while the actual administration would be in the hands of the local institutions—in the case of Lithuania, in the hands of the General Advisers. Actually, these so-called reforms did not change much.

On the other hand, the institution of General Advisers tried to hinder German decrees which were directed against Lithuanian national interests. Several advisers resigned when it became clear that the Soviet nationalization would remain in force. For resisting German measures against the higher schools of Lithuania, the General Adviser for education was sent to a concentration camp, where he perished. The adviser for administrative control met with the same fate when he refused to comply with German orders to declare a mobilization in Lithuania. Two other advisers were sent to concentration camps, but they were fortunate enough to survive.

THE COLLAPSE OF NAZI GERMANY

During the first days of the Russo-German War when the revolt took place, it was felt that the provisional government would be able to form a national army. Lithuanian self-defense units sprang up spontaneously, and grew into battalions. But when the Germans obstructed the restoration of independence, the further existence of the self-defense battalions was no longer linked up with the political aspirations of the nation. Several battalions fought against the Red Army, but they were used for the most part as rear-echelon defense forces. The Germans on their own initiative tried to declare a mobilization of Lithuanian men, but it did not meet with success, for the Lithuanian underground leadership boycotted the plan.

During the winter of 1942-43, when the course of the war took a turn for the worse for the Germans, the Nazis tried to organize SS Legions in Lithuania and the other Baltic States. In February, 1943, Reichskommissar Lohse and Generalkommissar von Renteln issued an appeal urging Lithuanian youths to join a "Lithuanian Legion." In order to put the Balts in a favorable mood, Rosenberg's order to return their property to the Baltic States was announced on February 18, 1943. On March 1, the regulations were issued. But it soon became obvious that the Rosenberg decree was essentially a propaganda play. The regulations and the actual practice were applied in very few cases. The return of property was a form of gratuity on the part of the Germans. In the property documents, it was emphasized that "the owner is duty-bound to use his property for the public good. He must understand that his property is based on a proviso —the sacrifices and victory of the Germany army."

Announcement of the mobilization of the young men by the Germans was a fiasco. The underground organizations issued directives to the youth not to join the Legion, for its creation had nothing to do with Lithuania's future or national interest. The political leadership held the view that the Lithuanian army should only be used for the protection of Lithuanian state interests. The failure to create a Lithuanian SS Legion infuriated the German administration. In the middle of March, 1943, announcements were made that "the process of registering the men called up was hindered by certain intellectual elements. Therefore the formation of the Lithuanian Legion is postponed." In reprisal, the Germans meted out their vengeance for the failure of the plan: All of the higher schools were closed, and the return of private property was halted. As for return of property, it was announced that "reprivatization will only apply to those persons who themselves or their families aid the war effort against Bolshevism."

The Germans took reprisals against intellectuals, i.e., professors, students, civic leaders and even several General Advisers. The arrested were sent to concentration camps where a number

of them perished. Executing reprisals against Lithuanian intellectuals, a decree was promulgated whereby taxes on higher
education were raised. The students were urged to join trade
schools. Even earlier, the German administration hampered higher
education; the liberal arts faculties were hindered, and new students were not permitted to matriculate. Using the pretext that
the "intellectual elements" had obstructed the formation of the
Legion, the German officials thus had an opportunity to deal a
blow to Lithuania's higher schools which, according to the pre-
cepts of Naziism, had to disappear anyway.

While attempts were being made to create a Lithuanian
Legion, the German administration announced that all Ostland
inhabitants between the ages of eighteen and forty-five had to
fulfill "work duties." Lithuanian youth were sent to various
German military, paramilitary and technical details or to factories
directly. Yet, direct mobilization was not undertaken.

During the winter of 1943-1944 when the Soviet Army began
to press the Germans militarily, questions arose in Lithuania regarding Lithuania's active participation in the struggle against the
USSR, but beforehand an agreement had to be reached with the
Germans on the manner in which the Lithuanian army would be
employed in the war. General Povilas Plechavičius was chosen to
head the army. He began to confer with the proper German
agencies which ended in a written agreement in January, 1944,
according to which the Lithuanian units would be used only in
the war against Soviet partisans and against bandits on Lithuanian territory. The units were to be officered by Lithuanians and
to be subject only to their commands. The units were to be
recruited on a voluntary basis only, and were to be called the
Lithuanian Home Formation (Lietuvos Vietinė Rinktinė).

When, in February, 1944, the registration of volunteers was
announced, about 20,000 men signed up within a few days.
Further registration was halted, for only 5,000 men were needed
at first. In view of the mass registration, the number of men for
the units was raised to 12,000. Immediately, however, quarrels
began with the Germans, who demanded that the recruitment
continue and that a mobilization be announced; those men who
could not be enrolled in the Home Formation were to be turned

over to the German army. General Plechavičius and his chief of staff, Colonel Otto Urbonas, did not agree, and friction developed over the arming of the Formation. The Germans tried all means to take over the command of the units, continuing to demand a mobilization of between 70,000 and 100,000 men for the German army. When the command of the Home Formation resisted this demand, the Germans announced a mobilization in May which ended in a fiasco. Then the Germans arrested Plechavičius, Urbonas and the staff officers; some of them were sent to concentration camps or prisons. Part of the Formation scattered, some were sent to Germany. Thus ended the last Lithuanian effort to form their own armed forces in the fight against Bolshevism. The Germans retreated and in July, 1944, the Soviet army crossed the Lithuanian frontiers.

The German Nazis vent their fury on the Lithuanians of East Prussia. In August, 1941, the Nazis killed the Jagomastas family in Vilnius. Jagomastas was a Lithuanian activist from Tilsit. Erdmonas Simonaitis, the chairman of the 1923 insurgent Directory in Klaipėda, and the former Presidents of the Directory, Martynas Reisgys and Eduardas Simaitis, were arrested and sent to a concentration camp. The same fate awaited Albertas Jonušaitis another former member of the Directory, and the Lithuanian educator Mikas Slaža. Martynas Žvilius, a member of the directory, was persecuted. Reisgys, Simaitis and Jonusaitis died in concentration camps. Simonaitis and Šlaža survived. Also, two famous activists of Lithuania Minor—the artist Adomas Brakas and the former President of the Directory Endrius Borchertas, were deported to Siberia during the first Soviet occupation.

As the second Soviet occupation drew near, several score thousands of Lithuanians fled to the West and sought asylum abroad. In view of the imminent Soviet reoccupation, they chose the hard lot of the political emigrant. A large percentage of them were intellectuals. After the second World War the refugees (displaced persons) were cared for by the International Refugee Organization. A large part of the immigration went to the United States as well as to Canada, Australia, New Zealand and the countries of Latin America. The largest emigre colonies in Europe concentrated in England and Germany. These emigres actively joined the fight for the liberation of their homeland.

On July 13, 1944, the Soviet army took Vilnius; on August 1, it drove into Kaunas, and on January 28, 1945, it took Klaipėda. In the wake of the Soviet army came Lithuania's Communist party and Soviet government, with the same people at its head that were in power in 1940. The First Secretary of the Lithuanian Communist party remained Antanas Sniečkus. The Chairman of the Council of Commissars (since 1946 Council of Ministers, after the example of Moscow) was Mečys Gedvilas. The Chairman of the Presidium of the Supreme Soviet was Justas Paleckis. The Soviet-Lithuanian leadership was bent on restoring the order that had been imposed by force on the country in 1940, and was prepared to cooperate to the fullest extent with Moscow.

By occupying Lithuania with military force, the Soviet Union once again violated her treaties with that country as well as international commitments, including the Atlantic Charter, according to which the Allies were to refrain from territorial conquests. Ignoring all of these promises, the Kremlin not only repeated the annexation of the Baltic States, which was a result of the Ribbentrop-Molotov Pact, but also annexed part of the Old Prussian and Lithuanian lands of East Prussia.

Moscow herself took an active hand in the introduction of the Soviet order in Lithuania, assuming an auxiliary role to the Lithuanian Communist party and the local Soviet government there. The task of sovietization was assigned to a special emissary from Moscow, Mihail Suslov, a high party functionary, who was well-qualified for the task of sovietization, for he had distinguished himself in the North Caucasus by destroying small anti-Soviet nationalities there for having cooperated with the Germans.

The introduction of the Soviet order in Lithuania faced many obstacles, for a partisan war was being waged against the Communists there. The Soviet regime thus for a long time merely controlled the cities and towns, whereas whole areas of the coun-

297

tryside were controlled by the partisans. During the second Soviet occupation the Klaipėda region was returned to Lithuania. This time, there was no restraining issue of autonomy, especially since the German elements left for the West.

COLLECTIVIZATION OF AGRICULTURE

The Soviets quickly introduced a more radical land reform than that of 1940. On August 30, 1944, a decree was passed "For the Liquidation of German Occupational Achievements in Agriculture," according to which decree all land that had no owners was placed in the "state land fund." (Most of the owners of these lands had fled to the West, others had been deported by the Communists in June, 1941.) In a similar manner, the land norm was lowered so that the maximum farm was to be twenty hectares, "according to the class of land and locale," while those farmers who aided the Germans were limited to five hectares. The nationalized lands were given first of all to Soviet sympathizers, demobilized soldiers, etc. The new land reform, which affected about 600,000 hectares, was therefore purely political in nature; it atomized further agrarian property and created a larger class of agrarian proletarians. Its aim was the creation of conducive conditions for the collectivization of the land.

The Communist party, in view of the partisan war, delayed the introduction of the *kolkhoze* system. As a first phase in collectivization, the government, in 1945, passed a decision for the encouragement and support of "agricultural cooperatives." This method of transition had as its purpose the urging of farmers "to go to the higher forms of land cooperation—to agrarian collectivization." In 1947, a systematic campaign was begun for the introduction of *kolkhozes*. (Before this, a campaign was waged against the "kulaks." They were burdened with progressive taxes and were forced to make large requisition payments in kind.) However, only twenty *kolkhozes* were formed.

In March, 1948, a resolution was passed "For the Organization of Collective Farms in the Republic." In February, 1949, the Lithuanian Communist party congress was devoted to a large extent to *kolkhozes*. It was decided that "in the near future a full victory of the collective system would be achieved in the Republic."

However, the disdain for *kolkhozes* was so universal among the Lithuanians that the Russian government took to reprisals— mass deportations of farmers and others to the slave labor camps of the Soviet Union. According to available statistics, the deportation took place in several mass waves. The deportations were begun immediately after the Soviet regime returned, and afterward, mass deportations took place in February, 1946, (they were repeated between 1947 and 1950). Every year, in conjunction with the liquidation of private farming and with the intense collectivization, thousands were deported. According to witnesses, the last mass deportation took place in 1951. Whole villages were left without inhabitants. In addition, the NKVD, later the MGB, continually arrested individuals or groups, especially students, senior high-school students and patriotic youth, for anti-Soviet activities: the issuance of proclamations, the printing of underground newspapers, the raising of flags at night just before the holidays of Independent Lithuania, national demonstrations in cemeteries by the monuments of soldiers on All-Souls Day, and the like.

There are no exact figures on how many were deported. It is estimated that during the 1944-51 period, about 350,000 persons were deported, which would comprise about twelve percent of Lithuania's population. The unfortunates were sent to Soviet "work camps" in the Soviet Union's far north or east, where the cruel climate, hard work and meager rations caused the death of most of them. The deportations began under emissary M. Suslov. He was assisted by the deputy chief of state security, USSR General Kruglov, who led the action and repressive measures against the partisans. In 1946, Suslov returned to Moscow; he was replaced by another Soviet emissary, V. V. Shcherbakov.

The destruction of Lithuania's farmer class could only be accomplished by these mass deportations and other methods of terror. Whenever possible, the farmers resisted collectivization. Soviet sources also recognize this fact by placing the blame on the "kulaks," priests and "bourgeois nationalists." The farmers sold their livestock and other property rather than have it collectivized. They supported the "bandits" (i.e., partisans), who fought against collectivization. Only in the wake of the wave of terrorism was collectivization speeded up. In 1950, about half of the farmers were herded into *kolkhozes*. In 1952, the percentage reached 96 percent. Shortly thereafter, no free farmers remained in Lithuania.

As elsewhere, so in Lithuania during the postwar era, especially during the Khrushchev era, various experiments were made in agriculture. The *kolkhozes* were joined into larger units (the agrograd); at times smaller units were favored. Such experiments caused a decrease in agricultural output. In addition to *kolkhozes,* which according to official statistics for 1967 numbered 1,700, there were 260 *sovkhozes.*

Soviet statistics themselves show that the production of the *kolkhozes* is low in comparison with the free-farming countries. The agricultural sector remains the weakest point of Soviet economy. Sovietologists are in agreement that the agrarian elements in the Soviet Union are the most exploited, and thus have to provide the most in labor and resources in order to increase industrialization and military potential. The inhabitants of Lithuania were also forced to experience the same conditions, especially those who worked the land. In spite of forced industrialization and urbanization, more than half of Lithuania's population is still engaged in agriculture.

Every expert on Soviet life knows that the source of food and income for the *kolkhozniki* is the strip of land allowed for private use (in Lithuania this so-called orchard lot is up to 0.6 hectares). These private strips produce meat, eggs, potatoes, vegetables and fruits for the local market; these important food-stuffs, produced by the so-called *privatniki* on their strips, are much greater than the amount produced on the *kolkhozes* and *sovkhozes* whose arable land is twenty times greater. This proves that the Soviet agrarian system is poor, in spite of mechanization and allied methodology.

FORCED INDUSTRIALIZATION

Following the lead of the Soviet Union, the Soviet Lithuanian regime began to industrialize the country. The dictatorial state, concentrating in its hands the monopoly of power, had the means to direct the material resources in any direction it saw fit. It drastically curtailed the requirements of consumers, unilaterally setting high prices on consumer goods and thus guaranteeing a huge profit for the state. By setting guaranteed wages to workers which would meet their minimum requirements for existence, and by forcing the people to work hard, the Communist state, un-hindered by public opinion or workers' strikes, was able to invest huge sums into those industries which it wanted developed. Thanks to these investments, Soviet Lithuania was able within twenty years to create new branches of industry and to set up new factories.

Soviet statistics, in comparing industrial production in inde-pendent Lithuania with that of the Soviet regime, show an extra-ordinary industrial growth. Lithuanian industry between the wars was not very developed, even though some branches of industry, such as agricultural production and that of raw materials, textiles, lumber products and paper, had reached a high modern level. As in the other free-market countries, especially those of Western Europe, which experienced phenomenal growth after the second World War, industry in the nation had all of the possibilities to grow.

Lithuania, under the Soviets, created factories that produced electronics, radio, television, computers, electromotors, adding machines, smelting apparatus, refrigerators and other metal and machine products. Several chemical industries (artificial ferti-lizers) and plastics plants were built. Shipbuilding was expanded. A number of industries were set up which did not even exist in Lithuania before. The field of energy was developed; several hy-droelectric and thermoelectric plants were set up. Natural gas was piped in from the Ukraine. According to Soviet statistics, on the 1960 averages, Lithuania produced 90 percent of the electric meters of the Soviet Union, 50 percent of the electromotors for regrigerators and washing machines, one-third of the electrical soldering devices, and one-third of the metal-cutting presses. Ac-cording to Soviet statistics, in 1965, 50 percent of Lithuanian production was in industry.

Together with forced industrialization, the cities grew: 45

percent of the nation's inhabitants now live in cities and large towns. During the past few years, new industrial centers mushroomed. Yet, under Soviet conditions, industrialization and urbanization does not by any means guarantee the increase in material well-being for industrial workers or urban dwellers.

One of the motives for forced industrialization is the desire to create an industrial proletariat, which, according to Soviet ideology would form a basic and viable buttress for the Soviet regime. Forced industrialization also has another motive which has nothing to do with Soviet Marxist theory. By developing industries which require raw materials from abroad, and by producing items for a market that depends on Moscow, Lithuania is being economically chained to the Soviet Union and is being made an economic dependency of the USSR. In this manner, a new type of Soviet colonialism is developing. Bearing in mind that economic planning is centralized in Moscow, industrial branches are being developed which will gradually increase Lithuania's dependency. As far as present dependency is concerned, 30 percent of Lithuania's industries come under the direct supervision of Moscow's central ministries; 50 percent of the industries belong to subsidiaries of those ministries. Only 20 percent of the industries belong to the Soviet Lithuanian Republic. Light industry accounts for only one-fourth of the nation's industrial production. Bearing in mind also the fact that there is a chronic shortage of goods in Lithuania, and that only some of the products of light industry remain in Lithuania while the greater amount is shipped to Russia or the markets of the Communist Bloc, it follows that Lithuania does not enjoy the fruits of her labor. For example, the inhabitants of Lithuania have difficulty in purchasing fish, while Klaipėda is one of the largest fishing centers of the Soviet Union.

Light industry, which should serve the needs of the local market, does not enjoy much approval from the Moscow planners; it is heavy industry that must serve the Soviet market. The number of workers in the machine and metal industries between 1950 and 1967 rose from 15.8 percent to 29.6 percent of the total labor force. Lumber, paper and wood-products accounted for a diminution of the labor force of from 24.4 percent to 12.3 percent.

The number of workers in food production declined from 17.5 percent to 14.0 percent. Light-industry figures, however, represent only an increase of from 24.4 percent to 26.4 percent during the fifteen-year period.

Other industries, which are not integral parts of the country's economy, are the result of the large influx of foreign elements. Since the industrialization of the country is executed at a fast tempo that requires a labor force which cannot be satisfied by the annual increase in population, it is necessary to import labor from other areas of the USSR to service the new industries. This immigration comes from the Slavic republics of the USSR, from Russia for the most part. In this manner, the Slavic element is on the rise in Lithuania, settling in those centers where new industries are being created, namely, in the cities. The result is that the cities are becoming more Russian, which is a political factor. According to official statistics, more than one-third of the inhabitants of Vilnius are Russians. The port city of Klaipėda has become a large shipping and fishing center. These industries are almost completely in the hands of the Russians. Klaipėda, which hardly had any Russians before the second World War, is now half Russian. West of Lithuania, the so-called Kaliningrad district (the former East Prussia or Lithuania Minor with the city of Koenigsberg) is annexed directly to the Russian SFR, and is being intensely Russified.

RUSSIFICATION

The first mass deluge of Russians and Eastern Slavs came at the close of the war, when many people moved from the devastated war areas to the east. Lithuania, like the other Baltic States, did not suffer as much from war as did the Slavic lands, in addition to which the standard of living was much higher in the Baltic than in the Soviet republics. Therefore, many Russians moved to the West. These uninvited immigrants called Lithuania "Little America." In addition to this chaotic immigration, an organized group of colonists came with Suslov's bureau whose task it was to Sovietize Lithuania. The leading positions in the Communist party, government and planning staffs were taken over almost exclusively by Russians: although the nominal heads of the Soviet

303

institutions were Lithuanians, behind their backs stood the Russian "deputies." Large in number, they formed the leading cadres of the Russian colonists. In 1949, 50 percent of the members of the Central Committee of the Lithuanian Communist party were non-Lithuanians. Only after Stalin's death did the Lithuanian Communists gain some autonomy.

A totalitarian regime, like that of the Soviet Union, has sufficient means to halt a mass influx from the East to Lithuania, especially to the cities where it was impossible to get quarters without a special permit. The local agencies could not halt the influx even if they wanted to, because to deny entry to Russians would be construed as a "national deviation," which would have led to repressions from Moscow.

One could not have the least doubt that the settling of Russian and Eastern Slavic elements went according to preconceived USSR plans. A phenomenon like the intrusion of people of a nationality into the Baltic States by no means can be interpreted as a spontaneous, grassroots manifestation. This phenomenon originated in the premeditated decision of the Kremlin to settle huge numbers of Russians in the Baltic cities in order to dilute the compact mass of autochtons. But the influx of Russians could be discerned in the smaller towns as well, where new industries were created. Soviet sources do not hide the fact that parallel to the industrialization of Lithuania, a resettling of "specialists" is taking place.

Statistics show that Lithuania's industrialization is taking place at a faster rate than in the other republics of the USSR. Between 1960 and 1967, Lithuania's industrial increase averaged about 12.6 percent per annum, while a similar increase for the rest of the USSR was 9.1 percent. Branches of machine industry which require much labor are encouraged. Regardless of the natural increase of the work force and the intense infiltration by Russians into the labor force, Moscow has purely political motives which have nothing to do with Lithuania's economic growth. Industrialization is a veiled pretext for the colonization of the country. As Walter C. Banaitis in his article "Die Industrialisierung Sowjetlitauens" in *Acta Baltica* states: "For the Soviets, industrialization is synonymous with Russification, not in the economic sense so much as in the critical demographic sense."

While on the one hand, the systematic settlement of Russians in Lithuania is taking place, the Lithuanian youth is urged to seek work in the Soviet Union. This mission is assigned to the Komsomol Youth organization, which periodically puts pressure on Lithuanian youth to sign up "voluntarily" for work in the far-reaches of the Soviet Union. During the Khrushchev era, campaigns were undertaken to draw them to the "virgin lands" of Central Asia. Young people were also recruited for the Donbas mines, for railroad construction, the construction of industries in remote areas of the Soviet Union, for lumber work in Karelia, etc. Although they were promised short-term contracts for labor, the real aim was to draw Lithuanian youth away from their homeland, to be Russified and to be subjected to conditions which would detain them for an indefinite period away from their place of birth. On the other hand, Russian youth is directed to infiltrate into Lithuania, to study in Lithuania's higher schools and specialist institutes. The infiltration has reached such a level that a number of courses have to be offered in Russian. The Academy of Sciences must print works in Russian as well as in Lithuanian.

Russianism is foisted in other ways. Although, according to the constitutions of the Soviet Union and of the Lithuanian SSR, all nationalities are equal, in reality, this provision, like many of the other provisions of the constitution, is merely of a declarative nature designated for propaganda purposes. In reality, the Russian nation, language and everything that is associated with Russianism is given the primary role. The Russian language is foisted upon all of the non-Russian nations, including Lithuania. Russification is advanced through the schools, theaters and literature.

The Russian language is introduced in the first year of primary school and is taught through all of the classes to the university level. A great number of lessons are devoted to the Russian language. The same is true of Russian literature, history and geography. The tendency in schools is to establish a bilingual system. In some classes, native children are placed with the children of Russian colonists and forced to learn Russian. Russian songs are even taught in nursery schools.

305

Textbooks are for the most part translations from the Russian language and are steeped in that culture. At the same time, the Lithuanian past is depicted in a bad light as a feudal epoch, whereas Russian history is accorded the role of "progress." In recounting Lithuania's history, an attempt is made to create the image that in the past there was harmony between the Lithuanian and Russian nations, which does not conform to the actual facts. Lithuanian history is falsified. Even the incorporation of Lithuania into the Czarist Empire is viewed as a progressive measure.

The glorification of Russianism borders on paradox. The Russian nation is more often referred to as "the Big Brother" than as the "Great Russian Nation," to which the Lithuanian nation must be always grateful even for the 1940 occupation and the destruction of the independent state, for this was "liberation from the yoke of the capitalists and bourgeoisie." Russification is also fostered through contemporary literature, which favors Russian works and their translations, through the theater, radio, television, the press, etc.

Only the Russian colonists enjoy the exceptional privilege of having schools in their native language. The colonists of other nationalities do not have this right; they are forced to send their children to Russian schools. A paradoxical situation develops: the children of non-Russians, settled in Lithuania, are Russified in a non-Russian country. Only the Russians are permitted to have their own press, theater and schools.

Contrary to the provisions of the USSR constitution regarding the equality of the nationalities, the Russian nation has special privileges while the other nations are deprived of their cultural heritage. The aim is quite clear: the Russification of non-Russian nationalities. During the transitional period, the non-Russian people are to be made bilingual, whereby the Russian language would be accepted on an equal footing with the native tongue. In the future, the priority would be given to Russian. The final goal is the melting of all nationalities into a single "socialist nation" with one common language, which would be the Russian language. This process is considered as a road to "progress." The Soviets encourage proletarian internationalism and the harmonious existence of the "fraternal socialist nations."

306

Of course, the Soviet Union would never publish a law openly favoring Russification, but the Russification goes on according to the directives of the Kremlin, which bypass the equitable provisions of the Soviet constitution. Since the individual Soviet Republics do not have any real right to complain or to appeal to courts on this matter, they are defenseless against the arbitrariness of the Soviet rulers and their local satraps.

Nevertheless, from the many manifestations that occur, one can see that Moscow has obstacles to overcome. Loyalty to the native land and language is very much alive among the Lithuanians, who still desire to break away from the domination by Moscow. This can be seen from the relentless struggle of the Communist party and government with "bourgeois remnants" and "nationalist ideology," which to this day are condemned at every party congress and which even solicits public statements from the Soviet dignitaries. Resistance can be discerned even among Party members. Although the Lithuanian Communist party and government has shown an extraordinary amount of servility and sycophancy to Moscow, and although Lithuanian Communists did not resist Moscow to the extent that the Latvian Communists did (which led to the dismissal of the party and government leadership in 1959 in Riga), there has been a spectacular purge of party members for opposing Russification. In 1959, the rector of Vilnius University, Juozas Bulavas, was dismissed from his post and expelled from the party for not catching "ideological mistakes" which were being made by lecturers and for catering to "revisionist tendencies." In March, 1960, during the Twelfth Congress of the Lithuanian Communist party, much time was devoted to the fight against "ideological deviation." On that occasion, it became apparent that "national communism" had developed in the party. Party Secretary Antanas Sniečkus attacked not only former Rector Juozas Bulavas, but also Dr. Juozas Laužikas, the deputy director of the Vilnius Pedagogical Institute, who was also dismissed from his post.

But all of these "purges" were unable to hide the fact that among the Eastern European satellites, as among all peoples subjugated directly by the Soviet Union, a reevaluation was taking place. The satellites are in a better position to openly resist Moscow's domination, which is still not the case in the captive nations. The Soviet-occupied nations only use indirectly to their advantage the splits in the Soviet Bloc and the developing polycentrism. At least in the cultural sphere, they have won more autonomy in relation to the period of Stalinist terror.

RELIGIOUS PERSECUTION

The Soviets fought with considerable fierceness against religion in Lithuania. During the first year of occupation, they began to execute their program against religion. Although during the Nazi occupation (1941-44) the Church did not receive favorable treatment from the occupational authorities, nevertheless the antireligious restrictions that had been imposed by the Soviets were lifted and religious life returned to more or less normal conditions. When, in the summer of 1944, the Communists returned they renewed their tactics in the religious field as well. When the Soviet constitution was made operative, the Church was separated from the state and the schools from the Church. Although according to the constitution "the right to practice religious cults and the right to antireligious propaganda is guaranteed to all citizens," in practice antireligious propaganda is encouraged by all means and supported by the regime, while religion is held to be an outmoded "superstition" against which a relentless struggle must be waged.

During the Stalin era, physical terror was used against the clergy and the faithful. Priests were accused of aiding the partisan movement. In connection with these accusations, immediately after the war 180 priests were arrested and sent to slave labor camps. The bishops were requested to publically denounce the partisans. When they refused they were arrested (in 1946) and condemned to prison and to death. The following Church dignitaries were condemned by the Communists: Archbishop Mečislovas Reinys of Vilnius, Bishop Teotilius Matulionis of Kaišiadoriai, Bishop Vincentas Borisevičius of Telšiai and his auxiliary Pranas Ramanauskas. In 1955, the two surviving bishops, Matulionis and Ramanauskas, were permitted to return to Lithuania, but they were forbidden to perform their duties. Elevated to

Archbishop, Matulionis died. In 1966, Bishop of Telšiai Maželis also died, leaving only one bishop, Juozapas Labukas-Matulaitis, who was also apostolic administrator of the Kaunas and Vilka-viškis dioceses. In 1953, Archbishop Reinys died a martyr's death in the Vladimir Prison.

After the death of Stalin there was a temporary "thaw," during which religious life was not hindered as much as before. In September, 1955, two new bishops were appointed: Julijonas Steponavičius and Petras Maželis. Shortly thereafter, Bishop Step-onavičius was not permitted to fulfill his duties and he was placed under house arrest in Žagarė. Religious affairs were turned over to a special government commissar.

The period of the "thaw" lasted for three years. In 1957, antireligious measures were hardened. Although direct physical terror was no longer employed, as during the Stalin era, all other forms of repression and persecution were applied with severity. During the last decade antireligious propaganda has been stepped up intensely. Communists, Communist Youth, and the Profes-sional Unions are employed in the war against religion. Intellec-tuals are recruited for the propaganda fight. Religious instruction in school is prohibited by the criminal code. Schools have to serve atheistic ideology. The press, radio, television, art and literature is used in the antireligious propaganda campaign; antireligious lectures are delivered throughout the country. According to So-viet sources, in 1963 alone, 150,000 antireligious lectures were delivered in Lithuania. Between 1945 and 1965, 2,500,000 pieces of antireligious literature were published in Lithuania. Since 1964, a specific antireligious publication, Ateistas, has been published. Civil servants and civic leaders are prohibited from going to church. The Soviet periodicals attest to the repressions taken against people who attend services. In 1962 the director of the Skapiškis high school was dismissed because two of his graduates entered the priests' seminary. A number of churches were pro-faned and turned into museums, warehouses and even dance halls; forty-two of the fifty-one churches and chapels in Vilnius are shut down; only eight of the twenty-nine in Kaunas remain open.

Pressure is being brought against the clergy. It is ridiculed and persecuted, while no rights are granted for their protection against such actions. The clergy is threatened with severe penalties for "transgressing the separation of church and state and the separation of schools from the church." The priests are not allowed to visit their parishioners, take the Church census, or even grant the last sacrament without permission from the local government.

All church property and rectories are nationalized and the priests have to pay high rents for their use, in addition to being burdened with the highest taxes in the land. One seminary remains, and it cannot have more than twenty-five seminarians at any time. Thus, the Church is faced with a severe shortage of priests.

In spite of systematic restrictions and persecutions, religion has not been eradicated within the Lithuanian nation. The Communist press itself attests to this by complaining that not only elderly people but the youth as well are tied to the beliefs of their fathers. *Komjaunimo Tiesa* (No. 66 1964) stated that the youth of historic Trakai on Sundays "desert the cultural home and rush to the churches of Semėliškis, Vievis and Trakai." There are many more such complaints in the Soviet press.

THE FACADE OF SOVIET FEDERALISM

Lithuania was incorporated into the Soviet Union as a federal republic. There are fifteen such republics. The constitution declares that Lithuania, like the other federal republics, can "freely" leave the Soviet Union. Under the existing circumstances, this provision of the constitution is pure sham.

Lithuania sends its representatives to the All-Union Supreme Soviet and to the Soviet of Nationalities. According to the constitution, the Soviet Union itself reserves the right to handle state matters, leaving to the federal republics matters of lesser importance. Even according to the letter of the law, the competence of the federal republics have little practical value. In practice, the Soviet constitution in all matters leaves the decisive voice to Moscow. In reality, Soviet federalism is a facade, while the Soviet Union is a highly centralized monolithic state. In every democracy, even the lowest units enjoy more autonomy than do any of the republics of the Soviet Union.

A federal republic like the Lithuanian SSR is completely tied to Moscow, regardless of constitutional provisions. This is due to extraconstitutional factors, the most important of which is the Communist party. The Communist Party determines state policy in all matters, while the state organs, from the Supreme Soviet down to the lowest-echelon committee, are mere executors of these policies. The Lithuanian Communist party is a separate entity in name only. In reality, it is part of the All-Union Soviet Communist party. All other Communist parties of the Soviet republics have in common the fact that they are all part of the Russian Communist party. The All-Union Party directs the affairs of the RSFR—in other words the All-Union and the Russian Communist Parties are one and the same. From this situation, it follows that not the Lithuanian Communist party but also the organs of the Lithuanian SSR do not exercise any real competence. They are organs approved or appointed by Moscow, and therefore cannot make independent decisions.

During the period when it was illegal, the Lithuanian Communist party did not have more than 2,000 members, its majority comprised of non-Lithuanians. Soviet falsifications of history to the contrary, the Lithuanian Communist party was never really an important political factor until the military occupation imposed by the Soviet Army. Only after the occupation was the Lithuanian Communist party made part of the All-Union Communist Party. It was immediately purged by the heavy hand of Stalin, and by the spring of 1941, it lost about 50 percent of the old revolutionaries who had been active during the illegal period. In February, 1941, six months after the Soviet occupation, the party had only 3,133 members and candidates. In 1952, party members and candidates numbered 36,693. Membership increased in 1967 to 71,316, which is about 2.5 percent of the population of Lithuania. The dominant elements in the party are the Russian Communist immigrants in Lithuania.

During the 1961 congress of the Soviet Union Communist party, resolutions clearly enunciated the goals of the USSR policy toward the non-Russian nationalities, who were told that the national principle under all circumstances must be subordinated to the class principle. According to the *History of the Lithuanian*

311

SSR published by the Historical Institute of the LSSR Academy of Sciences in 1958, Lithuania had already "formed a Lithuanian socialist nation, which was a member in equal standing in the fraternal family of Soviet socialist nations." This was an assertion, however, which the realities of life reject.

Antanas Sniečkus has been the First Secretary of the Lithuanian Communist party since 1936, although the real boss was and is the Second Secretary (a post which has had several occupants, all of whom were Russian). The composition of the heads of government had changed several times. In 1956, in place of Gedvilas, M. Šumauskas was appointed as prime minister. In April, 1967, Juozas Maniušis became prime minister, when Šumauskas was appointed to the post of President of the Supreme Soviet of the Lithuanian SSR; he replaced Paleckis who left for Moscow to assume the post of chairman of the Supreme Soviet of Nationalities of the USSR. In a brochure published in 1959 —"Thoughts About the Senior Brother" (*Mintys apie vyrensniji broli*)—Paleckis demonstrated once again to Moscow's satisfaction that he was a partisan of the Russian domination of Lithuania, and that he remains a faithful executor of Moscow's policies.

Lithuanian Resistance, 1940-52

by ALGIRDAS BUDRECKIS

For twelve years, a nation of 3-million refused to accept the fact that its sovereignty had been usurped and trammeled by the mightiest totalitarian power in the world. Lithuania's geopolitical position in the open southeast Baltic region made it an easy prey to powerful neighboring aggressors and, what is more unfortunate, its geographic isolation kept it from making its position known to world opinion.

It should be noted from the outset that the resistance against the Soviets, and later against the Nazis, was of an intensely nationalistic character. A century of fervent national revival, culminating in the reestablishment of an independent state, produced strong commitments to national ideals and the national state. The younger generation was sensitive to the medieval grandeur of Lithuanian statehood; it took modern Lithuania's independence as an axiom, and therefore refused to reconcile itself to its loss. This dedication to national Lithuanian deals, combined with the traditional hatred of Russian rule and the reaction to the alien totalitarian regime introduced by the Russian communists, crystallized into active opposition to the Kremlin's occupation.

Who comprised the rank and file of the resistance movements and the partisans? Soviet writers claim that they were fascist adventurers and criminals, lackeys of first the Nazis and then the Western imperialists. If this were true, then how could the anti-Soviet armed resistance survive for twelve years, especially since it was impossible to keep the movement supplied with outside arms and materiel? If the resistance fighters were mere "bandits" as the Soviet claim, then why did they enjoy the sympathy and

313

the support of huge segments of the population? The fact that the Soviets had to deport over 400,000 farmers (one-fifth of the rural population) because of anti-Soviet sentiments shows the extent of support that the partisans enjoyed.

Julien Amery, a former French Resistance leader, defines resistance as "operations directed against an enemy behind his lines by discontented elements among the enemy or enemy-occupied population." The enemy may be a conventional belligerent, an enemy in cold war, a malevolent occupant. According to Amery, resistance can take the form of revolt, sabotage, guerrilla bands, terror or civil disobedience, spreading propaganda or harboring escaped prisoners. Lithuanian resistance went through all phases for twelve years. It was primarily directed against the Soviet Union.

"Resistance," wrote George Bidault, head of the World War II French underground National Council, "is first of all a state of mind, reinforced by an act of faith. A spirit of refusal—refusal to become dishonorable, to collaborate, to despair in the face of the misfortunes befalling the country. An act of faith—faith in a few virtues perilously preserved: honor, courage, the spirit of sacrifice, love of freedom." To the Lithuanians, just as to the French, resistance meant a national decision, the categorical NO of a whole nation. It meant more than simply an armed action against the aggressor—it was a viewpoint which made the struggle of every individual meaningful and inspired the nation—the anonymous populace—to an active part in history.

THE FIRST RESISTANCE, 1940-41

The loss of independence on June 15, 1940, was a bitter experience. The Soviet occupation turned out to be more than merely a military occupation. Through the use of force and terrorism, drastic social and economic changes were carried out, a totalitarian dictatorship was introduced, and the country was annexed to the Soviet Union. Under these conditions, the usual forms of resistance against wartime military occupation were well-nigh impossible. No help was expected from the Western democracies. However, resistance to Soviet oppression occurred as early as the very first days of occupation. President Antanas

Smetona, feeling that he no longer would be able to exercise his constitutional prerogatives under duress, left the country to carry on the struggle from abroad. As a token of resistance, President Smetona, on June 16, gave orders to the Lithuanian garrisons at Marijampolė and Tauragė to cross the frontier into Germany, fully equipped and armed. On June 16, Colonel Antanas Gaušas led the garrison regiment out of Marijampolė and marched toward the German frontier; but, for some inexplicable reason, the regiment turned back at the last moment. Resistance by the political parties and the cultural elite was nipped in the bud when the Communist Director for Security, Antanas Sniečkus, on July 11-12, 1940, ordered the arrest of leaders and active members of all non-Communist political parties. The NKVD quickly rounded up 2,000 political, cultural and civic leaders in Lithuania.

RESISTANCE ON THE CULTURAL LEVEL

Plans for liberation from abroad would have been futile if the populace in the country had remained docile and servile to the Soviet occupant. Resistance in Lithuania, at first, was passive and sporadic. It manifested itself in the boycotting of the so-called elections to the Peoples' Diet, the boycotting of Soviet holidays (May 1st and November 7th), and in large-scale religious and national demonstrations during All-Soul's Day (November 2).

In August, 1940, the student body at the University of Vytautas the Great demanded non-Communist student candidates to the student council. The teachers' congress in Kaunas demanded a Lithuanian cultural program and sang native folk songs instead of Communist hymns. Primary- and secondary-school pupils, returning to school in September, manifested a form of resistance to the new Soviet order. They sang paraphrased versions of Communist songs, circulated ciphered poems, and defaced portraits of Lenin and Stalin. They even composed "prayers," as for example:

Hail Russia, full of woe, Stalin is with thee. Mocked art thou in Europe and mocked is your uncouth fruit Stalin. Holy Lithuania, our Mother, save us from the Asiatics. We will be grateful now and at the hour of our death.

315

The farmers resisted all orders to supply empty Red trains with grain. All deliveries of compulsory grain taxes were conducted as propaganda cavalcades, with red banners in the van. The farmers in their own way were able to ridicule this propaganda. For example, in the district of Marijampolė, of the thirty loaded grain carts scheduled to put in an appearance on an appointed day, only three arrived, and these three carts with red banners were escorted by a band to the city and jeered by the local populace. The rest of the farmers brought their grain quotas to Marijampolė the next day.

In the words of the NKVD memorandum of April 14, 1941, signed by NKVD Commissar Aleksandras Guzevičius and Director Todes, regarding the distribution of "Counterrevolutionary Leaflets in the Territory of the Lithuanian SSR": "The authors and disseminators of anti-Soviet leaflets and anonymous letters appeared to be members of the counterrevolutionary formations among former members of the anti-Soviet political parties and organizations, nationalistic school youths and university students." The memorandum continued with the following details: "From the moment of the establishment of Soviet rule in Lithuania, the counter-revolutionary nationalist element developed an active anti-Soviet activity, choosing as the basic method of its hostile subversive work, the distribution of counter-revolutionary leaflets and anonymous papers. In the main, the leaflets called for the overthrow of the Soviet government, sabotage, the boycott of the elections to the Supreme Soviet of the USSR, spreading angry lies regarding the party and government leaders. They also disseminated provocative rumors of a coming war between the USSR and Germany, etc. Mass dissemination of counter-revolutionary leaflets took place in all of the counties of the Lithuanian SSR."

In Kaunas, beginning in September, 1940, handwritten and multigraphed anti-Soviet leaflets began to appear systematically on the streets and in the educational institutions with the slogans: "Long live independent Lithuania," "Down with the Communist Terror," "Lithuania for the Lithuanians." Anti-Soviet leaflets in the city of Vilnius were disseminated in the main by Polish anti-Soviet organizations, mostly among the student body. There were also instances of dissemination of leaflets in Yiddish, distributed by Zionist organizations. A series of parallel Polish and Lithuanian organizations existed in the city of Vilnius, and each one of them published independently its own anti-Soviet leaflets, proclamations, and appeals.

Similar incidents occurred throughout the whole of Lithuania. In addition to the city and county of Kaunas, and the city and county of Vilnius, underground activities were reported in fifteen counties. A number of diverse and often uncoordinated underground groups sprang up among them: the Lithuanian Independence Party, Lithuanian Activists, *Soyuz Osvobozhdeniia Litvy*, Committee for Liberation of Lithuania (in Vilnius) Lithuanian Activist Union (LAS), Committee to Help Lithuania (LKG), LIG Committee (in Rokiškis), Exterminators of Parasites, Saigūnas (group in Telšiai, named after a prince of Žemaitija), Lithuanian Patriots, Committee No. 27 (in Šakiai), 118th Brigade of the Iron Wolf, Punitive Detachment of Lithuanian Fascists (in Tauragė), Union of Patriots of the Fatherland, Mirties Batalionas, etc. The background of the membership of these groups was even more diverse: high-school and university students of peasant, worker, professional and civil service families, *šauliai* (Riflemen), scout leaders, leaders of Catholic groups (like the Pavasaris and Ateitis movements), Young-Lithuanians (jaunalietuviai), Nationalists, former members of the nationalistic Iron Wolf, nationalist liberals. For the most part, the members of the resistance groups were young people, between the ages of seventeen and thirty years.

The following conclusions can be drawn from this passive phase of Lithuanian resistance: 1) An anti-Soviet resistance in Lithuania rose from the very beginning of the occupation and quickly spread throughout the country. 2) Youth, students, workers, farmers took a most active part in this resistance. 3) the resistance was directed against the occupation and for an independent Lithuania. Diverse slogans and plans show that the activities were not dictated from above or made according to a set plan. The frequent cross-purposes indicate that they arose from

317

different groups. Sporadic and universal, the Lithuanian resistance movement became more intense as the Sovietization of Lithuania proceeded. What was needed now was a unified underground command and a timetable for an armed insurrection. The Lithuanian Activist Front gave both to the resistance movement.

THE FORMATION OF THE LITHUANIAN ACTIVIST FRONT

The first steps to unite the separate nuclei of resistance and form an organized network under a single command were undertaken at the beginning of October, 1940. Of momentous importance was the October 9th meeting in Vilnius of the resistance leaders of Kaunas and Vilnius: Leonas Prapuolenis, X.X., major Vytautas Bulvičius, Juozas Vėbra, Dr. Adolfas Damušis, and Dr. Pranas Padalis. A centralized underground was formed. The objectives of the underground were as follows: first, to rationalize resistance operations, in order to protect the people from NKVD provocations; second, to aid and shelter persecuted patriots; third, to maintain contact with the free world, and finally, to organize an insurrection at the most propitious time.

The first concern of the centralized resistance was to anticipate and avoid NKVD provocations. For this reason, the underground was organized on the revolutionary Communist party basis, i.e., small cells of five (*penketukas*). In other words, from the command down, each member of the initial *penketukas* was responsible for five men, who in turn were responsible for five others. Only the cell leader knew who his immediate superior was. The underground was first organized in small villages, then in towns, then in Kaunas and Vilnius. At first, this organization, which came to number approximately 2,000, liquidated local Lithuanian traitors but did not touch Red army personnel. A court of three was set up to mete out justice to traitors. The military staff of the organization collected information on traitors, who because of their activities caused Lithuanians to be killed or arrested and deported.

There was a dual underground center—one in Kaunas and one in Vilnius. The Kaunas sector staff, headed by Damušis, Vėbra, and Prapuolenis, had fifteen members, mostly from the

318

Kaunas Technological Faculty. It concerned itself with organizational affairs and contacts with the countryside. The Vilnius sector staff, headed by X.X., and assisted by Bulvičius, Padalis, and
Stasys Žakevičius, concentrated its attention on political and
military matters. It maintained contact with Lithuanians abroad,
especially in Germany. Padalis was its political advisor, basing
his policies on German and BBC broadcasts and on advice from
former political leaders. The Lithuanian Activist Front Staff was
split, so that if one were captured by the Soviets, the other could
continue its functions, in addition to taking over the liquidated
group's duties.

As more escapees from occupied Lithuania began to enter
Germany and arrive in Berlin, some steps had to be taken to unite
them into the Resistance movement. There were some political
refugees of all political shades. The majority of escapees were belligerent young men, determined to aid their fatherland at all costs.
Among the escapees were former government officials, well-
known civic and political leaders, former army officers, etc. The
majority of these Lithuanians in Berlin agreed to cooperate with
the former Minister to Berlin, Colonel Kazys Škirpa, regardless
of former political affiliations. Škirpa carried on preliminary discussions with these groups and formulated a political action program. On November 17, 1940, Škirpa called together the nucleus
of his resistance group. Twenty-eight persons attended this first
meeting in his home, among them former ministers, noted civic
leaders, scientists, priests, lawyers, economists, writers and officers.
Škirpa read his "Ideas for the Platform of the Lithuanian Activist
Front," which emphasized the following ideals: 1) the preservation of Lithuanianism, perpetually developing Lithuanian nationalism; 2) Christianity, as the cornerstone of the nation's morality;
and 3) social justice, progressively attained by consideration of
changing social and economic conditions. The LAF platform was
accepted by those present, and the executive group of the Lithuanian Activist Front (Lietuvių Aktyvistų Frontas) was created,
with Col. Škirpa as its leader. In due time, the centralized resistance movement in Lithuania acknowledged the supreme leadership
of the Berlin group and adopted the name: Lithuanian Activist
Front (LAF).

The Berlin LAF, by following the trends of German diplomacy and relations with the Soviet Union, diagnosed the probability of a Russo-German war in the near future. It was fully aware of the totalitarian nature of National-Socialism, but preferred to have Lithuania occupied by the Nazis than to be physically and economically destroyed by the colonial policies of the Soviet Union. The LAF felt that the Western powers would ultimately defeat Nazi Germany and that Lithuania would re-emerge as an independent state. The immediate menace to this goal was the USSR; thus, it had to be destroyed. The LAF did not doubt that the Germans could defeat the Russians. But, in terms of long-range objectives, Lithuania's siding with the Germans would be frowned upon by the ultimate victors, Great Britain and the United States. The Lithuanian activists were faced with a dilemma; nonetheless, they chose a difficult middle course —they would rise against the Russians at the outbreak of Russo-German hostilities and present the world with the fact of a restored Lithuanian state, regardless of the consequences. The LAF in Berlin and Lithuania made plans for such a revolt.

A dichotomy of views on the political system of the restored Lithuanian state developed prior to the revolt. The Berlin LAF, operating in a totalitarian atmosphere and having a number of Lithuanian Nationalists on its staff, adopted an authoritarian platform with totalitarian leanings as a matter of expediency, so as not to antagonize the Germans. The LAF in Lithuania, unaware of the plans for the future by the Berlin LAF, because of the difficulty of communication, developed in a different direction: the leadership in Vilnius and Kaunas was more idealistic and democratic. It made plans for a coalition-type provisional government, so that all political ideologies would be represented. The youthful leaders of the LAF at home were not afraid of social innovations, and favored democratic political institutions.

As the LAF began to operate conspiratorially, maximum initiative was left with the local underground leaders. Only the overall network was coordinated from above. In order to confuse the Soviets, individual LAF units took different names or maintained old ones. The Germans, on their own initiative, succeeded only in setting up a movement in Samogitia (Žemaitija) called the "Black Swastika."

Consolidation and centralization processes of the Resistance had to be careful; therefore, it proceeded slowly. For example, the Lithuanian Freedom Fighters Union, formed on December 26, 1940, joined the LAF only in April of 1941. Some units only grouped together on the eve of the Revolt.

In order to maintain contact between the Berlin LAF Staff and the Kaunas-Vilnius centers, and to coordinate their activities, special messengers were sent across the frontier into Lithuania. Several of these were captured and became martyrs, not disclosing their secrets to the NKVD. For security reasons, the Berlin LAF avoided corresponding with the underground leaders in Lithuania. All communiques were transmitted orally. *Noms de guerre* were assumed to conceal the leaders' true identities. On December 5, 1940, couriers brought the Berlin LAF brochure "Out of Bolshevik Slavery to a New Lithuania" into Lithuania; it gave somewhat accurate information about German-Soviet relations, as well as suggestions regarding the revolt and the establishment of a government at the outbreak of war.

Attempts were made to unite all in the LAF ranks, and qualifications for entering the LAF were predicated on a membership limited to Lithuanians who were actively striving for Lithuanian independence and who were willing to make sacrifices, regardless of political and religious beliefs. High-school and university students (neolituanai, ateitininkai, varpininkai, etc.), workers, sons of workers, young intellectuals, and poor but idealistic individuals formed the backbone of the Lithuanian Activist Front. Through their efforts, all of Lithuania was covered by a network of underground contacts and presses, which regularly circulated thousands of pamphlets to the population.

In anticipation of the revolt, small military units were organized throughout the country. Partisan bands were comprised of young men who had fled to the forests. The biggest problem was obtaining arms and ammunition. A number of machine guns, rifles and revolvers had been cached by the former members of the Riflemen's Association (Šaulių Sąjunga), reserve officers and members of the Iron Wolf shortly after the Soviet invasion. Nevertheless, the majority of the population had been forced to turn its arms over to the police. The German military and the Gestapo sent small caches of arms to the Lithuanians. The LAF had reliable members in the Communist police, the Militia, the Postal Administration, the military ranks, and in hospitals and similar administrative positions. Important military points of contact were planned and determined.

In regard to the creation of a government, the actual selection of its members was left to the underground centers. An attempt was made in Lithuania to enlist leaders of the major political parties (Christian Democrats, Nationalists, Populists and Socialdemocrats) in order to form a truly coalition government. By May, the LAF had a complete list of "Ministers" for this provisional government.

The Resistance movement aroused the fears of the NKVD. On April 5, 1941, it was discovered that 500 grenades had been stolen from the Vilnius City Militia depot. NKVD Commissar Gladkov issued an order on April 7 to the effect that all police, army units and auxiliary police should prevent any Lithuanian revolt on May 1. Commissar Gladkov, in his April 7th Order, especially emphasized that

> it is established that counter-revolutionary organizations existing on the territory of the Lithuanian Soviet Socialist Republic—as well as individuals among the counter-revolutionary elements—are collecting and striving to procure weapons and cartridges in order to organize an armed struggle against Soviet rule.

When the Russians put into operation (June 14-18, 1941) the long-planned policy of mass deportations, youths and ex-soldiers who survived the June 13-14 dragnet flocked to the forests to take up arms. Rebel groups began revolting in remote areas as early as June 17.

Although the mass deportations disrupted ties between leaders of the underground and even eliminated some key personalities, the whole nation was aroused against the cruelty of the Russians. During the deportations, word was received from Berlin that the war would actually begin between June 18 and 26. The Vilnius staff was given an approximate date. Since the Nazis preferred Sundays for commencing invasions, it was decided to be especially alert on Sunday, June 22.

THE 1941 REVOLT BEGINS

At dawn, on Sunday, June 22, 1941, German airplanes bombed the Kaunas airport. All along the German-Lithuanian frontier, German artillery opened a barrage. The Russo-German conflict had begun. The inhabitants of Kaunas secretly rejoiced in the fact that war had broken out, because it meant the hour of deliverance.

Leonas Prapuolenis and Pilypas Narutis, together with the LAF staff, established themselves in the Žaliakalnis Old Folks Home in Kaunas. Part of the LAF staff established itself in the Kaunas Chemical Institute. By evening, LAF groups sallied forth with grenades to blow up strategic telephone and telegraph points. Telephone communications were cut. The Soviet military telephone exchange in Vilijampole suburb was dynamited.

The LAF also aroused panic in the ranks of the Kaunas Russian garrison, which was beginning evacuation operations. This move encouraged the activists. Around midnight, the Red Army began loading trains in Kaunas Railway Station. Units started pulling back toward Ukmerge.

LAF MOBILIZATION IN KAUNAS

The LAF and other partisan groups mobilized. Medical students, radio specialists and reserve units of fighters scurried to pre-designated points. During the night, the activists repaired the Kaunas Radio Station which had been abandoned by the Russians.

Sunday night was moody: The Kaunas streets were filled with retreating Red soldiers and would-be insurgents lacking weapons. Trustworthy militiamen turned over small caches of rifles to activist platoons. The *penketukai* (units of five) were uneasy; they requested orders from the centers. At dawn, the revolt began in earnest. Prapuolenis phoned Ambrazaitis, ordering his unit to seize the first police precinct in the Old Section of Kaunas. A platoon quickly occupied the premises, and this was the start of the Old Section partisan staff. Over 300 partisans registered there.

About 3:00 A.M. on June 23, Adolfas Damušis, Leonas Prapuolenis, Juozas Vėbra assembled in the provisional headquarters and edited the act of reestablishing Lithuanian independence and a short appeal to the nation. About 6:00 A.M., the radio station was ready to broadcast. A small armed group of activists guarded the station (the most effective weapon there was a mounted antiaircraft machine gun). A larger Soviet unit could have wiped out the LAF group at the station if it chose to mount an attack. The Ąžuolynas Park near the transmitter was crawling with Russian soldiers, but there was not enough time to await a larger LAF guard. The rebels had to broadcast quickly. Because it was impossible to delay, Prapuolenis ordered the small LAF unit at the transmitter to prepare for broadcasting. As a security precaution the street microphones were not hooked up.

At 9:28 A.M., LAF plenipotentiary L. Prapuolenis announced to the nation the restoration of Lithuanian independence in the name of the Lithuanian Activist Front staff.

> The Red executioners having brutally tortured our land are at present fleeing in disorder . . . the hour of liberation of all Lithuanian lands is at hand . . . Brother Lithuanians, to arms . . . Long live independent Lithuania!

He then went on to name the members of the provisional government which was to be headed by Kazys Škirpa. Adolfas Damušis repeated the announcement in German, and Professor Zenonas Ivinskis did so in French. Then the national anthem was sung. Thus was given the signal to start the insurrection.

THE REVOLT IN KAUNAS

Before noon, the first shots of the revolt in Kaunas were heard. Seventeen armed youths, backed by several thousand unarmed rebels, stormed the Panemune arsenal and seized 3,000 rifles and several machine guns. Ammunition was lacking. The activists also seized the Vilijampolė arsenals—2,500 automatic rifles and many revolvers, grenade-launchers and machine guns fell into the LAF hands. A large ammunition dump was also seized. Under Russian machine-gun fire, the Panemune activists ferried several hundred rifles across the Neris by motor launch to the Vilijampolė rebels, the launches returning with ammunition. (Other Panemune activists sent weapons to the freedom fighters in Freda and Aleksotas suburbs.) As LAF first-aid ambulances carried rifles to the important rally points, rebel groups continued to grow in size. The Kaunas activists also attacked the Soviet guards at the railroad bridges to protect them from destruction, and workers and civil servants began to organize the defense of important buildings (the Chamber of the Ministry of Justice, the Jewish Bank, etc.) At midnight the Freedom Bell (Laisvės Varpas) was heard over the Kaunas radio, and the Lithuanian Tricolor flew over the War Museum. Armed activists seized the telegraph-telephone exchange, ties were established with the suburbs. The Red Army did not know that the LAF was utilizing the repaired telephone network to coordinate separate LAF commands in the city. When the Security Police Building was occupied, former police officers began to organize the nucleus of a provisional police. At 1:00 P.M. bloody clashes occurred in the streets of the suburbs, Vilijampolė, Panemune and Aleksotas between the Red Army and the LAF. The rebels of the Kaunas center attacked state offices, and after several hours of brutal fighting seized them. Machine-gun and rifle fire echoed in the streets. The foundry workers of Metalas captured three Soviet tanks. Unfortunately, no one knew how to operate the tanks, therefore, the tanks' machine-guns were dismantled and given to other insurgent fighters.

The first victims of the Lithuanian revolt were young people: V. Živatkauskas, A. Norkūnas, P. Savulionis and J. Milvydas. The insurgents often would waylay Russian soldiers and overwhelm them. Armed with captured weapons, the partisans defended stores and buildings, and protected innocent civilians, even liberating 2,000 political prisoners in Kaunas, the majority of whom joined the partisan ranks.

Although the Russian guards blew up the bridges across the

Nemunas, this premature action probably saved Kaunas from destruction by a retreating Red army from Suvalkija, which was forced, under the circumstances, to detour the city. In the afternoon another danger was averted when activist machine-guns forced Red Army formations back as they attempted to cross the Nemunas at Panemune. In this engagement German bombers came to the aid of the Lithuanian insurgents.

The booty of the Lithuanian activists grew. Automobiles, trucks, machine-guns and even artillery and tanks fell into their hands. The night of June 23-24 was utilized for arming the activists in the suburbs. Weapons were ferried to Aleksotas and Freda across the Nemunas under intensive Russian machine-gun fire. Colonel Jurgis Bobelis, recently released from prison, became the military commandant of Kaunas. He ordered the inhabitants to register their weapons and report any Communist partisan activities. A directive was issued ordering all officials and civil servants to return to the posts they occupied prior to the Soviet occupation. Within a day, almost all of the units were under the direction of the unified command.

A crisis arose when the news reached Kaunas that large Red Army forces were moving toward Kaunas from Jonava, and it was suggested that the radio be used to contact the German Luftwaffe for assistance. In forty-five minutes a German bomber squadron headed toward Jonava, the Red armor was smashed, and the crisis was averted. (This was the first instance of coordinated operations with the Germans.) Two Soviet battalions surrendered to the partisans; on the whole, however, the Red soldiers avoided surrender, having been told by their officers that the Lithuanian rebels would cut out their tongues. There were instances where Red Army units fired upon each other in panic.

Since there was a shortage of experienced officers, at first the LAF in Šančiai had a poor organization, consisting primarily of young people and workers. Nevertheless, they succeeded in thwarting the entry of three Soviet divisions into the area. During the night of June 23-24, the LAF drove the remnants of the Red army out of Kaunas and took over the strongholds of the Communist partisans. In the fight for Kaunas, 200 Lithuanian partisans were killed and an additional 150 were hospitalized.

By 6:00 P.M. on the 24th, Kaunas was completely in the hands of the LAF. For three days, the Lithuanian activists fought with the Russians for Kaunas without any German assistance; thirty-six partisan groups operated in the city. On June 24, the partisans began mopping-up operations against the last nests of Communist resistance, and within forty-eight hours they had done likewise in the Kaunas suburbs.

THE REVOLT IN THE REST OF LITHUANIA

The revolt spread throughout the entire country. An important role was played by the soldiers of the Lithuanian army, which had been officially incorporated into the Red army on September 30, 1940. The resistance of the soldiers was spontaneous, and in some instances they were joined by the partisans. Almost all soldiers of the 184th Division in Camp Varena succeeded in freeing themselves, whereas those of the 179th Division in Švenčionėliai-Pabradė had a difficult time. Also, part of the student body of the Vilnius military school were deported to Russia before they had an opportunity to defect. Of the 7,000-8,000 Lithuanians in the so-called 29th Red Corps at the outbreak of the war, some 5,000 soldiers and 500 officers succeeded in breaking away from the Russians and regrouping into their old units, while several hundred others deserted from the Red Army and went home. Suffice it to say, a number of Lithuanian soldiers fell in battle against the Russians.

On June 23, in Druskininkai, the Lithuanians organized a local partisan militia. Although the Communist party leaders succeeded in escaping from the city, they did not get far; the Lithuanians captured them on the road to Parieše. Utena was seized by the partisans and spared the ravages of Russian plundering. In Aukštadvaris, the partisans, having only four revolvers, disarmed the Communists and hoisted the Lithuanian flag. In Prienai, the partisans began organizing a local administration on the second day of the war, and by the beginning of July they managed to clear the local forests of Red soldiers. In Subačius, a platoon of Lithuanian soldiers executed their Russian officers and joined the partisans. Similar incidents could be accounted for the whole of Lithuania.

Generally speaking, when the Red Army units began evacuation operations, brave youths grouped together, obtained motley
collections of arms and attacked the Russian rear guards. Often
the partisans, identified by white armbands, succeeded in saving
towns and villages from the reprisals of fleeing Russians. On June
22 at 10:00 A.M., the Russians began evacuating Šiauliai. The
following day, panic ensued in their ranks, and Communist party
officials began burning documents. Two days later, the Red army
fled from the city. The following day, rifle and machine-gun fire
was heard in the city, and at dusk the German Army arrived to
find Šiauliai in the hands of the partisans.

THE INTENSITY OF THE REVOLT

According to Professor Kazys Pakštas, a total of 131,000
armed and unarmed Lithuanians took part in the revolt; K. Pelekis
puts their number at 125,000; while General Stasys Raštikis and
Professor Juozas Brazaitis give a more conservative estimate of
upwards of 100,000 rebels. Though the insurgents were not properly armed or organized, their greatest asset was their determination to drive the Russians from the homeland.

The revolt completely demoralized the retreating Red army
and occupational officials. Bloody battles were fought in Vilnius,
Kaunas, Varėna and Ašmena. The heroism of the poorly armed
insurgents impressed neutral correspondents accompanying the
Wehrmacht through Lithuania. Unfortunately, the losses were
tragic: on the Lithuanian side 4,083 were killed and 8,000
wounded, and the fleeing Red army and NKVD butchered an
additional 1,500 persons. Also, the attacking Germans massacred
several hundred partisans whom they had disarmed, and later
excused these atrocities by stating that these incidents were
"mistakes."

What were the Russian losses as a result of the revolt? We
will probably never get the actual figures; however, having in
mind the suddenness of the revolt, one can assume that the Red
army suffered two or even three times as many casualties as did
the Lithuanians.

The preparation and execution of the revolt was successful. In one week (June 22-29) the Russians were driven out of Lithuania. Political prisoners were liberated. The majority of industries and towns were saved from destruction at the hands of the retreating Red army. The revolt averted reprisals and atrocities against the inhabitants of Lithuania. By the same token, the Germans were unable to justify their position that they had occupied Lithuania as Soviet territory. The Germans were forced to reckon, whether they liked it or not, with a functioning local government.

What were the results of the revolt? First, in the whirlwind of several days of fighting, over 2,000 freedom fighters fell. This number was greater than that of the Independence Wars of 1918-20. The greatest casualties were suffered by young soldiers, students, sons of farmers and even high-school students. These casualties attest to the intensity of the Lithuanian nation awareness. Although there had been shortcomings during the independence period, Lithuania's youth knew how to express its love of freedom and fatherland and to sacrifice for these ideals.

Second, during the revolt a provisional government was set up. The creation of this government shows that the revolt was not the product of chaos arising as a result of local disorders caused by the outbreak of the war. Nor was the revolt an outburst of a desire for revenge. The creation of a provisional government comprised of representatives of the major political groups shows that the aim was independence. This goal, however briefly, was realized by force of arms. The revolt exploded the Soviet lie that Lithuania had voluntarily joined the Soviet Union.

The provisional government considered it its duty to protect the regained independence. Therefore, this government did not agree to make any concessions which would compromise independence, although the Germans resorted to coaxing, temptations, threats and blackmail in order to bring about a compromise.

The six-weeks period of the provisional government is noted for its resistance to the German occupational authorities, who did not recognize the government. The Germans did not permit Prime Minister Škirpa and Foreign Minister Skipitis to leave

Berlin for Kaunas, in addition to forbidding any means of communications with Lithuania. The provisional government was not permitted to print its decrees and appeals in newspapers. The Nazis provoked friendly Lithuanian elements into signing petitions against the Government, and when this failed they persuaded pro-German elements to stage a putsch against the provisional government.

The Germans resorted to these measures in order to force the government either to liquidate itself or, if this were impossible, to transform itself into a "Trusted Council" which would be subordinated to the occupational authorities.

The government solidified under such conditions. Since Škirpa was unable to leave Berlin, Education Minister Juozas Ambrazevičius performed the functions of prime minister, and enjoined others to complete the cabinet. A meeting of civic leaders was held to show the solidarity of the country with the government. Sixty civic and cultural leaders, including former President Kazys Grinius, decided unanimously to support the decision of the provisional government regarding the Germans, to wit: "The Provisional Government will not liquidate itself. If they so desire, let the Germans liquidate it."

In the end, the Germans announced creation of the administration of Ostland (including Estonia, Latvia, Lithuania and Byelorussia) on July 28, 1941. On August 5 the last meeting of the provisional government was held, at which it was decided that, since the Germans had placed all sorts of obstacles in its way, the government was forced against its own will and the will of the nation to cease functioning. One could not assert that the government betrayed the mandate given it by the insurgents. It was forced to submit to brute force.

However, the administrative apparatus created by the provisional government continued to function. The majority of the administrative personnel was loyal to the nation, and supported a Lithuanian line rather than a pro-German line.

With the suspension of the provisional government, the concern for a unified political line and a unified political leadership did not disappear. Lithuanian political activity again went underground.

II. Resistance to the Nazi Occupation, 1941-44

During the period of the provisional government, no preparations were made for underground resistance against the German
occupation. Nonetheless, it arose spontaneously because of the
German refusal to recognize the right of the Lithuanian nation to
independence. Reestablishment of national independence was
thus the ultimate objective of the resistance movement. The two
enemies of national independence were Nazi Germany and the
Soviet Union, against both of whom the resistance movement directed its activities.

Great hopes were placed on the Atlantic Charter by the underground leaders. It was generally assumed that the Charter
summarized the real objectives of the Western Powers. An additional incentive was the fact that the Lithuanians knew the nature
of Soviet imperialism from direct and bitter experience.

The underground movement had to solve a difficult dilemma
—how to resist effectively against the Germans without helping
the other enemy, the Soviets. The first underground publications
emphasized the Lithuanian determination to regain freedom;
they informed the people about the objectives of the German policies and protested against their crimes—but, alas, there were no
concrete proposals for action.

1. Uncoordinated Resistance, 1941-43

Four or five weeks passed following liquidation of the provisional government. The public showed overt hostility to the
German-imposed Zivilverwaltung or Administration which reintroduced a totalitarian socio-economic order. Though looting had
been tolerated as an unavoidable consequence of military operations, the conspiracy against Lithuanian sovereignty and the rein-
troduction of a totalitarian regime by the Nazis alienated whatever
sympathies the Lithuanians may have felt for them.

The LAF, still operating in the open, felt duty-bound to raise
its voice in protest against the policies of the Zivilverwaltung. It
drafted a memorandum directed to Hitler, Ribbentrop, and Field
Marshal Wilhelm Keitel. The LAF submitted the memorandum
to the *Feldkommandantur* on September 20, 1941, in which com-

plaints were set forth pointing out that the Zivilverwaltung had disparaged Lithuanian independence, and had restored the Soviet system against which the Lithuanians had sacrificed so many lives; also, it accused the Zivilverwaltung of seizing Lithuanian property and discriminating against the Lithuanians by not giving them the same rations accorded to German civilians. The memorandum was signed by several score combatants against the Soviets—former members of the provisional government, high-ranking army officers, professors and civil servants. The *Feldkommandantur,* having acquainted itself with the contents of the memorandum, wanted to return it to the petitioners. But the latter had seen to it that there would be no agency available to receive the original document. Therefore, the contents of the memorandum became known to both the Lithuanians and the Germans.

Reprisals were quick in coming. On the following day, General Commissar von Renteln arrested LAF plenipotentiary L. Prapuolenis and sent him to Dachau concentration camp. It was only through the personal appeal of Minister Škirpa, to the German High Command, that Prapuolenis was released from the camp, though he was barred from returning to Lithuania. The other signatories were invited to the German security police where an SD official extorted promises from them that they would refrain from further political activities. The next day, the General Commissar closed the LAF and confiscated its property.

After the fading of the Activist Front, the resistance movement lacked a unifying organization and a single leadership. Thus, each underground group acted on its own. The overall impact of Lithuanian resistance was strong, but it was less effective than it might have been under a central leadership. Previously formed political groups and new resistance organizations began to manifest themselves. The Union of Lithuanian Freedom Fighters, the Lithuanian Front, The Socialdemocratic Party, the Peasant Populist Union, the Nationalist Party, the Tautininkai (Nationalist Union), the Christian Democrats—all these groups at first operated separately but subsequently formed joint organs.

The Union of Lithuanian Freedom Fighters (Lietuvos Laisvės Kovotojų Sąjunga or LLKS) was formed as a resistance organization on December 26, 1940. Its founders were youthful intellectuals of a liberal nationalist persuasion. During the first Soviet occupation, the LLKS mimeographed pamphlets entitled *LLKS Instructions*. In April, 1941, the Union joined the Lithuanian Activist Front and was active in the preparation and execution of the June, 1941, Revolt. In August, 1941, the Union broke away from the LAF. Some of the Freedom Fighters were active in the Nationalist Party, but began leaving its key posts when some of the Nationalists collaborated with the Nazis. The LLKS began its anti-Nazi activities, as mentioned above, with the open letter to the Councillors General. By the end of 1942, the LLKS was mimeographing an underground paper *Laisvės Kovotojas*. At intervals, the Union also published a survey of specific problems. In the struggle against the Nazis, the LLKS cooperated with all patriotic resistance groups; in 1943, it joined the Supreme Lith- uanian Committee (VLK) and by the end of 1943 it was a member of the Supreme Committee for Liberation of Lithuania (VLIK).

During the anti-Nazi resistance it established ties with the free West, sending a representative to Sweden who later (early 1944) became the VLIK plenipotentiary. The LLKS maintained a radio tie with its operative in Sweden and learned of outside develop- ments. The LLKS also established contacts with the Latvian and Estonian resistance movements.

At its zenith, the Union was one of the largest and strongest of underground organizations, its publications having a total cir- culation of a quarter of a million. In addition to the underground newspapers *Laisvės Kovotojas* and *Apžvalga,* the LLKS in Vilnius published *Laisvės Žodis*. Its local cells in the countryside printed or mimeographed countless brochures.

The Lithuanian Front, organized in 1941, was comprised of young Catholic activists and intellectuals, former members of the Ateitis Catholic organization. It observed and unmasked the plans and schemes of the occupant, and had a political-information sec- tion to form public opinion. The military section collected arms and organized military units in the eventuality that, when the Eastern Front collapsed, the Lithuanians would be able to defend their country with arms. In the information field, the LF began publishing *Į Laisvę* in 1943. It also published a weekly political survey, *Lietuvių Biuletenis.* Individual LAF units published *Vardan Tiesos,* the satirical *Pogrindžio Kuntaplis,* and *Lietuvos Judas* (a personal register of native traitors).

Preparations were made by the LLKS and the LF for an armed insurrection against the Germans, but the country had to be patient and to abstain from guerrilla warfare because it would aid the Soviet war effort. The policy of resistance enjoyed the general support of the people. During 1942, the movement grew until the entire country was covered by its intricate network. An absence of guerrilla action and of sabotage against the German war effort deceived the Germans; thus, the German administration underestimated the strength of the resistance movement.

The Lithuanian Unity Movement (*Vienybės Sąjūdis*) was organized by Kaunas students of varying political hues in the autumn of 1942. It published *Atžalynas* and amalgamated the Vilnius University students and the non-academic youth of the cities. At first, it was a heterogenous movement, but when the Germans arrested and deported one of its two principal leaders, the Unity Movement became an integral part of the Christian Democratic Bloc.

An active and large organization that stayed clear of party politics was the Lithuanian Freedom Army (*Lietuvos Laisvės Armija*). This resistance organization was created in February, 1942, by former Lithuanian army officers, and was organized on a purely military basis until the end of the German occupation. At first, it consisted of small units, but later it expanded to company-size formations. The Lithuanian Freedom army had units throughout the entire country. It published secret bulletins.

The former Voldemarists or Nationalists (not to be confused with the Tautininkai or Smetona's Nationalist Union) played an ambiguous role during the Nazi occupation. Elements of the Voldemarists, designated the Nationalist Party, openly collaborated for a while with the Nazis; others were wary of German intentions from the start. The Nationalists helped raise five Self-Defense Battalions (Savisaugos Batalionai) to combat Soviet partisans and to protect eastern Lithuania's communication lines. When the Nationalist Party formally presented the German authorities with a memorandum protesting the excesses of Nazi rule, the Party was officially closed. The Nationalists joined the anti-Nazi underground.

2. *Resistance of the Local Administration*

With liquidation of the Lithuanian provisional government, the Nazis set up a puppet Council General to direct the administration of the country with indigenous civil servants. The Councillors General were headed by the Voldemarist General Kubiliūnas. Theoretically, the Councillors General were to follow the directives of the German General Commissariat, the highest occupation authority in Lithuania. In a number of instances, the Councillors General playing the role of pro-Nazi sycophants actually worked for the interests of their nation. They were, so to speak, latter-day Konrad Wallenrods.

The most heroic case was that of Dr. Pranas Germantas-Meškauskas. Appointed Councillor-General for Education, Germantas-Meškauskas made the Germans believe that he was serving them loyally, when in fact, for two years, he did everything in his power to protect Lithuanian cultural interests against Nazification. After two years, the Germans discovered his ties with the underground. He ended up in the notorious concentration camp at Stutthof near Danzig—from which he never came out alive.

The Councillor General for Labor, Dr. Jonas Paukštys, was considered to be least impervious to German demands. Yet, even he showed signs of resistance when the General Commissariat demanded that 100,000 Lithuanian laborers be sent to Germany; he refused to sign the order, explaining that he could not compromise himself because he knew that such a number could not be raised. The Nazis gave him an "extended leave of absence" and ordered an assistant to sign in his stead.

As a result of this conflict of interests between the Commissariat and Councillors General, out of the nine Councillors General five of them ended their careers in Stutthof concentration camp when it eventually came to light that they were systematically contravening Nazi orders. Dr. Pranas Germantas-Meškauskas (Education), Mečys Mackevičius (Justice), Jonas Paukštys (Labor), Major Stasys Puodžius (Comptroller), and Colonel

Juozas Narakas (Internal Affairs) were sent to Stutthof. The Councillors General and other native administrative personnel were able to resist the Nazis because they felt the moral support of the Lithuanian public and of the popular underground.

For the task of preserving public order in Lithuania, the Nazis lacked a sufficient number of their own men. Therefore, they used a supplementary contingent of Lithuanian policemen. The task of the Lithuanian police was extremely difficult. They were always confronted with the duty to the occupant and to their own people. Next to their direct duty to fight criminals, they were forced to assist the Germans in collecting men for various services in the interest of the Reich, also to bring in compulsory deliveries. Yet, they secretly informed the population of the German plans in advance, so that the people affected would have enough time to hide their property before the German expeditions arrived. After unsuccessful "hunts," the Gestapo always tried to find a scapegoat among the Lithuanian police. As a result, many policemen became victims of Nazi vengeance.

Nepriklausoma Lietuva (No. 17-18, 1943) gives an example of the travails of the Lithuanian police:

> After the hunt in the Vilnius territory, the Gestapo went on arresting those of the Lithuanian policemen who they suspected of having warned the population before the hunt started, so that the people might be able to hide themselves and thus be saved. In this manner, the chiefs of police at Švenčionys and at Trakai, and the chief of the Lithuanian police and the chief of the railroad station at Varėnai have been arrested.

Here is another example of the solidarity of the Lithuanian police with the people: on the way from Vilnius to Kaunas, passengers in a bus were searched by a German and a Lithuanian policeman. Not only were identity documents examined, but all the bags were searched. There was one passenger on this bus who felt himself caught in a tight corner. In his seemingly hopeless situation he turned to the Lithuanian policeman: "Help me or I'm done for!" "What's the matter?" "My attache case is full of Lithuanian clandestine newspapers." "Put it next to me," was the suggestion. At a favorable moment, the Lithuanian policeman took the case under his arm. On leaving the bus, he warned the passenger in question that he must come to the police station the next day to "renew your passport." When the passenger appeared next day at the police station in Kaunas, the policeman, with a wink, apologized for the fact that the bag was no longer quite full. He had distributed half of its contents among his friends! Such incidents were by no means exceptional.

3. The Underground Press

The underground press was no new device to the Lithuanians. During the Soviet occupation, they had already published various proclamations and periodicals against the Russians. The origin of the underground press during the German occupation may be traced to the first memoranda, which were signed by prominent Lithuanians and entitled *pro memoria* for presentation to the occupation authorities. These *pro memoria* began to appear at the end of 1941, when Nazi violence had already become unre-strained. The *pro memoria* embodied protests against Nazi exploi-tative tactics in agriculture, industry and commerce; against a solution of the problem of land ownership in a manner wholly at variance with the interests of the native population; and against the murder of Jews, as well as generally evident plans for the abolition of Lithuania's independence. The substance of these *pro memoria* can be thus summarized: "Herren Germans, restore our independence and we shall be able to arrange the life of our country far better than you intruders from abroad can possibly do." The originals of these memoranda went through official channels to the German authorities, the Reich-kommissar, and copies were mimeographed and circulated throughout the country. They were constantly increasing and passed swiftly from hand to hand. From these leaflets the people learned the truth about the occupation. Although not strictly secret, these memoranda were not wholly public. Their contents, directed against the Nazis, faithfully reflected the feelings of the inhabitants and were there-fore very popular. In due course, commentaries on these memo-randa appeared. Secret printed proclamations followed. In the end, they gave birth to a copious clandestine press.

Clandestine newspapers representing all parties were printed in specially constructed cellars well hidden from the prying eyes of the Gestapo. It was no easy task to organize their publication and to provide them with paper, which, of course, could not be obtained in the free market, when the entire country was covered with a network of German spies. Well trained assistants were needed; a system of counterespionage against the Gestapo had to be organized; and data provided compromising the Nazis. Moreover, after printing, the distribution of these newspapers was both difficult and dangerous. It often happened that to avert detention entire issues had to be destroyed and then reprinted. Money too had to be found. It is indeed noteworthy that there was never any lack of men willing to risk their lives in this perilous undertaking. No sooner had one underground paper been discovered by the Gestapo than another of the same name would spring up in its place. Even humorous and satirical periodicals were printed and widely circulated, and special publications warned the people against German agents, spies and traitors.

Circulation of the clandestine press, in spite of difficulties, was quite extensive. In some cases, as many as 5,000 to 10,000 copies were printed. *Laisvės Kovotojas* circulation reached 20,000. The total issue of all secret newspapers would be almost equal to that of the so-called legal press. Considering that every copy of a secret paper passed from hand to hand, it is safe to assume that the clandestine press reached most of the inhabitants of the country. And there were always many people only too willing to write for this press without payment.

The Nazis both feared and hated the underground press. Experienced Gestapo agents were put on the track and did their best to trace the secret press centers and pressmen, editors, readers and contributors. Nor were they particular in their choice of means. The faintest suspicion sufficed to send the victim to a concentration camp. A solitary copy of a paper or proclamation would be regarded as sufficient evidence of guilt. Many Lithuanians died in these camps of sinister repute on the strength of such flimsy evidence. But new men were always read to come forward and take the place of the fallen.

Unable to break the spirit of Lithuanian resistance, the Nazis resorted to a fresh ruse: The Gestapo started publishing its own illegal newspapers in Lithuania! In August, 1943, the Gestapo succeeded in discovering one Lithuanian underground printing press which they confiscated. However, the next day the same periodical appeared again, printed in another secret place. The periodical *Laisvės Kovotojas* stated in its editorial:

> To chasten the Gestapo self-complacency a little, we promise, should the Gestapo be able to discover one more Lithuanian secret printing press, to publish two new periodicals in its stead. All preparations for that purpose were made half a year ago. We await their decision.

Now the Gestapo took up the idea—to fight against the underground press by means of an underground press of its own. In pursuance of this policy, they adhered to their principle that the end justifies the means. Their newspaper was given the name of the confiscated *Laisvės Kovotojas*; it was of the same size, printed in the same letters; only the motto was changed a little, i.e., "Published by the Young Generation of the Union of Lithuanian Freedom Fighters." Of course, the contents of the paper were thoroughly reformed. For instance, the Gestapo journalists went so far as to reform thoroughly the issue No. 21 of the real *Laisvės Kovotojas* of March 11, 1944, reprinting the text of the paper in their publication with changed and falsified contents. For example, they re-edited the proclamation of the Supreme Committee for Liberation of Lithuania, printed in the original *Laisvės Kovotojas* on the occasion of Lithuanian Independence Day. All democratic ideas expressed in the proclamation were thoroughly Nazified. The genuine *Laisvės Kovotojas* answered the Gestapo with stinging sarcasm.

Another incident, but of a different nature, happened in February, 1944. It serves to show that in the fight for freedom the customary rules of utility and austerity do not necessarily apply. The German authorities strictly forbade the observance of Lithuanian Independence Day, but with characteristic disregard for German susceptibilities the underground newspaper *Laisvės Kovotojas* decided to celebrate the occasion in its own way: the paper

339

appeared in gilt letters and with the national flag, reproduced in color—this in spite of the additional work, time and danger involved. It was surprising that this incident caused the German authorities much annoyance and irritation, for they considered, perhaps rightly, that it was meant to add insult to injury to their dignity and authority.

It is amazing to what extent the Lithuanian people followed the instructions and advice of the underground press. This press was the authentic voice of Lithuania, representing the true spirit and feelings of the nation. To what extent the underground press was alert and efficient under most trying circumstances may be judged by the following example:

On April 28, 1944, the German authorities announced the mobilization of all Lithuanian officers and some classes of enlisted men. On the very next day, there appeared extra issues of the underground newspapers advising the people not to comply with the mobilization order. Here are some characteristic quotations from *Nepriklausoma Lietuva*:

> The Germans intend to use our men in the West, in dangerous areas and cities of Germany where the Allied bombing is going on. In fact, they demand that we should fight not against Bolshevism but against the English and Americans. In this way our nation would be placed in danger of becoming an enemy of England and America, an enemy of those very countries which recognize our independence and in whose capitals even today there are our diplomatic legations . . . adhering to our undoubtedly right attitude—not to give a single man of our nation to die for the interests that are foreign to our nation and to our state—we are going to husband strongly and with determination our young men for the coming struggle in defense of the freedom of our people and our country. We were, we are, and we shall continue to be steadfast and unbending in this attitude . . . countrymen! When the proper moment for active fighting actually faces our nation, we shall be called to it by those who are really expressing the will of the nation—by the Supreme Committee for Liberation of Lithuania and by the free Lithuanian press.

The valuable service rendered by the underground press in the struggle against the Nazis may be summed up as follows: 1) the press united the Lithuanian nation into a single body. Although the people necessarily comprised various ideologies and political tendencies, with one wing of the underground press occasionally attacking another, the press as a whole was unified in leading the struggle against the Nazi occupants. 2) The press was the only channel through which the supreme political body VLIK could make known its will at that time. 3) The press succeeded in combining Lithuanians of all parties. Its will was to some degree accepted as a command to the nation. 4) It inspired the masses of the population to resistance; it warned them against being drawn politically, economically and culturally into the German war machine. 5) For some time, until the end of the Nazi occupation, it saved many Lithuanians from deportation to forced labor in the Reich. 6) The underground press and foreign radio services were the only sources of reliable information available to the Lithuanians. 7) By explaining to the people the Nazi plans for extermination of the conquered nations, the underground press was able to educate them in the spirit of the Western democracies.

Also, in German-occupied Lithuania, the sole underground transmitter in all of occupied Europe began to operate, a fact which astonished the Western Allies. All other transmitters operated from places other than countries which were under German military occupation.

4. Resistance by the Intellectuals

The Lithuanian educator deserves profound gratitude and much praise for his role in the anti-Nazi resistance. He, together with his students, stood resolute during the entire period. Attempts were made to force the students to conform to Nazi demands, but they did not obey these demands and dissuaded others from doing so. They published secret newspapers, spread the proclamations of VLIK, and assisted in many other ways such as instructing the nation how to resist the Nazis. The professors secretly read lectures to their students and examined them. United in anti-Nazi organizations, professors and students did their best in preparing the youth of Lithuania for the struggle against their oppressors.

The German administration tried to use the schools to spread National-socialism. In the event this would not work, they were prepared to limit and even eliminate higher education and capture the youth by other devious means. The goal of the Lithuanian educators was diametrically opposed to this; therefore, the struggle for the youth and for the spirit of academic freedom in the schools was dogged and dramatic. The higher schools, reorganized by the provisional government in 1941, functioned until March 16, 1943. During this period, they rallied the youth and gave them a na- tional direction by shielding them from the warped philosophy of Naziism. The higher schools completed their national mission by the time the General Commissar dealt them a fatal blow.

Other educational and cultural organs were actively par- ticipating in the struggle. The public press, which succeeded in avoiding final absorption by Nazi agents, was suffering under a very strict censorship. Contributors to these papers tried to write so that the readers could read between the lines. Thus, some editors of the public newspapers were arrested and deported. Pub- lication of books was very much hampered; only books and pam- phlets for German propaganda could be printed. Here, too, a way was found: fiction, poetry, and scientific works were secretly pub- lished. Paper, printing material, and printers were available when the object was to serve the interests of the people.

The most dramatic struggle between Lithuanian educators and the Nazis was over the use of Lithuanian youth for labor services in Germany. The *Arbeitsdienst* hunted the young people down, carried them off to Germany, tried hard to make Nazis out of them; once re-educated, these new Nazi-adherents were to be returned to their country of origin.

The first Lithuanian "evangelists" having graduated from the *Arbeitsdienst* "academies" returned home and gave such an ac- count of the working conditions in Germany, that no new volun- teers for the *Arbeitsdienst* presented themselves. Then the Ger- mans began to tempt the young people with all sorts of privileges: those who had not quite finished high school or had failed in their examinations were offered diplomas; those who received bad marks were told these marks would be changed. In effect, all sorts of trickery was resorted to, even to the forging of the signatures of well-known people to articles in the press urging the young people to enter their names for the *Arbeitsdienst*.

When all these measures failed, reprisals were resorted to. All young people over sixteen years old who had not performed their obligatory labor service in Germany were ordered dismissed from the high school. Many young people left high school but still refused to serve in the *Arbeitsdienst*. Meanwhile, the high-school authorities found a way out of their difficulties; they dismissed the pupils as ordered, but taught them secretly and allowed them to present themselves for examinations in the spring, and gave them certificates. And so the Nazi orders were again sabotaged.

In 1942, the Germans tried to gather all the students for labor service and thus undermine the universities. The order was given that the universities and other institutions of higher learning were to accept as students only those who had served their term of forced labor or in any other official service. This order did not increase the number of volunteers for the *Arbeitsdienst*, while students continued to be accepted in the universities. The Nazi authorities ordered a drastic investigation of the university activities, and were highly disappointed to find that they could not make a case against the universities. The latter had found a few loopholes in Nazi orders. The universities were forbidden to accept students who had not fulfilled their labor service—but nothing was said about auditors; so a considerable number of students were redubbed auditors, which was strictly according to the universities' statutes. Again, some sort of "official service" could take the place of the *Arbeitsdienst*. So hundreds of students presented to the universities duly signed certificates showing that they were working in the various local self-government administrations or in Lithuanian concerns as secretaries, bookkeepers, etc.

In the end, German patience was exhausted and the Nazis resorted to savage repressions. In March, 1943, the Lithuanian universities and the Lithuanian Academy of Sciences were closed. The War Museum and the Lithuanian Folklore Archives were looted, and many of the exhibits were wantonly destroyed. On

343

March 25-26, 1943, professors, intellectuals, priests and others were deported as hostages to German concentration camps.

5. *Two Resistance Centers*

By the beginning of 1943, the resistance movement reached such a point, that a coordinated center for all groups was conceivable. The center was formed by the representatives of the Tautininkai, Populists, Nationalists and Socialdemocrats. This center called itself the Supreme Lithuanian Committee (Vyriausias Lietuvos Komitetas, to be called henceforth, VLK). The first VLK secretary was Bronius Bieliukas, one of the staunchest and most active advocates of the consolidation of the resistance. VLK published its first declaration to the nation—*Laisvės Kovotojas* carried its text—on March 1, 1943. The declaration stated that the Lithuanian state still existed juridically, that the Soviets were driven out of Lithuania with the assistance of Lithuanian partisans. Since the country had no official organ to express the will of the nation, the need to establish VLK had arisen. Favoring unity and the conservation of all forces for a future Lithuania, VLK declared: "The reestablishment of Lithuania's freedom is the task of all inhabitants of Lithuania. We do not condone the use of brute force against Lithuania's minorities and we will strive to unite all dutiful citizens for the reestablishment of independence and for the reconstruction work."

When the Nazi plans for the colonization of Lithuania were uncovered, VLK immediately drew attention to this scheme and published a proclamation in the June 1, 1943, issue of *Nepriklausoma Lietuva*, pointing out that first the Germans planned to colonize the counties of Marijampolė, Vilkaviškis, Kaunas, Kėdainiai, Šakiai, Raseiniai, Biržai, Šiauliai, Telšiai, Tauragė, Mažeikiai, and Kretinga. In some places, colonization had already begun.

When it was discovered that the Germans were importing Latvian and Estonian SS units to impress Lithuanian men into the Wehrmacht, and that some Lithuanian Self-Defense companies were to be transferred to other countries, VLK quickly issued a new declaration in the October 15, 1943, issue of *Nepriklau-*

344

soma Lietuva, warning that Latvian and Estonian SS battalions were being sent to Lithuania to seize young men, and that Lithuanians are being sent to foreign countries where the inhabitants were resisting the occupants. It mentioned that in the Vilnius region the Nazis had shot ten prominent Poles and had deported a hundred others to concentration camps, and that the Jews of Lithuania were being ruthlessly exterminated. The inhabitants were warned to watch out for provocations and divisions among the local populace. The declaration categorically condemned Nazi atrocities. (This was the last declaration of VLK, for it soon afterward merged into VLIK.)

Coordinating the life-and-death struggle against the occupants and orientating the line to pursue in the light of Nazi designs, VLK tried to establish contacts with the free world. The Union of Freedom Fighters designated Algirdas Vokietaitis as its liaison man with the outside world. Having reached Sweden on July 20, 1943, in a fishing boat, he was authorized to negotiate in the name of the VLK.

On August 2, 1943, a Lithuanian Committee (Lietuvių Veikėjų Komitetas) was set up in Stockholm consisting of Vytautas Gylys, Ignas Šeinius, Vladas Žilinskas and Algirdas Vokietaitis. Vokietaitis enlightened the Committee about the situation in the homeland and distributed underground periodicals. The "Swedish Committee" immediately contacted the Lithuanian Minister in Washington, P. Žadeikis. Since Latvians and Estonians were able to reach Sweden much easier, Vokietaitis used their channels to maintain contact with the VLK. He also used Morse code to report on the international situation to partisans in Lithuania.

The second foray to the West was prepared by Vokietaitis in a declaration dated October 14, 1943, signed by the political parties and resistance. The original was initialed by Steponas Kairys (Socialdemocrat), Juozas Audėnas (Populist), Balys Gaidžiūnas (Tautininkas) Jonas Deksnys (LLKS), K. Brunius (Nationalist), Stasys Lušys (Christian Democrat) and Juozas Ambrazevičius (Lithuanian Front). (Two groups not represented by VLK also signed.) The declaration briefly recounted the relations between Lithuania and the USSR, the Reich occupation and the destruction of Lithuania's inhabitants (over 250,000).

As an antipode to the VLK, the Clerical Bloc formed the National Council (Tautos Taryba). This Council was little known and its activities *per se* were limited. The Lithuanian Front on its own was much more active. The leaders of the National Council were former members of the Christian Bloc and activists of the LF. Most leaders belonged to the Ateitis Catholic Action organization. The Tantos Taryba was homogenous, it had three basic groupings—Christian Democrats, Lithuanian Front and the Unity Movement. The Council wanted to introduce the principle of personalities instead of politically representative groups into the central resistance organs.

6. *Establishment of the Supreme Committee*

For a while, the two centers were unable to coordinate fully their actions or to avoid friction between themselves, even though they were fighting a common enemy. Gestapo officials in Lithuania were understandably gratified by the friction and hoped for its intensification. The Lithuanians themselves, realizing the pernicious efforts to find disunity, redoubled their efforts to find a common platform, but a basis of mutual understanding eluded them for some time.

The VLK took the initiative in trying to reach mutual agreement. The first talks were held on July 3, 1943. Negotiators voiced their regrets about the present situation and expressed determination to do everything possible to achieve unity. When the discussion turned to the essence of the problem, the representatives of the Supreme Lithuanian Committee proposed that one of the two active resistance centers cease its activity and join the other, with the number of its representatives in the new body agreed upon in advance. Their opinion was that the National Council should liquidate itself, because it was the later of the two to be organized. After further discussions, the conference ended with an agreement to consider the ideas raised.

Toward the fall of 1943, due to Nazi oppressive measures, the consolidation of the two centers became a necessity. After

346

long negotiations the VLK special representative, Juozas Audėnas, and the T.T. representative, Stasys Lušys, finally reached an agreement and VLIK was born. (The defunct Clerical Work Federation [Darbo Federacija] was revived and enrolled in VLIK as a concession to the clerical groups.) Thus, on November 25, 1943, the Supreme Committee for the Liberation of Lithuania (Vyriausias Lietuvos Išlaisvinimo Komitetas) came into existence as the highest political institution for the preservation of national rights and interests and for the direction of the restoration of independence. The country was soon covered with a network taking directives from VLIK.

The underground press disseminated the word of VLIK to the people. VLIK categorically opposed the German plans to mobilize Lithuanian men, the deportation of workers and the extermination of the country's Jewry. It concerned itself not only with political resistance, but also made plans for the reconstruction of an independent Lithuania. (The Supreme Planning Commission was set up with subcommissions on the constitution, social order, education, etc.)

On February 16, 1944, VLIK issued its declaration, expounding the principles it was fighting for. The citing of the entire text at this point is in order, for it sheds a light on the spirit and thinking of the coordinated resistance in Lithuania.

To the Lithuanian People!

The Lithuanian nation, endeavoring to liberate Lithuania from the occupation and to restore the functioning of Lithuania's sovereign organs, temporarily impeded by foreign forces, stands in need of a united political leadership. With this aim in view, the Lithuanian political groups, as exponents of the nation's political thought and as instruments of its application, have agreed to unite all forces for common action and have created the Supreme Committee for Liberation of Lithuania.

The Supreme Committee for Liberation of Lithuania, entering upon its duties, declares that:

1. The freedom of the Lithuanian nation and the inde-

347

pendence of the Lithuanian state are indispensable conditions for the nation's existence and well-being.

2. The sovereign State of Lithuania has not disappeared by reason of its occupation by the Soviet Union on the 15th of June, 1940, and the diverse other acts perpetrated by force and fraud under cover of that occupation resulting in disruption of the functions of the sovereign organs of the State, were brought to an end by the popular revolt of the Nation on June 23, 1941, and the functions of the sovereign organs of the State were temporarily resumed by the Provisional Government.

3. After the liberation of Lithuania from the occupation, the Constitution of 1938 will remain in force until it is appropriately amended in a legal manner.

4. A Provisional Government of the Republic will be organized when the proper time comes, within the Supreme Committee of Liberation of Lithuania on a coalition basis and by agreement of the political groups.

5. The democratic organization of the State of Lithuania will be effected in conformity with the interests of the people as a whole and with general post-war conditions.

6. The laws governing the election of the President of the Republic and of Members of Parliament will be modified in accordance with the principles of democratic elections.

7. The Supreme Committee for Liberation of Lithuania, having undertaken leadership in the struggle and labor for the liberation of the country, for the restoration of the functions of the sovereign organs of the State, for the restoration of the democratic order and for defense of the country against Communism and other life-disrupting factors, will endeavor to bring about the broadest possible consolidation of the community, at the same time eliminating misunderstandings among the political groups.

8. Recognizing the great importance of the national armed forces in the struggle for liberation of Lithuania, the Committee will by all available means support the restoration of the Lithuanian army.

9. The Committee will maintain close contact with Lithuanian Legations and Consulates and will collaborate with Lithuanians abroad, especially with Lithuanian-Americans, as well as with all nations that recognize the

principle of self-determination of nations and the right of Lithuania to independence.

10. In order to facilitate the cultural and economic progress of the nation and to accelerate the country's return to normal life, the Committee will collect and arrange the appropriate material for the use of liberated Lithuania's administration, as well as for regulation of the national economy, social life, justice and education.

The Supreme Committee for Liberation of Lithuania, in making this declaration to the Lithuanian people, invites all Lithuanians of good will of all poltical parties to imbue themselves with the spirit of unity and collaboration in this unequal struggle for the liberation of Lithuania.

"For the sake of Lithuania
Let the unity of her people flourish!"
(From the Lithuanian National Anthem)

THE SUPREME COMMITTE FOR LIBERATION OF LITHUANIA

In addition to its representative in Sweden (Vokietaitis), VLIK also planned to send its military representative Colonel K. Ambraziejus to Stockholm but he was captured by the Gestapo in Tallin and interrogated. As a consequence, on April 29-30, 1944, arrests of VLIK personnel took place. A. Damušis, B. Gaidžiūnas, J. Katilius, K. Brunius, A. Tumėnas, K. Valiulis, J. Deksnys and B. Bieliukas were arrested and sent to various German prisons. The political groups appointed new men to take their place.

The reconstituted VLIK issued a declaration on May 25, 1944, and, foreseeing the inevitability of a new Soviet occupation, appointed Mgsr. Mykolas Krupavičius, Rapolas Skipitis and Vaclovas Sidzikauskas as its delegation in Germany. While evacuating Lithuania, VLIK appointed three plenipotentiaries to remain in the homeland (Tautininkas, Socialdemocrat, and member of the Lithuanian Front). Only the plenipotentiary of the Lithuanian Front remained; the other two left the country. This was a strategic loss for VLIK, for the country was now left without a competent political leadership to cope with the new Soviet

349

invasion. The resistance movement was fragmented, lacking orientation and coordinated direction.

7. *German Attempts and Failure to Mobilize Lithuanians*

After the battle of Stalingrad, the military situation suddenly changed. The Germans realized that it might be difficult to conquer the Soviet Union singlehandedly. Their arrogance received a hard blow and they began to look for allies in the eastern countries. Now the Germans remembered the Lithuanian offer to raise a national army for participation in the war against the Soviets, and proposed the formation of a Lithuanian SS Legion.

The first step toward general mobilization was an appeal to some prominent Lithuanians for their support. The answer was negative. The reason given was that, although Lithuanians would be ready to defend their country against a repetition of the Soviet invasion, only a legitimate government of independent Lithuania could declare mobilization. After this, the Germans turned to the Lithuanian Counsellors General but even they refused to obey such instructions. As a result of this refusal, most recalcitrant Counsellors were arrested and some deported to Germany.

The Germans then decided to do the job themselves. They made three separate attempts at mobilization of the Lithuanian nation, and each time in a somewhat different manner. They invariably failed, each successive failure exceeding the previous one in intensity. Unfortunately, each abortive attempt was followed by harsh reprisals.

The first order of general mobilization was issued for the formation of a Lithuanian SS Legion to fight on the Eastern Front. Guided by the underground press, the Lithuanians with few exceptions stayed away from the registration centers and the attempt had to be abandoned. This recalcitrance brought severe reprisals in its wake. Scores of intellectuals were deported, some executed; both universities and all colleges were closed.

The Germans then tried to implement another plan for the mobilization of manpower, this time not for the armed forces, but ostensibly for the so-called *Baubataillone* ("Construction Battalions"), which would have to go outside the country to work.

The Lithuanians saw clearly what was really behind the Nazi ruse. 60 percent of the men mobilized dispersed. The Germans had no better success with the mobilization of another contingent, as the May 5, 1943, issue of *Į Laisvę* clearly stated:

> How is the mobilization progressing? By crawfish steps only. The men born in 1919-1924 remain faithful to their original decision—to enlist only when they will be called by the government of independent Lithuania. To registering offices come only a few men. In the towns more men are enlisted than in the villages.

Reprisals followed this failure. Relatives of those who failed to register and were hiding were arrested. Manhunts were conducted. Punitive expeditions were sent to scour the countryside and press-gangs sought young men. The Germans then formulated a plan to revive the Lithuanian Riflemens Association, which had existed prior to the war and was known as *Šauliai*—the national guard of the country. The Riflemen's Association was to have ostensibly only one task—to rid the country of the Soviet parachutists. The idea was a clever one: the Lithuanians were anxious to form some kind of military organization to meet possible eventualities which in due course might offer them the opportunity for getting rid not only of Soviet parachutists but of the German occupants as well.

The German Zivilverwaltung wanted to entrust the former leader of this organization, Colonel Kalmantas, with the task of reviving the Riflemen's Association. He rejected this proposal, giving as his reason the fact that according to the statute of the Association, their purpose and task were "to defend and to preserve the independence of Lithuania," and this condition was not implied.

Other forces were at work, however, which necessitated the formation of military units. In the latter half of 1943, Soviet partisan activities increased in the northern and eastern parts of the country. They looted and killed the inhabitants who were not friendly toward their cause. Bandits joined the Soviet partisans. The Germans placed the responsibility for the defense of railroads and bridges on the local authorities, but the local Lithuanian police

351

were too weak to protect the Soviet-infested areas. In this atmosphere, on November 24, 1943, Kubiliūnas' Council General conferred with forty-eight Lithuanian civic leaders about Lithuanian military formations. The Germans rejected the Lithuanian conditions.

On the Lithuanian side, the discussions were continued by General Plechavičius. He had been a popular figure during the fight for independence. The following demands were submitted to the Germans: 1) to allow a voluntary mobilization of 10,000 men; 2) to establish Lithuanian headquarters in the district centers; 3) Lithuanians were to fight only against outlaws in their own country; 4) the Germans were to supply arms to the Lithuanian Home Formation, but the leadership was to remain in Lithuanian hands.

Most of these conditions were unacceptable to the Germans, and the negotiations were broken off. On January 30, 1944, they finally agreed to the formation of a local Home Formation. General Povilas Plechavičius was to form fourteen battalions, to wit, thirteen battalions of 750 men each and the fourteenth (a training battalion for non-commissioned officers) of 1,800. Besides, there was to be a cadet school for officers with a complement of 1,200. Two principles prompted General Plechavičius to give his consent to the plan: 1) It was felt that the war was entering a decisive stage fraught with uncertainties, thus rendering it highly advisable for a dependable Lithuanian armed force to be at hand for the protection of the country; and 2) the promise exacted from the German authorities they would give up further recruiting for any other units. The staff of the formation started its work on February 8, 1944, and eight days later the first proclamation was issued.

General Plechavičius issued a call to join his battalions and in a very short time, by April, 1944, he had formed fourteen battalions up to strength. It is reported that the response to his call produced some 20,000 volunteers—double the number required. But here German duplicity once more manifested itself. The weapons were old and there was a minimum supply of ammunition. The enlisted men lacked clothing and footwear. Most of the officers wore their old uniforms of the former Lithuanian Army.

The very name of the Home Formation is evidence that the Lithuanians and the Germans understood the aims of the mobilization in two different ways. The Germans called the local formation "Litauischer Sonderverband" and, while denying clothing for the men enrolled, secretly stored uniforms of their Luftwaffe and planned one day to make them German soldiers. The Lithuanians were sure that Germany was on the bring of collapse, and that the formation would soon be needed for the restoration of Lithuania. Very soon, however, the Germans began to disrupt the formation by attempting to send Lithuanian battalions to various places without the knowledge of the leaders. The battalions refused to obey. They changed garrisons only with the approval of their Lithuanian leaders.

Sent to the Vilnius region, the soldiers were given only ten cartridges each, and soon they had to fight against certain Polish partisan bands secretly armed by the Germans themselves. Many Lithuanian soldiers died in the traps laid by the Germans.

The first group of 5,000 men having been formed, the Nazis allowed another 5,000 to be called up. About 1,000 men were allowed to stay with local commanders; about 1,200 men were in the training battalion at Marijampolė. The Germans were very suspicious of the training battalion; however, they were calmed by the apparent lack of young officers and sergeants.

Little by little the Home Formation went on its own way, contrary to the German designs. Very often, patriotic dispositions of the officers and soldiers were openly manifested ("We'll tan the German hide!"). For example, a large group of recruits embarked on a steamer from Jurbarkas to Seredžius. At their departure, the Lithuanian National Anthem was played and a group of Germans who did not take off their caps were badly mauled by the crowd. The enlisted men did not hide the fact that they had no intention of fighting for the Reich.

The Germans grew more and more suspicious of the Home Formation. At the end of April, 1944, the Gestapo had discovered the existence of VLIK. (A document carried by Colonel Ambraziejus contained information on the situation in Lithuania, to be dispatched to foreign countries.) As a result, the Nazis informed Plechavičius that they were taking possession of the battalions of the Home Formation. The district commanders were to be replaced by District Commissars (Nazis). General Plechavičius said to the officers of his staff: "Think of this 'honor' bestowed upon us, and let everyone come to his own conclusion."

Many small groups of the Home Formation split into squads and melted into the countryside, taking their weapons with them. The soldiers who escaped from the Germans reorganized into combat groups for guerrilla warfare and prepared themselves for action against the approaching Soviet Army.

The Germans soon realized that all of the Lithuanian soldiers might disperse, so they attempted to deceive them by saying that the order for taking possession of the battalions was a misunderstanding, and that on May 15 there would be a final conference. Meanwhile, they secretly prepared for the arrest of the staff and the takeover of the battalions. Thus, the battalions were not properly informed, and events overwhelmed them completely.

On May 15, 1944, General Plechavičius and his Chief of Staff, Colonel Urbonas were invited to a conference by the Germans. When they came, they were arrested and ordered to sit quiet, facing the wall they were properly scolded. At 3:30 P.M., the entire staff was arrested. At 7:30 P.M., the officers of the staff were addressed by SS Generals Jeckel and Hintze in the following words:

> You were given the last chance to join the task of creating the New Europe; you were trusted with arms. However, it became evident that you Lithuanians did not deserve this confidence. You think that the might of Germany is on the decline and that the old generals will be able to return to their posts. You are in the wrong. Our power is strong enough, and we shall bring you to reason. Some of you will be put to death today, others will get long prison terms.

After this sermon, they were brought to the Gestapo. On May 16, all twenty-four officers of the staff were deported to Riga and subsequently to Kirchholm.

At the same time, the order for disarmament of the Home

Formation was given. On May 16, early in the morning, German armored cars attacked the Lithuanian barracks at Marijampole. The men of the military school were no longer there. The officers had granted them leave of absence at an earlier date. The company of the local commander and the remaining cadets organized a defense. There were casualties on both sides. On the other hand, the seven battalions in Panevėžys and other eastern posts escaped into the forests.

The process of disarming the battalions in the Vilnius region was much more cruel. For example, when disarming one battalion, the Germans executed without any reason thirteen privates. On May 17, at Paneriai, near Vilnius, seventeen men of the 306th Battalion were executed.

Of the 10,000 soldiers of the Home Formation, the Germans succeeded in capturing only 3,400 men. But for every deserted soldier, they shot every tenth soldier or sergeant. The captured men were put into German uniforms of the Luftwaffe and dispersed throughout Germany. All told, during the three and a half years of rule the Germans succeeded by various means in impressing 25,000 Lithuanians into their military services, instead of the 250,000 men they had planned to mobilize for war.

8. *Collapse of German Rule*

The years 1944-45 in Lithuania were tragic. On the one hand, the Lithuanians, having stood by the side of the Western democracies and having resisted the Nazi occupation, were eager to believe that when the Western democracies won the second World War, Lithuania, like the other European countries, would regain her independence. The Atlantic Charter had promised them this. On the other hand, knowing well the Soviets and their true aims, the Lithuanians anticipated with fear and dread a possible second occupation, which they were firmly convinced would bring in its train renewed dreadful enslavement for them.

The struggle of the Lithuanian resistance could not achieve its ultimate objective; there was no possible course of action which could have brought freedom. All conceivable alternates would have led to substantially the same result. With the end of

the German occupation only the enemies changed, but the Lithuanian struggle for freedom continued without interruption.

III.   The Partisan War, 1944-52

1. *Motives and Scope of the Partisan Movement*

After more than three years of Nazi occupation, the exhausted Lithuanian people expected an Allied victory and a
reconstitution of their independent state. Unfortunately, the Lithuanians were fated to fall under a second, harsher and crueler
Soviet occupation. Those people who remained in Lithuania
suffered a vengeance exacted by the returning Soviet occupants.
Following on the heels of the Soviet Army, NKVD units executed hundreds of people in Svyriai, Kaunas, Vilnius, Biržai,
Ukmergė, Šiauliai, and elsewhere whom they deemed to be anti-
Soviet activists. (See *Baltiska Nyheter,* September 26, 1944 for
sordid details).

Invading the territory for a second time in the summer of
1944, the Russians did not consider Lithuania an independent
country, and treated her as Soviet territory legalized by the first
occupation. Furthermore, encouraged by their victory over the
Germans, the Soviets began to rule without caring about any
international responsibility for their actions. They began to probe
in a most cruel manner every Lithuanian inhabitant's behavior
with respect to the Soviet rule and their behavior during the
German occupation. The pretext for all sorts of charges were
found under convenient labels of a "Peoples' enemy" or "war
criminal."

The result was an undeclared war between the Lithuanian
people and the USSR. The scope of the resistance movement may
be determined from the number of partisans killed and the size
of the Soviet armed and security forces employed to maintain
control over the country. There is some disagreement as to the
exact number of casualties among the partisans. In all probability,
during a decade of fighting the number of partisans killed or later
executed is between 30,000 and 50,000. The number of active
partisans at any time varied between 25,000 and 40,000. In 1948,

eight divisions of the Red army and units of the Soviet Air Force, at least 30,000 MVD troops and 40,000 MGB forces, were stationed in Lithuania. In addition, the MVD was supported by "Peoples' Militia" and the MGB by the "destroyers" or *istrebiteli*. The armed forces were seldom used against the partisans; nevertheless, they did constitute a potential aid to the security forces and provided a wide margin of safety for the Communist regime. The security forces, totaling up to about 100,000 men, motorized and with air support, alone suggest the grave threat to the Soviet regime; this is especially evident if we remember that Lithuania was a country of about three million people. All in all, the partisan movement enjoyed the material or moral support of 85 percent of the populace.

What motivated this extensive resistance movement? Although motivation is individual, several factors may be discerned which caused so many Lithuanians to flock to the ranks of the partisans. First of all, since the Lithuanian nation had experienced Soviet rule and terror in 1940-41, no one had any illusions as to the nature of Soviet totalitarianism. To many, it was a matter of self-preservation to join the partisans. Among such people may be considered all former officials of the Lithuanian republic, leaders and activists of the former political parties, owners of large farms and businesses, and outspoken individuals of known patriotic and nationalistic disposition.

Another factor which swelled the ranks of the partisans was the mobilization of men born in 1909 to 1926 into the Soviet army, which was declared immediately after the re-occupation of Lithuania. To those who evaded the press gangs, the forests provided the only alternative to the hazards and misery of serving in the Soviet ranks. In a word, many preferred the partisans to becoming Soviet cannon fodder. Furthermore, Soviet terror instituted immediately after the occupation contributed to the reaction against the regime. Families and relatives of known partisans had no alternative but to join the underground. Similarly, those who were discovered to be aiding the underground joined the partisans as the only way of escaping total annihilation. Many soldiers and officers of Lithuanian units, armed by the Germans, refused to follow the orders of German generals and took to the woods, providing the nucleus for an armed resistance.

The most important factor for the mass resistance movement was the mood of the nation, the evaluation of the world situation, and accepted illusions. Many, including the new leaders of the underground, believed that armed resistance was necessary and meaningful since the occupation could last only a limited period. The expectation that the Western allies would make an early peace with Germany and turn against the Soviet Union was wishful thinking accepted by many. Thus, the conclusion was drawn that the nation had to resist Sovietization at all costs, and preserve a national movement and an armed force for the limited time until the Soviet Union would be defeated and the independence of Lithuania restored.

Finally, the Roman Catholic Church in Lithuania, experiencing extreme persecution, was forced to support actively the resistance movement. Many priests served as leaders and chaplains of partisan units and supported the resistance in many ways. Involvement of the Church in the freedom struggle brought people from all social and political sectors into the ranks of the partisans. The defense of national values became identified with the defense of one's faith.

Organizationally, the partisan membership was structured like most underground groups. There were three layers. Its visible part constituted the real underground of active fighters. Their weapons were of German and Soviet manufacture. They also had machine guns, heavy machine guns of the Soviet "maxim" type. The German machine guns were manufactured in the Skoda works in Czechoslovakia. Some of the partisan units were also armed with light artillery. These were the frontline soldiers and lived in forests or farm shelters. Their ranks were continually changing—the average life span of an active fighter was only two years. Passive fighters were armed but stayed at home, on their jobs, or at school; they were called upon only occasionally, for a variety of tasks. The supporters also lived "legally." Although they did not bear arms, their contribution to the cause was important; they provided supplies and shelters, and they gathered intelligence.

Unlike the European anti-Nazi movements of the second World War, the Lithuanian partisans sustained themselves without support or supplies from abroad, that is, from the Western powers, although they did maintain some contacts with Swedish, American and British intelligence. Liaison men sent from Western Europe penetrated the Lithuanian Iron Curtain in 1945 and 1946 and established contact with the partisan leadership. The Western intelligence agencies were only interested in culling information about Soviet military installations and troop dispositions. They did not really contribute to the movement materially. The actual extent of American and British involvement was, therefore, limited.

The Soviet charge of German sponsorship and inspiration for the resistance movement is false, because such a link did not exist. The Soviet Union fabricated the charge for political purposes, as a part of an extremely intensified Communist propaganda campaign in Lithuania, designed to create a pro-Nazi image of the partisans and to destroy existing nationalist influences by indiscriminately identifying all nationalists with the German occupational regime. The few cases of collaboration among the partisans produced by the Soviets usually involved Lithuanian rebels against the Soviet regime in 1941 and former soldiers in German uniform. Interestingly enough, the Soviets have not produced specific collaborationist or war-crime charges against any of the better known partisan leaders. It would be unreal to assume, however, that among the more than 30,000 active partisans that there was none who compromised personal or political integrity. However, even on the basis of Soviet information, such cases were minimal.

Organized as conspiratorial groups, the partisans were dedicated to the restoration of Lithuanian independence. True to the traditions of the previous nationalist underground groups, the partisans maintained that, according to international law, their country had not lost its sovereignty. They set up their own courts, issued credit script, passed decrees and enforced their regulations. Until 1952, they maintained an underground leadership.

Shades of political opinion and, at first, ethnic background were not important so long as a member's loyalty belonged exclusively to the partisan organization. A good number of freedom

359

fighters and most of their leaders had borne arms against the Soviets in the revolt of 1941, and later had worked against the Germans in the anti-Nazi underground. A handful were persons originally parachuted into the country as German intelligence agents; their joining the ranks of the Lithuanian resistance had given the partisans access to valuable German caches of ammunition, weapons and other needed supplies. Moreover, escaped German POWS and Soviet army deserters were also found in the ranks. The partisans from the beginning had disqualified those German agents who refused to subordinate themselves completely to the partisan command. Furthermore, beginning in early 1945, membership was confined exclusively to ethnic Lithuanians, with occasional exception made for Latvians and East Prussian Germans.

Most partisans came from the working and small-farmer classes. Many were of varied backgrounds: officers, civil servants, students, high-school students, sons of peasants, laborers. There were also a sprinkling of priests and veterans of the independence wars of 1918-20. Youth was most sympathetic to the partisan cause—in some places, entire classes of high-school students flocked to the partisans. Women partisans were not only medics and couriers but also numbered in the ranks of the fights.

A number of partisan leaders subscribed to the principles of Christian ethics and Western democracy, to charity, social reform, humanism, justice, tolerance and freedom of conscience, speech and thought. Law based on the principles of Christian morality was declared to be the only norm of personal and group behavior. The use of force was held to be a necessary evil.

The statute of the Tauras Region of Partisans enumerated the moral qualifications for partisan candidates: The freedom fighters are to be Lithuanian men and women, regardless of age; they are to be of high moral principle, brave, determined, without any past blemishes against the nation in the past, and they are to be totally committed to the liberation of Lithuania. Those joining the partisan organization had to take the following oath:

> I   swear before God Almighty, in the name of the
> fallen brothers for Lithuania's freedom and independence, to

work with fortitude for the reconstruction of independent Lithuania, committing all my strength and life, follow strictly the orders of the leadership, keep my activities in the greatest secrecy, avoid contact wits the enemy and report everything to my superiors. It is known to me that if I break this oath I will be punished by death. All this that I swear let God help me do.

The partisan could not leave the organization until Lithuanian independence was regained. Even then, he could not leave until permission from the leadership was granted. The partisan leadership tried to create an organization with high qualifications from the gray mass of men who had fled to the forests or who were willing to collaborate with the partisans.

To identify themselves with Lithuanian nationalism and its military traditions, the partisans wore uniforms of the Lithuanian army, with insignias of rank and merit. This, along with the wearing of decorations for valour or service that were occasionally bestowed on individual fighters or supporters, emphasized the military nature of the movement and helped maintain discipline. In most cases, commanding officers were elected. Leaders of the primary units were elected from the ranks; other commanders were elected by officers of subordinate groups. Only staff officers were appointed. Thus, there was a close relationship between the leaders and the ranks; the quality of the ranks and leadership tended to correspond.

The concrete objectives of the partisans were obstruction of the Soviet regime in all its aspects, emphasis being laid on preventing the reestablishment of local soviets and impeding the work of other Soviet institutions, notably the NKVD. The other partisan activities included: punishment of suspect native collaborators with the Communists; dissemination of information; documentation of Soviet crimes and practices; protection of the lives and property of the civilian population. Sentences were passed and publicly announced by partisan courts, with the accused usually absent from the proceedings. One of the partisan leaders, Žaliasis Velnias (Jonas Misiūnas), personally executed a number of traitors in eastern Lithuania, showing his responsibility for the sentence by attaching a calling card on the bodies of the executed persons.

2. Early Groupings, 1944-45

The forests of Lithuania were full of nationalist partisans toward the end of the Nazi occupation whose objectives were to stop the demolition of buildings, factories and railroads by the retreating Germans, to protect the inhabitants from German looting, and to fight German press gangs attempting to deport Lithuanians to the Reich. The Swedish newspaper *Baltiska Nyheter* reported on September 26, 1944, that the partisans attacked a one hundred-man SA unit and forced it to retire from Plateliai. This SA unit's objective had been to requisition horses and cattle. The partisans also attacked another large SA unit and forced it to retire from Darbėnai, thus frustrating German attempts to recruit Lithuanian laborers for Germany. All in all, in September, 1944, Lithuanian partisans were victorious against the fleeing Germans in Šiauliai, Panevėžys, Ukmergė, Plateliai and Darbėnai. They seized arms and foodstuffs.

During the first partisan-war phase, roughly from the summer of 1944 to the summer of 1945, the best organized freedom fighters were the Samogitians (Žemaičiai). They first grouped while the Germans were still in Samogitia in order to protect the populace from looting. A large number of former army officers, including General Motiejus Pečiulionis, had been part of the Lithuanian Freedom Army during the Nazi rule. From the first, when the Soviets returned, they began to organize and coordinate the partisan movement. Almost all of the Samogitian guerrilla bands were united into the LFA "Vanagai" or Hawks; they numbered several thousands. The Soviets did not try to reckon with the formidable Vanagai in open combat. They resorted instead to provocations.

In February, 1945, in the environs of Tauragė and Raudondvaris, there appeared an NKVD unit of several hundred men disguised as diversionary partisans. The provocateurs killed Soviet officials, ignoring the merits of these Communists. They also liquidated officials known to be friendly with the local inhabi-

tants. After several weeks of slaughter and rapine, this unit disappeared. It reappeared after several days, but this time in the
uniform of the NKVD. Larger massacres now occurred. The
people who had inadvertently aided the provocateurs, either
through fear or sympathy, were punished. Many farms were
burned, many innocent people shot or arrested. Many fled to the
partisans to escape from this terror.

In the districts of Kaunas, Pakuonys, Prienai, Punia, Butri-
monys, Aukštadvaris and Rumšiškė, a former army officer known
as "Beržas" unit liquidated several NKVD informers, executed
several active Communist district chairmen and several bands of
outlaws. In December, while liquidating an armed Russian ma-
rauder band, Beržas was killed. The unit was taken over by a
man known as "Aras."

In northeastern Lithuania the huge forests from Vilnius to
Lake Narutis concealed large partisan forces. For this reason, the
largest engagements were fought here by formidable units. In
March, 1945, Captain "G.'s" force of 800 freedom fighters
fought a pitched battle with two NKVD divisions, who sustained
losses of 800 men and were scattered, losing much equipment.
The partisan dead numbered 150 men. During the day-long battle,
the partisan leader was wounded; his command was taken over
by a leader known as "Žalgiris." After the battle, the partisans
shook off pursuit and fled as far as Lake Narutis and the Byelorussian frontier, where they made contact with Byelorussian partisans. The Byelorussians lacked good leadership and organizational
ability, and were poorly organized starving marauders without a
clear political objective. They were in reality the product of dissatisfaction with the Soviet system. Žalgiris, who had grown up
in the eastern area of Lithuania, spoke their language and knew
their idiosyncracies. He used the interlude from fighting in reorganizing and cementing the diverse Byelorussian guerrills into a
fighting force with political objectives, teaching them Lithuanian
partisan organization, methods of operation and national objectives. The Byelorussians at first fully adopted the "Lithuanian"
system and even formed a regional command. This order, however, lasted only as long as Žalgiris and his Lithuanian partisans

363

were in the district—when Žalgiris returned to Lithuania, the Byelorussian command collapsed.

In the area encompassing Penevėžys, Ukmergė, Kėdainiai and Kaunas, Vaitelis and his group drove fear into the local Communists. The base of operations for this numerous force were the Žaliosios Girios forests. Frequently, Vaitelis' units penetrated into large cities, e.g., Panevėžys and Kaunas. Often the Panevėžys NKVD forces panicked when rumors spread that Vaitelis would "call" with his group. Vaitelis tried to live up to his legend. His men secretly infiltrated into Kaunas and attacked NKVD precincts in broad daylight. One such attack was directed against the NKVD headquarters in Kaunas. Vaitelis struck to free captured comrades; the successful attack lasted only several minutes —afterward, the group quickly retreated by automobile.

The most legendary freedom fighter was the former policeman Misiūnas, Žaliasis Velnias, who operated in the counties of Trakai, Vilnius, Kaišiadorys, Ukmergė and northeast Kaunas. His bravery and audacious operations were a bane to local communists and the NKVD. The peasants enshrouded him in mysticism.

In December, 1944, activists of the Nationalist party (Nacionalistai) and members of the secret nationalistic society Geležinis Vilkas returned from Berlin to Lithuania to participate actively in their country's struggle for freedom. This formation, known as the Iron Wolf Regiment (Geležinio Vilko Pulkas), was active in Garliava, Prienai, Gudeliai, Sasnava and Balbieriškis. In the spring of 1945, the Iron Wolf command was taken over by a leader known as "Briedis." Before then, the individual units operated separately, coming together only for concerted efforts. Later neighboring groups joined the Iron Wolf nucleus. In January, 1945, the Iron Wolf Regiment purged its district of Communist activist centers, and attacked NKVD bases (viz., Šilavotas). A force of fifteen men surprised eighteen NKVD soldiers and *istrebiteli* requisitioning grain in Ingavangis. In half an hour they forced the NKVD to flee; only three Communists reached Šilavotas alive. The NKVD garrison left their base and fled to Marijampolė. The partisans collected discarded NKVD weapons and seized Šilavotas. Much Communist booty was taken: the partisans cleaned out all government buildings and cooperatives, collected documents and destroyed records of grain requisitions. After this operation, the partisans left the town and blended into the forests. Shortly thereafter, seven members of the unit attacked a Red convoy near Prienšilis. The NKVD escorts were wiped out and the grain seized. In February, 1945, eight freedom fighters unexpectedly clashed with six MGB troops in Dumiškiai. The fight lasted several hours. Five MGB men were killed; the sixth was captured.

In Polish-held Suvalkai (Suwalki) Lithuanian partisans operated under orders from the Vytautas Formation (Vytauto rinktinė). Their primary function was to maintain contact with the outside world. Not having direct contact with Lithuania for a while, they cooperated with Polish partisans, but when the latter "legalized," they again operated independently.

In January, February and March of 1945, the Germans parachuted agent-spies, radio-operators and saboteurs, mostly of Lithuanian origin, into Lithuania. They also dropped arms, munitions and explosives. Most of these diversionists were pro-Lithuanian in orientation and had chosen German assistance, not from love of Naziism, but on the assumption that by receiving German training and materiel, they would be able to help the partisans and their own country. After reaching Lithuania with German help, they cut off contact with their sponsors. Pro-German diversionists also landed in Lithuania, but they were not aided by the partisans and were isolated. The pro-German diversionists were rare and they did not hold out long in isolation.

By the beginning of 1945, partisan units of varying sizes were operating in Lithuania. The movement continued to grow until it covered all of Lithuania, except for those areas where large Red army units were stationed, i.e., near the Prussian frontier and the Baltic Sea. Forested areas like Rudninkai, Prienšilis, Kazlų Rūda, Žaliosios Girios, Labanoras, and Tauragė hid large combat forces of guerrillas, ranging from several dozen to several hundred men. At this time, there was no centralized partisan command. Units operated in small areas. Before undertaking larger operations, the leaders of one unit would invite another for assistance. After the operation, the units would split up again and return to their bases. Each command understood organization, operations and objectives in its own manner. Nonetheless, even in this first phase of the war the basic objectives were clearly understood: paralyze the activities of local Communists, obstruct their plans, and destroy NKVD forces which are raging in the provinces.

These spontaneous groupings of freedom fighters—(laisvės kovotojai), miško broliai (forest brothers), žaliūkai ("greenies") or partisans ("partizanai") as these guerrillas were called—earned the respect of the local populace through their legendary exploits against the native traitors and the NKVD. Many local Communist leaders and officials were executed. In the vicinity of Karmėlava, for example, seventeen Party cell bosses were exterminated in one year. The Sovietization of the Lithuanian countryside was thwarted. The local population was awed by the exploits of the partisans. By April, 1945, the partisans numbered about 30,000. Since the local Communist administration often simply ceased to exist for months at a stretch, the countryside and villages were actually governed by the partisans. In some areas, the Communists ruled by day, the partisans by night. The Communists were secure only in the large cities and in areas which had strong Red army or NKVD units close by. Even then, they did not dare appear in the countryside, except in company and battalion strength. What hindered the consolidation of partisan gains was the absence of a centralized or coordinated leadership.

3. The Spread of Armed Resistance, 1945

To recapitulate in any detail the exploits of the Lithuanian freedom fighters would call for much more space than the present study could provide. It was a valiant and brutal struggle. In the spring of 1945 the guerrillas came out of winter hiding and began a multitude of attacks against the NKVD and local Communist authorities. Being familiar with the local terrain and being armed with automatic weapons and machine guns, the partisans tackled Soviet forces three, five and even ten times their size. Using ambuscades and night raids, the partisans inflicted huge casualties on the occupants.

In southern and western Lithuania, the partisans operated in small units of twenty to fifty men. They struck hard, inflicted losses and quickly broke off actions before the Soviets could rally or bring up reserves. In the east and north, where large tracts of forestland and natural cover could be found, the partisans operated in groups of several hundred. For instance, Žalgiris led a force of 800 fighting men. Bands of 500 men were not uncommon. Since it was hard for large formations to avoid detection, the eastern partisans were prone to fighting pitched battles with regiments and even divisions of NKVD troops. Of course, such large-scale battle tactics led to huge expenditures of ammunition and frightful losses.

A few examples of engagements between the Lithuanian partisans and the NKVD troops will suffice to demonstrate the mode of fighting employed.

The NKGB forces received heavy losses at the hands of the partisans at the village of Budninkai. When the partisans of the Iron Wolf formation were in Budninkai, word reached them that enemy forces numbering 300 NKGB troops were approaching. The eighty-man partisan force commanded by "Briedis" deployed itself in a kilometer-wide perimeter and quietly awaited the enemy with fifteen machine guns. The NKGB, uncertain as to the actual whereabouts of the partisans, approached in trucks along the road. When the trucks came within gun range, the partisans opened fire along the entire perimeter. Thirty Russians were killed before they could alight from the trucks; the others attacked the entrenched partisans in waves. Although the partisans were outnumbered four-to-one, they calmly mowed down wave after wave of NKGB troops. With short breaks, the assault lasted several hours. The enemy were unable to dislodge the partisans from their positions. Toward evening, when the NKGB tried to flank them from the woods, the partisans retired, having lost only one fighter—a female medic. The NKGB lost over one hundred troops.

One unit of the Iron Wolf had as its base an island in the swamps at Paliai. For a long time the Communists failed to notice this camp. The unit would make sorties at night all over the district and return at dawn safely. (The approaches were difficult to the uninitiated.) After a while, the Soviets were able to pinpoint the base of partisan operations; after several months, NKVD agents detected the location of the swamp. At the beginning of August, 1945, large NKVD forces were assembled, and light artillery began to shell the swamp; but the shelling went amiss. After several hours of shelling, they sallied forth with boats into the swamp in search of the partisans. The "forest brothers" who had remained quiet until then, opened fire on the boats, sinking them with deliberate aim. In a short while, the swamp was filled with wounded and drowning NKVD troops. This slaughter lasted until dusk, when the partisans escaped using underwater bridges. Their losses were seventeen; 200 Soviet troops went to the bottom of the Paliai swamps.

Not all engagements were forced on the partisans. "Short excursions" were often undertaken by the freedom fighters against the enemy camp. These sorties were audacious, if not foolhardy; yet, they served a purpose. The repeated sorties and surprise attacks drove fear into the enemy. For example, in March, 1945, six men of the Iron Wolf, led by "Merkys," entered Prienai. Dressed in Russian overcoats, they came into town on market day, where they found five notorious Communists, who had murdered patriots. The partisans gunned them down on the spot. Later, these same men came to the market place posing as *istrebiteli* and began to check food prices. They confiscated the foodstuffs from those merchants who were sympathetic to the Communists or the *istrebiteli*. The provisions were brought back to the other partisans.

One battle in southern Lithuania which gave rise to legends and songs was that Kalniškės. There, in May, 1945, eighty partisans led by "Lakūnas" wiped out 400 NKVD troops. In this battle, women fought alongside the men. Lakūnas' wife, a former teacher, bravely operated a machine gun after the gunner was felled, in spite of being wounded in both legs. The woman partisan Pušelė showed equal bravery under fire. In the high grounds of Kalniškės forest the partisans were attacked by 800 NKVD troops. The battle lasted several hours which the enemy trying to take the partisans' positions. All attacks were beaten back by dogged resistance. The enemy dead fell in heaps. When the partisans began to run low on ammunition, they used their last cartridges in an assault whereby they broke through the surrounding NKVD rings. They left behind the leader "Lakūnas," his wife, Pušelė and many other dead comrades.

In February, 1945, in another part of Kazlų Rūda forest, near Gerčiai, a force of 2,000 NKVD troops attacked the camp of Captain Meilus. The partisans, numbering about 150, were entrenched on a hill with strong bunkers for their ammunition. The engagement lasted eight hours. By nightfall the enemy lost 290 men and the Lithuanians only thirty-three. As darkness fell, the partisans left their positions and pulled back into the forest.

The list of engagements is extensive. What is characteristic is the fact that the partisans, using assault tactics or ambushes, usually inflicted losses on the enemy that were several times larger than their own. The proportion of losses recorded was as follows: at Daukšiagirė the Communists lost ten, the Lithuanians none; at Žemaitkiemis the Communists lost twenty-seven, the partisans three dead and five wounded; at Alsininkai the Communists lost twenty-three, the partisans five; at Paverkniai, where seventy-nine fought against a NKVD division, ninety-four Communists and eleven partisans fell; at Raišupys, all six partisans perished, but the NKVD lost sixty-seven. For obvious reasons, the freedom fighters hid their identity under the cloak of strict anonymity and served their cause under assumed names often borrowed from nature, i.e., plants and animals, the elements, and names from Lithuanian history or folklore.

During the first year the partisans fought mostly against the so-called istrebiteli (Russian for "destroyers"), who had been organized in the fall of 1944 by the local Communist authorities for the defense of the Communist party aparatus and for the collection of requisitions. The istrebiteli (the Lithuanians called them stribai, strebokai, skrebai and stribikauliai) were a Communist defense force, in the main comprised of criminals, vagrants and local dregs, who volunteered for service in order to avoid conscription in the Soviet army or for ration cards. Each township was to form a unit of thirty istrebiteli, commanded by NKVD officers. Since they received no allowance, except a uniform and rations, they took to pillage. They were also used in operations against the partisans in order to create the impression that the anti-partisan struggle was a "civil war between bourgeois nationalists and the working people."

The partisans used flexible tactics against the *istrebiteli*. First, the native *istrebiteli* were contacted personally and warned. In some cases, partisans infiltrated their ranks and discouraged service. They were forced to work for the partisans. If they did not heed the partisan warnings, force was used. The partisan clashes with the *istrebiteli* and NKVD became legendary. The partisans used machine guns, mortars and bazookas (German *Panzerfausts*) to demoralize the *istrebiteli* who were poorly equipped. The annihilation of the *istrebiteli* at Gižai, Kačerginė and Žalioji completely demoralized the remainder. They deserted wholesale or even sought asylum with the partisans. Only the criminal element and Lumpenproletariat remained. (This group too was soon distrusted by the Communists.) With the liquidation of the *istrebiteli*, it was easy to disrupt the local administration, stop deportations, the cutting of forests and the collecting of grain requisitions.

What is more significant is the fact that the elimination of the native Lithuanian element from the *istrebiteli* was a blow to the Soviet myth about the "civil war" in Lithuania. The destruction of the *istrebiteli* showed the lack of support that the native Communists had among the local people. "The peoples' democracy" was forced to rely entirely on its true sponsor, the NKVD and the Red army.

4. *Desperate Resistance, 1945-46*

The years 1945-56 saw the rising storm of partisan engagements and NKVD-MVD counter-operations. In July, 1945, more than 10,000 fresh NKVD troops arrived in Lithuania. The following month, NKVD provocateurs were sent into the forests of Kazlų Rūda in southern Lithuania. In September, NKVD-NKGB units occupied all the cities and *raion* towns. Nevertheless, Lithuanian guerrillas dared to attack Communist headquarters and installations in the cities. In October, street fighting at night still occurred in Kaunas and Vilnius between partisans and NKVD forces. In October, rumors spread that the partisans were concentrating around Kaunas for a mass assault on the city. In reality, the basis for the rumor was the fact that the Lietuvos Išlaisvinimo Taryba (Lithuanian Council of Liberation) had succeeded in establishing connections between the partisans in Panevėžys, Kėdainiai, Kaišiadorys, Trakai, Kaunas and Marijampolė. As a result, in October and November the Soviets sent three infantry divisions reinforced by tanks and airplanes to scour western Lithuania.

During the first six months of 1946, more than 800 cases of serious sabotage were reported by the occupation authorities. The NKVD offered rewards up to 10,000 rubles for information leading to the arrest of the saboteurs.

The guerrillas were now almost exclusively comprised of Lithuanians of all ages and walks of life, with an occasional German or Dutch prisoner of war, Latvian, Polish or Byelorussian freedom fighter. In one Samogitian unit there was a sixty-year old farmer with his three sons; this family "squad" constantly volunteered for the most dangerous assignments. The old guerrilla was a good shot and he accounted for a number of NKVD men. In a Sudavian unit was a twelve-year old boy whose father was executed by the Communists and whose family was deported to Siberia. The guerrillas adopted the boy and employed him as a messenger. One night he was wounded by Soviet sentinels. When the wounded boy refused to betray his friends in the forests, the Soviet troopers crushed the boy's frail body by running a tank over him.

In the spring of 1946, the NKVD began to press and persecute the partisans with more intensity than in the previous year. The long winter and late snows kept the partisan units penned up in their old bases and lairs, thus exposing them to grave danger. Following NKVD General Bartašiūnas' order of February 15, 1946, the NKVD sought out the bogged-down partisans. Every day, NKVD units clashed with uncovered or fleeing partisan bands.

During the summer of 1946, the Soviets attempted to "purge" Lithuania three times. In the first operation, between June 28 and July 16, 4,000 NKVD troopers scoured western Lithuania, and 3,000 NKVD men searched the forests of Alytus and Seinai in southern Lithuania. Two hundred Soviet troopers were killed and thirty-one partisans perished in the skirmishes. The corpses of the "white bandits" were publicly displayed in the Prienai, Marijampolė and Veiveriai market places.

The second operation was effected between August 12 and 16. The task force included 15,000 NKVD troops and auxiliary units. Major General Juozas Bartašiūnas took personal command of the operation. The enemy scoured the counties of Kaunas, Trakai, Marijampolė, Alytus, Vilkaviškis, Ukmergė, Panevėžys and Utena. This time, the guerrillas suffered heavier casualties— about 200 men perished, including several staff officers. The Soviets, however, suffered considerably heavier losses, including 1,400 men killed. The third operation was carried out September 12-16 in Samogitia. The Russians lost 560 men, the guerrillas lost thirty-nine men.

The extent of this warfare on the local level may be gleaned by studying the "War Communiques of the Lithuanian Guerrilla Radio," broadcast almost daily by clandestine radio to listening posts in Sweden and West Germany. While the sources cannot be verified, very often the facts recorded corresponded with data received from other more reliable sources. The citation of a few radio communiques for August, 1946 give a vivid picture of the war situation:

August 12—a "strib" unit of 700 men proceeding along the Aukštadvaris-Semeliškės highway (Central Lithuania) was destroyed.

August 14—a Peoples' Militia unit was destroyed on the Klovainiai-Pakruojus highway (Šiauliai county). Partisan booty: three trucks, twenty-eight motorcycles and one light automobile with radio-broadcasting apparatus.

August 15—partisan units operating in the area of Valkininkai and Varėna (north of Marcinkonys) destroyed a unit of nearly 700 istrebiteli.

August 18—in the Augustavas Forest (on the Polish frontier) partisan units were encircled by NKVD detachments. When the partisans eluded the enemy by secret passages, the NKVD opened crossfire on their units and battled each other, until the partisans formed battle lines and destroyed the rest of them. The booty included ample supplies of firearms and cartridges, twenty-six field kitchens, a number of trucks in operating condition, and three tankloads of gasoline.

August 25—on the highway between Bubiai and Šiauliai, an *istrebiteli* unit of 250 men was annihilated within three minutes. The partisans suffered no casualties. The booty: forty trucks, one field kitchen, one truckload of food, arms, various grenades and a radio broadcasting-receiving set.

August 26—a NKVD unit of 150 men was exterminated in the Karsokiškės Forest. The partisans had no casualties. The booty: seven heavy machine guns, four light machine guns, many tommy guns with cartridges.

August 28—between Vilnius and Švenčionėliai, several Peoples' Militia and road guard units comprising 628 men were annihilated. In Gardinas (Grodno) Lithuanian and Byelorussian units in a jointly executed operation blew up the railroad station and set fire to various warehouses. The partisans retired from the city without casualties.

August 29—on the Tilsit Turnpike, between Šiauliai and Kelmė, an echelon of *istrebiteli* troops transported in thirty-six trucks and two automobiles was ambushed. The convoy was annihilated by partisan machine gun fire. All of the trucks were damaged beyond repair. Each truck carried fourteen *istrebiteli,* besides the chauffeurs and relief drivers (a total of 576 men). The two passenger automobiles carried eight officers. According to the testimony of survivors, the unit was on its way to mop up the forests of Viduklė. The partisan booty: 504 tommy guns with ammunition. Partisan casualties: one of the men was burned by gasoline through negligence.

August 30—partisan units operating the area of Tauragė-Raseiniai dynamited the Lydavėnai railway bridge. In the neighborhood of the Kaunas-Babtai highway, a militia unit of 182 men guarding the highway was destroyed. Partisan booty: fifty motorcycles, 172 tommy guns, more than 500 hand grenades and much ammunition. On the Samogitian Turnpike, five militia units of road guards, each operating in groups of twelve motorcycles with sidecars, were destroyed. The booty: forty usable motorcycles, sixty tommy guns and 200 rifle grenades.

August 31—railway bridges at Jonava and Kalnėnai were blown up. Three trains were wrecked and looted for munitions and canned foods.

Throughout 1946, in spite of large-scale search operations, the partisans were still able to inflict heavy losses in men and materiel on the enemy, as can be seen from the above-mentioned clashes. According to *Pergalė* No. 7 (Vilnius, 1961), one partisan platoon leader, Vytautas Gavėnas, personally liquidated 1,000 enemies in his various engagements. According to other Soviet sources, between June, 1944, and June, 1946, 9,000 Lithuanian partisans perished; 20,000 farmers sympathetic to the underground were summarily executed by the NKVD.

As the winter of 1946-47 approached, the partisans were again faced with the serious problem of finding quarters and stocking provisions. They began to loot Communist warehouses and *kolkhozes*. A typical operation was undertaken by the Iron Wolf Regiment. Fifty men of the Dešinys and Šarūnas companies, led by "Uosis," cleaned out the *sovkhoze* at Pagermonys, a former estate, and carried off enough food to supply the formations for the winter.

5. Unification of the Resistance, 1946-47

During the second Soviet invasion, the Supreme Committee for Liberation of Lithuania in the homeland fell apart; within six months many of its leaders were either killed or arrested.

Several political organs were formed to give direction to the underground. In the spring of 1945 there appeared a Lithuanian Council of Liberation (Lietuvos Išlaisvinimo Taryba or LIT) which tried to inform the nation about international developments and to give guidelines to the underground and populace. It tried to help fugitives re-enter "legal life" under assumed guises. Unfortunately, the LIT operated only until May, 1945. When the NKGD discovered its operations and rounded up the key personnel, the survivors fled to Vilnius and tried to set up a new center, the Committee of Unity (Vienybės Komitetas). This Committee of Unity was liquidated when the NKVD rounded up 16 leaders.

The new attempt to centralize the resistance was taken by the Sudavian partisans. On June 19, 1945, a secret meeting of partisan leaders was held in the church rectory at Skardupiai to form a staff uniting the local partisan groups. At the beginning of July a meeting of four organizers was held and they formed a partisan staff: "Vampyras" (Gavėnas), the new chief of staff, contacted groups in Kazlų Rūda and Paliai. Taunys contacted the resistance in Alytus. On August 25, 1945, a conference of southern Lithuanian partisan leaders was held at Skardupis. They agreed to form the Tauras District (Tauro Apygarda) consisting of the Vytautas, Iron Wolf, Žalgiris, Šarūnas, and Perkūnas formations (rinktinės). Each formation was to have an area of operations. The Tauras District was to encompass the counties of Marijampolė, Šakiai, Lazdijai, Vilkaviškis and Alytus. The district leader was to be "Mykolas Jonas" (V. Bacevičius); the chief of staff was to be "Vygantas." In addition, the staff was to have combat, mobilization, intelligence, supply, medical, and communication sections. There were also suggestions to revive the Lithuanian Council of Liberation (LIT). *Laisvės Žvalgas* (Freedom Scout) became the official newspaper.

Tauras District decided to contact the partisan leadership in Vilnius, Kaunas, Panevėžys, Raseiniai, Telšiai (Samogitia) and Dzūkija. The Tauras people helped the Kaunas partisans organize a district. The intelligence section leader made contact with two officers in Vilnius who had a radio receiver. Rev. Ylius traveled to Kaunas, Telšiai and the Samogitian towns. The LFA in Samogitia had collapsed when its leaders were captured. Nonetheless, the Samogitians were encouraged to form the Kęstutis District. The Dzūkai formed the A District. Contacts were established with "Beržas" (Jakštas) in central Lithuania, and the LIT was revived. A meeting was to be held on November 11 in Kaunas. Since *Laisvės Žvalgas* carried on appeal signed as "VLIK," the NKVD became interested, and as a result, on October 18, seventeen leaders of the newly formed partisan staff were arrested. The district staff, however, was not liquidated.

On April 23, 1946, the Tauras and "A" District partisan leaders met and formed the south Lithuanian Partisan Region (Pietų Lietuvos sritis). Colonel Kazimieraitis (Vitkus) was chosen regional leader; his adjutant was "Mykolas Jonas." The new group took the name "The Lithuanian Partisan Movement" (Lietuvos Partizanų Sąjūdis—LPS). Its purpose was to establish contact with all partisan units, merge them into larger formations and then form a unified partisan command. On June 7, 1946, Jonas was surrounded by NKVD troops and committed suicide. Kazimieraitis, leader of the Iron Wolf formation, fell in battle in July, 1946.

In spite of these losses, the consolidation continued. In October-November, 1946, the Supreme Armed Partisan Staff (Vyriausias Ginkluotų Partizanų Štabas—VGPS) was formed with a military college and political committee. On November 1, Colonel Vytis was appointed chief of staff; "Daumantas" (Juozas Lukša) became his adjutant. On January 12, 1947, a conference of the leaders of the Tauras, A. Dainava, Kęstutis BDPS Committee and VGPS was quickly called in Vilnius to reorganize the complete centralization. Two couriers were to be sent to the West.

Actually, the centralization was never really completed, because leaders and liaison men were continually being arrested or killed. Contacts had to be renewed frequently.

Each district (apygarda) adapted to local conditions. For the most part, the districts followed the model of the Lithuanian army or the Riflemen's Association.

The best known partisan organization was that of Tauras District. The leader's staff had two sections—a military staff and a political section (for propaganda, information, press). The military staff had four units: combat, mobilization, intelligence and supply. The district was divided into four formations, with a doctor and a chaplain. The formation was divided into three or four companies (kuopos), with three or four platoons (būriai). The platoon consisted of three squads (skyriai) and had from eight to ten fighting men. Therefore, the Tauras District consisted of between 1,080 and 1,920 fighters. As the underground became more centralized, small groups armed with weapons and dressed in uniforms with prewar Lithuanian Army insignias, being acquainted with the local terrain, solved problems of supply and permitted local initiative. In the words of the Soviets: "they worked in the *kolkhozes* by day, and went out at night as bandits."

On June 10, 1946, representatives of the political under-ground agreed to form a new resistance organization—the Common Democratic Resistance Movement (Bendrasis Demokratinio Pasipriešinimo Sąjūdis or BDPS). According to the agreement, a political leadership was also created—the Supreme Committee of Lithuanian Restoration (Vyriausias Lietuvos Atstatymo Komitetas or VLAK)—to be comprised of armed forces, resistance organizational unions, and old political parties. The armed forces sent one representative, the BDPS, three representatives, and the Christian Democrats, Socialdemocrats, and Populists, one each. (The Tautininkai were excluded.) The VLAK was to be the parliament, BDPS the government, and the VGPS the army. This structure, however, was not popular with the partisans. During the January 12, 1947, meeting VLAK was criticized for being an academic creation having no ties with the realities of the situation. It is hard to determine how the BDPS operated. The name lasted until June, 1948. On February 16, 1949, the Common Democratic Resistance Movement fell away from the partisans. The BDPS preferred infiltrating the Communist system. The partisans, led by the Tauras District Staff, favored con-tinuation of active armed resistance. In 1949, the partisans formed a new organization—the Movement of the Struggle for Lithuania's Freedom (Lietuvos Laisvės Kovos Sąjūdis—LLKS)

In 1946-47, the unified partisan command was concerned with the obstruction of the so-called elections to the Supreme Soviet. The first election in Lithuania occurred in February, 1946. Dep-uties to the Supreme Soviet of the USSR were to be elected. On this occasion, the strategy of the partisans was to destroy communication lines, to fire on Soviet armed posts in election districts and thus tire out the NKVD groups that were to collect votes, as well as keep them in one place, and to liquidate all Communist officials and to provide suitable excuses for the popu-lace not to appear at the polling places (i.e., the danger from attacking partisans). The result of this election was that only about twenty-eight percent of those eligible to actually cast their votes. The remaining votes were cast by the election officials themselves. The official announcement, however, was that over ninety-six percent had voted. This announcement was carried by *Tass* twenty-four hours before the polls opened!

Having learned their lesson from the disaster of the first election, the Soviet authorities did not dare hold elections to the Lithuanian Supreme Soviet until February 9, 1947. Far more careful preparations were made on this occasion. (Until 1947 the formal legislative duties were performed by a Supreme Soviet elected in 1940; thus the election was long overdue.) The election is a good illustration of the ineffectiveness of the local Soviet authorities and of the role of the Lithuanian underground. A formal report on the election, drawn up by the Lithuanian underground, states that besides the 50,000 MVD troops and detachments of the Red army stationed in the county just before the election, approximately 60,000 additional regular army troops were brought in. From twenty-five to fifty armed Soviet troops were stationed in each of the 2,277 electoral districts. Furthermore, in county and district centers reserve motorized troops were ready to provide additional support. (The additional troops were brought into Lithuania from Poland, where they had performed similar duties and had engaged in fierce fighting with the Polish resistance forces.) On the election day the populace, at least in the rural areas, simply stayed home. Facing a total boycott of the elections, the Soviet authorities sent out election committees, actually ten to fifteen armed men, to collect the votes. The armed committees in many cases simply dropped into the urns the number of votes corresponding to the number of voters on the list. Thus only about fifteen percent of the votes were cast freely, the rest being obtained either through threats and coercion or through simple stacking of the ballot boxes by the election committees.

The partisan supreme leadership, following the suggestion of the Tauras District, planned to gather the signatures of Lithuania's inhabitants to a memorandum, whereby the nation, in accordance with the provisions of the Soviet constitution, would secede from the USSR! This memorandum was to be presented by a special courier to the United Nations, the journey to be made in an airplane seized from the Soviets. A special group in

Telšiai, led by Jakštas and Juozas Jurkus, was to prepare the mem-orandum. This fantastic scheme leaked out to the NKVD and was nipped in the bud.

Up to 1947, the partisans obstructed the collectivization of the land and the settlement of Soviet *kolkhozniki* on vacated farms. The partisan command also directed its energies against local evils: in 1946 the distilling of moonshine was forbidden, as well as fraternization with Communist colonists. Thieves, bandits, traitors and Communist lackeys were punished. The population was informed through leaflets and cartoons how to conduct itself.

From 1944 to 1952 the Lithuanian underground press was very much alive. Twenty clandestine newspapers were published, giving proof that the Lithuanians never accepted the Soviet occu-pation, and turned to their own sources for information and guidance.

The press had two main divisions—periodicals publications; and non-periodical appeals, reports and posters. The paper short-age presented the greatest difficulty. During the first several post-war years, the entire Soviet Union was utterly stripped of paper. The partisans obtained their paper mainly by raids on offices of the Soviet administration.

In 1945-46, the publication of the underground press was centralized, but this soon proved to be impractical—NKVD forays would interrupt publication for long stretches. In 1947, the press was finally decentralized and apportioned among the larger units, each unit having its own facilities and information department to disseminate publications throughout the surround-ing territory. The decentralization proved especially useful, as it lessened the work of delivery and risk to the messengers, and made publication immune to NKVD raids. While an affected unit organized itself in a new location, neighboring units would main-tain press coverage for the area. Each unit published at least one issue of its periodical monthly, in a circulation of some 1,000 copies. (The circulation of appeals and posters varied widely.)

In comparison to the periodicals of the Nazi occupation, the clandestine press during the second Soviet occupation was poorly printed. Most of the newspapers were not printed on a press, but run off on mimeographing machines; others were mere carbon copies prepared on typewriters. The quality of the paper was poor; some sheets were even printed on wrapping paper. But all of the newspapers showed a tremendous fighting spirit. Characteristic of the partisan press was the March 22, 1947, editorial of *Kova*, entitled "Lithuania militans—Fighting Lithuania":

> Fighting Lithuania is alive and is here where the Nemunas flows and winds, where the enslaved Lithuanians grieve, for blood flows here, for the lives of the fighters for freedom are being extinguished, like candles, for here are the graves of giants and their descendants—Lithuania militants.

The unified resistance also maintained contacts with abroad. The first contacts were made by couriers from the West. In the fall of 1945 two couriers (Daunoras and his companion) arrived in southern Lithuania and made contact with Colonel Kazimieraitis. Daunoras returned to the West shortly thereafter. When he returned in May, 1946, Colonel Kazimieraitis was dead. Daunoras then contacted the Tauras Staff and talked the leaders into accepting a twofold organizational structure—BDPS and VLAK. Agreeing to maintain radio ties, Daunoras returned to the West, taking with him authorization papers for seven men to set up a BDPS delegation abroad. The radio ties were never established. Not receiving further word from the West, the partisan leadership sent its own courier, who reached Danzig in May, 1947, and reestablished contact with Daunoras. The latter convinced him in not going any farther west, by promising to come to Lithuania in the fall. The partisan courier safely returned home on June 6. Radio contact, however, was still not established; two partisan radio operators perished while beaming communiques to the West.

In December, 1947, the partisan leadership sent a group of couriers led by Daumantas to the West via East Prussia. Two people managed to reach the free West. Daumantas and his companion brought much documentary material—the "Appeal of Enslaved Lithuania to the Free World," the "Letter of Lithuania's Faithful to the Holy Father," etc. The special courier operating in the name of the BDPS Presidium had authorization to check on the representatives of the underground abroad and to seek aid for the underground. Daumantas transferred the representation from the BDPS delegation to VLIK (the 1948 Baden Baden Agreement) and set up special-resistance liaison.

The ties with the West did not give the partisans what they wanted, and did not fortify their belief in the West. In fact, they were gravely disappointed. By reading information received from the West, the partisans drew the following negative conclusions: "They gave us away to death at Yalta, Potsdam. . . . The same mistakes are being repeated. The West does not dare raise a voice in protest against the destruction of nation, it does not even want to know that we have lost confidence in them, that we are continuing the struggle against their allies. . . . Long and terribly bloody is the path of the struggle before our eyes. . . . We can only continue the struggle by the most ingenious methods which would give us the necessary conditions to continue this struggle until the necessary moment."

In the special report of Daumantas that reached the partisan leadership in 1949, the courier complained bitterly about the free Lithuanians. In a special note to VLIK, he also complained about certain VLIK operatives through whose negligence a new courier from Lithuania was killed while trying to reach the West.

He and Jonas Deksnys—two essential couriers—had influence over the resistance. The first came from the West to Lithuania, the second went to the West. They were not the only ones. From the West via Stockholm through Deksnys' channels, a group led by the freedom fighter Neris reached Lithuania, but while landing on the coast near Palanga, it was detected by the NKVD and wiped out. In 1949, Jurgis Rimvydas left Lithuania and safely reached Poland, but because of the procrastination of the VLIK operative who was to take him out of Poland, Rimvydas also perished.

One of the primary aims of the resistance was to weaken the fighting capacity of the NKVD, to demoralize NKVD soldiers in every possible way. According to the data of the partisans, the losses of the NKVD in its war against the partisans during

1944-49 were in the vicinity of 80,000 men, most of whom were killed in attacks against partisan units.

Though no major battles occurred after the fall of 1946, individual MVD-NKVD troopers, MGB investigators, Communists and militiamen were killed daily. On May 8, 1947, the partisans attacked MVD forces in wooded Eisiskes; 600 partisans fell; the Russians lost three times as many men. In the summer of 1947, the Šiauliai Headquarters of the MVD were blown up. Again in November, 1947, in Šimonys Forest near Lake Narutis, a pitched battle was fought. The Lithuanian guerrillas lost 200 men, while the MVD suffered 2,000 killed; the partisans grabbed three mortars, destroyed twenty-five jeeps and five small tanks. In December, the Panevėžys MVD Headquarters were blown up by the partisans. Such spectacular operations, however, were not typical. For one thing, the partisans were weakening in men and materiel to carry on such struggles. In January and February, 1948, they continued to blow up railway bridges and bushwack small enemy security units.

Continuous armed clashes eliminated many officers from the ranks of the freedom fighters, and by 1947 the shortage was keenly felt. In August, 1947, the armed resistance organized courses for officers; seventy-two selected freedom fighters graduated from the first partisan cadet school. The second course was to take place in 1948, but the Soviet security forces attacked the training camp and forced it to disperse.

6. Soviet Counter-Insurgency

Moscow was alarmed from the start by the tenacious partisan movement. In the fall of 1944, Deputy Minister of the Interior Lieutenant General Sergei N. Kruglov came to Lithuania to organize cleaning-up operations.

On a dark September night in Panevėžys, Kruglov called a top secret operational meeting at which were present commanders of the units of NKVD troops, and deputies of these commanders for political affairs and intelligence, as well as the chiefs of staff of territorial units of the NKVD in Lithuania. In this meeting, Kruglov summarized the results of the fight against the so-called bandit movement in Lithuania and said that up to the present time the measures which had been employed had not proved to be realistic; that the Politburo of the Soviet Union, and Stalin and Beria themselves, were not satisfied with the results achieved in Lithuania; that it was time to change from words to sharp measures; that order must be restored in Lithuania, and that the Communist party and the administrative Soviet apparatus must be reestablished in Lithuania. In the name of Stalin and Beria, Kruglov gave a concrete order that the work of intelligence agents had to be intensified and activated.

Kruglov then ordered the chiefs not to spare any efforts or money in creating a network of agents, to learn the leadership of the movement, and to liquidate this base of operations. All necessary measures were to be used in order to get all the information from the partisans themselves, from their relatives, or from the people whom the partisans use for liaison purposes. He also ordered the troops to become more active in their fight against the "bandits." Anyone found under suspicious circumstances was to be brought before the NKVD. Knouts, rubber-covered steel truncheons and bundles of ramrods were to be used to extract information. After interrogation, the friends and relatives of the known bandits were to be exiled to Siberia. Anyone fleeing arrest was to be shot on sight, and the farm or house from which he was fleeing was to be burned to the ground, and its inmates turned over to the NKVD.

Former NKVD Colonel Burlitski, who later defected to the West, reported on the operations:

> It was like beating the forests for wild game, except that the game was human. Day after day we formed long lines and combed the forests and the swamps, arresting, shooting, burning. If there was any doubt left about escaping from Russia, my experiences in Lithuania put an end to it. Even my well-disciplined soldiers were sickened by their jobs. Often after a particularly grim manhunt I would find them in their quarters half mad with drink; whatever was left of their human feelings were drowned in alcohol.

To direct the sovietization of Lithuania, the Kremlin established (1944) an Organizational Bureau for Lithuania of the

Central Committee, CPSU. Colonel General Mikhail Suslov was appointed head of this bureau, which exercised the supreme power in Lithuania and directed the struggle against the resistance, as well as the reestablishment of Soviet and Communist party apparatus. Suslov was well qualified for this assignment—during the second World War, he directed partisan activities against the Germans, and was quite familiar with resistance tactics. This Orgburo existed until 1947, when the Soviet apparatus had been firmly reestablished, after which his functions were taken over by a plenipotentiary of the Central Committee, CPSU. Vladimir V. Shcherbakov.

This Orgburo had as its principal aim the liquidation of the resistance movement; in actuality, it took over the entire political administrative and economic life of the Republic. Any orders or directives which were issued by Suslov were a "must" for the Government of Soviet Lithuania. Since the search-operations were unsuccessful, the NKVD became suspicious of the Lithuanian militiamen, officials and even Komsomols. They believed that these elements were employed in purging these groups and officials.

In February, 1945, General Bartašiūnas, with the approval of the Soviet government, issued a declaration to the effect that if the Lithuanian partisans were to leave their underground lairs and report to the territorial organs of the NKVD in Lithuania, with a statement that they were repenting their sins, they would receive amnesty. They were told to give up their arms and to indicate to the territorial organs of the NKVD where the headquarters of the partisans were located, where depots of arms were located, who the leaders were, etc. Some partisans who complied were dressed in partisan uniforms and used for provocations. Captured partisans were tortured by the NKVD to betray their comrades. One was cut into three parts with a power saw for remaining adamant; when another refused to speak, the NKVD cut out his tongue; others were flayed alive or buried head down in ant hills. In order to demoralize both the resistance and the populace, in 1946 the bodies of dead partisans were desecrated in public places in the towns.

In nothing perhaps so starkly as in their treatment of the bodies of the fallen partisans does the ineffably vile nature of the

Russian NKVD and Communists reveal itself. A few examples taken at random from the ghastly record should suffice.

In one case, after the destruction of an armed resistance staff bunker in which the combatants had blown themselves up with grenades, the Communists tried to wash the bodies and to stitch on the detached parts, especially of the faces, and to stuff them into discovered uniforms. Then the corpses were photographed several times, conveyed to Veiveriai and dumped down near the former vicar's hen coop. Here the local Communists assembled with whoops of joy. They also rounded up suspected inhabitants, drove them to where the corpses were lying, and with blows and curses demanded that they should reveal the surnames and living relatives of the dead partisans. Yet it was out of the question for even those desirous of doing so to identify them, because two of the corpses had had their skulls split open.

In the second case, the Russians conveyed the bodies of the partisans to the town of Kazlų Rūda. Here they were subjected to those hideous forms of desecration of which the Russian Communists were past masters. The bodies were, so to speak, "bridled" with the rosaries found on them, into the mouths of others were stuffed prayerbooks, and the revered Lithuanian emblem of the "Gediminas Pillars" was cut into their flesh.

Generally speaking, it was the custom of the *enkavedists* (security troops) to collect the bodies or parts of bodies of Lithuanian partisans on the battlefield, load them haphazardly into carts and transport them to the nearest town to be thrown out in the town square. There the Communists of the commune would gather, kick and beat the corpses, spit on them, drag them through the streets with horses and do everything that a degraded wretch of fanatical Communism could do to vent his fury on the victims. Then the desecrated bodies would be cast at night into ditches, trenches, swamps, lakes, rivers or onto dunghills. At best, the bodies might be covered with a few spadefuls of earth in the outskirts of a town or village, and the first rains would at once wash them away. In winter, abandoned corpses were not buried at all, and were thus speedily dismembered by dogs, wild animals and birds. And where the bodies of slain freedom fighters had been buried, skulls and the bones of arms and legs protruded from the earth—if wild animals had not already carried them away.

A favorite Soviet strategem devised to facilitate the discovery of the relations or friends of Lithuanian guerrillas whose mutilated bodies were exposed in some town square, was for a few leading Red activists or perhaps members of the militia to take up a point of vantage at the window of a nearby house and from there, through field-glasses, scan the facial expression of wayfarers passing by these sad relics of humanity. Should anybody betray signs of distress by shedding tears or in any other way, his or her arrest would almost certainly follow and not infrequently lead to an orgy of torture and maltreatment during an "inquisition" for the purpose of extorting the required information.

On July 10, 1947, 15,000 NKVD troops surrounded the staff of Dainava District in a forest near Punia. Eight partisans held out in the staff bunker for several hours until they were killed. Among the dead were Azuolas, the District leader; Senis, the intelligence chief; Linas, the District adjutant. Two of the men in the bunker were only stunned by grenades and captured alive. The NKVD signed an appeal in their name addressed to the other freedom fighters to put down their arms.

When Archbishop M. Reinys announced from the pulpit that his name was being falsely used by the NKVD in appeals to the partisans to cease fighting, he was deported to Siberia. Bishop V. Borisevičius suffered a similar fate.

The partisan leadership tried to alleviate the terror from the start. During the August 25, 1945, meeting of the Sudavian leaders, it was decided to permit partisans to make use of Bartašiūnas amnesty. Men willing to seek amnesty were stricken from the roster and permitted to go. Then the ranks of the partisans were tightened up, because the remaining men were the hard core. The Soviets saw that these tactics were not breaking up the resistance, and therefore continued applying harsh methods.

In the main, brutality and terror were most widely employed by the Soviets against the partisans and their supporters. Mass deportations of supporters and possible supporters of the partisans were undertaken. It is known that during the period of 1944-50, eight mass deportations were carried out. According to the under-ground reports and the testimony of eyewitnesses, the dates of deportations and the number of victims are as follows:

August-September, 1945 60,000
February, 1946 40,000
Second Half of 1947 70,000
May 22, 1948 70,000
March 24-27, June, 1949 50,000
March, 1950 30,000

To these 320,000 deportees must be added 20,000 farmers executed by the NKVD between 1944 and 1946 for supporting the partisans. Soviet terror did not end with deportations; entire villages that supported the underground were burned, armed men were liquidated on the spot. Provocateur partisan bands were trained and sent out to discredit the resistance movement. These bands and individuals of provocateurs tried to discover the sup-porters of the partisans among the populace. But the most treach-erous aspect of the provocateur band activities was that they attempted to confuse the populace by plundering, stealing, and by the murder of peaceful inhabitants. While the well-organized partisans could unmask the provocateurs and spies, the populace in many instances was confused and fearful.

An armed force of such magnitude as was the Lithuanian resistance could only exist if the people provided the basic support in food, clothing and shelter. As long as private farming and iso-lated homesteads existed, the armed forces had plenty of food, clothing and hiding places. Contrary to Soviet contentions, al-most a universal national support, transcending class and social positions, was necessary to maintain the armed struggle. The Soviet regime was well aware of this and acted accordingly. By pauperizing the Lithuanian farmer through result of state requi-sitions and the disorganizing effect on the land reform and subse-quently instituting collectivization, the Soviet regime was able to deprive the armed partisans of their main source for subsistence.

The new offensive, prepared by Mikhail Suslov, started in February, 1946. This was a year of great importance to Communist leaders. The fourth Five Year Plan (*Petiletka*) was announced and the Lithuanian economy was to be integrated into this all-union program. Though collectivization of farms was not publicized as one of the goals of this plan, it was obvious that to participate in it effectively, the republic would need domestic peace and a measure of socialization to provide the necessary funds for the scheduled industrial investment. Suslov's was a furious frontal attack, combining the peace offensive with military action of increased cruelty and thoroughness.

By 1949, the collectivization of Lithuania destroyed the economic props of the partisan movement. The tremendous bloodletting and disillusionment with the West further sapped the movement. During 1950-51, the entire fight against the partisans was entrusted to two NKVD units—the 2nd and 4th Special Tasks Divisions. The headquarters of the 2nd Special Tasks Division was located at Vilnius and the commander was General Vetrov; the 4th Division was located in Šiauliai and the commander was General Piashov. These forces were engaged in what can sadly be called mopping-up operations.

7. The Phasing-Out of the Resistance, 1949-52

The newly-formed Movement of Lithuania's Struggle for Freedom (Lietuvos Laisvės Kovų Sąjūdis) united the entire underground in 1950. The information given to the West by "Daunoris" gave a different picture, namely, that the resistance had split into the BDPS and the LLKS. Regardless of what actually happened, it is significant to note that resistance continued on two planes—there was an active resistance which continued to wage guerrilla warfare, and a passive resistance which hid under the cloak of legality and waged a propaganda struggle. The partisans who had adopted the name freedom fighters (laisvės kovotojai) functioned in nine districts (apygardos). By 1951, there were still three regions with two districts each.

In October, 1949, the Algimantas District of eastern Lithuania lost its staff and most of its effective forces. It never revived after this calamity.

During 1952, in the northeast, in the Kalnai Region, two

388

districts (Vytis and Vytautas) persevered. Vytis District still had three formations—Briedis, Krištaponis and Algimantas. Vytautas District also had three formations—Liūtas, Tigras and Lokys. The freedom fighters in both districts still numbered 200. The regional leader was a former teacher, Siaubas. Although the regional staff no longer had any officers, Siaubas' authority and ingenuity kept the movement viable. MVD infiltrators and agents were quietly and quickly liquidated.

In the Jūra Region (Samogitia) there were still three districts—Jungtinė Kęstutis, Žemaičiai, and Prisikėlimas. "Germantas" was the regional leader. The Supreme Partisan Command was also located in this Region. The Žemaičiai District pursued a careful policy, while the other two used aggressive tactics which led to harsh Soviet reprisals in their area.

The saddest fate of all was suffered by the Nemunas Region, comprised of the Tauras and Dainava Districts. The region was rather active in 1950-51, suffering great losses. Moscow sent its new minister of security, General S. N. Kruglov, to handle operations. He was particularly interested in eliminating the legendary Skirmantas-Miškinis who had been parachuted from the West (see below). In 1951, the entire Dainava staff with its leader Diemedis perished. Afterward, the Dainava freedom fighters tried to change their tactics and reorganize. Tauras District was practically annihilated, and the survivors continued in small isolated squads.

The creation of the LLKS led to a change in tactics from open resistance to sabotage and tactics more suitable to small conspiratorial groups. Resistance took the form of infiltration and obstruction of the *kolkhozes, sovkhozes* and Communist administration from within. Frequently, the very offices of farm and factory chairmen and militia precinct headquarters were used by the partisans. This organized resistance continued until 1952.

The LLKS presidium had its headquarters in Samogitia. Its leader was "Vytautas" (Captain Jonas Žemaitis), who had collaborated with Germantas. The LLKS leadership in 1951 still published two underground newspapers—*Laisvės Varpas* (Freedom Bell) and *Prisikėlimo Ugnis* (Fire of Resurrection). *Laisvės Varpas,* the organ of the Kęstutis District, first came out in 1945, and was published for seven or eight years, and was perhaps the longest-lived clandestine paper in resistance history. Vytautas' adjutant was Vanagas, who also headed the underground army and operated in Dainava. Vanagas, whose real name was Adolfas Ramanauskas, was an American-born school teacher who had fought with Vytautas in the Lithuanian resistance since 1941. When Vytautas was paralyzed in 1951 in Raseiniai, he turned the supreme leadership over to Vanagas.

Attempts were made to bolster the partisan movement by dropping specialists into Lithuania who had been trained by American intelligence. Their task was twofold—to reorient the resistance leadership, and to try to change its mode of operations.

Jonas Deksnys returned with Rimvydas (a former resistance courier) to Lithuania for a third time in 1949. The two men quarrelled and separated; Rimvydas was killed in Poland shortly thereafter; Deksnys was captured by the KGB and defected to them. He helped the KGB infiltrate the underground in the West. Thanks to him, the Soviets knew about two subsequent drops.

Daumantas-Juozas Lukša completed a two-year intelligence course in America, and on October 2, 1950, he was parachuted back into Prienai Forest with Širvys-Sakalas and Benediktas Trumpys-Vytis. A second group followed on April 19, 1951, consisting of Julijonas Butėnas and Jonas Kukauskas. Trumpys died in combat, and Širvys was captured. Lukša assumed the name "Miškinis" and continued his activities. The second group searched for Lukša for several weeks after landing. They were surrounded in a bunker; Butėnas committed suicide and Kukauskas was captured. He betrayed Lukša. As a result Juozas Lukša, alias Daumantas-Skrajūnas-Miškinis-Skirmantas, died in October, 1951. He was the most respected, feared freedom fighter leader. General Kruglov personally sought out this "Miškinis." There are two versions concerning Lukša's death: first, that he was surrounded in Prienai Forest by numerous NKVD forces and, seeing that all was lost, committed suicide. The second version speaks of a rendezvous which was a trap—Lukša was trapped in a restaurant and forced to commit suicide. Lukša's death was a great blow to the partisans, but it did not destroy the movement.

In 1951, the partisans succeeded in eliminating a number of

traitors and security agents. Only in 1952, when collectivization was completed, did organized resistance collapse, though individual squads continued to operate for a while. In the spring of 1953, "V" took over the remnants of the Iron Wolf. "V" and four others blew themselves up in a bunker near Vilkaviškis when they were surrounded by KGB men. In the fall of 1952, in Šaukotas Forest, the Iron Wolf unit, led by "K," was surrounded by the militia of Radviliškis, Dotnuva, Tytuvėnai and Raseiniai and was wiped out.

Even then, the partisans did not completely disappear, as was confirmed by the fact that on October 19, 1955, the Soviets issued an amnesty declaration over Radio Vilnius to "the men in the forest." Party Secretary Antanas Sniečkus admitted to the press that there were still "bourgeois nationalist bandits lurking in the forests." On March 22, 1956, the KGB appealed to the persons "still hiding" to avail themselves of the amnesty offer. The last resistance leader, Vanagas, evaded capture until 1956; he was seized and hanged in Kaunas. In 1957, people were arrested for engaging in partisan activities. Even as late as 1959, in Samogitia, three partisans were surrounded and shot. Armed resistance, however, had collapsed; resistance now took different forms.

The years of war against Soviet forces had thinned the ranks of the freedom fighters. One detachment of partisans, for instance, had lost seventy-two men and suffered fifty-nine wounded in the course of one year. The average yearly losses in dead and wounded can be set at almost 5,500. The entire war, 1944-54, probably cost the partisans something more than 40,000 men. Most painful was the fact that the death toll took 90 percent of the cadres. The training of new cadres became impossible without outside help. According to available data, in 1944-45 the number of active armed partisans stood between 30,000 and 50,000. By 1949-50, this number had dwindled to 5,000, and by 1951-52 to 700. Furthermore, plentiful supplies of light arms and ammunition which had fallen into the hands of the partisans after World War II became exhausted. The annual losses of one partisan detachment, for instance, averaged out to fourteen machine guns and seventy-six other firearms. On this basis, the yearly losses of the guerrillas must have reached over 500 machine guns and over 3,000 other firearms, while the entire war must have consumed a total of 4,000 machine guns and 25,000 other weapons. The only remaining sources of replenishment of arms supplies were NKVD or Soviet Army munitions depots. The raids, however, on these depots were becoming more and more costly.

It was a brutal war with no quarter shown on either side. No pity was shown to Russian and Lithuanian Communist activists who were carrying out the Soviet policy of oppression and genocide. From 1945 to 1952, the partisans put to death about 4,000 Communist activists, and in battle, the guerrillas killed 100,000 MVD, NKVD and Soviet Army troops. In spite of these staggering losses, the Soviets were able to draw upon limitless manpower resources. They could afford heavy losses as long as they were able to bleed the Lithuanians white.

There are two cardinal reasons for the failure of the anti-Soviet resistance. First, the leaders miscalculated partisan resources and the chances of political victory. They misinterpreted international developments and the intentions of the Western powers, and thus wrongly counted on the support of the United States and Great Britain. The first anti-Soviet and the anti-Nazi resistances also made these same naive mistakes of misunderstanding world politics and of counting on Western help. Also, without support from abroad, a long guerrilla war against the total-war strategy of the Soviets became militarily impossible, especially under conditions of complete sovietization. The partisans lost after ten years of war. It is amazing that they were able to hold out so long, a tribute to their strong will, dedication and idealism.

Liberation Attempts from Abroad

by ALGIRDAS BUDRECKIS

I. An Idealistic Crusade, 1940-45

1.

Almost one million Lithuanian immigrants and their descendants lived in the United States before World War II. Numerous
communities of Lithuanians, numbering an additional 100,000,
were living in Great Britain, Canada, and the countries of South
America. Most of them had their own cultural and religious
organizations, as well as thirty-five newspapers. The Lithuanians
abroad reacted most strongly against the Soviet invasion of their
homeland. Special committees for Lithuanian liberation were organized in Argentina, Brazil, Uruguay, Canada and the United
States. It is the activities of the major liberation movements with
which we will be concerned in this study.

While the Lithuanians did not despair and were determined
to continue their opposition to the Kremlin's domination by all
available means, they also realized that, by themselves, they were
too weak to throw off the rule of the Soviet Union. Their eyes,
therefore, turned toward the international sector. They refused
to believe that the free world would remain passive spectators to
the unprecedented Lithuanian tragedy, especially since the occupation of their country was not of their own choosing.

The Lithuanian people were encouraged by the indignation

and protest expressed in behalf of the United States government by the then Under-Secretary of State, Sumner Welles, in June, 1940, and by the assurances given to the American Lithuanian Council several months later by United States President Franklin Delano Roosevelt. They had an almost naive belief that Nazi Germany would first crush the Soviet Union and then, in turn, be defeated by the Anglo-American alliance, which would restore Europe on an *ante bellum* status. The Lithuanians in the Nazi-occupied homeland and abroad believed in the sanctity of the wartime legal commitments and political pledges of the great Western powers, as set forth in the Atlantic Charter. The Atlantic Charter, proclaimed by President Roosevelt and the prime minister of Great Britain, Winston Churchill, brought new hope to the Lithuanians. It stipulated that no territorial changes should take place unless freely accepted by the clearly expressed will of the interested populations (Article 2 of the Charter). Referring to the old democratic principle of the right of all people to self-determination, the leaders of the Anglo-Saxon democracies pledged themselves, in Article 3 of the Charter, to respect the right of all people to choose the form of government under which they will live; and declared it to be their wish to see sovereignty and self-government restored to those who had been forcibly deprived of them. These principles apply in every respect to Lithuania.

The free Lithuanians believed in the sanctity of the United Nations Declaration and the Yalta Declaration on liberated Europe, which promised the restoration of independence to nations which had fallen victims to aggressive powers. They believed with a crusading ardor that the universal application and implementation of the right of all people to self-determination does not stop at the Iron Curtain.

Their optimistic enthusiasm suffered a setback on February 11, 1945, when a communiqué was issued making known the results of the conference held at Yalta in which the participants were President Franklin D. Roosevelt, Prime Minister Winston Churchill and Joseph Stalin. The Yalta Agreement, confirming the division of Europe into military zones previously adopted at the Conference at Teheran, ultimately decided the fate of Central and Eastern Europe, as Soviet military occupation was bound to turn into Communist political domination. By the same token, the fate of all nations of Central and Eastern Europe was sealed.

2.

At the beginning of Soviet-Lithuanian friction in 1940, the Lithuanian Foreign Ministry felt that arrangements should be made to continue government functions in case the Soviet Union occupied Lithuania. The post of diplomatic chief was conceived in conjunction with Telegram 288 sent by the Lithuanian Foreign Minister Juozas Urbšys on June 2, 1940, to Stasys Lozoraitis, envoy to Rome: "If we are met with a catastrophe, Stasys Lozoraitis is to be held chief of the remaining diplomatic corps abroad." Two alternates were also designated—Jurgis Šaulys in Switzerland and Petras Klimas in France.

Although the Lithuanian state continues to exist, there is no organ which could exercise further the rights deriving from its continued legal existence. Nevertheless, certain ministers plenipotentiary and other diplomatic representatives of Lithuania were still recognized and continued to fulfill certain functions deriving from state sovereignty. But they were executive bodies, and not sovereign political representatives. As such, they were subordinated to central government. No organ existed any longer, however, capable of concentrating in itself the execution of sovereign rights in their completeness.

The Lithuanian diplomats abroad considered the Merkys cabinet left behind by President Smetona to operate in the face of the Soviet invasion, as provisional in nature, in no way hindering President Smetona's freedom to appoint a new ministry. Smetona, while still isolated in East Prussia following his flight, informed Minister to Berlin Kazys Škirpa that he planned to form a new ministry, with Lozoraitis, the minister to Rome, at its head (the so-called Kybartai Protocol which dismissed Merkys from the Premiership).

Since the last legal government of Lithuania had not made any formal protest against the Soviet aggression, its inaction automatically hindered such protests by the Lithuanian diplomats abroad. The occasion came one month after the Soviet occupation.

When the Soviets convened the puppet "Peoples' Diet" in Kaunas on July 21, which announced that it had petitioned for admission of Lithuania into the USSR, the Lithuanian diplomats protested.

On the basis of a communication between the Lithuanian diplomats, it was felt that corresponding notes should be presented on July 22 in all of the capitals in which Lithuania was represented. Lithuanian diplomats in Washington, London, the Vatican, and Rome protested the republic's incorporation into the USSR. Similar notes were sent to the governments of Argentina, Brazil, Denmark, France, Germany, Hungary, Portugal, Rumania, Sweden, Switzerland, Uruguay and Yugoslavia. Simultaneously, the diplomats presented their protests against the falsification of the will of the Lithuanian nation directly to the puppet government of Soviet-occupied Lithuania. These protests, on the one hand, formally exposed to the world that the Soviets were attempting to mask their aggression against Lithuania; on the other hand, the diplomatic protests authoritatively encouraged the Lithuanian nation to have hope and to wage resistance against the USSR. The diplomats were deprived of Lithuanian citizenship by the puppet regime on August 14, 1940. This was the only way the Soviets could mete out punishment for the diplomats' bold stand.

3.

A plan to organize the Lithuanians under a united front for the struggle was formulated as early as July, 1940, while Minister Kazys Škirpa was still at the Lithuanian Legation in Berlin. President Smetona, whom Škirpa informed about his projects, approved of the plans in principle, informing Škirpa that he would give him a mandate to form a new ministry if the Lithuanians succeeded in restoring sovereignty in "at least one township."

From September 19-25, 1940, Lithuanian diplomats Stasys Girdvainis, Stasys Lozoraitis, Petras Klimas, Eduardas Turauskas and Kazys Škirpa held a conference in Rome. Petras Klimas suggested the formation of a national committee, modeled after Masaryk's Czech National Committee, which at the appropriate moment could become the provisional government. Such a committee was set up in Berlin, based on the legal authorization by the republic to its legations to protect Lithuanian interests abroad. Ernestas Galvanauskas, who had recently fled to Germany, was appointed chairman. His *ipso jure* alternate was Stasys Lozoraitis. Eduardas Turauskas and Kazys Škirpa were to be permanent members. Later, Minister to Washington Povilas Žadeikis was designated as a second alternate. The Lithuanian envoys, by con-certed action, approved of the formation of the Lithuanian Na-tional Committee as the unifying agency for the restoration of independent Lithuania.

On August 11, the Soviets pressured the Germans to force Škirpa and his staff to vacate the Lithuanian Legation and turn over the property to the Russians. President Smetona also had problems. He wanted to remain in Europe, close to Lithuania; however, since his presence in Germany threatened to complicate Nazi-Soviet relations, the unsympathetic German government coaxed him into leaving the country. Smetona received his dip-lomatic visa on September 19 and immediately left for Bern, Switzerland.

The Lithuanian diplomatic corps made contact with Spanish Foreign Minister Colonel Juan Beigbeder y Atienza, a personal acquaintance of Škirpa's, to allow some ten Lithuanian political leaders, including Galvanauskas, to reside in Spain until the opportune moment when this group, without any hindrance, could set up a provisional government. Foreign Minister Beig-beder was willing to give his consent to this plan, but the Nazis would not permit Galvanauskas to leave Germany.

While in Switzerland, Smetona decided that he could serve the cause of Lithuanian freedom better in the United States. On February 14, 1941, the Smetona family sailed to Rio de Janeiro. While in Brazil, the president appointed Frikas Meieris to the post of Lithuanian Minister to that country.

On March 10, 1941, President Smetona landed in New York, and immediately began organizing the nationalistically-minded Lithuanian-Americans. On April 1, he visited Sumner Welles in the State Department. Through the efforts of Minister Žadeikis, he had a private audience with President Roosevelt, whom he thanked for the United States government's firm stand against Lithuania's occupation.

On May 4, the Mayor of Chicago, Edward Kelly, at a special reception in honor of the Lithuanian President, declared: "To President Smetona we offer the solemn pledge of our continuing resistance to the oppression that snatched liberty from Lithuania."

During 1941, the exiled president's supporters flocked to the Lithuanian Liberation Alliance (Lietuvai Vaduoti Sąjunga). He visited the larger cities—New York, Newark, Elizabeth, Phila-delphia, Baltimore, Pittsburgh, Detroit, Cleveland—urging his nationals to organize for liberation.

Smetona found a temporary haven on Mr. Joseph Bachunas' Tabor Farm in Michigan. Finally in May, 1942, he settled down in his son's home in Cleveland, and devoted his energies to writing a study about Lithuania's boundaries, making speeches concerning Lithuania's restoration. As Lithuania's President-in-exile, he con-tinued to exercise a moral force as a symbol of Lithuanian state sovereignty. The case for the continuity of government met with complications when he died in a fire in his son's home on January 9, 1944. His last testament to the nation was the advice given to friends on January 2, 1944, to wit: "One must go down various routes to the one goal—restoration of Lithuanian Independence. One must not be discouraged, if everyone does not fit into one or-ganization." (Reikia eiti visokiais keliais prie vieno tikslo—kad Lietuvai būtų iškovota nepriklausomybė. Nereikia nuleisti rankų, jeigu nesutelpama į vieną organizaciją.)

In addition to the National Committee, the Lithuanian po-litical exiles in Berlin organized a liberation movement, which was headed by Kazys Škirpa. On November 17, twenty-eight exile political leaders met and formally established the Lithuanian Ac-tivist Front (LAF or Lietuvių Aktyvistų Frontas). The LAF had two purposes: to fight for the restoration of independence and to prepare a program for the organization of the restored state. Among the refugees who fled to Germany were many Lithuanian statesmen, famous civic and cultural leaders, former officers and civil servants. They all supported the plans and activ-ities of the LAF, in spite of prior political differences. In order to prepare for the revolt, the LAF established contact with the underground in Lithuania, providing it with necessary informa-tion for the preparation of the armed revolt.

The Lithuanian resistance movement with its centers in Kau-nas and Vilnius, acknowledged the Berlin LAF as its center. The entire resistance movement merged into the LAF. The Berlin staff maintained precarious relations with the German foreign ministry and the army high command. Škirpa formulated instruc-tions and plans for the eventual revolt; he even drew up a list of ministers for the provisional government, which was accepted with slight alterations by the Lithuanian underground. He soon realized that the Germans intended to use the Lithuanian resist-ance to help establish German rule in the Soviet-occupied Baltic States. He therefore proceeded to instruct the underground to quickly set up a functioning Lithuanian administration at the outbreak of the Russo-German conflict, in order to confront the Nazis with an independent state.

When, on June 22, 1941, Nazi Germany invaded the USSR, a spontaneous revolt against the Soviets erupted, and a Lithu-anian provisional government was proclaimed in Kaunas, naming Škirpa its head. The Berlin LAF publicized these events to the world through American, Swiss and Swedish correspondents in Berlin and through operatives in Sweden and Switzerland. The Nazis retaliated by placing Škirpa under house arrest. Other pro-visional ministers in Berlin were detained from returning to Kaunas. Only General Raštikis, provisional defense minister, was permitted to fly to Kaunas. He informed the provisional cabinet, presided over by Education Minister J. Ambrazevičius, of German designs to set up a protectorate. On August 5, after six weeks of administration, the provisional government was suppressed by the Nazis. Members of the Berlin LAF were deported to German provincial towns or to concentraton camps by the Gestapo. Sev-eral LAF operatives abroad, such as Albertas Gerutis in Bern, Switzerland, continued to inform the Lithuanian diplomats of developments in Lithuania.

Immediately after the Soviet invasion of Lithuania, the diplo-matic and consular representatives protected the properties of the Lithuanian Government as well as the properties of their na-tionals "by all legal means." First, there were the deposits of the state and private banks as well as those of corporations and Lithuanian nationals in the United States banks. There were also several ships under the Lithuanian flag in foreign ports and on the high seas. The Lithuanian representative, Mr. Povilas Žadeikis, requested the United States Government to safeguard and secure these deposits and property.

In a memorandum on July 15, 1940, Loy W. Henderson, Assistant Chief of the Division of European Affairs of the U.S. State Department, after describing and evaluating the Soviet activities in the Baltic States, stressed that "the recent events in the Baltic States have raised a number of rather important questions," the first of which was the basic policy and the political philosophy of the United States toward these countries. The problem concerning this basic question was worded in a memorandum as follows:

> Is the Government of the United States to apply certain standards of judgment and conduct to aggression by Germany and Japan which it will not apply to aggression by the Soviet Union? In other words, is the Government of the United States to follow one policy with respect to, say, Czechoslovakia, Denmark and German-occupied Poland, and another policy with respect to Latvia, Estonia, Lithuania and Finland? Is the United States to continue to refuse to recognize the fruits of aggression regardless of who the aggressor may be, or for reasons of expediency to close its eyes to the fact that certain nations are committing aggression upon their neighbors?
>
> The United States will probably not receive one cent of the several million dollars which the governments of these three countries owe us. Furthermore, American interests in those three countries will probably be a total loss.

The Treasury Department acted on the same day and decided to block all the accounts of the three Baltic countries in the United States. Title to the assets remained in the names of the non-Soviet governments of Estonia, Latvia, and Lithuania. The protests which followed from Soviet Russia and its three new "republics" did not change the U.S. position in this matter.

Although the assets were "frozen," disbursements from them were subsequently accorded to the Baltic diplomatic and consular missions in order to support their continued operations, not only in the United States but also in the other countries which had not recognized the Soviet occupation of the Baltic States.

Following the declaration of the puppet Diet in Lithuania for union with the Soviet Union, the U.S. Undersecretary of State, Sumner Welles, issued (July 23, 1940) a statement condemning the deliberate suppression by "devious process" of the independence of the Baltic States. He went on to say to the press:

> During these past few days the devious processes whereunder the political independence and territorial integrity of the three small Baltic Republics—Estonia, Latvia, and Lithuania—were to be deliberately annihilated by one of their more powerful neighbors, have been rapidly drawing to their conclusion. From the day when the people of these republics first gained their independence and democratic form of government, the people of the United States have watched their admirable progress in self-government with deep and sympathetic interest.
>
> The policy of this government is universally known. The people of the United States are opposed to predatory activity no matter whether they are carried on by the use of force or by the threat of force. They are likewise opposed to any form of intervention on the part of one state, however powerful, in the domestic concerns of another state, however weak.
>
> These principles constitute the very foundations upon which the existing relationship between the 21 sovereign republics of the New World rests.
>
> The United States will continue to stand by these principles, because of the conviction of the American people that unless the doctrines in which these principles are inherent once again governs the relations between nations, the rule of reason, of justice, and of law—in other words, the basis of modern civilization itself—cannot be preserved.

This declaration constituted the basis of the policy of nonrecognition of the annexation of the Baltic States. The example set by the United States in this nonrecognition has been followed by the majority of those nations which have expressed an attitude in regard to this problem. The United States government reem-phasized on subsequent occasions its nonrecognition of the incor-poration of the Baltic States into the Soviet Union. In view of this American position, Lithuanian diplomatic and consular rep-resentatives have continued to function in the United States, enjoying all rights usually accorded to such representatives.

The attitude of Great Britain toward Lithuania's status was less clear than that of the United States. During World War II, Great Britain extended *de facto* recognition of Lithuania's incor-poration into the USSR. However, the British government re-fused to accord *de jure* recognition to the annexation. The problem of the Baltic States was raised during the Soviet-British negotiations for a friendship and alliance treaty (December, 1941, to May, 1942). The Soviet government exerted pressure upon Great Britain to include in the treaty a clause which would have recognized the Soviet frontiers of 1941, i.e., including the Baltic States. Mainly due to the unswerving attitude of the United States government against any territorial changes during the war period, the British government refused to accede to the Soviet wishes, and the treaty was finally signed without any territorial clauses. Lithuania was listed in the British official *Foreign Office List and Diplomatic and Consular Year Book 1942* alongside its colleagues. The Lithuanian diplomats' names appeared under the name of their respective country. This has also been true in all subsequent editions.

In 1942, the names of the ministers of the Baltic States and their staff members were placed by the *Diplomats' Annual* in a separate category at the end of the official diplomatic list, without any indication of the country they were representing, under the caption: List of Persons No Longer Included in the Diplomatic List But Still Accepted by His Majesty's Government as Per-sonally Enjoying Certain Diplomatic Courtesies. In a letter on this occasion from the Foreign Office to the Latvian Minister, it was stated that it was "felt desirable and in fact necessary to take into account the anomalous situation in which you and your Estonian and Lithuanian colleagues find yourselves as a result of having no government to represent." In the House of Commons on December 21, 1944, Sir Henry Williams asked the Foreign Secretary "Whether His Majesty's Government still recognises the Governments or republics of Latvia, Estonia, and Lithuania?" Answering for Secretary Eden, Mr. George Hall said: "His Majesty's Government has not recognised any Government in the Republics of Latvia, Estonia, and Lithuania since the changes occurred in June, 1940."

The position of the French government was subject to more fluctuation. At least *de facto* recognition to the annexation was accorded by the French in 1940, but the Lithuanian Legation was closed on August 15, 1940, and Minister Petras Klimas was subsequently arrested by the Germans. The request by the diplomatic representatives of the Baltic States for permission to continue their activities was denied after the departure of the Germans in September, 1944. Yet, there has still been no official announcement concerning the recognition of the annexation.

The attitude of Mussolini's Italy was not clear. In 1940, the Mussolini regime closed the Lithuanian Legation, but no formal declaration to this effect was issued. This act alone would infer a *de facto* recognition of the annexation.

Spain and Portugal, as members of the Savedra-Lamas Pact, assumed a mutual obligation not to recognize any territorial arrangement "which is not obtained by pacific means, nor the validity of an occupation or acquisition of territory that may be brought by force." Consequently, they have not recognized the annexation of the Baltic States. Although there were no official pronouncements by Latin-American states on the subject of their treatment of the diplomatic and consular representatives of the Baltic States and the nationals of these states, it is safe to assume that they have not recognized the annexation either *de jure* or *de facto*. In Argentina, Uruguay, Brazil and Colombia, Lithuanian diplomatic and consular officers continued to function and carry on their duties.

Sweden came closest to a *de jure* recognition of the Soviet annexation, although it has never officially affirmed it. According to the official Swedish point of view, Lithuania disappeared as an independent state and, accordingly, its incorporation into the

Soviet Union merited *de facto* recognition. Foreign Minister Gunther emphasized, in a statement in the upper house of the Riksdag, that practical considerations have led Sweden to such recognition. No Lithuanian nationality is recognized by the Swedish government, and former nationals are officially considered either Soviet citizens or stateless persons. They are considered stateless if they left their homeland before the enactment of the Soviet Nationality Edict of September 7, 1940, which declares the citizens of the Baltic States to be Soviet citizens.

All in all, the Lithuanian Foreign Service, in spite of the occupation, remained active. Under the leadership of Minister Plenipotentiary Stasys Lozoraitis, officially designated Chief of the Lithuanian Diplomatic Service Abroad, the following ministers continued their functions during the war years: Povilas Žadeikis—Washington; Bronius Balutis—London; Stasys Girdvainis—the Holy See; Kazys Graužinis—Buenos Aires and Montevideo; Frikas Meieris—Rio de Janeiro. For a while in 1940, the following ministers continued in quasi-official capacities: Kazys Škirpa—Berlin; Petras Klimas—Paris; Jurgis Šaulys—Berne; Vytautas Gylys—Stockholm. Lithuanian consuls also continued at the following posts: Consul General Jonas Budrys—New York; Vytautas Stašinskas, consul—New York; Anicetas Simutis, vice-consul—New York; Julius Bielskis, honorary consul—Los Angeles; Anthony O. Shallna, honorary consul—Boston; Aleksandras Polišaitis, consul—Sao Paulo; Friedrich Simon, consul general—Zurich; Dr. N. Rachmilevičius, consul—Tel Aviv; Colonel Grant-Suttie, consul general—Toronto.

4. *The Lithuanian American Council—ALT*

When the Soviets occupied Lithuania on June 15, 1940, the Lithuanian-American community in the United States began organizing to protect Lithuania's interests. The prevailing mood was to form one organizational center to coordinate the work. The Lithuanian American Roman Catholic Federation, convening in Pittsburgh on August 10, 1940, voted in favor of an intergroup center. In September, the Socialists reorganized into a Democratic Lithuanian Independence Alliance (Demokratijos ir

Lietuvos Nepriklausomybės Sąjunga) whose purpose was to fight for a democratic Lithuania.

After Sumner Welles' pronouncement, the idea was conceived to visit Washington and thank President Roosevelt for his condolences to enslaved Lithuania. Spokesmen of the three main ideological groups Socialists, Catholics, and Liberal nationalists formed the delegation. The delegation had an audience with President Roosevelt on October 15, 1940, at which time Dr. Pijus Grigaitis bemoaned the fact that Lithuania had lost her independence and urged that the President help the nation. President Roosevelt outdid the Lithuanians in his reply:

> I understand perfectly your feelings concerning the fate of Lithuania. Let me tell you that you have made here two mistakes: the first mistake is in your address that you gave me. It is stated here that Lithuania has lost her independence. It is a mistake to say so. Lithuania did not lose her independence—Lithuania's independence was only temporarily put aside. Time will come and Lithuania will be free again. This will happen sooner than you may expect. The other mistake as I observed was made by one of your speakers when he referred to Lithuania as a very small state. Look at the Latin American Republics and you will see that there are even smaller states than Lithuania, but they live a free and happy life. It is not fitting to even talk about the smallness of Lithuania for even the smallest nation has the same right to enjoy independence as the largest nation.

He went on to say that the United States would do everything in its power to hasten that day, and that after the war Lithuania and the other enslaved nations would be free. (When he subsequently received President Smetona, on April 18, 1941, President Roosevelt assured him of American support for Lithuanian independence.)

After the audience with President Roosevelt, inspired by his assurances, the delegation met at the Lithuanian legation and decided that the remarks had opened the way for further Lithuanian-American action. That same day, they formed the intergroup Committee to Aid Lithuania (Lietuvai Gelbėti Taryba).

This was just the beginning. There were no by-laws, guide-lines, treasury or chapters as yet. The Lithuanian-American political leadership did not have a popular attractive name for their nucleus. The problem faced them as to how and on what basis to coordinate the thirty-four patriotic Lithuanian newspapers and 2,000 societies.

On May 15, 1941, when the delegation met in Chicago for deliberations, the name Lithuanian American Council (Amerikos Lietuvių Taryba) was accepted.

On June 7-8, 1941, the Lithuanian Nationalist leaders held a convention in Sodus, Michigan, and decided to form the Lithuanian Liberation Alliance (Lietuvai Vaduoti Sąjunga). The first chairman was the brilliant young Lithuanian-American lawyer Anthony Olis of Chicago. In 1942, the center was reor-ganized and moved to Cleveland, to the *Dirva* newspaper office. For three years the LVS chairman was Dr. Stasys T. Tamošaitis; he was followed for three years by Pijus J. Žiurys; the last chair-man was Dr. Motiejus J. Colney. The long standing secretary was the editor of *Dirva,* Kazys S. Karpius. The LVS or Alliance formed chapters in the Lithuanian communities, organized Presi-dent Smetona's lectures among Lithuanians and Americans, and published literature on Lithuania. In 1943, money was raised for the publication of the book *Timeless Lithuania* by the former American Minister to Kaunas, Owen Norem, which was distrib-uted to American government officials, diplomats and civic leaders.

In order to inform the American public about Communist methods of terror, the LVS translated and published Colonel Petruitis' book *Kaip jie mus šaudė.* The LVS later published an anthology by Lithuanian journalists entitled *Lithuania in the Chains of Tyrants.* During the February 5-6, 1944, Congress in New York, a special commission was formed to present the Lith-uanian problem to the American public. This commission was designated the Lithuanian American Mission (Amerikos Lietuvių Misija); the executive board consisted of Anthony Olis (chair-man), Antanas G. Kumskis and Pijus J. Žiurys.

The Lithuanian American Mission was the political action organization of the Nationalists. Its purpose was to work for

Lithuanian freedom and independence. In order to realize this aim, it established close ties with members of the United States Congress and periodically visited the State Department. On March 21, 1945, then Vice President Harry S. Truman received the Mission's executive board. On March 23, the Mission organized a reception in Washington for members of the United States Congress and American statesmen, and the speeches made at that reception and later in Congress were recorded in the *Congressional Record*. (This tactic, developed by Anthony Olis, was later adopted by the Lithuanian American Council). The Mission had numerous articles about Lithuania published in the American press. When, in May, 1945, the United Nations Organization met in San Francisco, the Mission organized a press conference, and informed the American and other Western delegations about developments in Lithuania. It also organized a solemn mass for Lithuania in the local cathedral.

When the Nationalists rejoined ALT in November, 1948, A. Olis became a member of the Executive Committee of ALT (he was succeeded by Eugenijus A. Bartkus after his death). The Nationalists maintained their LVS ties until 1949.

On January 8, 1943, the Lithuanian American Council held a conference in New York and decided to place the entire organization on a firm footing by preparing by-laws, setting up a treasury, authorizing an executive committee to act in the organization's name, and to incorporate in the state of Illinois as a non-profit organization.

The agreed purpose of the Lithuanian American Council was to unite all of the democratic forces of Lithuanians in the fight for basic human rights, and to support world efforts to establish permanent peace based on justice, democracy and freedom; to work for the realization of the Atlantic Charter and to see to it that its provisions were applied to Lithuania which would restore her independence with historical-ethnographic boundaries; to give moral and material aid to Lithuania's people in their struggle for freedom and to aid refugees from oppression and Lithuania's exiled citizens, to disseminate to the public at large truthful information about Lithuania and to protect the latter from the lies and calumny of her enemies.

407

The executive committee of ALT was comprised of three members, who lived in Chicago, all three of whom were editors and represented three ideological newspapers: Pijus Grigaitis—socialist *Naujienos,* Leonardas Šimutis—Catholic *Draugas,* and Mykolas Vaidyla—liberal nationalist *Sandara.*

The January 8, 1943, ALT conference issued an appeal to the Lithuanian Americans to organize commemorations of Lithuanian Independence Day on February 16 in the various communities, and to collect money for the liberation of Lithuania. Since 1943, all of the Lithuanian communities have observed February 16, during which commemorations money is still raised to support the activities of ALT. These commemorations have featured prominent Americans as key-note speakers.

On September 2-3, 1943, ALT called a national convention in Pittsburgh attended by 400 delegates from various organizations, all of whom put aside their ideological differences and agreed to better intergroup relations for the common cause. They established a solid front against Lithuanian Communists, who supported the Soviet occupation. The Pittsburgh convention also authorized ALT to set up an information bureau and to establish a fund to help refugees. As a result, the following year the Lithuanian American Relief Fund (Bendrasis Amerikos Lietuvių Šalpos Fondas—BALF) was created, which helped bring to the United States over 30,000 Lithuanian displaced persons.

As its activities increased, the structure of ALT expanded. Two huge fraternal alliances—the Lithuanian Alliance of America and the Lithuanian Roman Catholic Alliance of America—joined the Council. With the return of the Nationalists in 1949, the Lithuanian American Council consisted of thirty-four representatives. The Executive Board was chosen for one year. Local ALT chapters were created in the Lithuanian communities, comprising representatives of the four major ideological groups as well as representatives of local societies.

In April, 1944, ALT founded the Lithuanian American Information Center (LAIC) in New York City, which maintained ties with American Senators, Congressmen and government officials, providing information for newspaper men and various agencies which sought news about Lithuania. It also published the

Lithuanian Bulletin which contained news about current developments in Lithuania, about Lithuanians and their activities. The original publisher was the Lithuanian National Council (Lietuvių Tautinė Taryba) which in 1943 printed ten issues, and many more followed in succeeding years. The LAIC also published twelve books in English on various questions dealing with Lithuania. When the United Nations met in San Francisco, the LAIC sent a delegation which informed the various government members and world press about Lithuania. For a while, the LAIC had a correspondent-observer at the United Nations; it cooperated with R. Lemkin in preparing a detailed report on genocide which he presented to the Senate Foreign Affairs Subcommittee, and also urged the United States Congress to investigate officially the Soviet occupation of Lithuania.

The overall concern of the Lithuanian American Council during the war was to counter Soviet pressure in Washington to recognize the Soviet incorporation of the Baltic States. On March 4, 1945, any doubts on this subject were dissipated by the declaration of the United States Secretary of State in Washington that "as far as the United States is concerned, the status of the Baltic States has not altered in any way, not even after the Yalta Conference."

ALT also saw to it that Lithuanian interests would be protected at the San Francisco meeting and that the United Nations not recognize the incorporation of the Baltic States into the USSR.

5. *The Lithuanian Council of Canada*

The idea to form a uniting body was conceived by a group of Toronto Lithuanians in 1940. The conference took place in September, 1940, and voted to form the Lithuanian Council of Canada to fight for the liberation of the homeland. The Council gained the support of all patriotic groups scattered throughout the Dominion. In order to coordinate activities, an official weekly paper, *Nepriklausoma Lietuva,* (Independent Lithuania) was started.

The Lithuanian Council of Canada was comprised of thirty

representatives of various organizations. It organized Lithuanian Independence Day commemorations every year in the cities and issued protest resolutions denouncing the Soviet occupation of Lithuania to the Ottawa Government. It also took concrete measures to keep Canada from recognizing the Soviet occupation of Lithuania.

6. The Supreme Committee for Liberation of Lithuania

With the death of President Antanas Smetona in 1944, the last executor of the sovereign rights of the nation disappeared. Since there were no constitutional organs to continue the executive functions, the Supreme Committee for Liberation of Lithuania (Vyriausias Lietuvos Išlaisvinimo Komitetas or VLIK), as a revolutionary organ, took over the political leadership of the nation. VLIK, as supreme underground center of the resistance to the Nazi occupation, through its operative in Sweden, Algirdas Vokietaitis, kept the Lithuanian diplomats abroad informed of developments in the homeland. VLIK sent its military representative, Kazys Ambraziejus, to Sweden, but he was arrested by the German Gestapo in Tallinn, Estonia, and returned to Lithuania for interrogation. As a result, the Nazis began to arrest members of VLIK and its operatives on April 29-30, 1944. The Lithuanian political groups appointed new representatives in their stead. This reconstructed VLIK saw the inevitability of a second Soviet invasion and occupation; the threat was spelled out in the May 25, 1944, appeal to the nation. As a positive measure, VLIK appointed a delegation in Germany, while three authorized members of VLIK were to remain in Lithuania; the rest withdrew to carry on the struggle in the West.

The VLIK delegation abroad held its first meeting in Berlin on October 3, 1944, and decided to enlist more members. On October 25, the expanded delegation decided to use the full title Supreme Committee for Liberation of Lithuania, since only one of the VLIK plenipotentiaries remained in Lithuania. On December 14, VLIK spoke out against the conference called by the Nazis to mobilize Lithuanians for the war effort. As the Eastern Front fell back toward Berlin, the group moved to Würzburg, which was soon taken by the American army. Under these new conditions, the group called its first meeting on March 9, 1945, and held its last meeting five days later, when the president of VLIK, Steponas Kairys-Kaminskas, arrived.

After the American occupation of Würzburg, this supreme Lithuanian political organization began its operations in the free world, convinced that the free world would help Lithuania regain its freedom and independence. The Teheran and Yalta conferences, however, had dimmed the hopes of immediate Western aid.

President Kairys called a meeting of the reconstituted VLIK, into which the Lithuanian Peasant Party and Lithuanian Peasant Union were admitted. The basic problems under discussion were: 1) communication with Lithuanian representatives in Washington, London, Paris, Rome, the Vatican, Montevideo and elsewhere, and 2) the quick preparation and presentation of a memorandum to the Allied Supreme Commander General Eisenhower. This memorandum introduced VLIK to General Eisenhower as the only Lithuanian political and resistance center in exile, and presented Lithuania's case. Subsequent memoranda spelled out the deportees and displaced persons problems of security and subsistence, and the question of prisoners of war captured by the Allies.

II.   THE STRUGGLE BASED ON WESTERN HELP, 1945-56

1.

The Lithuanians were especially hopeful in the monocentric era that immediately followed the end of the second World War. Because of its atomic monopoly, the United States was at that time the dominating, if not the only, center of military strength and political and economic power. A peace conference, the Lithuanian exiles and immigration thought, would have to include on its agenda the righting of the wrongs done to the Baltic States by the Stalin-Hitler conspiracy. This hope vanished when it became obvious that, because of Soviet machinations, no peace conference was in sight.

When the Soviet deceit and hypocritical policies became

known, the United States reacted. On March 12, 1947, President Harry S. Truman announced that the purpose of American policy was to help the free nations resisting conspiracies to enslave them by internal revolts, by armed minorities or by external aggression. This was the beginning of the so-called Truman Doctrine. A new period was ushered in when the United States gave aid to Greece, then fighting against Communist insurgents. Help was also given to Turkey. The Truman Doctrine slowly evolved into the so-called policy of "containment" or "stop Russia."

The bipolarization of the world that followed, when the Soviet Union became a nuclear rival of the United States, brought promise of the early liberation of the captive nations of East-Central Europe by peaceful and legitimate means. Such a liberation, the Lithuanian exile and immigration leaders had been assured, "has been, is and, until achieved, will be the major goal of United States policy."

A number of pronouncements by the administrations of Presidents Truman and Eisenhower affirmed this stand. For example, on November 20, 1953, Secretary of State John Foster Dulles stated before the House Select Committee to Investigate the Incorporation of the Baltic States into the USSR that "the United States for its part maintains the diplomatic recognition which it extended in 1922 to the three Baltic nations. We continue to deal with their diplomatic and consular representatives who served the last independent governments of these states."

In spite of hopeful promises by the Eisenhower Administration, Lithuanian hopes for vigorous Western aid ended when Soviet tanks brutally and with impunity crushed the Hungarian Revolution of November 1956.

2.

During the period under consideration, the attitude of Great Britain toward Lithuania's status was not as clear as that of the United States. At the Nuremberg War Trials, the representatives of Great Britain made the same reservations as the United States concerning the Soviet listing of the Baltic States in the indictment as part of the Soviet Union; England emphasized that such a listing had no relation to the British position on the question of Soviet sovereignty in the Baltic States. An official statement about the *de facto* recognition was given on May 23, 1947, in the House of Commons by Undersecretary of Foreign Affairs Mayhew, who stated that "it is necessary for us to deal with these facts as we find them. We have not however recognized these countries *de jure*." As recently as 1954, the joint Parliamentary Undersecretary in the Foreign Office, Dodds-Parker, declared in response to an inquiry in the House of Commons that "Her Majesty's Government are not prepared to take any steps which would imply or constitute *de jure* recognition of the Soviet annexation of the Baltic States."

The Lithuanian Legation in London continued to function as in the past, and the Foreign Office maintained relations with it. Members of the British Commonwealth—Australia, Canada and New Zealand—for the most part adopted the same attitude as Great Britain. Lithuanian, Latvian and Estonians consulates also functioned in Toronto, Canada. (When Grant-Suttie died on May 24, 1949, Minister Stasys Lozoraitis appointed Vytautas Gylys to succeed him as consul general. When Mr. Gylys died on June 14, 1953 the consulate general was vacant until Prime Minister Diefenbaker recognized the appointment of Jonas Žmuidzinas on February 10, 1962.)

In 1948, when the Soviet government attempted to induce Lithuanian citizens in Canada to register at Soviet consulates as Soviet citizens, the Canadian government issued statements to the effect that the Soviet government in Lithuania was not a *de jure* government. This position was further confirmed in a governmental statement in the House of Commons on May 17, 1954:

> There has been no occasion when the Government of Canada considered it necessary to reaffirm or withdraw formally *de jure* recognition of these Baltic States.

Because the Lithuanian Legation in Paris remained closed, it would appear that the French government recognized the annexation. The Supreme Court of France, however, in its decision in

413

the case of *Gebraud v. de Medem* (1951), rejected such an interpretation regarding the Baltic States:

> Considering that no act of international significance has intervened to obliterate the recognition of the Latvian State as a holder of rights and liabilities to legal obligations; that the Court of Appeal rightly decided that so long as the peace treaty has not determined the fate of Latvia, it is impossible to say that Latvians at present have no nationality.

The position of the Belgian government is based on a statement of the High Court in Brussels in its decision in the case of *Compagnie Belgo-lithuanienne d'Electricité v. Société des Centrales electriques regionales* (October 26, 1946), in which it was stated that Belgium has not recognized the annexation of Lithuania *de jure* and that "no document issued by the Department of Foreign Affairs and Foreign Trade establishes that the Belgian Government considers such annexation recognized *de facto*." Mention in this connection should be made also of the fact that the government in 1945 refused to repatriate to the Soviet Union nationals of the Baltic States then in Belgium.

A *de facto* recognition of the Soviet annexation may be inferred from the acts of the Swiss government. The Federal Government of Switzerland decided on November 15, 1946, to take under its trusteeship the assets of the Baltic States and the archives of their former missions in Switzerland. The diplomatic missions of Estonia, Latvia and Lithuania had not been recognized as such by the Swiss government since January, 1941, but the final change in policy came when Switzerland exchanged diplomatic notes with the Soviet Union on March 18, 1946.

The Government of the Federal Republic of Germany has not publicly stated its position in regard to the annexation of the Baltic States. Its actions, however, did not leave any doubt that it did not recognize the annexation either *de facto* or *de jure*. A circular letter of the Ministry of Internal Affairs of September 12, 1952, stated that the republics of Estonia, Latvia, and Lithuania are still legally existing. Furthermore, the Bonn government honored passports issued by the consular representatives of the Baltic States, and showed its willingness to accept semi-diplomatic representatives of these countries. On April 29, 1953, the Foreign Ministry of the Federal Republic of Germany notified the judicial organs of the city of Berlin that it considered Latvia to be still in existence, since neither the German Reich nor the present Federal government had ever recognized that state's annexation. In the circular letter of March 2, 1953, the same ministry stated that, since the annexation of the Baltic States was not recognized in international law and the citizens of those states had not become the citizens of the Soviet Union, the citizenship of those persons remained unchanged; hence, passports issued by the diplomatic and consular services of Estonia, Latvia and Lithuania were valid as long as they conformed to the usual regulations.

The Latin American states, signatories of the Savedra-Lamas Pact, like Spain and Portugal, did not recognize the annexation of the Baltic States. Peron's regime in Argentina alone suspended the functioning of the Lithuanian Legation in 1948, until the question of the Baltic States is solved by the United Nations. The Lithuanian Legation under Dr. Kazys Graužinis was then transferred from Argentina to Uruguay where it continued to operate. Through the efforts of Mr. Stasys Lozoraitis, a Lithuanian consulate under Dr. Stasys Sirutis was opened in Bogota, Colombia, in 1954.

After the war, the Lithuanian Diplomatic Service Abroad reestablished a close-knit organization in the West. Stasys Lozoraitis, with his office in Rome, was acknowledged by all as the diplomatic chief. He wrote notes, protests, and memoranda to states which did not have official Lithuanian representatives. He also designated Lithuanian consuls (e.g., Vytautas Stašinskas' elevation to consul general in New York in 1964) and transfer of diplomatic officials (e.g., Stasys Bačkis from Paris to Washington). The Lithuanian diplomats had power to issue or confirm Lithuanian passports. They also retained the right to attend conferences and receptions. The consuls handled court cases dealing with Lithuanian property and wills. (The honorary consul in Boston, Anthony O. Shallna was instrumental in forging legal decisions regarding Lithuanian property that are still cited as precedents in American courts.) The consuls also handled searches for missing persons and confirmed documents. For example, the consulate general in New York catalogued a file of over 100,000 Lithuanian names and addresses for such purposes. As one could see, in addition to preserving the symbol of Lithuanian sovereignty the Lithuanian diplomats also served a useful purpose.

The Lithuanian diplomats and their staffs were financed by the interest accrued on the Lithuanian gold assets frozen in the United States. The United States Department of the Treasury, together with the State Department, administered the reserves of the Lithuanian Republic. The Lithuanian Legation in Washington submitted budgets for all of the Lithuanan overseas missions.

The Lithuanian Legation in Washington published a bulletin in English *The Lithuanian Situation*. The first issue appeared on August 3, 1940; the second issue was much larger (44 pages) and appeared on June 15, 1941. The third issue was called *The Current News of the Lithuanian Situation*. This name was used until 1955, when the former name was readopted. Altogether, twelve volumes or 145 issues of this information bulletin were published until the fall of 1957. At first, it appeared twice a month. Since 1946, it has been a bi-monthly publication. In addition to articles about the plight of Lithuania, *The Lithuanian Situation* expounds the views of prominent statesmen on pertinent questions as well as on bibliographical reviews.

3. American-Lithuanian Council

Both ALT and BALF were instrumental in the passage of the Displaced Persons bill by the U.S. Congress, which eased the way for the immigration of 30,000 Lithuanian refugees to America from Western Europe. This immigration was a vital factor for the continuation of the Lithuanian cause. Some 75 percent of the nation's intellectuals had escaped to the West, along with 85 percent of the republic's municipal and government employees; close to 80 percent of the physicians, lawyers, teachers, engineers, artists, writers and businessmen. The intellectual calibre and scope of activities in the decade following the 1949-50 period of immigration was quite marked among the Lithuanian-Americans as a result. Eventually, many of the displaced persons became the dynamic civic and cultural leaders of the ethnic community in the free world. This transition, of course, took place with some friction and misunderstandings, because of the difference in climate between the old and new immigrants.

ALT also held annual conventions at which time the political goals were formulated and the work of the past year was ratified. Between conventions, a four-man Executive Committee handled all of the financial matters and executed the plans. Leonardas Šimutis was president during the 1945-56 period. Dr. Pijus Grigaitis, serving at times as vice president or as secretary, was the leading political light of ALT. When the Nationalists rejoined ALT in 1949, Anthony Olis also played a prominent role. A loose network of chapters, following local by-laws, functioned under various names, such as New York Lithuanian Council, ALT Cleveland Chapter, Committee to Aid Lithuania (in Elizabeth, N. J.), etc.

In addition to organizing conventions and congresses, the ALT Executive Board continually felt the official pulse in Washington—ascertaining whether the American government was planning policy changes in regards to the Baltic States. This question plagued ALT when Hitler declared war against his former ally Russia, which made the USSR a wartime ally of the United States and the West. Relations between the United States and the USSR became so cordial that it took courage to speak out in public against Russia or even to raise the question of Lithuania. Returning from the Potsdam Conference, President Truman said the following about Stalin: "I like Joe, he's a good fellow. . . ." Since Berlin had been turned over to the Russians, ALT feared that the Baltic States would also be recognized as part of the USSR. ALT tried to ascertain policy in this matter. On October 29, 1946, an ALT Delegation visited President Truman and asked him if his administration had not changed its policy toward the Baltic States. President Truman reassured them that it had not. ALT visited President Truman on two other occasions; each time it received the same assurance.

ALT used the 1952 American presidential elections to gain party pledges from both the Democrats and the Republicans that the Baltic States would not be recognized as part of the Soviet Union. Its representative also paid visits to the State Department and to Capitol Hill. In the fall of 1951, a project for the codification of "international crimes" was raised in the General Assembly of the United Nations. There was a threat that this code would be used against resistance movements in opposition to Soviet occupation; ALT took vigorous measures to have this project stricken from the Assembly's agenda. On January 13-16, 1952, ALT representatives paid a visit to the State Department with a memorandum concerning Soviet genocide in Lithuania. ALT also organized a letter-writing campaign directed at the United States Senate over the ratification of the United Nations Genocide Convention; 36,000 letters were sent. Unfortunately, the Senate did not ratify this convention.

ALT also organized press conferences in New York and Washington, when the VLIK representatives, Mykolas Krupavičius and Vaclovas Sidzikauskas, first visited the United States, when former President Kazys Grinius came to America, and when three fishermen fled from occupied Lithuania to the free West. In order to solicit public opinion against genocide in Lithuania, the ALT chapters organized June Commemorations to observe the first mass deportations of 1941.

ALT was instrumental in the establishment of a Lithuanian Section of the Voice of America. On February 16, 1951, the first Lithuanian broadcast over the Voice took place; these broadcasts took place twelve times a day. The former head of the Lithuanian-American Information Center, Dr. Kostas Jurgėla, became its director. The broadcasts were heard in Lithuania, America and Australia; Munich broadcasts were heard three times a day. These were the more popular of the two Lithuanian-language programs of the Voice of America. (It was discontinued in 1958.) Following the ill-fated Hungarian revolution, the Washington broadcasts became innocuous, carefully omitting aspects of Lithuanian political activities.

The ALT Executive Committee also visited President Eisenhower on several occasions, presenting its views on the Lithuanian situation, and memoranda were submitted to the State Department, a complete collection of which would fill a huge volume.

Of course, these various activities required a substantial war chest. Money was raised by the ALT chapters during rallies and mass meetings. Between 1943 and 1952, the Lithuanian-American community contributed $353,501.33.

All in all, the most important victory of ALT was the creation of the so-called Kersten Committee by the United States Congress. The idea was conceived by a Brooklyn lawyer and member of ALT, Stephen Bredes. It was imperative to put the facts of the Soviet occupation on record in order to bolster the claims for restoration of independence. Although the Lithuanian-Americans knew how their mother country had been enslaved, the Soviet government always dangled the rebuttal that the so-called Peoples' Diet of Lithuania had voted for incorporation into the USSR. The Soviets asserted that they had merely complied with the wishes of the Lithuanan people!

The American diplomats did not believe this lie, however, they did not know how to refute it. It is for this reason that ALT suggested the creation of a Congressional Committee to investigate the facts. On July 27, 1953, the United States House of Representatives passed a resolution by virtue of which the House Baltic Committee was created to investigate the seizure and forced incorporation of Lithuania into the Soviet Union and the treatment of the Baltic peoples during and following the occupation by the Soviets. Congressman Charles J. Kersten was designated chairman. Later, this bipartisan committee was expanded into the Select and Bi-Partisan House Committee on Communist Aggression. President Eisenhower supported this project and Congress appropriated $30,000 for its hearings.

The investigations began in Washington, where Lithuanian Minister Povilas Žadeikis, Secretary of State John Foster Dulles and others testified. Lithuanian witnesses were later questioned in New York, Detroit and Chicago. The Lithuanian-American Council also collaborated by gathering documents, classifying and registering witnesses, and translating these testimonies into English and sending them to the Kersten Committee. ALT gathered data from over 1,000 witnesses who had experienced Soviet terror in Lithuania.

After questioning Eastern European witnesses in America,

the Kersten Committee went to Europe to gather further material. Back in the States, the Kersten Committee prepared a report of its hearings and on August 9, 1954, submitted the report to Congress. But the report was incomplete because more witnesses appeared. As a result, the Kersten Committee held further hearings in New York, Wilkes Barre, Chicago, Milwaukee and elsewhere. Much valuable material was collected. ALT submitted a list of more than 18,000 Lithuanians who were deported to Siberia during the first Soviet occupation.

After the hearings, the Kersten Committee compiled a three-volume report containing documents and testimony on the enslavement of Lithuania. This report was submitted to the State Department, to the United States Mission to the United Nations, and to the United States Congress. On October 28, 1954, the Select House Committee submitted to the Secretary of State its third Interim Report. The findings, conclusions and recommendations contained in this report are explicit and categorical: "The Soviet Union is guilty of unprovoked aggression against the Baltic States and inhuman treatment of the population of these enslaved countries."

4. The Lithuanian-Canadians

After the war, when thousands of Lithuanian refugees crossed over to the new world, the Communists took steps to have Canada prevent their entry by accusing them of being fascists and Hitlerites. The Lithuanian Council of Canada worked hard to have these false accusations dismissed, and a special commission was formed which traveled to Ottawa and demonstrated to the Canadian government that these accusations were without foundation. The Council won the fight, and thousands of Lithuanian immigrants were admitted into the country.

The newcomers began to organize the ethnic community or *Bendruomenė*, which soon became interested in political activities and for a while competed with the old Council. In 1948, the Council during its convention voted to support VLIK, and became the National Fund Delegation in Canada.

As time passed, the predominantly cultural *Bendruomenė*

420

formed a political committee which became its political arm. This political committee evolved into the Lithuanian institution which spoke on behalf of the community to other ethnic groups and to the Dominion and provincial governments.

5. VLIK

The Supreme Committee for Liberation of Lithuania (VLIK), in preserving its continuity of authority from Lithuania, during this period was based exclusively on former VLIK members or alternates from the homeland who retained their citizenship.

On July 5, 1945, VLIK proclaimed the following guidelines for its activities: 1) to prepare for the peace conference, 2) to study the question of Lithuania's boundaries, 3) to study the former system of government in the country and to prepare a new constitution, 4) to organize the tabulation of losses sustained by the Lithuanians, and 5) to plan for the reconstruction of the country's economy. Commissions were created to study these plans. In conjunction with the Potsdam Conference, VLIK (July 10, 1945) sent a lengthy and detailed memorandum to the President of the United States and the Prime Minister of Great Britain, calling upon them to: 1) not recognize the unilateral act of the Kremlin which incorporated Lithuania into the Soviet Union, 2) demand that the Soviet Union remove its forces from the country and allow the Lithuanians to re-establish without hindrance their sovereign institutions, 3) stipulate that until such time, Lithuanian displaced persons should be sheltered by the Allies, and 4) force the Soviet Union to return all Lithuanians deported to Siberia, the operation to be supervised by the International Red Cross.

In order to bolster the case of Lithuania, VLIK decided to prepare a petition to the Pope and other heads of state, and to prepare appeals to academicians of the world's institutions of higher learning and to world student groups. VLIK also urged the various writers and journalists' organizations, to issue similar appeals.

Since there were two institutions that represented Lithuania's interests—VLIK (the Nation) and the Diplomatic Service (the

State)—a number of questions arose concerning parallel activities, jurisdiction, methods of operations, etc. There was a need to coordinate the two institutions. For this reason, the VLIK leaders, diplomats, signatories of the Lithuanian Declaration of Independence, former ministers and parliamentarians, party leaders and activists met in Berne, Switzerland, in July, 1946. This conference, which lasted several days, agreed to accept the following points: 1) to form a nucleus of the Lithuanian delegation which would attend the peace conference, 2) to unite both representative institutions into one organ—the VLIK Executive Council (Vliko Vykdomoji Taryba) which was to function as the exile Lithuanian government, and 3) to consider VLIK as a parliamentary and research institution which would be supervised by the Executive Council. On November 16, 1946, VLIK formed this Executive Council. On August 5-15, 1947, a second conference was held with the Diplomatic Service in Paris to discuss the problems of the liberation organization, political-diplomatic action, information and propaganda, the resettlement of the refugees, and the financing of operations.

On October 30, 1946, VLIK sent a memorandum to the Lithuanian Minister in Washington, Povilas Žadeikis, which pointed out that the Soviet Union by use of military and police coercion had deported 115,000 inhabitants of Lithuania to Siberia. In 1947, VLIK sent a supplementary memorandum to Minister Žadeikis with lists of deportees, who for the most part were government, educational, journalistic, religious, military, labor and agricultural people. Minister Žadeikis utilized these memoranda in the United Nations and the American press, creating a stir.

On September 17, 1949, VLIK prepared and sent to the United Nations a memorandum signed by the exile organizations of Lithuania, Latvia, Estonia, Byelorussia, Czechoslovakia, Hungary, Poland, Slovakia, the Ukraine and Yugoslavia. This memorandum pointed out that human rights were being violated in the countries occupied by the Soviet Union.

Between 1947 and 1950, VLIK sent seven memoranda to the United Nations through the intercession of the then Secretary General Trygve Lie. Between 1950 and 1954, VLIK sent twenty memoranda to the United Nations Organization, fifty-two notes to the U.S. Delegations, 132 letters to parliamentarians, seventy-two letters to universities and political parties, twelve to Austria and 1,075 letters to French dignitaries. In addition, during this period VLIK participated in the United Baltic Bureau, the European Movement, the Council of Europe, and exiled anti-Communist movements in Germany and France. It had connections with the Christian Democrats, International Peasant Union, Social Democrats and European press and radio.

The Duties of the Executive Council included executing the decisions of VLIK and maintaining relations with other exile organizations and occupational authorities in Germany, with the Bonn Government, and with Lithuanian refugees. Other duties included the supervision of the Lithuanian, German, and Italian language ELTA information publications, radio scripts and information for the Lithuanian-language broadcasts of the Vatican, Rome and Madrid radios. It also supervised the monitoring of the broadcasts of Radio Vilnius. The Lithuanian radio programs were broadcast daily into Lithuania (Radio Rome—20 minutes, Radio Vatican—15 minutes). The Council also gave information on Lithuania to the Rias and Stuttgart radio stations.

After the signing of the Moscow-Bonn Reparation Agreement, Lithuanian residents of German origin were allowed to emigrate to West Germany (over a thousand of them took advantage of this agreement). The VLIK Executive Council maintained regular contact with the repatriates, some of whom had spent up to ten years in the Siberian labor camps, and received from them extensive authentic data on life under Soviet occupation. The Council also added to its store of information about Lithuania under Soviet rule by closely studying periodicals published in the occupied country. The extensive documentation in the Council's hands served as a mine of useful material for the press of the free world and for academic studies.

The information service of VLIK is one of the most important tasks in the struggle for independence. In 1945, VLIK began publishing short daily ELTA news items (the name ELTA is a contraction of Lithuanian Telegraph Agency). In 1946, it began publishing ELTA bulletins, which have continued to the present every seven to ten days. The Lithuanian press abroad utilized its news extensively. (The bulletin was published in Reutlingen, Germany.) It was essential for VLIK to inform the world press as well about occupied Lithuania. As a result, VLIK published a monthly in German entitled *ELTA Pressedienst*. Since 1954, VLIK has published an Italian edition (*ELTA Press*) and since 1956 an English monthly (*ELTA Information Service*). In 1961, the VLIK operatives in Buenos Aires, Argentina, began a Spanish edition. Since 1964, Polish diplomat Sigismund Zawadowski has published an Arabic edition in Beirut, Lebanon. For a while, a clandestine ELTA in Lithuania was published every three months and smuggled into the occupied country. VLIK has also published a number of books; among them, A. Šapoka's *Lithuania Through the Ages,* J. Audėnas' *Twenty Years Struggle for Freedom of Lithuania,* and Milovan Djilas' *Naujoji Klasė* ("New Class").

In order to raise money for the activities of VLIK, an autonomous institution, Tautos Fondas (National Fund) was set up.

One of the theoretical tasks of VLIK was to plan for Lithuania's reconstruction. As early as 1943, VLIK had organized the Lithuanian Planning Commission, set up the Committee to Study the Technical and Economic Reconstruction of Lithuania under the chairmanship of Dr. Petras Karvelis. The reports, discussions and resolutions were published in the conference work book *Išlaisvintos Lietuvos ūkis* (1949).

In 1946, VLIK prepared a statute for the Lithuanian Community (Lietuvių Bendruomenė) which was accepted by the convention of Lithuanian refugees March 1-3, 1946, in Hanau, Germany. VLIK also formulated a plan for the World Lithuanian Community, the purposes and organization of which were spelled out in the introduction to the plan. This plan became the basis for the Lithuanian Charter (Lietuvių Charta), promulgated on June 14, 1949. This worldwide organization, the Bendruomenė, owes its conception to VLIK which sought to preserve an organized Lithuanian cultural nucleus in exile.

The first goodwill mission of the Supreme Committee in North America took place from January to May, 1949, when the President, Msgr. Mykolas Krupavičius, and the chairman of the Executive Council, Vaclovas Sidzikauskas, visited the United States and Canada. The visits sought to establish closer contacts with the leading foreign policy officials of the two countries, to exchange views with Lithuanian Minister Povilas Žadeikis, to discuss problems of Lithuania's liberation with ALT and to visit the larger Lithuanian colonies.

Their first stop was in Washington, where Minister Žadeikis received them with warmth. Accompanied by him, the two VLIK executives were received at the State Department, where they submitted a comprehensive memorandum, "On the Restoration of Lithuania's Independence." The VLIK spokesmen then went on a tour of Lithuanian communities, following an itinerary arranged by the Lithuanian American Council. At the same time, they joined actively in the ALT fund-raising campaign, which coincided with the thirty-first anniversary of Lithuanian independence, the proceeds of which were earmarked for liberation activities. They also visited Canada.

In 1955, VLIK moved to America. The presence of VLIK in New York City made possible the strengthening of the ties with the Lithuanian Minister in Washington and the establishment of permanent contacts with the United States State Department. VLIK now not only stood on firm ground, but also enjoyed a solid backing, which was confirmed in the frequent visits of its president to Washington. New York's position as a hub of international policies enabled VLIK representatives to meet ambassadors and high officials of many countries and to brief them on matters concerning Lithuania. To avoid duplication of effort VLIK left such activities within the United Nations to the ACEN (see below), of which the Lithuanian Delegation, appointed by the Committee for a Free Lithuania, is an active member.

In the decade under consideration, VLIK had met with many obstacles, but did not let any opportunity go by without reacting or raising the Lithuanian case. Thanks to these ceaseless efforts, Lithuania has remained a factor in international relations.

7. Two Secessionist Political Centers

Two groups seceded from VLIK just prior to its moving to New York and established their own political centers. They were the Lithuanian Front and the Lithuanian Independence Alliance.

The Lithuanian Front was a resistance movement of Catholic activists who had been associated with the LAF in 1941. Unlike the traditional Christian Democrats, they believed in a corporate state based on Christian and "organic democratic" principles. In the free world, this group was designated the Friends of the Lithuanian Front (Lietuvių Fronto Bičiuliai).

The Lithuanian Independence Alliance (Lietuvos Neprik-lausomybės Talka) was an alliance of four political organizations seeking restoration of Lithuania's independence through coordinated efforts. The sponsoring members of the Alliance were the Lithuanian Regeneration Movement, the Freedom Fighters Union, the Lithuanian Resistance Alliance of America and the Lithuanian National Movement, each retaining its individuality and freedom of action in all other fields. The member groups of the Independence Alliance or *Talka* were nationalistic and liberal resistance groups or political organizations.

8. *Committee for a Free Lithuania*

The Committee for a Free Lithuania was the result of concerted Eastern European exile activities. At first, the Lithuanian politicians called themselves the Lithuanian Advisory Group (Patariamoji Lietuvių Grupė) which was set up on May 24, 1951, with the support of the Committee for a Free Europe. This group joined other exiles in picketing the visit of the Soviet delegation to the United Nations Plenary session on October 14, 1951. At that time, protest notes were submitted to fifty-five members of the United Nations, reminding them of the 1951 memorandum urging the world organization to raise the question of Soviet genocide. The Lithuanian Advisory Group, together with the Lithuanian Minister in Washington, prepared a memorandum for the United Nations on Soviet aggression and violation of treaties.

In December, 1952, after an agreement was reached by Lithuanian Minister Povilas Žadeikis and the Committee for a Free Europe, the Advisory Group became the Committee for a Free Lithuania, in order to coordinate its work with similar committees of Soviet-enslaved European nations. Its main purpose was to work toward the eventual liberation of the enslaved nation and, in the meantime, to maintain hope and give moral support to the

426

democratic forces in Lithuania itself. The Committee for a Free Lithuania was composed of eight members, each of whom represented one of the more popular ideologies or factions.

While preserving its independence, the Committee for a Free Lithuania cooperated with ALT, the Lithuanian diplomats and VLIK both in planning the guidelines for concerted action and in executing plans. The Committee's main task was to observe and analyze developments in Lithuania and to prepare annual surveys for the Assembly of Captive European Nations (ACEN), as well as to participate in the work of the ACEN through the Lithuanian Delegation. The Committee, together with similar Latvian and Estonian committees, edited the *Baltic Review* in English, French and Spanish. For a brief time, it published a political journal, *Lietuva*. The Committee, on its own and in conjunction with the ACEN, disseminated information to the United Nations delegations of the free world, members of UNESCO, the Interparliamentary Union, governments of the free world, the European Movement, the Council of Europe, Pan-American Congresses, and international organizations opposed to communism, by means of memoranda, reports, declarations, appeals, protests, personal contacts, and the press and radio.

In order to appreciate more fully the work done by the Committee, a brief survey of the activities of the ACEN is in order. Founded on September 20, 1954, the ACEN (Assembly of Captive European Nations) is primarily an organization for joint political action, and its program is designed to offer a meaningful contribution to the captive peoples' quest for self-determination and enjoyment of their inherent rights. The ACEN is composed of member and associate member organizations, which are represented by accredited delegations (Albanian, Bulgarian, Czechoslovakian, Estonian, Hungarian, Latvian, Lithuanian, Polish and Rumanian). The international organizations of Central and Eastern European political parties or movements are the associate members.

Apart from its New York headquarters, ACEN has centers in Paris, London, Bonn, Latin America, and elsewhere. Judging by ACEN's activities, the scope of their work can easily be assessed: 1) regular visits to Washington and other capitals; 2) permanent lobbying in the United Nations and at various international conferences; 3) appeals to world organizations; 4) supplying information (surveys) on the captive countries to the Council of Europe and other organizations; 5) appearances on television, radio shows and panels, including lecturing both in the United States and elsewhere; 6) dissemination of information throughout all available communications media both to the free world press and, through radio, to the captive peoples themselves; 7) publications, such as *ACEN NEWS,* and books and pamphlets sent to thousands of organizations, libraries, universities, and key personalities in all fields; 8) demonstrations organized periodically to urge the settlement of topical issues; 9) protecting the interests of exiles and promoting their entry into the countries of their choice.

III. The Struggle Based on Lithuanian Resources, 1956-66

1. *The Climate*

The recent Sino-Soviet rift has destroyed the myth of the Communist monolith and caused confusion among the Communist parties everywhere in the world. Some of them have aligned themselves with Peking, while others have remained faithful to Moscow. This rift, the emergence of Western Europe as an independent military and political center, the political ferment in Latin America, the political transformation of Africa and Asia, and the wave of neutralism which has made considerable inroads in many areas of the world, have created a polycentric world.

Polycentrism brought in its wake new concepts and new trends; it engendered Western policies designed to ease East-West tensions in the spirit of "coexistence and accommodation," and encouraged at least a policy of gradualism. The Western powers hoped that an improvement of relations with the Soviet-imposed Communist puppet regimes and intensification of trade and cultural exchanges would bring more independence and freedom to the captive nations of East-Central Europe. Yet, the captive peoples and their exiled leaders knew from bitter experience that the

Communist regimes set definite limits to any evolution toward genuine freedom, since a transgression of these limits would mean the collapse of Communism in Eastern Europe. It was for these reasons that the Polish Communist regime reintroduced repressive measures, as did other Communist regimes, whenever the score of liberalization threatened its totalitarian rule.

If the fallacy of gradualism, based on the assumption of step-by-step liberalization and spurious betterment, was evident in the satellite countries of East-Central Europe, it was glaringly obvious in the Baltic States, isolated by a double Iron Curtain. There, the winds of Russification and economic exploitation were on the rise. Stalinist stooges and methods continued to reign supreme in Lithuania. Emboldened by the Western quest for normalization and "package deals" for Europe, as well as escaping with impunity for their international crimes, the Soviet leaders did not relax their grip on the Baltic States, but on the contrary, strove to destroy the very national identity of those nations. The polycentric era is thus fraught with the gravest dangers for the Baltic states.

Lithuanian political circles have come to realize that the West, especially the United States, will no longer pursue "liberation" policies. Slowly, they have come to accept the harsh reality that further action—both political and information—will have to depend exclusively on Lithuanian financial contributions and volunteer support of the ethnic communities. Since resources are limited, the political leaders have ceased paying mere lip-service to the need for unity and have begun to seek ways of consolidating the leadership and organizations.

3. The Supreme Committee for Liberation of Lithuania

Upon moving to the United States, VLIK drew closer to the large communities of Lithuanian immigrants in Canada and the countries of Latin America. In 1957, the president of the Supreme Committee, Antanas Trimakas, made a goodwill tour to Brazil, Uruguay, Argentina, Chile, Peru, Bolivia, Venezuela, and Panama. The Conference of Latin American Presidents, which was taking place in Panama at the time, provided Mr. Trimakas with an excellent occasion to meet a number of Latin American leaders. These acquaintances proved to be very useful door-openers to the cabinets, press and other institutions during the subsequent visits to the capitals of the respective countries. During this Latin American tour, the president held over forty press conferences and gave several radio and T.V. talks.

During this period, relations with the Diplomatic Service were improved, VLIK conferred with the diplomats on important matters, made all diplomatic *demarches* through the diplomats in countries which still recognized the Lithuanian Republic. In those countries where there were no Lithuanian legations, VLIK approached the governments concerned directly.

The most important developments in VLIK occurred in the early 60's when the major political groups were reunited in that body.

The new president, Vaclovas Sidzikauskas, appeared before the Congressional Foreign Affairs Subcommittee headed by Congresswoman Edna Kelly in 1965, testifying about recent attempts at Russification in Lithuania. In his capacity as chairman of the Assembly of Captive European Nations, he also made a visit to Europe in April, 1966, and raised the Baltic question with German and French statesmen and parliamentarians.

After the resignation of Vaclovas Sidzikauskas, a new executive board was elected on December 10, 1966. Dr. Juozas Kęstutis Valiūnas was elected president. All in all, with its expanded base of representation, VLIK received more support from the Lithuanians of the free world. It showed more activity in the information sector and a concern for Lithuanian public opinion and the needs of those in exile.

4. The Lithuanian American Council

The Lithuanian American Council joined the Conference of Americans of Central and Eastern European descent (CACEED) on January 28, 1956, when representatives of several nationwide organizations of American citizens of Central and Eastern European background gathered in New York for the purpose of devising a common instrumentality which would speak on behalf of the 15,000,000 Americans whose ethnic origins were rooted in

430

Eastern Europe. CACEED is a coordinating body of organizations whose membership maintains a keen interest in the plight of the captive nations. In integrating and coordinating the efforts of American citizens of Albanian, Bulgarian, Czechoslovak, Estonian, Hungarian, Latvian, Lithuanian, Polish, Rumanian and Ukrainian descent, CACEED seeks the attainment of objectives common to all. Msgr. Jonas Balkūnas headed the five-man ALT delegation. He was elected president of the Conference, and has held that post for the last ten years.

In 1958, when the American press carried items on the forthcoming summit conference, rumors spread to the effect that the United States was going to accept the status quo for the Baltic States. The ALT Executive Committee in May presented John Foster Dulles, then Secretary of State, with a memorandum. The plenipotentiary of ALT, Dr. Pijus Grigaitis, used the occasion to testify before the Congressional Subcommittee headed by Rep. Wayne L. Hays.

When, in August, 1958, President Dwight D. Eisenhower issued the Captive Nations Proclamation, ALT immediately took steps to inform the United States public that Lithuania is indeed a captive nation. During the same year, when President Eisenhower invited Soviet premier Khrushchev to visit the United States, promising in return to visit the USSR, ALT issued an appeal to the Lithuanian community urging mass protest meetings.

The Executive Committee visited the State Department twice in 1959: January 11-14 and July 4-5. Memoranda were submitted to the President, to Secretary Herter, and to the State Department as a unit. The first memorandum touched on the subject of the draft code of offenses against peace and security of mankind; this was a Soviet proposal designed to stop anti-Soviet activities. ALT also encouraged a letter-writing campaign directed at the President and the United States Congress to proclaim Captive Nations Week 1959. At the beginning of 1960, ALT asked for a liberalization of immigration quotas. It also ordered 5,000 copies of the reprints of the *Congressional Record* which carried the February 16 (Lithuanian Independence Day) speeches in Congress.

On April 23, 1960, Miss Mary Kizys, director of the Lithuanian Information Center, informed the Director of the Eastern European Division of the State Department about developments in Lithuania just prior to the summit conference.

During the 1960 Presidential campaign, ALT sent representatives to the conventions of both parties to have the Lithuanian question considered in the platform. After John F. Kennedy's election, ALT received a declaration from the new Secretary of State, Dean Rusk, that the United States government does not and will not recognize the annexation of Lithuania by the USSR.

5 The World Lithuanian Community

Bendruomenė is a hard term to translate into English. While it conveys the thought of community (German *Volksgemeinschaft,* French *communauté,* Russian *obshchina*) it is more. It is an organized and directed community. The struggle for liberation stretching beyond the postwar years needed a permanent organization to preserve the emigre national and cultural identity. It was inevitable that this largest of Lithuanian organizations in the free world, the World Lithuanian Community (Pasaulio Lietuvių Bendruomenė), would become a political factor in the liberation cause during the 1956-69 period. Bendruomenė was a new social phenomenon in the postwar Lithuanian immigration movement.

The idea for a World Lithuanian Community grew out of the prewar World Lithuanian Union which had been formed in Kaunas. With the return of the Soviets to Lithuania in 1944, some 100,000 Lithuanians fled to the West. The majority of them wound up in DP camps in Germany and Austria. In the immediate postwar years, in spite of anxiety and hard conditions, Lithuanian cultural life flourished in these camps. Through the initiative of VLIK, the first displaced persons convention was held in Hanau, Germany, on March 4, 1946. The convention drew up the constitution of the Lithuanian Exiles Community (Lietuvių Tremtinių Bendruomenė). The purpose of the Exiles Community was 1) to preserve a healthy segment of the nation in exile; 2) to protect the good name of the Lithuanians; 3) to care for the health, education, cultural and social affairs of the exiles; 4) to prepare the re-education of displaced persons for useful occupations and professions; and 5) to foster national solidarity, democratic ideals and work.

In the field of education, the Lithuanian Exile Community performed wonders. In 1947-48 there were seventy-six kindergartens with 2,280 children and 148 teachers; eighty-eight primary schools with 3,655 pupils and 364 teachers, and forty high schools with 3,122 students and 713 teachers. The secondary schools had 799 graduates, a number of whom entered the Baltic University at Pinneberg and German universities. The Exiles Community also ran a technical school in Nuertingen and Schwaebisch Gmuend, higher vocational courses at Kempten, a fine arts school in Freiburg, and a commercial school at Ravensburg.

When it became apparent that there would be no immediate return to the fatherland, the cultural and civic leaders began to plan a permanent organization that would preserve Lithuanian culture on a high level. Between 1947 and 1949, VLIK and cultural leaders worked on a plan for a permanent cultural organization. The idea of the World Lithuanian Community (PLB) was conceived. Its purpose was defined in the preamble to the project; this preamble was later modified and became the code of every patriotic Lithuanian displaced person. After much study and work, VLIK promulgated the Lithuanian Charter (Lietuvių Charta) a thirteen-point manifesto of the World Lithuanian Community. Model by-laws were drawn up, which later served as a basis for setting up communities in England, France, Brazil, Argentina, Uruguay, Colombia, Venezuela, Australia, New Zealand, Canada, Switzerland, the United States, and in other countries which admitted refugees from Communism.

The Lithuanian Community organization was formed rather quickly in Germany, Austria, France, Sweden, Belgium, Canada, New Zealand, and Australia because its organizational principles were more readily acceptable to the Lithuanians in those countries. The Lithuanian-Americans, with their established organizations and traditions, only gradually came around to accepting the idea of unified, organized cultural activity that cut across ideological lines. ALT was especially jealous of Bendruomenė.

In December, 1951, the Temporary Organizational Commit-

433

tee of the Lithuanian Community (LOK) was formed. The prominent Lithuanian-American civic leader, Msgr. Jonas Balkūnas became its first chairman. LOK promised to reach an agreement with both ALT and BALF, agreeing to work in the ethnic-cultural field, leaving politics in America to ALT and relief work to BALF. Many of the old ALT and local club leaders still looked with suspicion upon this "Displaced Persons' organization." The initial work was not easy.

In 1952, the Bendruomenė by-laws were prepared, and it was incorporated under the name of "Lithuanian American Community of USA, Inc." Its purposes were listed: 1) to support the U.S. Constitution, follow the ideals of democracy and actively participate in American life; 2) to contribute to American society by introducing Lithuanian cultural and national traditions and customs; 3) to preserve Lithuanianism; 4) to maintain ties with Lithuanians outside of the United States, and 5) to support the fight for Lithuanian liberation and aid the suffering Lithuanian nation. This fifth purpose had political undertones which kept rising to the surface in succeeding years.

The first elections to the LB Council were held on May 1, 1955; there were ninety-five candidates. About 9,000 members voted; twenty-seven persons were elected to the Council, which met on July 1-2, 1955 and formed a presidium and an executive board of seven to serve for three years. Stasys Barzdukas became president. This first session of the Council also set up an auditors commission, and a five-man court of honor. Also, it decided to establish a cultural fund, form an educational board and cultural council, and levy a one-dollar solidarity fee on all active members. Active members had the right to vote and run for office; theoretically, members were all persons of Lithuanian descent.

According to the constitution, the cardinal purpose of the World Lithuanian Community is cultural activity and liaison among Lithuanians on a worldwide basis. Organizationally speaking, the PLB is a federation of autonomous Lithuanian communities operating in North and South America, Europe and Oceania. The most active communities are those of the United States, Canada, Australia, Germany, France, and Great Britain. In addition to preserving and fostering Lithuanian culture and

434

information, the organization in many countries performs two auxiliary functions, to wit, taking an active role in the struggle for Lithuania's independence, and organizing relief for destitute Lithuanians. In the field of political action, PLB recognizes the authority of VLIK, but in several countries where there are no representatives of VLIK, PLB organs act as political auxiliaries (e.g., in Canada).

The first PLB Congress in 1958 adopted the constitution and elected the first executive board which was comprised of Lithuanians of Toronto, Canada. The first PLB President was Jonas Matulionis.

The second PLB Congress, held in the autumn of 1963 in Toronto, decided to transfer the executive board to Cleveland, Ohio. The new president for five years was Juozas Bachunas of Sodus, Michigan. His executive vice president was Stasys Barzdukas of Cleveland, Ohio. Bachunas visited the Lithuanian Communities of Europe and Australia several times. During his presidency, the first World Lithuanian Youth Congress was held in 1966 in Chicago, in which several thousand Lithuanian youths from the United States and Canada, as well as 200 representatives from abroad, participated.

IV.   THE PROTRACTED SIEGE

1.

In spite of the fact that more than twenty years have elapsed since the occupation of Lithuania, the ardor and hopes of the Lithuanian-Americans, on the whole, have not diminished. The local civic leader as well as the erstwhile Lithuanian intellectual continues to show a deep concern for the plight of his homeland. However, it became apparent in time to all but the sentimental that Lithuania's liberation was not around the corner. A vague feeling of impotence and impatience set in. Many became impatient with the slow, diplomatic procedures of the Lithuanian diplomats and VLIK. Others felt that ALT had outlived its usefulness. By 1960, a number of young activists felt that the old politicians were unwilling to relinquish the leadership. A number of discontented activists, feeling excluded from the traditional political institutions, chose new avenues of activity, which they felt would hasten the day of Lithuania's liberation.

Grass-roots political action was not new to the Lithuanian-Americans. As early as 1946, the Knights of Lithuania (Lietuvos Vyčiai), a Lithuanian-American Catholic youth organization, set up a Lithuanian Affairs Committee, guided by a dynamic and astute priest, Rev. John C. Jutt-Jutkevičius of Worcester, Mass. Using modern American lobbying and public relations techniques, Rev. Jutt's committee, over the years, has helped mold official and public opinion regarding Lithuania.

The Lithuanian Affairs Committee had officers in the various councils of the Knights of Lithuania. The local operatives gathered articles and news on Lithuania and communicated this data to Rev. Jutt, who published a bulletin with instructions on how and to whom to write. Letters of protest or thanks, depending on the situation, were sent to congressmen, senators, governors, mayors, editors, writers, journalists, radio and television producers. Every year, 15,000 letters were sent out; by 1963, the Lithuanian Affairs Committee of the Knights of Lithuania had sent a total of 250,000. Rev. Jutt also realized the importance of incentives. In 1955, the Knights of Lithuania established a Medal and Scroll to be presented annually to a non-Lithuanian who has distinguished himself in the service of the Lithuanian cause. These medals were presented at the annual Knights of Lithuania conventions. Recipients include senators Paul Douglas and Thomas Dodd, among others.

2. A Single-Action Movement

In 1961, through the initiative of Leonard Valiukas, a grass-roots Baltic movement was formed in California called the "Americans for Congressional Action to Free the Baltic States." The purpose of this movement was to pass a resolution in the United States Congress urging the President of the United States to raise the Baltic question in the United Nations.

Leonard Valiukas, a young and energetic recent immigrant, active in the Knights of Lithuania and the Republican party of California, set up a Baltic Committee in Los Angeles.

The Americans for Congressional Action quickly set up *ad hoc* committees throughout the Estonian, Latvian, and Lithuanian communities to solicit funds and lobby senators and congressmen. The lion's share of the work was carried on by Lithuanians, especially by Leonard Valiukas and Dr. Petras Vileišis, chairman of the Connecticut Lithuanian Community. During the first session of the 89th Congress, seventy-three Senate and House resolutions were introduced on the Baltic States Question. Letter-writing campaigns directed at the American legislators and visits to representatives by local Baltic groups helped pressure Capitol Hill.

After a concerted campaign of nearly five years, a House resolution on the Baltic question was passed by the United States Senate in the waning hours of the 89th Congress. On October 22, 1966, Senator Mike Mansfield asked for unanimous Senatorial consent on House Concurrent Resolution 416, which requested the President of the United States to urge certain actions in behalf of Estonia, Latvia, and Lithuania. The resolution urged the President a) to direct the direction of world opinion at the United Nations and at other appropriate international forums and by such means as he deemed appropriate to the denial of the rights of self-determination for the peoples of Estonia, Latvia, and Lithuania, and b) to bring the force of world opinion to bear on behalf of the restoration of these rights to the Baltic peoples.

This resolution, sponsored by Congressman John S. Monagan, was passed in the House on June 23, 1966. Senators Thomas J. Dodd, Thomas H. Kuchel, Karl E. Mundt, Frank J. Lausche, Paul H. Douglas, and Everett M. Dirksen, were instrumental in its passage in the Senate.

The resolution did not have the force of law, it was an expression of the opinion of Congress on a specific issue; it was directed to the State Department. During the December 23, 1966, ACEN visit to the State Department, Vaclovas Sidzikauskas brought up the subject of the resolution. Vague promises were received that the matter would be directed to the United States Ambassador at the United Nations, to be raised "at an appropriate time."

3. The New Generation

Twenty years of struggle constitutes a generation. In the period 1940-60, in addition to the old generation of politicians and the interwar years generation of activists, a new postwar element appeared. Young Lithuanians, who began or completed their studies in the DP camps of Germany and in the United States, entered the political struggle for Lithuanian liberation. At first, these students publicized Lithuania's name in international student conferences or at international scout jamborees. Through the efforts of Vytautas Vardys and Vytautas Kavolis, the Lithuanian Student Association of the United States of America (Lietuvių Studentų Sąjunga) was formed. In its preamble, the Association, uniting all ideological shades of students, declared that it would work to preserve Lithuanianism and carry on the struggle for the restoration of independence. It also declared that the Student Association would coordinate its activities with Bendruomenė and the political institutions.

In 1954, the International Affairs Section of the Student Association was created for political activities. The first concrete undertaking was in the field of information. On November 24, 1954, the group began publication of the quarterly, *Lituanus,* whose purpose was to inform non-Lithuanian scholars about Lithuania and Lithuanians. The idea was conceived by Vytautas Vygantas. Although most of the contributors have been of the "older generation," *Lituanus* is still published quarterly, thanks to funds raised by the Lithuanian community. During the November, 1963, Student Convention in New York, a *Lituanus* Foundation was set up. On June 15, 1956, the students, under the leadership of Valdas Adamkavičius, collected 40,000 signatures and presented them with a petition to then Vice President Richard Nixon, urging the American statesman to use all means at his disposal to hasten the day of independence for Lithuania.

In 1960, the Student Association Foreign Affairs Section was reorganized by Algirdas Budreckis and contacts were established with the Lithuanian Student Associations in Canada, West Germany, Australia and New Zealand. In 1962, an attempt was made to form a World Lithuanian Student Association. In July of that year, the Student Association delegate Miss Birutė Augustinavičius attended the International Student Conference in Quebec. In 1963, the Student Association was admitted into ALT as a member organization. (In April, 1961, student representatives were invited to join the VLIK information committee.)

On May 25, 1965, activists of the "new generation" formed the Federation of Lithuanian Youth Organizations. This Federation maintained an informal tie with VLIK President Antanas Trimakas. Its approach was to publicize the Lithuanian case to the student unions and the United Nations Missions of the Afro-Asian Bloc. This Federation, using the secondary name of Anticolonial League of Lithuanian Youth, organized symposia with Latin American, Asian, and African students and sent out 100 photostatic copies of the infamous Ribbentrop-Molotov Pact to Afro-Asian student groups. It greeted new African states, receiving cordial replies from such dignataries as Premier H. K. Banda of Malawi. In December, 1964, the Federation sponsored a five-week political seminar for Lithuanian students. Because the Lithuanian community looked with suspicion upon these novel modes of operation, the Federation declined. In 1965, the new chairman Juozas Miklovas dropped the name "Federation" and applied the title "Anticolonial League." The Lithuanian community and student organizations were chary of such "radical names," and soon the Anticolonial League's activities became nominal. In 1966, the remnants of the League merged with young Latvian and Estonian activists to form the "Baltic Appeal to the United Nations" (BATUN).

A grass-roots movement initiated by the "new generation" was the so-called "March to the United Nations" (Žygis į Jungtines Tautas). The year 1965 marked the twenty-fifth anniversary of Soviet occupation and forced annexation of Lithuania. To add insult to injury, the USSR celebrated the anniversary by staging a "festival" in Vilnius. This carefully rehearsed mis-en-scene was to convey the impression that the Baltic peoples were merry and gay under their Soviet-imposed regimes. Of course, Estonians, Latvians and Lithuanians in the free world anticipated and challenged this Soviet propaganda. The traditional exchange of claims and counterclaims took place in the press and diplomatic circles. But the issue did not end there. Not content with verbal rebuttals or local political meetings, five young Lithuanians— Anthony Mažeika, Jr., Anthony Sniečkus, Algirdas Budreckis, Romas Kezys and Juozas Miklovas—advocated a mass march to the United Nations as the most effective answer to Soviet claims. Their plan called for the purchase of a full-page advertisement in the Sunday edition of the *New York Times* and in the Paris edition of the same newspaper, appealing to the conscience of the world. This was to be followed by a protest rally at Madison Square Garden. The rally was to be concluded with a dramatic march to Hammarskjold Plaza, in front of the United Nations, where a symbolic plea to the world organization was to take place. Later on, delegations were to visit member states of the United Nations and hand over a resolution passed at the rally. The ultimate aim of the rally and march was to raise the Baltic question before the United Nations Committee to Investigate Colonialism.

Grass-roots support sprang up practically overnight. The five youths brought their project to the attention of sixty-four representatives of major Lithuanian cultural and civic organizations. The presentation took place on June 25 in Brooklyn, New York, and the quintet received a mandate to carry out their project. Calling themselves the Committee to Restore Lithuania's Independence (Komitetas Lietuvos Nepriklausomybei Atstatyti), with little more than moral support from established Lithuanian institutions, they organized in two months fourteen commissions to handle various aspects of the project.

The "Appeal to the Conscience of the World" appeared in the November 7 edition of the *New York Times* and a day later in the newspaper's Paris edition. It carried the signatures of 130 noted American statesmen, political leaders, business and civic leaders, churchmen and educators. In spite of inclement weather on the day of the Rally (November 13) some 11,000 people thronged into Madison Square Garden. The ensuing march to the United Nations consisted of a train one and a half miles long (14,500 marchers). Radio and Television stations and networks, covering the event, commented favorably on the orderly fashion of the March.

The most challenging thought in a final analysis of this arduous and rewarding project deals with the fact that over half of the participants at the rally and march were people under thirty years of age. It heralds the advent of a new generation of activists, which has no personal memory of Soviet crimes and cannot be accused of harboring feelings of *revanche,* but which is eager and willing to take up the struggle for restoration of independence of Lithuania.

4. *Future Prospects*

In recapitulating the efforts over a period of twenty-six years of the Lithuanians abroad to liberate their homeland, one can discern certain salient features characteristic of most prolonged political emigrations, namely, an intensification of nationalistic idealism. There was and is a large measure of ideological speculation among Lithuanian emigres. Coupling this with a feeling of frustration in not being able to influence international forces, a proliferation of paper parties and competing political institutions arose. In spite of this negative phenomenon, one witnesses a certain rationalization, that is, a rational attempt to avoid duplication and an attempt to consolidate institutions. After so many years, the Lithuanian emigres have not given up hope in establishing a unified all-encompassing political leadership.

The last quarter of a century has had an erosive effect on experienced political institutions and leaders. A number of prominent leaders of the Republic period have died or become superannuated. It is only a matter of time before the remaining diplomatic offices will close with the demise of official representatives. If it wishes to prolong its existence, the Committee for a Free Lithuania will likewise have to admit non-Lithuanian citizens as members.

The Supreme Committee for Liberation of Lithuania has wisely admitted activists of the new generation, but unless it reforms its party representation to admit members of the World Lithuanian Community, it will be faced with a dearth of active and capable workers in the future.

The World Lithuanian Community is making belated attempts to gain the loyalty of the postwar generation; to a large extent, it has succeeded. Recent developments, however, have shown that even Bendruomenė is not a homogenous worldwide organization: both the American and Canadian Bendruomenės, during the January, 1967, political summit conference in New York, demonstrated their desire for political autonomy at the expense of the World Lithuanian Community (PLB) leadership.

President Lyndon B. Johnson's "Peaceful Engagement" speech of October 7, 1966, has conceptualized recent international trends. The era of "peaceful engagement" and "bridge-building" is fraught with uncertainties for the Lithuanian political emigres.

In spite of all vicissitudes and attrition, the Lithuanian political emigration continues to demonstrate extraordinary tenacity and vitality. The postwar generation, to a large extent, is integrated into the organization and leadership of the political movement. The cause will be secure for at least another generation. Unlike the White Russian emigres of an earlier era, the Lithuanian political emigration is keeping pace of recent developments in Soviet-occupied Lithuania and is adjusting to meet changing situations. And in the long run, dynamism, the vast store of political acumen and adaptability, will be the necessary factors in keeping alive an emigre political movement. The Lithuanians abroad will continue to be the spokesmen for Lithuanian sovereignty in a changing world.

The Prospects for Lithuanian Liberation

by STASYS LOZORAITIS

The road to the restoration of Lithuania's sovereignty will be determined by the trend of further developments in the international community, and by the characteristics of the Lithuanian nation. In other words, in considering the prospects of Lithuania's liberation from the Soviet occupation, one must answer the following questions: does the Lithuanian nation have the ability to govern itself, and does the moral-political development of mankind give hope for a favorable direction in international affairs?

There are objective instances which permit one to answer in the affirmative to the above questions.

The restoration of Lithuania's independence, declared by the State Council on February 16, 1918, was not an isolated episode, but the result of an historic process. The Lithuanian nation had a state tradition going back hundreds of years to the time of the Grand Duchy. The annexation of Lithuania by the Russian Empire at the end of the eighteenth century did not stultify this tradition. During the Russian rule, the nation successfully defended its individuality, its language and its beliefs from the attempts at Russification by the Czarist government. The nation also produced new intellectual cadres.

As a result of these developments, after the first World War, which saw the fall of the Russian Empire, it was natural for Lithuania to break away from this empire and to regain its independence. At this point, it should be noted that this event had the universal approval of the nation, without internal upheavals or civil strife which are characteristic of many countries that received their independence after the second World War.

By the same token, the organization of the Lithuanian republic showed that the restored state of independence was not a transient phase, but the product of the normal organic maturation of the nation. Social relations, the economic evolution, the cultural life were established on healthy foundations which guaranteed a continuous and marked progress based on the nation's tireless efforts to win for Lithuania her proper place among the countries of Europe. Progressing along this road, Lithuania was guided by the principles of Western civilization and rejected the guiles of the Soviet revolutionary political, economic and social rules.

At the same time, foreign policy was conducted on a healthy basis; it sought the solution of conflicts by international cooperation and peaceful means. Lithuania did not have any problems with other nations which could not be solved by peaceful and legal means. One of the rules of Lithuania's foreign policy was that in the event of war much could be lost, while peace would guarantee the future of the nation. One must remember that Lithuania won all of the cases to which she was party at the International Court of Justice at the Hague.

Under these conditions, there are arguments to maintain that inasmuch as it depended on the national characteristics of the Lithuanians, the state was capable of guaranteeing further progress. This peaceful evolution was disrupted by the Soviet Union when it invaded and occupied Lithuania in 1940.

However, the general course of development in human political morality, especially in international affairs, is based on the hope that the Soviet occupation of Lithuania, though it still continues, can only be an episode which must eventually end. The course of nineteenth- and twentieth-century history bears witness to the fact that the major idea, which cannot be hindered or stopped in its development, is that of personal and national freedom. Violations of this idea are mere episodes in the course of history. The pulling force of the idea of freedom is such that everytime the threat of enslavement menaces the world, the idea of freedom is used as the most important factor to rouse the people

444

to fight against aggression. This happened during the first World War when President Wilson announced his Fourteen Points, which included the principle of national self-determination. That political step not only decided the war politically, but also determined the peace which lasted until 1939. A similar course occurred during the second World War when the idea of freedom was declared in the Atlantic Charter, which drew to the side of democracy all of the European states then under German or Soviet occupation.

The power of the idea of freedom as a moral-political force is demonstrated by the fact that even the Soviet Union, whose order is the out-and-out rejection and denial of freedom, will never dare to admit this, but, on the contrary, will operate by means of slogans of freedom and will use these slogans to mask its aggressive expansion.

If the democratic world has committed a number of errors, if it was unable to win the peace after it won the war and was unable to force the Soviet Union to respect the Atlantic Charter and the international law then, on the other hand, its consistent refusal to recognize Moscow's aggression against the Baltic States is an event of historic importance. This stand will eventually contribute to the greater implementation of legal principles in international relations.

Another basic problem facing Lithuania's future is whether the idea of freedom be quashed by Communism or will survive and become stronger. During the fifty years since the Bolshevik Revolution, the Russians have been unable to destroy the quest for freedom in the countries taken over by the Soviet Union— and, for that matter, even in Russia itself.

The establishment of nation-states today has reached a degree of intensity and irreversible drive unknown to any other period in history. In 1945, the United Nations comprised forty-five states; there are now 122. This condition points out a significant fact, namely, that the Soviet Union and its captive countries is the only system of nations today based on coercion. It is an island surrounded by independent national states. This island will eventually be unable to hold out against the aspirations of the nations it holds captive to be free and independent of the Soviet Union,

The Soviet Union is essentially a federal state in name only. Its federalism is merely a facade. The equality of nations announced in the Soviet constitutions has no bearing on reality, for in reality the Soviet system is based on the domination by the Russian element. The non-Russian nations in the USSR do not have favorable conditions for improvement of their material well-being or for the development of their national cultures. The nations themselves know that only the formation of independent states can guarantee their existence and well-being. Therefore, independence is an elemental aspiration which conforms to the present-day principle of self-determination, which has become an irresistable force against which even the Soviet Union cannot fight.

Europe is a continent of small and medium-sized states. The idea of regional and Pan-European cooperation is alive among the Baltic peoples. As a free state Lithuania, without any hesitation, would join efforts to create a united European continent on the basis of equality and real freedom.

The power of the USSR today extends to Western Europe, to the Elbe, farther than even the most pessimistic statesman of the West would have dared to speculate prior to the second World War. Yet, no nation occupied by the Soviet Union has freely accepted the rule of Moscow and Communism. The expansion of the Soviet Union was executed by brute force alone, and is maintained by force. By the same token, the Soviet-imposed social and economic systems did not contribute to the well-being of any country and did not grant greater social justice than that country had enjoyed while still free. On the contrary, the Soviet rule has repulsed the people. In addition, if no country has freely accepted Communism, then by the same token, and this is significant, no country, if given the freedom to decide, would decide to maintain the system. The uprising in Lithuania in 1941 and the armed resistance of the Lithuanians from 1944 to 1952 attests to this. The Berlin, Poznan and Budapest uprisings also attest to this.

Finally, the expansion of the Soviet Union has produced negative results as far as cooperation and solidarity in the Social camp is concerned. The monolithic structure established by the

Soviets during Stalin's era did not mean unanimity of tactics for the spread of Communism. Trotsky's conflict with Stalin is the most prominent example of this lack of unity. After this followed the liquidation of Kamenev, Zinoviev and other first-rate Communists; later during Khrushchev's rule, the degradation of Malenkov, Molotov and Bulganin. Even though the accusations brought against these men may have been groundless, the fact that they were made points to the presence of widely divergent political attitudes among the Kremlin leaders, especially during the period that followed Lenin's death. It also suggests that the monolithic nature of Russian communism consisted of nothing more than adherence to the dictates of the majority of party members, along with effective elimination and suppression of opposing views. The same procedure seems to have been adopted by Communist parties throughout the world. The activities of these parties did not interfere with Moscow's monolithic system, since such parties were either under direct Moscow supervision—as in the case of satellite nation parties—or, if operating outside the USSR, without sufficient strength to move against Moscow's decrees.

The spread of the power of the Soviet Union beyond its frontiers brought the inner conflicts of Communism's contradictions to the international level. If there are contradictions among the Russians, then there must also be contradictions in their relations with others. The Russians made a mistake when they ignored historical processes in order to impose with brutality the Soviet system on other countries. Stalin made a mistake by "exporting" Russian Communism to other countries. His successors in the Kremlin are paying—and will continue to pay—the price for this. The deviation of the Yugoslav, Czechoslovak and Rumanian Communist parties from the Moscow line, although it does not touch on principles, shows that the Communist party of the USSR is not all-powerful and is forced to tolerate manifestations of opposition in the Communist camp. These developments must have repercussions in Russia itself, where there is much ferment against the dictatorship. This ferment is noticeable mostly in the cultural field, among the younger generation of intellectuals, writers, artists and scholars who desire spiritual freedom. This

447

movement, however, in spite of the government's repressions, continues to manifest itself through clandestine and through public means of protest, both of which phenomena are new in the Soviet system. These are signs of moral resistance which are important in that they come to the surface at the time of the fiftieth anniversary of the Bolshevik Revolution, when Communism, according to official Soviet affirmations, should have made deep inroads in the Russian character and should have eliminated altogether any resistance. The Kremlin did not succeed in enslaving the human spirit. All assertions that there can be a "Soviet man" are myths. A conflict between Moscow and Red China is also brewing. It is difficult to guess the final outcome of this conflict, but there are no doubts that it will affect profoundly the international political constellation.

The current situation in the Soviet Union supports the hope that the moral-political outlook of the people is gradually turning away from the Soviet System, and leaning towards conditions that would facilitate the liberation of nations heretofore forced to remain under Soviet rule.

One cannot refute the fact that in the field of armaments the Soviet Union has reached significant results. But as far as this question is concerned, there are grounds for waiting until the inevitable development of legal norms as a decisive factor in international relations becomes influential in this paradoxical era of nuclear arms. If the use of nuclear arms threatens the greater part of mankind with destruction, mankind will have no other alternative than the elimination of force from international relations and the ultimate application of law and justice as a means of deciding international disputes. In this manner, the weakening of force as a factor will strengthen the power of law and will lead to the creation of a democratic international order, which will not exclude the liberation of the nations enslaved by the Soviet Union. It will also have to include the restoration of Lithuania's independence.

The Lithuanian nation even today under the harsh conditions of the Soviet occupation and the oppression of the Communist system demonstrates its vitality, national fortitude, creativity and ability to govern its material and spiritual affairs in such a manner as to insure progress. The Lithuanian nation is always ready to return to the community of independent nations, from which it still awaits moral and political support in its quest for liberation and freedom.

Bibliography

THE ORIGINS OF THE LITHUANIAN NATION

I

Avižonis, K., "Lietuvių kilimo iš romėnų teorija XV-XVI a." (Roman theory of Lithuanian origins, 15th-16th cent.), *Praeitis*, vol. III, Kaunas, 1939.

Basanavičius, J., "Apie trakų prygų tautystę ir jų atsikėlimą Lietuvon" (On the Thracian-Prygian nationality and its appearance in Lithuania), *Lietuvių Tauta*, vol. III, Vilnius, 1921.

Bohusz, X., *O początkach narodu i języka Litewskiego* (On the origins of the Lithuanian nation and language), Warsaw, 1808.

Dlugosi sev Longini, *Historiae Poloniae* libri XII, Lipsiae, 1711.

Gabrys, J., *La parenté des langues hittite et lituanienne et la préhistoire*, Genève, 1944.

Hanka, V., *Königinhofer Handschrift. Sammlung altböhmischer lyrisch-epischer Gesänge, nebst anderen altböhmischen Gedichten*, Prague, 1829.

Hartknoch, Chr., *Alt- und neues Preussen oder preussischer Historien zwey Theile*, Frankfurt, 1684.

Jonynas, I., "Vytauto ženklas" / The seal of Vytautas /, *Vairas*, No. 6, Kaunas, 1930.

Kromer, M., *De origine et rebus gestis Polonorum libri XXX*, Basileae, 1568.

Lelewel, J., *Rzut oka na dawność Litewskich narodów i związki ich z Herulami* (A glance at the antiquity of the Lithuanian peoples and their ties with the Heruli), Wilno, 1808.

Lepner, T., *Der preusche Littauer*, Danzig, 1744.

Maciūnas, V., *Lituanistinis sąjūdis XIX amžiaus pradžioje* (The lithuanistic movement at the beginning of the 19th century), Kaunas, 1939.

Michalonis Lituani, *De moribus tartarorum, lituanorum et moschorum*, Basileae, 1615.

Narbutt, T., *Dzieje starożytne narodu Litewskiego* (The ancient history of the Lithuanian people), vols. I-IX, Wilno, 1835-1841.

Praetorius, M., "Historische Nachricht von der alten Preussischen Sprache," *Acta Borussica*, vol. II, Königsberg, 1731.

Puzinas, J., "Aušros laikotarpio archeologija" (Archeology in the period of Aušra), *Vairas*, No. 12, Kaunas, 1935.

Puzinas, J., "Lietuvių kilmės teorijos amžių būvyje" (The theories of Lithuanian origin in the course of history), *Literatūra, Lietuvių literatūros, meno ir mokslo metraštis* / Literature.Yearbook of Lithuanian Literature, Art and Science /, vol. I, Chicago, 1950.

Puzinas, J., "T. Narbutas mūsų prosenovės tyrinėtojas" (T. Narbutas, the investigator of Lithuanian antiquity), *Naujoji Romuva*, No. 7, Kaunas, 1936.

Puzinas, J., *Vorgeschichtsforschung und Nationalbewusstsein in Litauen*, Kaunas, 1935.

Račkus, A. M., *Guthones (the Goths) Kinsmen of the Lithuanian people*, Chicago, 1929.

Ruhig, P., *Von der Ähnlichkeit der litauischen Sprache mit den orientalischen Sprachen, insbesondere der hebräischen*, Königsberg, ca. 1781.

Stemmermann, P. H., *Die Anfänge der deutschen Vorgeschichtsforschung*, Leipzig, 1934.

Stryjkowski, M., *Kronika Polska, Litewska, Żmódzka i wszystkiej Rusi* (Chronicle of Poland, Lithuania, Samogitia and all Russia), Königsberg, 1582.

Vincentii, Magistri, Episcopi Cracoviensis, *Chronica Polonorum sive originale regum et principium Poloniae*, Cracoviae, 1862.

Watson, K. F., "Über den lettischen Völkerstamm," *Jahresverhandlungen der kurländischen Gesellschaft für Literatur und Kunst*, II, Mitau, 1822.

II

Bezzenberger, A., "Bemerkungen zu dem Werke von A. Bielenstein über die ethnologische Gestaltung des Lettenlandes," *Bulletin de l'Académie Impériale des Sciences de St. Pétersbourg*, vol. XXXVI, 1895.

Būga, K., *Aisčių praeitis vietų vardų šviesoje* (The Aistian past in the light of place-names), Kaunas, 1924.

Būga, K., "Die litauisch-weissrussischen Beziehungen und ihr Alter," *Zeitschrift für slavische Philologie*, 1, Leipzig, 1924.

Būga, K., *Kalba ir senovė* (Language and antiquity), I, Kaunas, 1922.

Būga, K., "Kann man Keltenspuren auf baltischem Gebiet nachweisen? (Aus Anlass der Arbeiten Schachmatovs über keltisch-slavische und finnisch-keltische Beziehungen), *Rocznik Slawistyczny*, vol. VI, Kraków, 1913.

Būga, K., "Šis-tas iš lietuvių ir indoeuropiečių senovės" (Remarks about the Lithuanian and Indoeuropean antiquity), *Tauta ir Žodis*, vol. 2, Kaunas, 1924.

Grinblat, M. J., "K voprosu ob uchastii v etnogeneze belorusov" (On the question on the role of the Lithuanians in the ethnogenesis of the Byelorussians), *Voprosy etnicheskoj istorii narodov Pribaltiki*, vol. I, Moscow, 1959.

Kiparsky, V., "The earliest contacts of the Russians with the Finns and the Balts," *Oxford Slavonic Papers*, vol. III, Oxford, 1952.

Kochubinskii, A. A., "Territorija doistoricheskoj Litvy" (The territory of pre-historic Lithuania), *Zhurnal Ministerstva Narodnogo Prosvesh-chenija*, vol. CCCXIX, Petersburg, 1897.

Pogodin, A. L., *Iz istorii slavianskikh peredvizhenii* (On the history of the Slavonic migrations), Warsaw, 1901.

Puzinas, J., "Kalbotyra apie lietuvių protėvynę" (Linguistical research on the homeland of the Lithuanians), *Lietuva*, No. 1, New York, 1952.

Schachmatov, A., "Zu den ältesten slavisch-keltischen Beziehungen," *Archiv für slavische Philologie*, 33, Berlin, 1911.

Sobolevskii, A. I., "Gde zhila Litva?" (Where did Lithuania exist?), *Izvestija Imperatorskoj Akademii Nauk*, Series VI, No. 12-18, St. Petersburg, 1911.

Thomsen, V., *Beröringer mellem de finske og de baltiske / litausk-lettiske / sprog* (Relations between the Finnish and the Baltic /Lithuanian-Latvian/ languages), Kopenhagen, 1890.

Toporov, V. N. and Trubachev, O. N., *Lingvisticheskii analiz gidronimov verkhnego podneprov'ja* (Linguistic analysis of river names of the Upper Dnieper basin), Moscow, 1962.

Trubetzkoj, N., "Zum Flussnamen *Upa*," *Zeitschrift für slavische Philologie*, 14, Leipzig, 1932.

Vasmer, M., "Beiträge zur historischen Völkerkunde Osteuropas. I. Die Ostgrenze der baltischen Stämme," *Sitzungsberichte der Preussischen Akademie der Wissenschaften*, Phil.-Hist. Klasse, Berlin, 1932.

Vasmer, M., "Die alten Bevölkerungsverhältnisse Russland im Lichte der Sprachvorschung," *Vorträge und Schriften der Preussischen Akademie der Wissenschaften*, No. 5, Berlin, 1941.

Vasmer, M., *Wörterbuch der russischen Gewässernamen*, Lieferung 1, Berlin-Wiesbaden, 1960.

III

Alseikaitė-Gimbutienė, M., *Die Bestattung in Litauen in der vorgeschichtlichen Zeit*, Tübingen, 1946.

Antoniewicz, J., *The Sudovians*, Białystok, 1962.

Arbusow, L., *Frühgeschichte Lettlands*, Riga, 1933.

Balodis, Fr., *Det äldsta Lettland* (The old Latvia), Uppsala, 1940.

Balodis, Fr., "Die baltisch-finnisch-ugrische Grenze in vorgeschichtlicher Zeit," *Mémoire de la Société finno-ougrienne*, vol. LXVII, 1933.

Balodis, Fr., "L'ancienne frontière slavo-latvienne," *Conférence des historiens des états de l'Europe Orientale et du mond slave*, Varsovie, 1928.

Balodis, Fr., *La Lettonie du 9me au 12me siècle*, Riga, 1936.

Biezais, H., *Die Religionsquellen der baltischen Völker und die Ergebnisse der bisherigen Forschungen*, Uppsala, 1954.

Bosch-Gimpera, P., *Les Indo-Européens, problèmes archéologiques*, Paris, 1961.

Engel, C., "Die baltische Besiedlung Weiss-und Mittelrusslands in vorgeschichtlicher Zeit," *Literarum Societas Esthonica 1838-1938; Liber Saecularis*, Tartu, 1938.

Engel, C., *Einführung in die vorgeschichtliche Kultur des Memellandes*, Memel, 1931.

Engel, C., *Vorgeschichte der altpreussischen Stämme. Untersuchungen über Siedlungsstetigkeit und Kulturgruppen im vorgeschichtlichen Ostpreussen*, Königsberg Pr., 1935.

Engel, C., and La Baume, W., *Kulturen und Völker der Frühzeit im Preussenlande*, Königsberg Pr., 1937.

Gaerte, W., *Urgeschichte Ostpreussens*, Königsberg Pr., 1929.

Gimbutas, M., *The Balts*, London, 1963.

Gimbutas, M., *The Prehistory of Eastern Europe. Part I: Mesolithic, Neolithic, and Copper Age cultures in Russia and the Baltic area*, Peabody Museum, Harvard University, Bulletin No. 20, 1956.

Gimbutas, M., *The Prehistory of Eastern Europe. Part II: Bronze Age cultures in Eastern Central Europe, the Baltic area and Russia*, Peabody Museum, Harvard University, Bulletin No. 21, 1963.

Harmjanz, H., "Volkskunde und Siedlungsgeschichte Altpreussens," *Neue Deutsche Forschungen*, vol. 100, Berlin, 1936.

Hoffmann, J., *Die spätheidnische Kultur des Memellandes (10.-12. Jahrh. n. d. Zw.)*, Königsberg Pr., 1941.

Indreko, R., *Die mittlere Steinzeit in Estland. Mit einer Übersicht über die Geologie des Kunda-Sees von K. Orviku*, Stockholm, 1948.

Jablonskytė-Rimantienė, R., "Kai kurie Lietuvos paleolito klausimai" (Several questions on the Paleolithic in Lithuania), *Lietuvos Mokslų Akademijos Darbai*, Series A 1 /16/, Vilnius, 1964.

Jablonskytė-Rimantienė, R., "Maglemozinė ankstyvojo mezolito stovykla Maksimonyse IV" (The Maglemose side at Maksimonys IV in the early Mesolithic), *Lietuvos Mokslų Akademijos Darbai*, Series A 3/22/, Vilnius, 1966.

Jablonskytė-Rimantienė, R., "Paleolitinės titnago dirbtuvės Ežerynų kaime" (Paleolithic flint-works in the village of Ežerynai), *Lietuvos Mokslų Akademijos Darbai*, Series A 2/21/, Vilnius, 1966.

Janits, L. J., "K voprosu ob etnicheskoj prinadlezhnosti neoliticheskogo naselenija Estonskoj SSR" (A contribution to the question of the ethnogenesis of the Neolithic people in Estonia), *Voprosy etnicheskoj istorii Estonskogo naroda,* Tartu, 1956.

Jaskiewicz, W. C., "A study in Lithuanian mythology. Jan Łasicki's Samogitian gods," *Studi Baltici,* vol. IX, N. S. I, 1952.

Kamiński, A., *Jaćwież. Terrytorium, ludność, stosunki gospodarcze i społeczne* (Jatvingia. Territory, population, economy and social structure), Lódź, 1953.

Kilian, L., *Haffküstenkultur und Ursprung der Balten,* Bonn, 1955.

Kiparsky, V., *Die Kurenfrage,* Helsinki, 1939.

Kulikauskas, P., Kulikauskienė, R. and Tautavičius, A., *Lietuvos archeologijos bruožai* (An outline of the archeology in Lithuania), Vilnius, 1961.

Kulikauskienė, R. and Rimantienė, R., "Senovės lietuvių papuošalai" (Ornaments of ancient Lithuanians); *Lietuvių liaudies menas* (Lithuanian Folk-Art), vol. I, Vilnius, 1958, vol. II, Vilnius, 1966.

Łowmiański, H., "The ancient Prussians," *Baltic Institute,* London, 1937.

Mannhardt, W., "Letto-preussische Götterlehre," *Lettisch-Literarische Gesellschaft,* vol. 21, Riga, 1936.

Moora, H., *Die Eisenzeit in Lettland,* vol. I, 1929, vol. II, 1938.

Nagevičius, V., "Mūsų pajūrio medžiaginė kultūra VIII-XIII amž" (The material culture along the Baltic coast in 8th-13th centuries), *Senovė,* vol. I, Kaunas, 1935.

Nerman, B., *Die Verbindungen zwischen Skandinavien und dem Ostbaltikum in der jüngeren Eisenzeit,* Stockholm, 1929.

Nerman, B., *Grobin-Seeburg Ausgrabungen und Funde,* Stockholm, 1958.

Nikolskaja, T. N., "Kultura plemen bassejna verkhnej Oki v I tysiacheletii n. e." (The culture of the upper Oka tribes in the first millennium A. D.), *Materialy i Issledovanija po Arkheologii SSSR,* No. 72, Moscow, 1959.

Puzinas, J., "Aisčiai istorinių šaltinių šviesoje" (Aistians in the light of history), *Aidai,* No. 12, 1948.

Puzinas, J., "Die Flügelfibel in Litauen," *Ur-und Frühgeschichte als historische Wissenschaft, Festschrift Ernst Wahle,* Heidelberg, 1950.

Puzinas, J., "In the search of the origin of the Lithuanian people," *Lituanus,* No. 1/10/, Brooklyn, N. Y., 1957.

Puzinas, J., "Naujausių proistorinių tyrinėjimų duomenys /1918-1938 metų Lietuvos proistorinių tyrinėjimų apžvalga" (Results of archaeological excavations in Lithuania from 1918 to 1938), *Senovė,* vol. IV, Kaunas, 1938.

Puzinas, J., "Sūduva naujausių archeologinių tyrinėjimų šviesoje" (Sudovia in the light of the recent archaeological excavations), *Aidai,* No. 4, Brooklyn, N. Y., 1965.

Puzinas, J., "Sūduvių problema" (The Sudovian question), *Aidai,* No. 2, 1965.

Schmittlein, R., *Études sur la nationalité des Aestii,* vol. I, Bade, 1948.

Spekke, A., *The ancient amber routes and the geographical discovery of the eastern Baltic,* Stockholm, 1957.

Šturms, E., "Der ostbaltische Bernsteinhandel in der vorgeschichtlichen Zeit," *Commentationes Balticae,* vol. I, Bonn, 1954.

Šturms, E., "Die ältere Bronzezeit im Ostbaltikum," *Vorgeschichtliche Forschungen,* 10, Berlin, 1936.

Šturms, E., "Regionale Unterschiede in den Beziehungen zwischen dem Ostbaltikum und Skandinavien in der Bronzezeit," *Contributions of Baltic University,* No. 53, Pinneberg, 1947.

Tarakanova, S. A. and Terent'eva, L. N., (ed.), "Voprosy etnicheskoj istorii narodov pribaltiki" (Problems of the ethnogenesis of the East Baltic peoples), *Trudy Pribaltiskoj Ob'edinennoj Kompleksnoj Ekspedicii,* vol. I, Moscow, 1959.

INDEPENDENT LITHUANIA

To the readers interested in delving into the problems of Lithuania's past and present, the bibliography compiled by Professor Jonas Balys is recommended. The name of the work is *Lithuania and Lithuanians, A Selected Bibliography,* New York, N. Y., 1961, published for the Lithuanian Research Institute by Frederick A. Praeger, New York. By the same token, the multivolume *Lietuvių Enciklopedija* (Lithuanian Encyclopedia) in Lithuanian has been completed. This set, being published in Boston, Massachusetts, contains many articles of value to the specialist as well as bibliographies of sources in various languages. In addition to these two works, the following is a list of major publications dealing with all facets of the history of the Lithuanian Republic.

Literature about the February 16, 1918, Declaration of Independence and the first years of that period includes:

"Vasario 16 d. aktas," *Lietuvių Enciklopedija,* Vol. XXXII (Boston).

B. Colliander, *Die Beziehungen zwischen Litauen und Deutschland waehrend der Okkupation 1915-1918,* Turku, 1935.

P. Klimas, *Der Werdegang des litauischen Staates,* 1919.

G. Linde, *Die deutsche Politik in Litauen im ersten Weltkrieg,* Wiesbaden, 1965.

E. Ludendorff, *Meine Kriegserinnerungen,* Berlin, 1919.

A. E. Senn, *The Emergence of Modern Lithuania,* New York, 1959.

Concerning the relations with Poland and the Vilnius Question, see "Vilniaus byla," *Lietuvių Enciklopedija,* Vol. XXXIV (Boston). The Lithuanian Ministry of Foreign Affairs published a collection of official documents in Kaunas under the title *Conflit Polono-Lithuanien, Question de Vilna 1918-1924* (Kaunas, 1924).

Other works include:

A. E. Senn, *The Great Powers, Lithuania and the Vilna Question, 1920-1928*, Leiden, 1966.

P. Lossowski, *Stosunki Polsko-Litewskie w latach 1918-1920*, Warsaw, 1966.

Concerning Lithuania's international recognition and the evolution of further relations with Poland, some of the material is contained in the above-mentioned *Conflit Polono-Lithuanien*. Other materials are contained in:

L. Natkevičius, *Aspect politique et juridique du différend Polono-Lithuanien*, Paris, 1930.

A. N. Tarulis, *American-Baltic Relations 1918-1922, the Struggle over Recognition*, Washington, D.C., 1965.

See the following articles in the Lithuanian Encyclopedia on the Lithuanian State Constitutions, Constituent Assembly, land reform, etc.:

"Konstitucija," L.E., Vol. XII.

"Lietuvos Bankas," L.E., Vol. XVI.

"Litas," L.E., Vol. XVI.

"Seimas," L.E., Vol. XXVII.

"Žemės reforma," L.E., Vol. XXXV.

For the Lithuanian Constitution see also A. Gerutis, *Die staatsrechtliche Stellung des Staatsoberhauptes in Litauen, Lettland und Estland*, Kaunas, 1935.

On land reform:

J. Krikščiūnas, *Agriculture in Lithuania*, Kaunas, 1938.

J. Krikščiūnas, *Die litauische Landwirtschaft*, Kaunas, 1933.

On Lithuanian currency and economic life:

K. Sruoga, *Die Wirtschaft der Republik Litauen und ihre Notenemission*, Kaunas, 1930.

A. Simutis, *The Economic Reconstruction of Lithuania after 1918*, New York, 1942.

J. Karys, *Nepriklausomos Lietuvos pinigai* (Currency of Independent Lithuania), New York, 1953.

On the union of the Klaipėda district with the Lithuanian State, see:

"Klaipėda," L.E., Vol. XII.

"Klaipėdos sukilimas," L.E., Vol. XII.

"Klaipėdos krašto konvencija ir statutas," L.E., Vol. XII.

The Lithuanian Ministry of Foreign Affairs published two volumes of official documents entitled *The Question of Memel*, London, 1924.

The Foreign Ministry also published two volumes in French: *Question de Memel*, Kaunas, 1924. A. Šapoka, *Lietuvos istorija*, Fellbach, 1950.

Concerning the internal policies of Lithuania, relations between the

457

political parties, and the December 17, 1926, *coup d'état* and its effects, see:

"Perversmas," L.E., Vol. XXII.

"Seimas," L.E., Vol. XXVII.

"Tautininkai," L.E., Vol. XXX.

A. Merkelis, *Antanas Smetona,* New York, 1964.

Mykolas Sleževičius, Chicago, 1954.

Pirmasis Nepriklausomos Lietuvos dešimtmetis, Kaunas, 1930.

Concerning church-state relations see:

L. Natkevičius, *Op. cit.*

"Katalikų Veikimo Centras," L.E., Vol. XI.

"Konkordatas," L.E., Vol. XI.

J. Prunskis, *Comparative Law, Ecclesiastical and Civil in the Lithuanian Concordate,* Washington, D.C. 1945.

Concerning cooperation between the Baltic States see:

B. Kazlauskas, *L'Entente Baltique,* Paris, 1939.

Concerning the Klaipėda Question and the German Ultimatum:

P. Mačiulis, *Trys ultimatumai,* Brooklyn, N. Y., 1962.

"Neumanno ir Sasso byla," L.E., Vol. XX.

The German thesis is defended in E. A. Plieg, *Das Memelland 1920-1939,* Wurzburg, 1962.

Concerning Lithuania's relations with the Soviet Union and the Soviet Ultimatum:

A. N. Tarulis, *Soviet Policy toward the Baltic States, Estonia, Latvia, Lithuania, 1918-1940,* Notre Dame, Ind., 1959.

"Inkorporacija," L.E., Vol. VIII.

Concerning Lithuania's education and cultural life:

"Literatūra," L.E., Vol. XVI.

"Mokykla," L.E., Vol. XIX.

"Vytauto Didžiojo Kultūros Muziejus,: Vol. XXXIV.

"Vytauto Didžiojo Universitetas," L.E., Vol. XXXIV.

"Žemės Ūkio Akademija," L.E., Vol. XXXV.

Concerning the First Soviet occupation (1940-41), the Studies Bureau of Kaunas published three volumes entitled *Lietuvių Archyvas, Bolševizmo metai* (Kaunas, 1942). (A new edition was prepared by Dr. J. Prunskis in Brooklyn, N. Y. in 1952.)

Concerning the German occupation, 1941-44 see:

J. Audėnas, *Twenty Years Struggle for Freedom of Lithuania,* New York, 1963.

"Ostlandas," L.E., Vol. XXI.

Soviet Lithuania published a number of works on the German occupation, but the majority of them are of a polemical nature. A good example of their work is *Hitlerinė okupacija Lietuvoje,* Vilnius, 1961.

German military operations in the Baltic States and the plans of the Nazis are given in W. Haupt, *Baltikum 1941, Die Geschichte eines ungelösten Problems, Neckargemünd,* 1963.

The Soviet occupation since 1944 is included in:

V. S. Vardys, *Lithuania under the Soviets. Portrait of a Nation, 1940-1965,* New York, 1965.

A. Gerutis, *Gedanken zur sowjetischen Russifizierungs-politik im Baltikum,* Königstein im Taunus, 1966.

"Genocidas," L.E., Vol. VII.

Liber Annalis Instituti Baltici, *Acta Baltica,* Königstein im Taunus, 1961-1967.

Lituanus, Lithuanian Quarterly, Chicago, 1955-1967.

The Baltic Review, New York, 1953-1967.

Dr. J. Savasis, *The War Against God in Lithuania,* New York, 1966.

LITHUANIAN RESISTANCE, 1940-52

Jonas Aistis, *Laisvės Kovų Dainos,* New York, 1962.

Kazys Ambrozaitis, "Aukos ir vilties dienos," *Į Laisvę,* No. 10, 1956.

Juozas Audėnas, "Vyriausias Lietuvos Išlaisvinimo Komitetas," *Lietuvių Enciklopedija,* XXXIV (Boston, 1966).

"Baltaraištininkai," *Mažoji Lietuviškoji Tarybinė Enciklopedija,* I (Vilnius, 1966).

Baltiska Nyheter, September 26, 1944.

B. Baranauskas, "Buržuaziniai nacionalistai-hitlerininkų talkininkai," *Tarybinis Mokytojas,* December 21, 24, 28, 1961 (Vilnius).

Hitlerininkų penktoji kolona Lietuvoje, Vilnius, 1961.

Major General Bartašiūnas, *Lietuvos TSR Vidaus Reikalų, Liaudies Komisaro Įsakymas,* February 15, 1946.

Juozas Brazaitis, "Insurrection Against the Soviets," *Lituanus,* No. 3, 1955.

"Lietuvių Aktyvistų Frontas," *Lietuvių Enciklopedija,* XVI (Boston, 1958).

"Partizanai," *Lietuvių Enciklopedija,* XXII (Boston, 1960).

"Partizanai antrosios Sovietų okupacijos metu," *Į Laisvę,* No. 24 (61), April, 1960.

"Rezistencija Lietuvoje," *Lietuva,* No. 8, 1956.

"Sukilimas ir tauta," *Aidai,* No. 2, 1962.

Algirdas Budreckis, "1941 metų tautinis sukilimas," *Į Laisvę,* No. 37-38 (74-75), June, 1965.

Thomas Chase, *The Story of Lithuania,* New York, 1946.

M. Chienas, K. Smigelskis, E. Uldukis, *Vanagai iš anapus,* Vilnius, 1960.

Communist Aggression Investigation, "Testimony of Colonel Burlitski," *Fourth Interim Report,* Washington, D.C., 1954.

Adolfas Damušis, "Kaip sukilome prieš bolševikus 1941 metais," *Į Laisvę,* No. 3, 1954.

Juozas Daumantas, *Partizanai už Geležinės Uždangos,* Chicago, 1950. *Par-tizanai* (Second Revised Edition), Chicago, 1962.

Stasys Daunys, "The Development of the Resistance and the National Revolt against the Soviet Regime in Lithuania in 1940-41," *Lituanus,* No. 1, 1962.

Dokladnaia zapiska o raspostranenii kontrrevoliutsionnykh litovsk na terri-torii Litovskoi SSR, April 14, 1941.

Karolis Drunga, "Antinacinės rezistencijos organizacija," *Santarvė,* No. 4-5, 1954.

Faktai kaltina, *Žudikai bažnyčios prieglobstyje,* II, Vilnius, 1960.

Kazys Gečys, *Katalikiškoji Lietuva,* Chicago, 1946.

Algimantas P. Gureckas, "The National Resistance During the German Occupation," *Lituanus,* No. 1-2, 1962.

E. J. Harrison, *Lithuania's Fight for Freedom,* New York, 1952.

"How the Kremlin Treats Its Own," *Readers Digest,* October, 1954.

Zenonas Ivinskis, "Lithuania During the War: Resistance Against the Soviet and Nazi Occupants," in V. Stanley Vardys, *Lithuania Under the Soviets,* New York, 1965.

Kazys Jurgaitis, "Ginkluotos rezistencijos žygiai laisvę ginant," *Į Laisvę,* No. 24 (61), April, 1960.

Albert Kalme, *Total Terror,* New York, 1948.

Mykolas Krupavičius, "Šiandieninė lietuvių tautos kova už laisvę," *Met-raštis 1950,* Kennebunkport, Maine, 1949.

Laisvės Kovotojas No. 21 (March 11, 1944) (Nazi Falsification).

Lietuvių Aktyvistų Fronto Vadovybė, *Lietuvai IšlaisvintiNurodymai,* Ber-lin, March 24, 1941.

Lithuanian American Information Center, *Lithuanian Bulletin,* Vol. III-IX (1945-51).

Stasys Lušys, "The Emergence of a Unified Resistance Movement in Lith-uania, 1940-1943," *Lituanus,* No. 4, December, 1963.

"The Origin of the Supreme Committee for Liberation of Lithuania," in J. Audėnas, *Twenty Years Struggle for Freedom of Lithuania,* New York, 1963.

Benediktas Maciuika, *Lithuania in the Last 30 Years,* New Haven, 1956.

Antanas Mažiulis, "Rezistencija," *Lietuvių Enciklopedija,* XXV, Boston, 1961.

Vincas Natkus, "Partizanas herojinėj ir realistinėj buity," *Į Laisvę,* No. 22 (9), October, 1960.

Nepriklausoma Lietuva, No. 17-18 (April 29, 1944), No. 9 (21) (June 1, 1943), No. 29-30 (October 13, 1943).

O kontrrevoliutsionnykh litovskakh za aprel-mai mesiatsy 1941 goda.

Kazys Pakštas, *Lithuania and World War II,* Chicago, 1947.

"Partizanų Vadas Juozas Lukša-Daumantas," *Į Laisvę* No. 28 (65), April, 1962.

460

K. Pelėkis, *Genocide, Lithuania's Threefold Tragedy*, Venta, 1949.

Perkūnas, *In the Name of the Lithuanian People*, Wolfberg, 1945.

J. Petruitis, *Lithuania Under the Sickle and Hammer*, Cleveland, 1945.

Vladas Ramojus, "Jauno vokietuko odisėja Lietuvoje," *Draugas*, May 26, 1959.

"Lietuva partizanų tinkle," *Draugas*, May 7, 1959.

Vincas Rastenis, "Lithuania : Three Years After Stalin," *Lituanus*, No. 2 (7), June, 1956.

Stasys Raštikis, *Kovose dėl Lietuvos*, II, Los Angeles, 1957.

"Recent Reports of Anti-Soviet Activity in Lithuania," *Lituanus*, No. 1-2, 1962.

Thomas Remeikis, "The Armed Struggle Against the Sovietization of Lithuania After 1944," *Lituanus*, No. 1-2, 1962.

N. E. Sūduvis, *Ein kleines Volk wird ausgeloescht*, Zuerich, 1947. *Vienų Vieni*, New York, 1964.

Svetur, Stockholm, 1945.

K. V. Tauras, *Guerrilla Warfare on the Amber Coast*, New York, 1962.

Oskaras Urbonas, "Vietinė Rinktinė, 1944," *Karys*, 1951-1952.

V. Stanley Vardys, "The Partisan Movement in Postwar Lithuania," *Lithuania Under the Soviets*, New York, 1965.

Romas Vaštokas, "The Image of the Partisan," *Lituanus*, Winter, 1966.

Julius Vidžgiris, "Lietuvių Pasipriešinimas Okupantams," *Į Laisvę*, No. 22 (9), October, 1960.

Henrikas Žemelis, *Okupantų Replėse*, 1947.

J. Žiugžda, ed., *Lietuvos TSR Istorija*, Vilnius, 1958.

Stasys Žymantas, "Aktyviosios Rezistencijos Tragedija," *Santarvė*, No. 4 (London, 1953).

Stasys Žymantas, "Karas, kurio niekas neskelbė," *Dirva*, No. 88, August-September, 1965.

"Lithuania Militans," *Lituanus*, No. , June, 1956.

"Twenty Years Resistance," *Lithuanus*, No. 2, 1960.

Pranas Zundė, "Lietuvos Rezistencija," (Lecture, May 5, 1962).

LIBERATION ATTEMPTS FROM ABROAD

ACEN File No. 4.351, *Lithuanian Delegation to ACEN, 1954-1961.*

ACEN File No. 4.350, *Committee for a Free Lithuania*, 1955, 1966.

Americans for Congressional Action to Free the Baltic States, *News Bulletin*, April, 1964 - April, 1966.

Amerikos Lietuvių Bendruomenė, 1957-1963.

Assembly of Captive European Nations, *First Session*, (New York) September 20, 1954 - February 11, 1955.

Audėnas, Juozas, *Twenty Years Struggle for Freedom of Lithuania* (New York, 1963).

461

Briggs, Herbert W., "Non-Recognition in the Courts : the Ships of the Baltic Republics," *American Journal of International Law,* XXXVII (1943).

Budreckis, Algirdas, "Idea That Caught Fire," *ACEN NEWS,* No. 121 January-February, 1966; "Lietuviškoji Politika," *Mūsų Vytis,* April, 1965; "Prezidentas Semtona Tremtyje," *Dirva,* January 18, 1964; *The Lithuanian National Revolt of 1941* (Boston, 1968); "Žygis į Jungtines Tautas," *Tėvynės Sargas,* No. 1 (27) 1966.

Chevrier, Bruno, "The International Status of the Baltic States," *The Baltic Review,* Vol. 1, No. 6. (Stockholm, 1946).

Churchill, Winston S., *The Hinge of Fate* (Boston, 1950).

"Dokumentų šviesoje," *Į Laisvę,* No. 1-38 (1953).

Dzikas, Stasys, "Pabaltijo Klausimas JAV Kongrese," *Tėvynės Sargas,* No. 1 (26), 1965.

Estonian Information Centre, *The Baltic States and the Soviet Union* (Stockholm, 1962).

Gečys, Kazys, *Katalikiškoji Lietuva* (Chicago, 1946).

Harrison, E. J., *Lithuania's Fight for Freedom* (New York, 1952).

Jurevičius, Juozas, "Amerikos Lietuvių Tautinės Sąjungos Veikla Laiko Perspektyvoje," *Dirva,* Nr. 30-3.

Kaminskas, Juozas, "Laisvinimo Organizacijos Klausimu," *Lietuva,* No. 2 (October-December, 1952).

Kasulaitis, Algirdas, "LF Bičiuliai Laisvinimo Klausimais," *Jaunimo Žygiai* (22-23), 1960.

Krivickas, Domas, "Lithuania's Struggle Against Aggression and Subjugation," in J. Audėnas, *Twenty Years' Struggle for Freedom of Lithuania* (New York, 1963).

Krupavičius, Mykolas, "Šiandieninė Lietuvių Tautos Kova už Laisvę," in Rev. L. Andriekus, *Metraštis 1950* (Boston, 1949).

Lietuvių Frontas ir Lietuvių Fronto Bičiuliai (Į Laisvę leidinys No. 1, 1958).

Lietuvių Kongresui Washingtone Vykstančiam 1964 m. birželio 26-28 Amerikos Lietuvių Tarybos Pranešimas.

Lithuanian American Council, *Lithuanian Bulletin,* (New York, 1945-1951).

Lithuanian Legation, *Current News on the Lithuanian Situation,* August 3, 1940-1954; *The Lithuanian Situation,* 1955 - July-December, 1957.

Lukacs, John, *A New History of the Cold War* (New York, Archer Books, 1966).

Lušys, Stasys, "Lietuvių Politinių Grupių Antrasis Apsijungimas Lietuvos Išlaisvinimo Darbui," *Tėvynės Sargas,* No. 1 (26) 1965 - No. 1 (27) 1966.

Merkelis, Aleksandras, *Antanas Smetona* (New York, 1964).

Michelsonas, Stasys, *Lietuvių Išeivija Amerikoje* (Boston, 1961).

Pakštas, Kazys, *Lithuania and World War II* (Chicago, 1947); *The Lithuanian Situation* (Chicago, 1941).

Pasaulio Lietuvių Bendruomenės Seimo Vadovas (New York, 1958).

Politinės Lietuvių konferencijos, įvykusios 1954 m. gegužės 18-19 d.d. New Yorke, Baltic Freedom House Protokolas.

Puzinas, Jonas, *Lithuanians in the Mosaic of Canada* (Toronto, 1967).

Raila, Bronys, *Tamsiausia prieš aušrą* (Chicago, 1960).

Raštikis, Stasys, *Kovose dėl Lietuvos*, II (Los Angeles, 1957).

Repečka, Juozas, *Der gegenwaertige voelkerrechtliche Status der baltischen Staaten unter besonderer Beruecksichtigung der der diplomatischen Vorgeschichte der Eingliederung dieser Staaten in die Sowjetunion* (Goettingen, 1950).

Riismandel, Vaimo J., "The Continued Legal Existence of the Baltic States," *The Baltic Review* No. 12 (1957).

Roosaare, Evald, "Consular Relations Between the United States and the Baltic States," *The Baltic Review*, No. 27 (June, 1964).

Sidzikauskas, Vaclovas, "Baltic States in the Polycentric Era," *The Baltic Review*, No. 27 (June, 1964); "25 Years of Baltic Freedom Struggle," *ACEN NEWS*. No. 120 (November-December, 1965).

Simutis, Anicetas, *Lithuanian World Directory* (New York, 1958).

Škirpa, Kazys, *Sukiliminės Vyriausybės Genezė* (Washington, D.C., June 15, 1961).

"Ties mūsų nesusipratimais," *Santarvė*, No. 4-5 (April-May, 1954).

United States Department of State, *Department of State Bulletin*, III, No. 27 (July 27, 1940).

United States Department of State, *Foreign Relations of the United States 1940*, I.

Vaitiekūnas, Vytautas, "Amerikos Lietuvių Taryba," *Lietuva*, No. 2 "October-December, 1952); "Homo Diplomaticus," *Lietuva*, No. 3 (January-March, 1953); "Kersteno Komisijos Darbų Rezultatai," *Lietuva* No. 7: "Lietuvos Laisvės Komitetas," *Lietuva*, No. 2 (October-December, 1952); *Lithuania* (New York, 1965); "Patariamoji Lietuvių Grupė, *"Lietuva*, No. 1, (1953).

Vyriausio Lietuvos Išlaisvinimo Komiteto Statutas (Mimeographed Draft).

VLIKO Grupių Komisijos Pranešimas (Cleveland, 1958).

Index

465

466

Douglas, Paul H., 437
Dovydaitis, Pranas, 191
Draugas, 408
Draugija, 142
Drevenca River, '64
Druskininkai, 327
Dukštas, 32
Dulksnys, Kostas, 282
Dulles, John Foster, 412, 420, 431

E

1863 Revolt, 125-129
1831 Revolt, 120-125
Eisenhower, Dwight David, 411-412, 419, 431
Eolians, the, 5
Erdvilas, 45
Estonians, the, 48, *passim*

F

Finno-Ugrics, the, 16, *passim*
Foch, Marshall, 167-168
Fourteen Points (of Wilson), 445
Freedom Fighters Union (LLKS), 410 *et seq.*
French Revolution, the, 108, 112, 120
Friends of the Lithuanian Front, 426
Funnel Beaker Culture, the, 23, 26

G

Gabrys-Paršaitis, Juozas, 9
Gaidžiūnas, Balys, 345
Gaigalaitis, Rev. Vincas, 151
Gailius, Viktoras, 210
Galdape, 38
Galindians, the, 20, *passim*
Galvanauskas, Ernestas, 192, 197, 214, 267, 397
Gardinas, '62, *passim*
Garmus, Antanas, 276
Gaušas, Antanas, 315
Gediminas, 50, 52-55, 67
Gediminas Dynasty, 50, *passim*
"Gediminas Pillars," the, 385
Gedvilas, Mečys, 267, 269, 277, 297, 311
Georgenburg (Jurbarkas), 47
Gepidae, the, 3
German occupation (post WWI), 145 *et seq.*
German Quendlinburg yearbooks, 43
German Red Cross, the, 291
Germantas-Meškauskas, Pranas, 334
Gerutis, Albertas, 399

Gestapo, the, 338, *passim*
Gibaud v. de Medem (1951), 414
Girdvainis, Stasys, 396, 404
Girėnas, Stasys, 264
Golden Horde, '63, 70
Goths, the, 9-10, 33
Grand Duchy of Lithuania, 50, *passim*
Grand Vilnius Assembly, 135-140, *passim*
Grant-Suttie, Colonel, 404
Graužinis, Kazys, 404, 415
Great Vilnius Assembly of 1905, 192
Greeks, the, 1, 4-5
Grigaitis, Dr. Pijus, 405, 408, 417, 431
Grinius, Kazys, 197, 217, 220, 33^, 418
Grobina, Latvia, 35
Grundstuckgesellschaft, 291
Gustav Adolf, King, 90
Guthones (Goths) Kinsmen of the Lithuanian People, 9
Guzevičius, Antanas, 273, 282, 316
Gylys, Vytautas, 242, 404, 413

H

Halich-Volynia state, 55, *passim*
Hall, George, 403
Hanka, Vaclav, 10-11
Hansa (city of), 53, 89
Hartknoch, Christoph, 10
Hays, Wayne L., 431
Hebrews, the, 3
Hedwig of Poland, 58-59
Heidelberg, University of, 84
Henderson, Loy W., 400
Henry of Bavaria, 54
Henrici Chronicon Lyvoniae, 37
Henry IV of England, 60
Henry of Valois, Prince, 82
Herodotus, 33
Herter, Christian, 431
Herulli (Herullians), the, 1, 7-8
Hindenburg, Paul von, 145-146
Historia Polonica, 1
History of the Lithuanian SSR, 311
Hitler, Adolf, 230, 246-248, 253, 417
Hohenzolern, Albrecht, 75-76
Hohenzolern, Vilhelm, 78
Horodle Union Act, 65, 73
Hymans, 170-174

I

Į Laisvę, 333, 351
India Septentrionalis, 87
Internal Refugee Organization, 296

International Court of the Hague, 166, *passim*
"Introductory Land Reform Law" (1920), 200
Ionians, the, 5
Iranians, the, 19
Isenburg-Berstein, Franz-Joseph, 148, 153
Italics, the, 19
Ivan III, 70-71
Ivan IV ("the Terrible"), 78
Iziaslav, 40

J

Jaknavičius, Jonas, 88
Jakštas, Juozas, 43
Jankus, Martynas, 208
Janulaitis, Augustinas, 188
Jaunius, Kazimieras, 19
Jaunutis, 55
Jesuits, the, 77, 84-88, 91-92, 97, 99
Jogaila, 56-61, 63, 65-66, 74, 84, 105
Jogailai dynasty, 4 (*see also* Jogaila, above)
John Kalita, 70
John of Luxembourg, 54
Johnson, Lyndon Baines, 441
Jonas Goštautas, 67-68
Jonušaitis, Albertas, 296
Juozapavičius, Antanas, 164
Jurgėla, Dr. Kostas, 419
Jurgutis, Vladas, 197
Jutt-Jutkevičius, Rev. John C., 435-436

K

Kabeliai, 22
Kaip jie mus šaudė, 406
Kairys, Steponas, 345
Kalinauskas, Kostas, 126
Kaliningrad district, the, 303
Kamšai, 22
Karevičius, Bishop Pranciškus, 152
Karpius, Kazys S., 406
Karvelis, Dr. Petras, 424
Katekizmas, 85
Katkevičius, Jonas, 81, 90
Kauener Zeitung, 291
Kaunas, 163, *passim*
Kaunas University, 260, *passim*
Kavolis, Vytautas, 437
Kazlų Rūda, 385
Kėdainai Agreement (1656), 95
Kellog-Briand Pact, 251
Kelly, Edna, 430
Kelmė, 77, *passim*

Kennedy, John Fitzgerald, 431
Kernavė, 49
Kersten, Charles J., 419
Kersten Committee, the, 491-420
Kęstutis, Grand Duke, 37, 56-57
Kettler, Gotard, 78
Kezys, Romas, 439
Khrushchev, Nikita, 431, 447
Kiev, University of, 124
Kievan Chronicle, 40
Kievan Russia, 36, *passim*
Kiparsky, Valentin, 16
Kizys, Mary, 431
Klaipėda, 21, *passim*
Klaipėda-Memel question, 179 *et seq.*
Klaipėda Statute, the, 234, 238
Klimas, Petras, 396, 403-404
Knights of Lithuania (Lietuvos Vyčiai), 435-436
Kochubinskii, Aleksandr A., 13
Koenigsberg, 69, *passim*
Koenigsberg University, 75-76, 84, 86, 113
Kojalavičius, Vijukas Albertas, 88
Komitetas Lietuvos Nepriklausomybei Atstatyti, 440
Komjaunimo Tiesa, 310
Konarskis, Simonas, 123-124
Kosakowskis, Simonas, 109
Kosciuška, Tadas, 109
Kova, 380
Kralovodvorski rukopis, 11
Kraševskis (Kraszewski), Ignas, 119, 124
Kražiai School, the, 125
Krėva Union Act, 59
Krėvė-Mickevičius, Vincas, 266-269, 272
Krikštonys, 38
Kronika Polska, Litewska, Žmodzka y wszystkiej Rusi. W. Krollewcu 1582, 3
Krupavičius, Rev. Mykolas, 215, 349, 418, 425
Kubiliūnas, Gen. Petras, 293
Kubilius, Juozas, 140
Kuchel, Thomas H., 437
Kulvietis, Abraham (Abraomas), 76, 86
Kumskis, Antanas G., 406

L

Lake Durbe, 48
Landbewirtschaftungsgesellschaft, 291
Laisvės Kovotojas, 333, 338

468

474

ABOUT THE AUTHORS

ALBERTAS GERUTIS (b. 1905) is a diplomat, a journalist and the author of several books on Lithuanian and Baltic issues. He received his doctorate in law at the University of Bern, Switzerland, in 1933, and subsequently joined the Foreign Ministry of Lithuania in 1936. After the collapse of the League of Nations, where he served as the Secretary of the permanent Lithuanian Delegation, Dr. Gerutis was transferred to the Lithuanian legation in Bern and, in 1948, was appointed Lithuanian representative to Switzerland.

JONAS PUZINAS (b. 1905), archeologist, curator and author, holds a doctorate in ancient history from the University of Heidelberg. He has published numerous studies, some of which deal with archeological excavations in which he had participated. For many years a professor at the University of Vytautas the Great in Kaunas, he served as its dean in 1941-1944 and was president of the Baltic University at Pinneberg, Germany, in 1948-1949. Dr. Puzinas has been living in the United States since 1949, and is one of the editors of the Lithuanian Encyclopedia, published in Boston.

JUOZAS JAKŠTAS (b. 1900), one of the outstanding Lithuanian medievalists, has studied in Berlin, Vienna and in Kaunas, Lithuania. A prolific author of articles concerning Lithuanian history, he has taught at several universities and was editor of the medieval section of the Lithuanian Encyclopedia, Boston. In the United States since 1949, he resides in Cleveland, Ohio.

STASYS LOZORAITIS (b. 1898) heads the diplomatic service of free Lithuania abroad. He was Foreign Minister of Lithuania from 1934 to 1938 and in this capacity Mr. Lozoraitis played an important role in the tumultuous international political conflicts of the Thirties, especially in defending his country's rights vis-a-vis national-socialist Germany. In 1940 Mr. Lozoraitis was entrusted with the guidance of the Lithuanian diplomatic corps outside Lithuania and led their protest action against the Soviet invasion and occupation of his homeland. A member of the International Diplomatic Academy in Paris, Mr. Lozoraitis now divides his time between Rome and the French capital. He has written many articles on the case and status of Lithuania.

DR. ALGIRDAS MARTIN BUDRECKIS (b. 1937) is the author of *The Lithuanian Revolt of 1941*. He has also contributed numerous articles concerning Lithuanian history and culture to various publications. Active in Lithuanian cultural and civic organizations, Mr. Budreckis is Executive Officer of the Supreme Committee for the Liberation of Lithuania, a member of the National Council of the Lithuanian Community of the U.S.A., Inc., and Treasurer of the Lithuanian Research Institute.

In addition, he is the Press Officer of the Assembly of Captive European Nations and has taught Russian and Modern European History at the Extension Division of Rutgers University.

Other Manyland Books Publications

BOBBY WISHINGMORE, by Stepas Zobarskas............1961 Cloth $1.95
MEMOIRS OF A LITHUANIAN BRIDGE, by Vincas Kudirka
                                                1961 Cloth $2.00
LITHUANIAN FOLK TALES, by Stepas Zobarskas......1959 Cloth $4.50
THE HERDSMAN AND THE LINDEN TREE, by Vincas Krévé
                                                1964 Cloth $3.95
HOUSE UPON THE SAND, by Jurgis Gliauda............1963 Cloth $3.95
LITHUANIAN QUARTET, by Stepas Zobarskas, ed.......1962 Cloth $4.95
MODERN STORIES FROM MANY LANDS, by Clarence R. Decker
    and Charles Angoff, eds. (out of print)............1963 Cloth $5.00
THE MOUNTAIN DOVES, by Nola M. Zobarskas, ed. 1964 Cloth $3.50
THE DELUGE, by Mykolas Vaitkus ....1965 Cloth $3.95
THE STOWAWAY, by Francisco Coloane............1964 Cloth $3.00
SELECTED LITHUANIAN SHORT STORIES, by Stepas
    Zobarskas, ed. ....1963 Cloth $5.00
NIMBLEFOOT THE ANT, by Vytas Tamulaitis............1965 Cloth $3.95
REJUVENATION OF SIEGFRIED IMMERSELBE, by Ignas
    Šeinius ....1965 Cloth $5.00
NOON AT A COUNTRY INN, by Antanas Vaičiulaitis
                                                1965 Cloth $3.95
FOOTBRIDGES AND ABYSSES, by Aloyzas Baronas...1965 Cloth $5.00
THE TEMPTATION, by Vincas Krévé............1965 Cloth $3.00
THE WAR AGAINST GOD IN LITHUANIA, by Dr. J. Savasis
                               Paperback $1.25; 1966 Cloth $3.00
THE BELL OF TIME, by Charles Angoff............1966 Cloth $4.00
THE TUNDRA TALES, by Nola M. Zobarskas, ed.......1967 Cloth $5.00
ESSAYS IN GREEK POLITICS, by Raphael Sealey........1967 Cloth $6.00
ALOHA POLYNESIA, by Joseph Joel Keith............1967 Cloth $4.00
AMENS IN AMBER, by Leonardas Andriekus............1968 Cloth $5.00
THE WINNOWING WINDS, by Gerald Earl Bailey...1967 Cloth $4.00
THE ORDEAL OF ASSAD PASHA, by Ignas Šeinius...1963 Cloth $2.00
THE SONATA OF ICARUS, by Jurgis Gliauda............1968 Cloth $5.00
THE THIRD WOMAN, by Aloyzas Baronas............1968 Cloth $5.00
TO REGIONS OF NO ADMITTANCE, by Danguolė Sealey
                                                1968 Cloth $4.00
FIVE POSTS IN A MARKET PLACE, by Algirdas Landsbergis
                                                1969 Cloth $4.00
LITHUANIA: 700 YEARS, by Albertas Gerutis, ed.......1969 Cloth $12.00
CULTURAL WELLSPRINGS OF FOLKTALES, by Vytautas
    Bagdanavičius ....1969 Cloth $6.00
AFRICAN WRITING TODAY, by Charles Angoff and
    John Povey, eds. ....1969 Cloth $6.00

BOOK SALES DEPT., MANYLAND BOOKS, INC.
Box 266, Wall St. Station, New York, N. Y. 10005